THE MAN IN THE BATH
Death of Trooper Rolfe
German Gas Victim
THE AUSTRALIAN
TRAVEL SERVICE
414/417, AUSTRALIA
An Australian firm
Australians.
"The Australian and New Zealand troops have indeed proved themselves worthy sons of the Empire."
GEORGE R.I.
Association of Centres for Soldiers' Wives and Mothers.
HE'S MINE!
I SAW HIM FIRST
WORSE THAN GALLIPOLI
POOR SOLDIER!
THERE AND BACK

WORLD WAR ONE

A HISTORY IN 100 STORIES

MURTAGH J.
MYERS C. R.
NASH T. W.
NAYLON T.
NAYLOR A. A.
NEVILLE
NEW H. C.
NEWBERY
NEWCOMBE
NEWLAND
NEWTON
NICOLL J.
NICOLL R. M.
NIX J. E.
NOBLE A.
NOBLE J.
NOLAN
NORMAN A. H.
NORRIS J.
NORTH C. R.
NORTH R. G.
NUGENT E.
O'BRIEN W. J.
O'CALLAGHAN
O'CONNOR
OFFORD
O'GORMAN
O'GRADY
O'SHEA
LEDDEN R.
LEWIS R. J.
LEWIS S. J.
LEWIS W.

WORLD WAR ONE

a history in 100 stories

BRUCE SCATES, REBECCA WHEATLEY & LAURA JAMES

VIKING
an imprint of
PENGUIN BOOKS

CONTENTS

for Isabella

The Great War tore us apart
INTRODUCTION

There aren't many books dedicated to the memory of a four-year-old child. But this one is. We don't know who Isabella Wilkinson might have become. We know nothing of the challenges she may have faced, the opportunities she might have seized, the hopes she might have harboured. Like every young life, hers was one filled with promise. Sadly, Isabella's life ended abruptly after four short years when her father smashed her skull in with a hammer.

Frank Wilkinson was what they called a nerve case. He was one of a generation of young men who came back scarred by the war – physically, psychologically and emotionally. Once, Frank was a hero. Bombardier Wilkinson was awarded the Military Medal at Passchendaele after taking part in some of the most terrible and costly fighting Australian soldiers endured. He survived the war but not the peace. Frank returned to Australia in 1919, took up land as a soldier settler at Stanhope, failed as a farmer, struggled against debt, illness and depression and, ten years after Passchendaele, took his own life. Before slitting his throat, Frank turned on those who loved him, bashing both his daughter and his wife to death.

No one hurried to condemn Frank Wilkinson in the 1920s. Perhaps because Australia was full of similar stories, equally tragic: good men undone by the horrors of war, brutalised by what they had seen and what they had done, unable to escape the nightmare of Passchendaele or the Somme, Gallipoli or Palestine. The question is, are we prepared to hear such stories today?

In 2012, the story of Frank Wilkinson and his family was presented to the Anzac Centenary Advisory Board in Canberra. It was one of one hundred stories developed by historians at Monash University – narratives designed to capture the true cost of war to our community. Fighting didn't just maim and kill Australian servicemen and women, though that price was staggering enough. The pain of war tore through townships large and small, cast a shadow of grief across many thousands of families, and left a crippling legacy of trauma. For families like the Wilkinsons, the Great War did not end in 1918. A hundred years on we, too, still live with its consequences.

Prior to Frank Wilkinson, Canberra had endorsed all our presentations. This was the story that went too far. 'Why was it necessary,' one board member asked, 'for historians to be so brutally honest?' As if a dishonest history would somehow be preferable. A senior civil servant told one of the authors of this book that all the public hoped for from the Anzac Centenary was 'a warm fuzzy feeling'; it was not the intention of his department to disappoint them. We were presented with an ultimatum: if Canberra was to adopt the 100 Stories project in its commemorative program, Frank Wilkinson's story would have to go. The tragedy of little Isabella would be quietly forgotten and replaced with what one board member called 'a positive nation-building narrative'.

There will be no shortage of nation-building narratives over the course of the Anzac Centenary. We will be told time and again a story of courage and sacrifice, fortitude and endurance, mateship and resolve. There will always be a space for such stories as Australia and Aotearoa/New Zealand remember the Great War. But perhaps a hundred years on there is space for other stories as well; perhaps we should seek out stories often marginalised in those 'nation-building narratives'. We believe the Centenary is a time to gauge the cost of war for our entire community, and we believe that far from building a nation, the Great War tore us apart.

By reading this book, you affirm the decision we made in Canberra. Frank Wilkinson's story is not one we can afford to cast aside. It stands alongside ninety-nine others, one hundred stories in all to mark the Centenary of Anzac. We have selected these stories from across Australia and Aotearoa/New Zealand. They highlight the experiences of women as well as men and recover Indigenous narratives too long ignored by mainstream histories. Amongst the cast of the 100 Stories are not just soldiers, sailors, airmen, nurses; but parents who lost their sons, wives who struggled with shell-shocked husbands; children who never knew their fathers; daughters like Isabella Wilkinson. The recent release of repatriation records has extended our understanding of war well beyond the battlefield. New sources (hitherto locked away in closed archives) offer fresh insights into the way war came home. Each story is a microhistory in itself, but all relate to larger issues during and after the fighting. The 100 Stories are not just about the lives of individuals but the experience of combat, the nature of loss and bereavement, the politics of gender, nation and empire, and the challenge of building a new society in the aftermath of war.

OPPOSITE **No one hurried to condemn:** The grave of Frank Wilkinson, his wife and daughter – all casualties of the Great War. These flowers were placed by the grave on Anzac Day, 2015. *Courtesy Tom Maher.*

We offer these stories as an insight into the generation of 1914–1918. But the 100 Stories are just the beginning. Within every community that suffered through the Great War there are hundreds of similar stories; the mass digitisation of papers, letters and journals enables researchers the world over to find an Isabella Wilkinson in Austria and Serbia, Turkey and Germany, Russia and France. We hope these stories suggest

1897 BOMBARDIER
F.E. WILKINSON MM
11 FIELD ARTILLERY BRIGADE
26TH AUGUST 1927 AGE 39
AUSTRALIAN IMPERIAL FORCE

ways we might extend this conversation beyond the narrow national and imperial boundaries that drove the world to war. And like every sample, this one has obvious limitations.

The stories we have chosen do not claim to be representative in any statistical sense; nurses, Indigenous soldiers and shell-shock victims are all over-represented here. We highlight their stories to redress what we see as a great imbalance in the way we remember that watershed in human history. And we contest the simple tallies that diminish the true cost of war. Officially, Australia's war dead numbers 60 000; New Zealand's around 20 000. But that counts only those who had died when our armies were formally disbanded. What of the tens of thousands who died of war wounds years after the fighting had ended; a 'burnt out' generation that lingered on in repatriation hospitals, whose lungs corroded away years after being gassed, cot cases confined to bed for most of their lives?

It is hard to say if suicide cases are over-represented in this collection. Many coroners left their findings open and we can never know how many desperate men took their own lives. What we can say with certainty is that for many, the nightmare of war never ended; thousands returned to Australia irreparably damaged. Many could never readjust to civilian life, some knew no other life than that of soldiering. And there were many other non-combatants who died as a result of hostilities, Isabella Wilkinson included. In a conflict of such catastrophic scale, the true number of casualties can never be counted.

BELOW **National and imperial boundaries:** Patriotic cards issued in support of the war effort. Transnational histories challenge older understandings of a conflict that shaped the modern world. *Courtesy Melbourne Museum and State Library of Victoria.*

ABOVE **Thousands returned:** A good luck token issued to men leaving Australia. This book's use of repatriation records offers new insights into the postwar period. *Courtesy Melbourne Museum.*

World War One: A History in 100 Stories is a collective endeavour. Authorship is shared here between senior and early career historians. All the stories have been painstakingly researched and, where possible, we have consulted the families concerned.

Conventional histories are bounded by the archives, and the 100 Stories respects that need for a verifiable 'truth'. But the writing of history is also a creative endeavour; a matter of perspective and choice. Very occasionally, we have embarked on what might be called an 'imagined history' – constructing the diary of a nurse from medical case notes, sketching the scene of a battle or a homecoming, imaginin g what one of Australia's first pilgrims might have thought as he prepared for a journey to war graves overseas.

We acknowledge our immense debt to the families, archivists and researchers who suggested stories in addition to those we found. Finally, we thank the relatives of Isabella Wilkinson and all those other families who have come forward in the course of this project. We have benefited immensely from their suggestions and welcome further comments from readers.

A hundred years after the end of the Great War, the telling of these stories aids in our understanding of that conflict. It widens the ambit of remembrance, beyond our blinkered vision of 1914–1918 to the broken years that lay beyond. And perhaps it helps to heal the pain of a past we never truly left behind.

Bruce Scates, Rebecca Wheatley, Laura James
Monash University, April 2015.

NOTES ON MONEY, MEASUREMENT AND TERMINOLOGY

To avoid anachronism, this book retains imperial units of measurement. Metric measures are used in any discussion of the late twentieth century and beyond.

MONEY

Australia and New Zealand used pounds, shillings and pence for much of the period covered by this book. There were 12 pennies (d.) in one shilling (s.) and 20 shillings in one pound (£). A guinea was £1 1s. When Australia adopted decimal currency in 1966, $2 was equal to about £1.

MEASUREMENT

The relevant metric equivalents to imperial measures are as follows:

1 inch = 2.54 cm

1 foot = 30.48 cm

1 yard = 91.44 cm

1 mile = 1.61 km

1 acre = 0.405 ha

1 pound = 453.6 g

1 stone = 6.35 kg

1 ton = 1016 kg

TERMINOLOGY

The Returned Services League has a long and complex genealogy. To simplify the narrative, the Returned Soldiers Sailors and Airmen's Imperial League of Australia (RSSAILA) and the Returned Soldiers and Sailors Imperial League of Australia (RSSILA) are, throughout the text, referred to as the RSL. By the same token, the Australian War Museum is referred to by its current name, the Australian War Memorial.

Anzac was originally the acronym of the Australian and New Zealand Army Corps but it also came to represent a place (the site where Australian and New Zealand troops landed at Gallipoli), a group of servicemen (initially those who served in the campaign) and a mythology or legend. In each case the meaning of Anzac is contextualised by the narrative to follow.

OPPOSITE **Raising funds:** Peg Agnes and Vi Deviney selling goods for the Comfort Fund Brisbane ca. 1917. Those who supported the war, as well as those who opposed it, are the subjects of this book. *Courtesy State Library of Queensland.*

Weary hours and days of pain

HAROLD CANDY

Harold lay awake. Neither his body nor his mind would let him sleep. On the other side of the bedroom his brother rested soundly. *Strange*, Harold thought, *Charles came home and left the war behind him*. But Private Harold Candy couldn't do that; he had been scarred by the fighting in more ways than one.

Harold sighed and turned over. His back was aching. Years before, he had been knocked by a shell at Pozières – it had twisted his spine like a corkscrew. He clenched his teeth against the pain and tried to think of something else, anything else.

Things could still be different for Harold. He was marrying his sweetheart in a few hours time, and she was the best thing that had happened to him. They'd walk down the aisle at St Xavier's, he'd lift her veil and kiss her pretty face, they'd honeymoon in Victor Harbor. Harold would never tell her of the girl he knew in France, or of the sexually transmitted disease he'd contracted. VD was stamped on his service record like a kind of stigma – uglier than the shrapnel wounds that cut across his hands and body, or all the horrid things he couldn't help remembering.

Harold Candy was a young man on the morning of his wedding, but wounds and disease had aged him prematurely. He could barely manage a shift now at the Grand Central Hotel – the latest in a string of dead-end jobs. The rheumatism was getting worse; the wet and cold of the Somme did that to soldiers. Last time Harold had been to the repat hospital, the doctor noted the 'gnawing' pains in his leg joints, the 'wasting' of his calf muscles and damage to his knees. He wondered if he could ever earn enough to keep a wife and perhaps a family.[1]

The doctors said some of his troubles might not be war related. That dose of the clap had counted against him. No one could explain the aching in his gut; a pain so intense it often left him doubled over. Despite being buried alive by a shell, despite that shredding by shrapnel, a partial pension was the best Harold might hope for. He sighed

OPPOSITE **A young man:** Harold Candy on the eve of his departure to war. On his first attempt to enlist he was rejected on the grounds he was underweight. Nearly four years of service took its toll on that slight figure. Harold received wounds to his spine, his right foot and wrist. He was hospitalised for venereal disease, developed debilitating rheumatism and suffered the effects of being gassed. *SRSA GRG26/5/4/1324 courtesy State Records Office South Australia.*

and turned again. A partial pension just wasn't enough to build a new life for anyone.

Harold got up and wandered about the house. The modest worker's cottage had been transformed. Wedding decorations lined the walls and the windows. In the kitchen a feast lay waiting . Soon enough the guests would arrive. But Harold would not be there to greet them.

It was August and freezing cold outside, so Harold put on his overcoat. Slowly and cautiously he untied a box of crockery hired for the wedding breakfast, careful not to crash the dishes together and wake his sleeping family. He pocketed the rope, and walked out into the dark morning. Wakefield Street was quiet and empty. To his left he could see St Xavier's Cathedral, not half a mile down the way. Harold turned and walked in the opposite direction, toward the nearby parklands.

They found Harold Candy's body hanging from a tree later that morning. The young man had climbed up a low-hanging branch, firmly fastened the rope to the branch above, then launched out into eternity.

That same afternoon, Charles went with the police to see where his little brother had killed himself. The tree was in a lonely corner of the park; its bark torn by the weight of a swinging body. Charles tried to understand, tried to find the words to explain, tried to comfort a bride bereft on her wedding day.

Private Harold Candy was buried in the Catholic section of West Terrace Cemetery in Adelaide. An oak leaf motif is etched on his headstone and 'In Loving Memory' carved as his epitaph. We do not know how Harold's fiancée remembered her lost love. We don't know if she married or moved on, if she recovered from shame and regret, if there was ever a second chance for her. And we do not know if she ever learned of Harold's secret – that terrible disease so many had but so few spoke of.

But we do know that Charles never judged his brother, never dismissed that short young life as cowardly or sinful. Men who had been to war knew what war could do to them. On the anniversary of Harold's death, Charles placed a memorial notice in the Adelaide papers:

His weary hours, his days of pain,
His sleepless nights are passed.
His ever-patient, worn-out frame
Has found sweet rest at last.[2]

BELOW **Sweet rest at last:** Harold is buried in the West Terrace Cemetery. His grave is in the Old Catholic section, on the opposite side of the cemetery to the AIF section where more than four thousand ex-service people are buried. Despite the stigma associated with suicide, Harold was buried in consecrated ground. Perhaps in death, the community could afford to be forgiving *Courtesy Rebecca Wheatley.*

SOURCES AND FURTHER READING: This story draws on Harold Candy's service dossier NAA: B2455, CANDY HJ; his repatriation file NAA: D363, R14615, CANDY, HAROLD JOSEPH; and the police report to the Coroner SRSA GRG 1/44, 242. The tragic death of Harold Candy was reported on widely in the press, and this story has drawn on contemporary newspaper articles. For further reading on postwar trauma see Jay Winter, 'Shell shock', in Jay Winter (ed) *The Cambridge History of the First World War*, vol. III (Cambridge: Cambridge University Press, 2014), pp. 310–333. The authors gratefully acknowledge the work of A.C. (Sandy) MacFarlane and Malcolm Sim, whose work explores the intertwined physical and psychological effects of war.

That Australian girl
LIZZIE ARMSTRONG

In London everyone seemed to know Miss L.E. Armstrong. They called her 'that Australian girl'. The society pages described her as strong, independent, and farsighted. 'A quick thinker,' one journalist noted, 'an inveterate worker . . . [and] a keen lover of her native land.'[1]

When hostilities began, most Australian women of her age and class settled for Red Cross work at home: knitting socks for soldiers at the front, writing letters of encouragement or raising money for 'their boys'.

But not Lizzie. Working as a typist, she saved every penny she could and spent it all on a passage to London. The young woman from Sydney volunteered to work in a hospital, trained as a first-class physiotherapist and massaged the limbs of men shattered by war.

Healing soldiers' bodies was not the only part of Lizzie's war effort. Convinced all Australians were great travellers, she organised sightseeing tours of the old country – history walks along famous London streets, rambles through the English countryside, motor tours to Devon and picnics on the Thames. 'The Anzac masseuse' became the 'guide, philosopher and friend'[2] to a great many lonely Australians, most eager to see all the wonders of Empire, many homesick for the land they'd left behind.

By the end of the war, Miss Armstrong's work as a masseuse had damaged her hands irreparably. But Lizzie was always a woman with a plan. She returned to Australia on a troopship and contrived to get an interview with Prime Minister Billy Hughes. Hughes spotted her talent and industry instantly. He encouraged her to return to London and offered her an office in Australia House. There, Lizzie Armstrong established the Southern Cross Information Bureau, a travel company run by Australians for Australians.

The Bureau offered assistance to Australians travelling overseas. In the 1920s,

ABOVE **A spirited example of the 'new woman':** A portrait of Lizzie Armstrong. Here, Lizzie adopts the guise of a London socialite but she was also a capable business woman, a skilled masseuse and considered by many an ambassador for Australia. Country Life Stock and Station Journal, *21 March 1924, courtesy National Library of Australia.*

ABOVE **An essential service:** A wartime photograph of North Beach at Anzac stands above the counter in Australia House, London. Gallipoli was almost impossible to reach in the early 1920s. Note the prominence of other Australian symbols, two kangaroos grazing at either side of the bench. The British Australian and New Zealander, *10 May 1928.*

over ten thousand Australians made their way to Britain and the Continent, many on their grand tour of Europe, some on a pilgrimage to a battlefield where a loved one lay buried. Miss Armstrong's travel bureau catered for the needs of all:

> *A program is drawn up for the best means of reaching much frequented beauty spots, timetables of road excursions, motor tours for weekends . . . are all to be found there. Theatre tickets are booked, tickets for tours arranged for, advice given on shopping centres, and enquiries of all kinds dealt with.*

But the most important service Miss Armstrong offered was a chance to visit the graves of Australia's war dead. The library at Australia House was:

> *converted to a Memorial Chamber, in which a card index [was] established giving particulars of every dead Australian soldier, together with maps . . . as complete a set of war literature as possible [and] mural paintings of battle scenes.*[3]

With these details in hand, pilgrims were directed to Miss Armstrong's office, where battlefield tours for groups, families, and individuals by touring coach, rail, and private motorcar were seamlessly arranged.

The Southern Cross Information Bureau was staffed entirely by Australians, most drawn from the huge expatriate community that had settled on the Strand. In an astute business move, Miss Armstrong also hired ex-AIF and New Zealand Army men as drivers, guides and companions.

However, services such as these didn't come cheap. A three-day trip to Amiens including a first-class return fare, hotel accommodation, private limousine and officer guide cost 15 guineas (sterling). That would amount to several weeks' wages for most working men.

Whatever the price, Miss Armstrong provided an essential service. Without her assistance, thousands might never have found a son's or husband's grave. On one hand, she was seen as 'an ambassador for Australia', and her 'first rate work' was one of the ways 'to keep the motherland and her dominions firmly knitted together'.[4] On the other, she was a spirited example of the 'new woman' of the interwar period: independent, mobile, enterprising and determined to build a life of her own. And her work is a reminder that then, as today, pilgrimage and tourism often travel together.

Lizzie never lost her love of travel. Determined to broaden her business, she toured Canada, Africa, New Zealand and all the far-flung corners of the Empire. The war had taken her far from that typist pool in Sydney; 'that Australian girl' had made the world her home.

BELOW **An Australian firm for Australians:** The Southern Cross Information Bureau became part of the Australian Travel Service in the mid 1920s. With branches in Sydney, Melbourne and Paris, as well as Australia House, it was an example of the global reach of the tourism industry. British Australian and New Zealander, *21 June 1928*.

SOURCES AND FURTHER READING: This story draws on contemporary newspaper reports detailing Lizzie's life and work and a detailed scan of the *British Australasian* and its successor, the *Brisitsh Australian and New Zealander*. For further reading on Lizzie Armstrong see Bruce Scates, *Return to Gallipoli: Walking the Battlefields of the Great War* (Cambridge: Cambridge University Press, 2006). For further reading on women's movement within the Empire see Angela Woollacott, *To Try Her Fortune in London: Australian Women, Colonialism, and Modernity* (Oxford: Oxford University Press, 2001) and for women's mobilisation during the Great War see Raelene Frances, 'Women's Mobilisation for War', *International Encyclopedia of the First World War* (eds) Ute Daniel, Peter Gatrell, Oliver Janz, Heather Jones, Jennifer Keene, Alan Kramer, and Bill Nasson (Berlin: Freie Universität Berlin, 2014).

ABOVE **Over thirty years to complete:** This drawing of Shrapnel Gully Cemetery appeared in a sketchbook of Gallipoli graves issued to grieving families. By the time it was sent out, Mrs Lyall was long dead. This booklet did not contain a sketch of Ari Burnu Cemetery. There are over twenty graveyards at Anzac alone and thousands of others on the Western Front. Not all could be pictured in the commemorative booklet. Where the Australians Rest *(Melbourne: Government Printer, 1920) courtesy Rare Book Room, Monash University.*

A sorrow unsaid

BRIAN LYALL

On 2 December 1915, Major G.F. Stevenson, Commanding Officer of the 6th Australian Battery at Gallipoli, wiped the grime from his hands and wrote a letter home to Australia. The letter began in the way so many others did, bearing the most personal of messages to a woman he would never meet. 'It is with extreme regret that I find myself called upon to write to you giving details of the death of your son . . . '

Brian Lyall had been killed on 29 November. That day, Turkish artillery swept the gullies and the ridges, pounding the Anzac position and breaking crucial communication lines with the beach. Major Stevenson detailed Gunner Lyall to find the break in the telephone wire and to mend it. Though 'fully aware of the danger', the young soldier went on his mission 'without hesitation or complaint'. Somewhere in the trenches, Lyall was struck down by a shell and buried alive.

It took them several hours to prize Gunner Lyall from the earth, and several hours more to carry his body to the beach. And although Major Stevenson broke the news as gently as he could, it was clear that it took Mrs Lyall's son several hours to die:

> *[I] . . . was informed that the poor lad had passed away at [two o'clock] that morning . . . This news, I assure you, was a great shock to me, as [I thought] his wounds would soon mend and that he would in all probability be sent home. However, God's will was otherwise.*

We don't know if Mrs Lyall found much comfort in the thought that God had taken the life of her loving son. But we can conclude, from that sheet of frayed and worn paper, that she (and probably those close to her) read the Major's letter time and time again. Somehow, knowing how her son died offered some consolation.

The Major was careful to choose words a grieving mother longed to hear. Gunner Lyall was:

> *the best liked man in the Battery and though one of the youngest he was the manliest of them all . . . the way he did his duty will help to sustain you a little in your grief.*

Much of Lyall's kit was 'sold by auction to his comrades who bought them up eagerly as mementos of one they all admired'. But personal things – a watch, some letters and a soiled pocket diary – were carefully set aside by the Major. 'I am [also] sending you a silver brandy flask with his name engraved thereon.' It was dated with the week that Lyall enlisted. 'You would value it more than anyone else [possibly] could.'[1]

No doubt Mrs Lyall also valued the description of her son's funeral, or what passed as a funeral on the shores of Gallipoli. The boy from Victoria was 'buried in a cemetery close to Ari Burnu on the beach'. The chaplain read a service and 'a wooden cross [was] erected'. Brian's mates stood quietly beside the shallow, sandy grave on the edge of the Aegean Sea; their last farewells laid that battered body to rest.

Today, Brian Lyall's remains lie in a peaceful corner of Ari Burnu Cemetery. All year round, the graveyard is tended as if it is a garden. Soft green lawns sweep between the regulation tombstones, and every spring, flowers spread a carpet of colour down to the

BELOW **A graveyard by the sea:** Ari Burnu is one of two cemeteries flanking Anzac Cove. Men who died throughout the entire campaign – from April to December – are buried here. *Courtesy Bruce Scates.*

ABOVE **The family's final message:** Loved ones sometimes found the words to say goodbye. This grave stands opposite Lyall's blank headstone. It suggests the family refused to accept the finality of this man's death. *Courtesy Bruce Scates.*

OPPOSITE **A peaceful corner:** Brian's remains rest beneath an oak planted at Gallipoli. This particular tree, as well as the English flowers dotted amongst the graves, were chosen to symbolise a living link with Empire. *Courtesy Bruce Scates.*

sea. But Brian's tomb also poses a question: why does this much loved man, admired by his mates, treasured by his family, honoured by all, have no personal epitaph on his grave?

In some ways this is not so exceptional. The graves of many soldiers killed in the Great War are marked by the barest of inscriptions; they record name and rank, date of death and sometimes an age, but nothing more. There is evidence that some families found the cost of inscribing a final message prohibitive. The Imperial War Graves Commission charged families three pence halfpenny for every letter and every space between words. The standard inscription could cost as much as nineteen shillings, and many families in the 1920s had not a penny to spare. To this day, the debtors files can be found in the National Archives of Australia office in North Melbourne. Vigilant officials pursued families who had failed to pay.

Nor were families entirely free to choose the inscription they wanted. The number of words allowed was strictly limited: sixty-six letters minus the spaces between each word. The Commission also reserved the right to veto any epitaph it deemed inappropriate. Suggested inscriptions were routinely sent back to families; grieving mothers, fathers, wives told their last message was too long, too cumbersome, 'inartistic', even 'sentimental'.[2] In such cases, the Imperial War Graves Commission sent families a list of approved epitaphs – comforting words plucked from the Bible, a passage from Binyon or Kipling, or the big words carved on memorials across the British Empire.

Perhaps some families baulked at this state sanctified grief. Perhaps for some, 'King and Country' no longer said enough.

There was a third reason why families chose no parting message. The cemeteries of the Great War took over thirty years to complete. Indeed the last memorials, at Vimy Ridge and Villers-Bretonneux, were not finished until 1938, on the eve of a new world war in Europe. Most families were invited to choose an epitaph in the early 1920s, and by that time many next-of-kin could not be found. Some no longer lived in the towns where their men enlisted, some had remarried and changed their names and lives accordingly, and some had simply passed away. Mrs Lyall died in 1917, a year before the end of the war, two years before the task of bringing in the dead at Gallipoli began, and five years before the cemetery at Ari Burnu was actually completed.

We will never know the epitaph Mrs Lyall might have chosen or if words in stone could offer any solace. Brian Lyall's grave at Gallipoli remains blank, but a few sheets of paper sealed away in the State Library of Victoria tell us something of his mother's grief.

SOURCES AND FURTHER READING: This story draws on Brian Lyall's service dossier NAA:B2455, LYALL BRIAN; and the Lyall Papers at the State Library of Victoria, MS 10132. For further reading on the Lyall story and the war graves of Gallipoli see Bruce Scates, *Return to Gallipoli: Walking the Battlefields of the Great War* (Cambridge: Cambridge University Press, 2006).

A useful citizen frustrated

DOUGLAS GRANT

April 1949: the Anzac Day Parade winds its way through the streets of Sydney. Seventeen thousand diggers from the First World War march alongside 19 000 soldiers from the Second. Despite the grey skies, 200 000 people turn out to witness the procession. Some wave, some applaud, an old woman in the crowd is seen to cry. But not everyone is welcome. Not far from the cenotaph in Martin Place, Douglas Grant, an Aboriginal man, stands alone, watching on dejectedly. A mate from his old battalion catches his eye and breaks away from the column.

'[We] were all marching in,' Allan Kinghorne remembered, 'and there he was, just with the crowd. So I left the boys and I went across and I said, "Come on Douglas, hop in."

'"Oh no," he said. "No, I'm not wanted any more . . . I think I'm better out here . . . I don't belong. I've lived long enough to see that I don't belong anywhere."'

But Kinghorne insisted. 'On a day like this,' he said, 'everyone wants you. Come on, hop in with the boys.'[1] With that, Douglas relented and, taking his friend's hand, joined him in the march.

Douglas Grant was one of more than a thousand Indigenous Australians who served with the First AIF. In many ways this was not his war. So called 'full blood' Aborigines were not permitted to serve in an army where recruits were required to be British subjects or 'of predominantly European descent'. Nor was Douglas actually a citizen of the country he fought for. Aboriginal people in early twentieth-century Australia were not allowed to vote, marry or work without special permission from the government. Often their land, their language and their culture were taken from them.

Douglas Grant was one of thousands trapped in the cultural limbo of colonialism. Born on the Atherton Tablelands, he had been 'smuggled out of Queensland' as

ABOVE **Trapped in the cultural limbo of colonialism:** Douglas Grant stands beside the white family who 'adopted' him. Douglas spoke with the same thick Scottish accent as his father. He was also taught to play the bagpipes. *SP1011/1, 2176 courtesy National Archives of Australia.*

OPPOSITE **Not a citizen of the country he fought for:** Douglas Grant in the uniform of the First AIF. Upon enlistment Private Grant enjoyed many of the entitlements of white soldiers, but these were concessionary. Under the Aboriginal Protection Act these privileges could be withdrawn, and many Indigenous soldiers faced discrimination on their return to civilian life. *SP1011/1, 2176/1 courtesy National Archives of Australia.*

an infant, taken from his Indigenous family by a white man, Robert Grant.[2] Robert believed he'd rescued the child from a life of violence and abuse. He and his wife had witnessed an Aboriginal trooper, working for the white authorities, beating the young boy.

Life with a white family was thought to offer hope and opportunity. But as one of Douglas' friends remarked in later life, it was all just a 'tragic experiment'.[3] Douglas would always be an outsider, not accepted fully by either world, black or white.

Adopted by the Grants, Douglas received a first-class education, trained in a technical school and qualified as a mechanical draughtsman. As he grew older, Douglas continued to stand out with his thick Scottish accent, his strong labour political views, and his love of the classics. Douglas recited Shakespeare in a thick Highland brogue.

When war broke out, Douglas believed it was his duty to enlist. He joined the AIF in 1916 but, after training with the 34th Battalion, was barred from leaving Australia because of his Indigenous descent. His father stepped in. A special dispensation was granted; Douglas was allowed to re-join his battalion and make his way to France.

Known as 'the black digger', Private Grant experienced barely two months of trench warfare in France before being wounded. He was struck by a shell at the Battle of Bullecourt and taken prisoner by the German Army.

Even as a prisoner Douglas stood out. He was sent to Berlin to be studied by anthropologists and scientists, a case study of the effects of western civilisation on 'a wild Cape York Bush Native.'[4] Seen as something of a curiosity, he was taken numerous times from his prison camp to be measured, photographed and questioned.

Separated from his fellow Australian prisoners and held with other 'coloured' Imperial troops, Douglas was given comparative freedom as a prisoner of war. He represented the British Help Committee, and organised and distributed Red Cross parcels to the other POWs. He corresponded tirelessly with London, thanking the Red Cross for their assistance and pleading the special needs of his comrades. The German authorities appear to have assumed that all 'coloured' people would be much the same and that Douglas would share the Indian troops' fondness for curry.

BELOW TOP **Prematurely aged:** Douglas Grant poses beside the memorial he designed at Callan Park. *P1 / 2079 by Sam Hood courtesy State Library of New South Wales.*

BELOW BOTTOM **A war memorial for his fellow patients:** Douglas Grant stands with a group of nurses and patients at Callan Park. The grounds and pond were thought to be therapeutic – all these men were psychologically damaged by the war. Sydney Morning Herald, *5 August 1931 courtesy National Library of Australia.*

Upon his return to Australia, Douglas appeared to readjust to civilian life. He became actively involved in numerous soldiers' associations, maintained a wide and diverse social network and even hosted his own radio slot – *The Diggers Session*. He believed, as many Indigenous soldiers did, that the war would bring change and sweep away prejudice and inequality. In that, he was sadly disappointed. Indigenous servicemen were often refused those things granted far more readily to their white comrades: soldier settlement blocks, access to pensions and medical entitlements.

During the years of the Great Depression, Douglas struggled. Finding work was hard enough for an able

ABOVE **Physically and mentally broken:** Douglas Grant's grave in Botany Cemetery. We do not know who placed the poppy there but Douglas Grant has now become a symbol of Indigenous service. Ironically, his grave overlooks Captain Cook's landing place in Sydney where the processes of colonisation effectively began. *Courtesy Bruce Scates.*

white man, let alone a black man hampered by a war injury. Douglas travelled extensively through country New South Wales and Victoria looking for work. He wrote one letter after another to the repatriation authorities, pleading for assistance. 'I must here state that I am really financially embarrassed,' he wrote to the pensions department. '[W]ith the exception of a day here and there all effort to find work has been futile.'[5] For an intelligent man, highly skilled and used to providing for himself, Douglas' unemployment was devastating.

Depression and hardship took their toll on Douglas, as it did for many returned diggers. In 1931, he was admitted to Callan Park Mental Hospital. The Department of Repatriation refused to acknowledge that Douglas' psychiatric problems were due to his war service. They denied him any increase in his war pension.

Douglas remained in Callan Park for over eight years. He struggled with alcoholism and bouts of mental instability. One repat doctor believed he was 'an incorrigible alcoholic with mild alcoholic dementia and will never improve'.[6] Another noted that despite being 'well nourished and well spoken' this prematurely aged man was prone to 'melancholic fancies'.[7] But even the asylum couldn't break Douglas' spirit. Nor did it crush his creativity. Whilst he was a resident, Douglas designed and constructed a replica of the Sydney Harbour Bridge and styled it as a war memorial for his fellow patients. Many men like himself had come back physically and mentally broken by war.

In the 1930s, Douglas Grant became a pioneer of the civil rights movement and advocated the cause of all Australia's veterans. He wrote a damning newspaper article entitled 'A Broken Pledge', claiming the government had wronged returned servicemen and had not delivered the 'land fit for heroes' they had been promised.

Upon his release from Callan Park in 1939, Douglas moved into the Salvation Army Home for Men in Dee Why, Sydney. Living unhappily on a pension, he was never able to find steady work, marry, or successfully negotiate the space between black and white Australia. He was often seen drinking alone or in the company of other 'burnt out' diggers. Douglas Grant died 'in loneliness and obscurity' in the Prince Henry Hospital, La Perouse in 1951.[8] After his death, a close friend remarked that his life was 'not a story that we have much to be proud of. A good brain wasted and a useful citizen frustrated.'[9]

SOURCES AND FURTHER READING: This story draws on Douglas Grant's service dossier NAA: B2455,GRANT D; his repatriation file NAA: C138, R70396 DOUGLAS GRANT; his Red Cross Wounded and Missing file AWM 1DRL/ 0428; 'The Story of Douglas Grant, the Black Scotsman' by John Thompson and Brian Hungerford [ABC Radio feature script, Box c21.] 1957, NAA: SP 1297/2 Grant, Douglas [Box 60218]; and Chris Clark, 'Grant Douglas (1885–1951)', *Australian Dictionary of Biography*, National Centre for Biography, Australian National University adb.anu.edu.au/biography/grant-douglas-6454/text11049, first published in hard copy 1983, accessed online 7 May 2015. For an introduction into the experience of Indigenous soldiers at war see Philippa Scarlett, *Aboriginal and Torres Strait Island Volunteers for the AIF: The Indigenous Response to World War One* (Canberra: Indigenous Histories, 2013).

A deeply damaged man

NOBLE BLACK

Noble Alexander Black was an office boy before he went to war. Raised in the pleasant seaside suburb of Manly, it was said he was spoilt as a child; a bit too bookish for his own good, leading too sheltered an existence. But France changed all of that. Black was just 18 years old when he enlisted. Despite his tender years, the young bombardier was sent into the thick of the fighting and soon gained a commission.

Then, in November 1917, Lieutenant Black was gassed and caught by a shell blast.

Sent home medically unfit, Black was no longer suited to clerking work in the city. The country air would do him good, the doctors said, and he was encouraged to try a new life as a grazier. Black married a Mudgee girl and took up a soldier settlement block.

Many thought the young man's prospects were good. Although Black had barely nine months' experience on the land, his father-in-law's money and practical assistance would help him. The country, too, was 'in very good heart'. An optimistic inspector, charged with valuing soldiers' blocks, boasted Black's run would comfortably carry five hundred sheep, and Black was just the fellow to work it. Five years of poor returns proved otherwise, and even the authorities admitted that sending a sick man to work poor land was nothing but 'a gross blunder'.[1]

In 1931, Noble Black was hospitalised in Randwick on four separate occasions, in part because of the residual effects of gas. Medical notes record that as well as 'harsh, vescular breathing sounds' in his back:

> *[Black] states he has been washing out his right nasal passage every two days since April but it always makes him feel sick. He does not get much hassle or mucous away but it is always mucky.*[2]

Alongside this rapid physical decline was a worsening in what medical staff called Black's 'mental condition'. An attending doctor noted:

> *This man was admitted in a very nervous and jumpy state. At the slightest sound or even the electric light being turned on or off, he threw his arms up trying to escape. He could not walk without assistance. His legs seem to have lost all power.*[3]

ABOVE **Hidden away in rigid isolation:** A view of Callan Park. This asylum for the mentally ill received hundreds of former soldiers in the postwar period, Noble Black included. Special facilities were provided by the repatriation authorities for 'nervy' and shell-shocked men. *4481_a026_000151 Callan Park Hospital, courtesy State Records Office, New South Wales*

Black was described as 'queer in manner', given to 'fits of crying', stammering and nightmares. He also experienced hallucinations, during which he relived the traumas of the trenches. 'He thought he could see ghosts,' the doctor noted, 'he was . . . throwing himself about in a frightened state . . . At times he is very violent.' Having failed to build a new life for himself on the land, Noble Black became one of the nervy, displaced men who haunted the cities and towns of interwar Australia.

Black often imagined violence committed against those he loved. 'He started to . . . yell out,' a disturbed doctor noted, 'when asked what was the matter he stated that men were stripping the flesh [off his wife's body] and crunching and eating the bones.'[4]

Damaged men like Black posed both a problem and an embarrassment for the authorities. At first, they were hidden away in rigid isolation, sent to special soldiers' wards in hospitals. Then they were locked up in institutions. In 1931, Black was finally certified. Admitted to Darlinghurst Reception House, he was diagnosed as 'delusional, restless and depressed'.

Throughout the 1930s, Black and thousands of others like him drifted in and out of one kind of institution or another – nerve homes, asylums, hostels for the homeless and incapacitated. These men, this deeply damaged generation, were effectively lost to the families and communities they came from. Mrs Black complained that her once attentive husband was now 'moody and bad tempered', given to violent outbursts against herself and her children. She lived in fear of the man she once loved. War had made a stranger of him.[5]

SOURCES AND FURTHER READING: This story draws on Noble Black's soldier settlement file State Records NSW: 12/7293, BLACK NA; his repatriation file NAA: C138/4 C29645, BLACK NA; his service dossier NAA: B2455, BLACK N A. For further reading about illness and disability after the war see Martin Crotty and Marina Larsson (eds) *Anzac Legacies: Australians and the Aftermath of War* (North Melbourne: Australian Scholarly Publishing, 2010); and Bruce Scates and Melanie Oppenheimer, *The Last Battle of the Great War: Soldier Settlement in Australia* (Cambridge: Cambridge University Press, forthcoming).

Almost within sight of Australia

NARRELLE HOBBES

In May 1918, the hospital ship SS *Kanowna* drifted to a halt in the Indian Ocean. The ship shut down her engines, and all who could gathered on the foredeck. *Kanowna*'s chaplain mumbled a few words to the swelling sea beneath him. Then a sheet containing Narrelle Hobbes' body slipped into the deep.

Narrelle was buried at sea just a few days sailing time from Australia. Her sister was beside her when she died. Elsie had been sent out to India to bring Narrelle home and had nursed her tirelessly while the ship ploughed its way through the ocean. But all to no avail. Narrelle lost her life to liver cancer. She was barely 39.

Narrelle's war had lasted four years; she had nursed the troops of the Empire in Malta and Sicily, India and Mesopotamia. Despite disease, exhaustion, danger and injury, she had been steadfast in her service. 'You see them brought in,' she wrote, 'stretcher after stretcher, in that endless procession, every man somebody's boy. I will never give up till we are not needed.'[1]

Narrelle was born in Tilba Tilba, New South Wales, and in her eagerness to serve she'd enlisted in the British rather than Australian forces. That meant Narrelle received none of the benefits extended to the men and women of the First AIF. It meant her pay was a quarter less, and that she was often set apart from the company of her fellow Australians. It also meant that the young woman who died in the service of her country would never be honoured in the cloisters of the Australian War Memorial. Narrelle Hobbes was not counted as one of our nation's 60 000 war dead. Like the names of all those who served with British units, her name was never set in bronze.

Narrelle left behind a close circle of friends, countless grateful patients and a loving family. Her letters remain, evoking memories of wattle in the wintertime, sunsets behind the mountains, wind rustling through forests of eucalypt, the scent of

ABOVE **Oceans of love:** A photograph of Narrelle Hobbes in her nurse's uniform. *PR03708 courtesy Australian War Memorial.*

summer rain. Every letter Narrelle wrote home ended with her characteristic farewell, pledging 'oceans of love' to Australia.

In 1919, the town of Tilba Tilba raised their war memorial. An obelisk of stone, it looks out across the fields and the mountains. The tall marble pillar carries its burden of names: farmers and carpenters, labourers and graziers. All were sons, some brothers – one in every four of Tilba Tilba's families lost someone in that war. But one name is missing: Narrelle Hobbes, a daughter of the district, whose body was committed to the deep almost within sight of the land she loved.

SOURCES AND FURTHER READING: This story draws on the extensive collections relating to Narrelle Hobbes at the Australian War Memorial PR3708 and 2DRL/0162; as well as Melanie Oppenheimer's fine book, *Oceans of Love* (Sydney: ABC Books, 2006). Narrelle's war service and her death just off the coast of Australia were reported on in the press and this story has drawn on these contemporary newspaper articles. For further reading on the work of nurses during war see Jan Bassett, *Guns and Brooches : Australian Army Nursing from the Boer War to the Gulf War* (Melbourne : Oxford University Press, 1992); and Kirsty Harris, *More than Bombs and Bandages : Australian Army Nurses at Work in World War I* (Newport: Big Sky Publishing, 2011).

BELOW LEFT **Every man, somebody's boy:** Narrelle with a party of Australian soldiers at St David's hospital in Malta. *PR03708 courtesy Australian War Memorial.*

BELOW **Looking out across the fields and the mountains:** The town of Tilba Tilba dedicates their war memorial in 1919. Narrelle's name does not appear on the obelisk, as she enlisted at Brewarrina, where she was nursing in the local hospital. Her name appears on the Honour Roll there. Sydney Mail, *21 April 1920 courtesy National Library of Australia.*

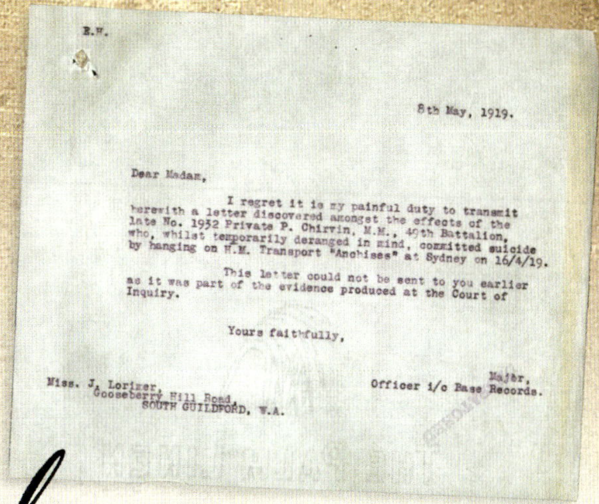

B.W.

8th May, 1919.

Dear Madam,

I regret it is my painful duty to transmit herewith a letter discovered amongst the effects of the late No. 1932 Private P. Chirvin, M.M., 49th Battalion, who, whilst temporarily deranged in mind, committed suicide by hanging on H.M. Transport "Anchises" at Sydney on 16/4/19.

This letter could not be sent to you earlier as it was part of the evidence produced at the Court of Inquiry.

Yours faithfully,

Major,
Officer i/c Base Records.

Miss. J. Lorimer,
Gooseberry Hill Road,
SOUTH GUILDFORD, W.A.

True to Australia

PETER CHIRVIN

Peter Michaelovitch Chirvin was born in Vladivostok, Russia in 1894. Eighteen years later, he immigrated to Australia; young, fit, confident, and keen to see the world. He worked as a reporter in Brisbane for a time before enlisting as an Australian soldier in the 9th Battalion in 1915.

Chirvin was one of around one thousand Russian Australians to serve in the First AIF, and one of over a hundred who saw action at Gallipoli. He was wounded twice during the course of the war and awarded the Military Medal for his bravery as a stretcher-bearer at Mont St Quentin. 'Private Chirvin,' the citation reads, 'displayed courage of the highest order, and was always the first to volunteer . . . By his splendid devotion to duty numbers of wounded were saved.'

Mont St Quentin was one of the last major battles the First AIF would fight, and it broke the German lines. In all, over three hundred casualties were brought in from the battlefield. Chirvin's 'bearing' in the face of danger 'was worthy of the highest praise'.[1]

Peter Chirvin survived the war and returned to Australia in 1919. The troopship HMAT *Anchises* took several weeks to reach Sydney. Throughout the voyage the young soldier counted the days. He 'appeared quite cheerful', a shipmate remembered, and was 'looking forward to returning' to the place he had made his home.

Then everything changed.

News of Bolshevik disturbances back home in Australia spread like wildfire through the ship. There had been riots in the streets of Brisbane as Allied armies began a new war in Russia, seeking to restore the old regime. Many in Australia's Russian community rallied beneath the Red Flag, calling for an end to foreign intervention in the affairs of that country and demanding the right to return home. Mobs of returned soldiers denounced the demonstrators as traitors and attacked the headquarters of the Russian Association. Police with rifles and fixed bayonets dispersed the angry crowd.

ABOVE **Written to Australian families:** One of the last letters that Peter Chirvin wrote was to Miss Lorimer in Western Australia. The two had corresponded often during the long years of war. In the final moments of his life Peter Chirvin tried to explain the circumstances that had driven him to suicide. Friends and fiancées often heard of the death of their soldiers overseas, but few received news like this. *NAA: B2455, CHIRVIN P courtesy National Archives of Australia.*

OPPOSITE **Courage of the highest order:** Will Dyson's famous image of Australian stretcher-bearers at work in France. Chirvin served in similar conditions to these, braving the elements and heavy enemy fire. *ART02266 courtesy Australian War Memorial.*

ABOVE **Buried in an unmarked grave:** The final resting place of Private Peter Chirvin. Like many returned soldiers, Chirvin was buried in what was commonly called a pauper's plot. His remains compete for space amongst hundreds of others buried at the Quarantine Station. This empty stretch of bush land is very different to the neatly aligned tombstones found in cemeteries in Flanders and on the Somme. *Courtesy David Little.*

In the tense postwar atmosphere, fear and suspicion grew. The men on the ship decided Chirvin might also be a 'Bolshie'. He was heckled, ridiculed and told that his Russian parentage somehow made him disloyal.

On the morning of 15 April 1919, as the men on the *Anchises* were nearing home, Private Chirvin asked to speak to his commanding officer. Lieutenant Colonel Denton later told a court of inquiry:

> *He was very moody and depressed. He told me that he intended to go overboard . . . His comrades were calling him a Bolshie . . . I tried to obtain the names of the offenders but he refused [to turn them in].*

Private Chirvin handed the Colonel two letters for safekeeping. They were written to Australian families he'd corresponded with during the long years of war. The next day Chirvin was found hanging from a beam in the ship's washroom. The court of inquiry into his death later returned a verdict of 'suicide whilst temporarily deranged'.[2]

One of Chirvin's last letters was written to a Mrs Bryan in Brisbane. He thanked her for all the gifts and the great kindness she had shown him. 'By the time you receive this I will be out of the world,' the letter continued, 'but do not think me a coward, not for a battlefield. If you see the 49th Battalion boys ask them about me, and they will tell you.'[3] Chirvin's last letter claimed he was 'true to Australia'. But had Australia been true to him?

In 1926, Peter Chirvin's mother made her way to the British Mission at Vladivostok. She said she'd received a letter from her son during the war, telling her that in the case of his death, she would receive 'one or two small trinkets', a ring and a watch, and whatever money he had. The last personal effects of Peter Chirvin were sent home to Russia, as were the decorations he had earned in the war. When the Victory Star arrived, the parcel had already been opened, the medal removed and only the ribbon remained. The authorities deducted the sum of two shillings and ten pence from the money Peter had left his mother – the exact cost of the medal being replaced.

Peter Chirvin's body was buried in an unmarked grave in the Quarantine Station at North Head in Sydney Harbour. Alongside him lie thirteen men of the First AIF who died of wounds and disease. No other man from the 49th Battalion lies there. And perhaps that is just as well.

The grave has no epitaph and Mrs Chirvin would never visit it. Like countless thousands of Australian mothers, her boy's body was buried oceans away. But she kept the letter the young soldier had written to her from France, where he went to fight for the country he'd adopted. 'I beg you once more not to worry too much, I think we shall meet each other again.'[4]

SOURCES AND FURTHER READING: This story draws on Peter Chirvin's service dossier NAA: B2455, CHIRVIN P. The death of Private Chirvin was reported on throughout Australia and this story draws on these contemporary newspaper articles. For further reading on Russian Anzacs see Elena Govor, *Russian Anzacs in Australian History* (Sydney: UNSW Press, 2005).

BELOW LEFT **Born in Vladivostok:** Private Peter Chirvin served as a Russian subject in the Australian Imperial forces. Imperial Russia was Australia's ally during the First World War. *The Imperial Standard of the Emporer of Russia (1858–1917), Creative Commons.*

BELOW **True to Australia:** Lieutenant Bond relates the background to Private Chirvin's death. Bond claimed that Chirvin got no more than the 'usual teasing that most foreigners get'. Northern Star *23 April 1918 courtesy National Library of Australia.*

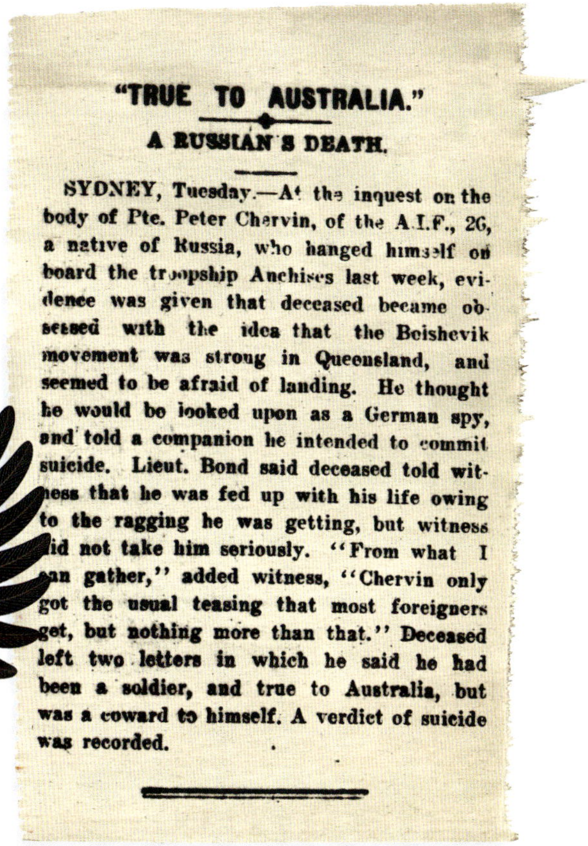

"TRUE TO AUSTRALIA."

A RUSSIAN'S DEATH.

SYDNEY, Tuesday.—At the inquest on the body of Pte. Peter Chervin, of the A.I.F., 26, a native of Russia, who hanged himself on board the troopship Anchises last week, evidence was given that deceased became obsessed with the idea that the Bolshevik movement was strong in Queensland, and seemed to be afraid of landing. He thought he would be looked upon as a German spy, and told a companion he intended to commit suicide. Lieut. Bond said deceased told witness that he was fed up with his life owing to the ragging he was getting, but witness did not take him seriously. "From what I can gather," added witness, "Chervin only got the usual teasing that most foreigners get, but nothing more than that." Deceased left two letters in which he said he had been a soldier, and true to Australia, but was a coward to himself. A verdict of suicide was recorded.

Inventing Anzac Day in England

ALFRED SHARP

Alfred Sharp described himself as an Australian, first and foremost. From a young age, he loved the bush. Growing up in Chilwell just outside Geelong, he spent every summer roaming creeks and hillsides; watching parrots darting colour through the trees, sketching flowers and animals. As a young man, Sharp joined the railways and devoted himself to public service. In 1912, he was appointed the Victorian Immigration Officer in London and sailed off to what was then called 'the old country'.

In England, Alfred Sharp advocated the cause of Australia through his work assisting emigrants about to take up a new life in Victoria, and played a part in establishing the first branch of the Australian Natives Association in England. Sharp was also at the centre of a vibrant expatriate community nestled then (as today) in the heart of London, a patron of every Australian artist, writer and celebrity to visit the city, a close observer of politics 18 000 miles away, an avid reader of every paper shipped in by steamer.

ABOVE **A separate grave:** Alfred Sharp inspects the grave of Private Samuel West at Lawnswood Cemetery in Leeds. West's grave is marked by a rough tilting cross, unlike the sturdy headstones that would be raised after the war. The grave is clearly neglected and scattered amongst civilian burials. Sharp believed all Australian servicemen should be buried in purpose-made cemeteries and was appalled by the practice of mass, common burials. West died of wounds in 1916, aged 24 years. Although he served in the First AIF he was born in England. *J00599 courtesy Australian War Memorial.*

Then came the war. Sharp was too old to serve in the regular army, and enlistment in the First AIF from London would have been a difficult matter anyway. So, he joined the British Volunteer Regiment and served in Middlesex with the Willesden Battalion. But being a weekend soldier was not enough for Alfred Sharp. In addition to his duties on the home front, and his demanding office at Australia House, he threw himself into volunteer work. In 1916, he helped establish the Anzac Buffet, opposite AIF Headquarters on Horseferry Road. 'A great centre for the Anzacs', it served hot meals, boasted a reading, writing and billiard room and hosted a live concert every evening. The atmosphere, Sharp noted, 'was distinctively Australian'; every service was free of charge and every volunteer hailed from Australia or New Zealand.[1]

During the war, Sharp's home was thrown open to his countrymen. Sharp was known as 'the diggers' friend', and he and his wife hosted visits from several hundred servicemen, Albert Jacka VC and Hugo Throssell VC amongst them. By 1918, Sharp

ABOVE **Distinctively Australian:** The Anzac Buffet in London. Originally located near AIF Headquarters in Horseferry Road, the buffet moved to Victoria Street in 1916. A 'live institution', in six months alone it served 177 000 soldiers with refreshments. *H18652 courtesy Australian War Memorial.*

was corresponding with around two hundred soldiers a week, in particular wounded men convalescing in England. But the hardest letters he wrote were sent home to Australia. 'Many of the mothers of Australian soldiers' who had died in hospital 'received a nice letter from this man saying that he or his wife followed their son to his last resting place'. One of their own had done all that could be done for them.[2]

As if caring for the living was not enough, Alfred Sharp also devoted himself to the dead. In early 1917, he revealed the scandalous treatment of the bodies of Australian servicemen buried in Britain. When a push was on in Belgium or France, hospital mortuaries in the south of England were stacked high with corpses; there was neither the space nor the time to bury them 'decently'. As many as twenty men were piled in a single grave, and graves were often left open awaiting the next fatality. Driver J.F. Naughton was one such case.

A baker from Charters Towers, John Naughton died of war wounds and kidney failure a year after leaving Gallipoli. Largely forgotten in life, he became a cause célèbre in death. Naughton's body was placed in an open grave in Kensal Green Cemetery. Exposure to the elements led to 'consequences better imagined than described' (as Sharp's anxious report to the authorities put it). It was several weeks before the plot was filled in and then it was only after formal protests by the London Branch of the Australian Natives Association. In 1921, Naughton's decomposing body was exhumed and placed in a separate plot for Australian soldiers.[3]

Sharp's protest shaped the protocols of remembrance; it set down the simple principle that made the cemeteries of the Great War possible. In time, the Imperial War Graves Commission would guarantee each soldier an individual grave, undertake to preserve each tomb in perpetuity, and assure families that all men were honoured equally. A forest of glistening white tombstones would rise up on Flanders and the Somme, ending the age-old anonymity of the war dead.

But not in 1916. When John Naughton was buried, troops killed overseas or who died from wounds or illness in Britain were only entitled to individual graves if they were officers. Enlisted men were often buried in common plots, usually with nothing to mark their graves and certainly no epitaph from grieving families.

The decent interment of the dead was the first task Alfred Sharp set himself, honouring the graves of Australia's fallen was the second. Few would contest the *Chronicle*'s claim that Sharp was 'the originator of Anzac Day pilgrimage in Great Britain', which began long before the war had ended.[4] In March 1918, Sharp called on Australian expatriates to honour the brave representatives of the Commonwealth who had died in their midst:

> *It is felt by the members of the London branch of the ANA that it would be very fitting if a pilgrimage was undertaken on Anzac Day (25th April) and floral tributes placed on various graves and, if possible, arrangements will be made whereby such tokens of remembrance will be renewed from time to time. Seeing the burials have taken part in so many localities it may perhaps be difficult to carry out the scheme absolutely, but much may be done.*[5]

Much was; Australian and New Zealand expatriates rallied around Anzacs' graves, bedecked them with springtime flowers, weeded and tended them. It was a massive undertaking. By the end of the war, 2135 members of the First AIF were buried in common or individual plots in some 343 graveyards scattered across England.

Peace hastened what Sharp liked to call 'the pilgrimage movement'. It was not just that the cessation of hostilities signalled the end to much other volunteer work, freeing time and resources for Anzac commemoration. Or that marking Australian war graves on Anzac Day laid our country's claim on a hard-won British victory. As early as 1919, Sharp warned of 'the inevitable pilgrimage' from 'down under', and by 1921 as many as 10 000 Australians a year were touring French and Belgian battlefields. The Anzac cemeteries in England, he explained, must be fit to receive them.[6]

This duty of care was not confined to graveyards

BELOW **From the sunny south:** Alfred Sharp's portrait of three Australian nurses, Sister Mabel Cameron from Tasmania, Sister Annie Foster from New South Wales, and Sister Clare Deacon, also from Tasmania. All survived the war. Sister Deacon was awarded the Military Medal for bravery during bombing raids at the 2nd Casualty Clearing Station near Armentières in July 1917. Nurses like these were recruited for the first Anzac pilgrimages, placing flowers on the graves of those they could not save. *J00721 courtesy Australian War Memorial.*

in the immediate vicinity of London. Supporters in Glasgow vowed to 'place a floral tribute on each Australian grave in that city'; and parties of pilgrims set out to Birmingham, Cardiff, Cheltenham, Lincoln, Portsmouth and the Australian camp at Salisbury. By 1921, Sharp had achieved his aim of a movement that extended 'the length and breadth of the old land'. Aided by 'the heartiest support of Australasian residents here and many others who do not hail from the Sunny South' he had placed a floral tribute on 'practically every [Anzac's] grave' in Britain.[7]

Amongst these surrogate mourners were British families whose sons had served alongside Anzac forces in Gallipoli, nurses who had cared for them in Britain, townsfolk with fond memories of 'the distinctive slouch hats [and one suspects bulging wallets] of the colonials'. Supporting the Anzac pilgrimage assuaged the common grief of Empire, as letters to 'My Dear Mr Sharp' clearly testify.

> *One is from the widow of a [British] soldier who . . . also took part in the landing at Gallipoli. He was subsequently killed but as she cannot put flowers on his grave, she intends visiting some Australian graves on Anzac Day thereby honouring his memory.*

Another was from a mother whose son was buried in France:

> *[she] wishes to 'adopt' a lonely Australasian grave in England, and keep in touch with the relatives overseas. People in France are doing the same for her.*

In both cases these women performed the role of what historians have called 'fictive kin'; their use of the term 'adoption' is telling.[8]

In a sense, Alfred Sharp, 'the diggers' friend', was also one of their family. He corresponded tirelessly with grieving mothers back home, assuring them that their boy was honoured and remembered, bridging (as one woman put it) 'such a great space of water between us'.[9] He welcomed many lonely men into his home, offering sage advice and cheering hospitality, treating them to the company of a fellow Australian. And he left a record of Australia's distant graves, a folio of photographs donated (on his death) to the Australian War Memorial.

Today few Australians would know the name of Alfred Sharp. But neither Anzac Day in Britain, nor indeed the cemeteries of the Great War, would have been quite the same without him.

ABOVE **Lonely Men:** A digger wanders the streets of the metropolis. This sketch, from the 'Anzac Series', features prominent London landmarks, St Paul's Cathedral on the city skyline and Ye Olde Cheshire Cheese, an inn favoured by Australian visitors. The image suggests the great city could be as alienating as it was exciting. Sharp offered visitors to London company, reassurance, and an element of moral guidance. *W. G. Alma Collection courtesy State Library of Victoria.*

SOURCES AND FURTHER READING: This story draws on Alfred Sharp's papers and photographs at the Australian War Memorial PRO4809; the service dossier for Driver J N Naughton NAA:B2455, NAUGHTON JN; Arrangements in connection with the graves of fallen soldiers buried in Europe general policy of Commonwealth Government NAA:A11849, 2350/2; Imperial War Graves Commission minutes of proceedings NAA:A209 A2909/2, A453/1/3; and a detailed survey of the *British Australasian*, journal of the expatriate community in London. For further information on the work of Australia House, see Olwen Valda Pryke, 'Australia House: Representing Australia in London, 1901–1939' (PhD thesis, University of Sydney, 2006) and Bruce Scates and Frank Bongiorno with Rebecca Wheatley and Laura James, '"Such a great space of water between us": Anzac Day in Britain, 1916–1939' in *Australian Historical Studies*, vol. 45, no. 2, June 2014, pp. 220–241. The authors thank Frank Bongiorno and Angela Woollacott for their insights.

Age shall not weary them

THE CARMAN BROTHERS

Port Broughton is a tiny farming community on the Spencer Gulf, some 170 kilometres from Adelaide. Forty-seven of the town's sons marched off to war; twenty-one never came home.

Elizabeth and David Carman sent three sons to France: Clement, who enlisted at 19, and was killed at 20; Roland, 22 when he joined up, dead a year later; and David, barely 20 when he died in the last year of the war.

The first telegram, announcing 'with deepest regret' that Roland had died, came in 1916. The grim pink envelope was carried to the Carman family's door by the local clergyman. He came again in 1917, for Roland, and the year after that, for their youngest boy, David.

Like thousands of other families scattered across the globe, Elizabeth and David Carman could never visit their sons' graves. So in the 1920s they gave what they could to help build the town's war memorial. The memorial took the form of a white stone soldier, set on a plinth, gazing down the same streets where townsfolk once gathered to cheer their men. It looks much the same as hundreds of other stone soldiers, mute with grief, scattered across the Australian countryside.

The names of Mr and Mrs Carman's three sons are carved on a panel near the feet of Port Broughton's stone soldier. These men, it tells us, 'made the supreme sacrifice'. But so too – in a sense – did the parents who raised them. David Carman Sr died in 1928. He had lived forty years longer than any of his sons. Two of his boys were underage when they enlisted. David Carman signed both their consent forms, unwittingly sending those he loved to their deaths.

A decade after the war had ended, the Carman family was still in mourning. The memorial medallions, issued in honour of each dead boy, were gathered together soon after David Carmen Sr died, and set in the marble pillar marking his grave. That chilling phrase, the same phrase used in those telegrams, was chiseled beneath their names: KILLED IN ACTION 1914–1918.

The Carman family had a passage based on Binyon's *Ode* carved at the base of the memorial:

> *They shall grow not old the same*
> *As we who are left grow old*
> *Age cannot weary them nor*
> *The years condemn.*

In the memory of those who loved them, Clement, David and Roland were still young men, frozen in the moment they marched off to war from Port Broughton.[1]

SOURCES AND FURTHER READING: This story draws on the service dossiers of each of the Carman boys NAA: B2455, CARMAN CC; NAA: B2455, CARMAN RC; NAA: B2355, CARMAN DW; the Red Cross Wounded and Missing file of Clement Carman AWM 1DRL/0428. For further reading on war memorials in the Australian landscape see Ken Inglis, *Sacred Places: War Memorials in the Australian Landscape* (Carlton: Melbourne University Press, 1998); Bruce Scates and Rebecca Wheatley, 'War Memorials' in Jay Winter (ed) *The Cambridge History of the First World War*, vol. III (Cambridge: Cambridge University Press, 2014), pp. 528–558. The authors warmly acknowledge the assistance of Nigel Starck and John Savage in researching the Carman brothers' story.

OPPOSITE **Mute with grief:** A stone soldier stands guard over Port Broughton War Memorial. *Courtesy John Savage.*

BELOW **That chilling phrase:** The Carman family tomb became a surrogate grave for bodies lost on the other side of the world. There is no actual grave for Roland and Clement – their names are listed on the memorial to the missing at Villers-Bretonneux. David was buried in Hangard Communal Cemetery, Picardie, France. *Courtesy Nigel Starck.*

I still have the bullet in my body

JAMES NEWMAN DANN

James Newman Dann, a labourer from Broome, enlisted the day after the Anzacs landed at Gallipoli. He arrived on the Peninsula just in time for the August Offensive. Private Dann went over the top at Lone Pine and was wounded soon after. He was hospitalised in Malta and sent home to Australia in 1916.

Like many of his generation, James Dann wasn't the sort to complain. 'I still have the bullet in my body,' he told the repat doctors, '[but] so long as I take things quietly I can keep going.' Even so, Dann just wasn't the man he once was: 'I cannot do any [heavy] work [now] . . . any exertion brings on severe pains in the stomach, tremors and . . . lung trouble.'[1]

The Repatriation Department put Dann to work weaving baskets for the Red Cross. It was light work that even he could manage but it paid him barely a pound a week.

Then, in 1921, they decided Private Dann might just be fit enough for farming. 'Inspector Hadlington has interviewed Dann,' an official from the soldier settlement scheme noted, 'and considers him a likely man to make a success of the holding.' The property was a poultry farm outside of Sydney, not too far from where Dann had grown up in Balmain. It was a five-acre block, one small enough (the Department reasoned) for even a weak man to manage. '[H]is experience is not great,' the report concluded, and Dann's health was not that great either.[2]

Within a year of taking up the block, Dann had developed pulmonary tuberculosis, a portion of his lung had collapsed and the bullet lodged in his body caused intense pain.

Medical reports chart the steady decline in his health: patient 'short of breath', one notes, 'sleeps badly', 'sweats very freely', and is 'pale and anemic'. Dann was assessed as 'totally incapacitated' and his pension set accordingly. The likelihood of further improvement was deemed 'problematical'.[3]

Sick and injured veterans were told that working the land would be a chance to regain their manhood and independence, and raising a few chooks was seen by some as therapeutic. But nervy men like James found otherwise. In 1923 he walked off the land.

'I frequently have to rest,' he explained:

> *the foreign body near my spine handicaps me considerably [and] I get severe backaches and pains in the neck and across the eyes after walking or sitting for any length of time.*[4]

Dann lost not just his farm but also his family. At risk of infection from tuberculosis, his wife and two children were 'living apart from him under a separation order'.

Tuberculosis was known as the wasting disease in the early twentieth century. It claimed the lives of thousands. In the hope of avoiding its spread, sufferers were often physically removed from their families. Many would die alone, far from the company of those they loved.

James and his family were eventually reunited. But, having survived the Great War, Dann then faced the Great Depression. Through the long dark years of the 1930s, he managed on a pension of a few pounds a week. He did what work he could for the Red Cross, but any heavy lifting brought 'a stabbing pain', sometimes for days on end.

James Dann died in 1953, almost thirty-five years to the day from when the Great War ended. Like hundreds of others, his last weeks were spent in the repat hospital in Concord, and he was buried in an unmarked grave.

SOURCES AND FURTHER READING: This story draws on James Dann's service dossier NAA: B2455, DANN J N; his soldier settlement file State Records NSW: 12/7293/08239; his repatriation file NAA: C138/4 C314427 DANN JD. For further reading on the soldier settlement scheme see Bruce Scates and Melanie Oppenheimer, *The Last Battle of the Great War: Soldier Settlement in Australia* (Cambridge: Cambridge University Press, forthcoming) and Glenys Allison, 'Shadows of the Great War: Group Soldier Settlement in Greater Sydney' (PhD thesis, University of New England, 2011).

BELOW **Put to work weaving baskets:** An image of one of the workshops designed to teach 'useful' trades to disabled men. Dann was incapable of doing any heavier work, but many men viewed weaving baskets as a slight on their masculinity. This picture was published on Anzac Day – an ironic homage to the men who returned. Sunday Times, *25 April 1920 courtesy National Library of Australia.*

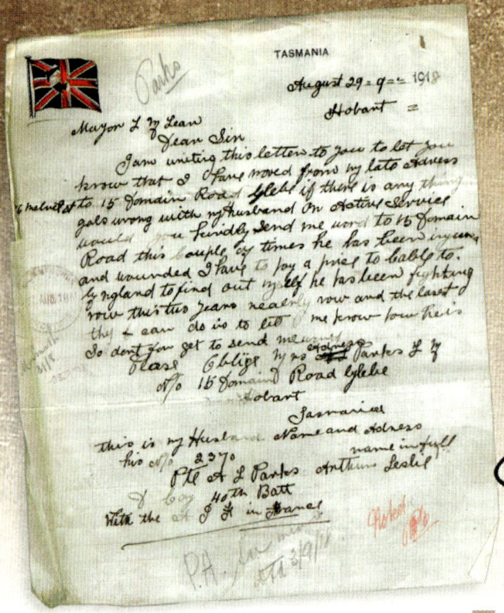

TASMANIA

August 29 - 9 - 1918
Hobart

Major L Mc Lean
Dear Sir
I am writing this letter to you to let you know that I have moved from my late address to 15 Domain Road Glebe if there is any thing goes wrong with my husband On Active Service would you kindly send me word to 15 Domain Road this couple of times he has been wounded and I have to pay a price to cable to England to find out myself he has been fighting now this two years nearly now and the least they can do is to let me know how he is So dont you get to send me word
Please Oblige Mrs Parkes L F
c/o 15 Domain Road Glebe
Hobart
Tasmania

This is my Husband Name and Address
his No 2370 name in full
Pte A L Parkes Arthur Leslie
D Coy 40th Batt
with the A I F in France

Such a small favour

EMILY LUTTRELL

They fashioned Hobart's Honour Board from the finest Tasmanian timber. The blackwood panels are a warm golden brown, shaped from sturdy trees, felled in the heart of the temperate rainforest. As you enter the Town Hall, Hobart's Honour Roll stands proudly in the foyer: 3500 names, the city's sons and daughters, who volunteered for service overseas.

It took years to complete the Honour Board. Each day, the master craftsman carved another name carefully in the wood. And many names are repeated – there are three Hanigans, four Hunts and five Luttrells.

Emily Luttrell first approached the Minister of Defence in June 1922. 'Please pardon me for taking the liberty of writing,' she began, 'if you could see your way to help me . . . I would deem it one of the greatest favours of my life'.[1] Mrs Luttrell longed to see the grave of her son Arthur. He had been wounded four times during the course of the war and died of influenza within a few months of the war ending. Her boy was buried in the south of England.

By any criteria, Mrs Luttrell must have seemed deserving. At 66 years of age, with a husband who was deaf and blind, there was no way she could afford the fare on her own. Mrs Luttrell had lived in Australia forty-nine years and raised fifteen children. Of these, seven were sent to war.

In October, she wrote again: 'I am not asking much from you.'[2]

By March the following year, the letters become both more pathetic and more insistent.

ABOVE **The least they can do is let me know:** Lillian Parkes, Arthur's wife, pleads for any news of her husband. Private Parkes had been wounded four times in battle – Lillian was obliged to cable the authorities in England for details. Like Arthur's mother, Lillian found herself disenfranchised by her grief. As late as 1947 she approached the authorities for a widow's badge. None were available. *NAA: B2455, PARKES ARTHUR LESLIE courtesy National Archives of Australia.*

> *I . . . beg that your Government will take into consideration my Appeal and try and help me to visit my Dear ones resting place, there was seven of our sons went to the war . . . Surely I have won the right to ask such a small favour which was promised by the late government.*[3]

But the government wasn't about to do Emily Luttrell any favours. A crisp memo to the Prime Minister declared:

> *. . . it would be rather dangerous to [agree] to these requests. The deaths overseas numbered [almost 60 000] and the burials took place in many different countries. There is a danger that such privileges might well be abused.*[4]

Just how these grieving women planned to abuse this privilege was never explained by the Prime Minister's Office.

Emily Luttrell died in October 1931. She was 75 years of age. She never visited the grave of her son.

SOURCES AND FURTHER READING: This story draws on Arthur Parkes' service dossier NAA: B2455, PARKES AL; and War Graves / Visits to Pt 1 NAA: A1608, F27/1/7 Part 1. See also Bruce Scates, '[It] ought to be as famous as the Statue of Liberty': The Forgotten History of Tasmania's Cenotaph – Australia's first State War Memorial', *Tasmanian Historical Studies*, vol. 14, 2009, pp. 53–78.

BELOW LEFT **Shaped from sturdy trees:** Hobart's Honour Board adorns the entrance of the Town Hall. 3500 men, almost 10 per cent of the city's total population, enlisted to fight in the Great War. Many did not return. *Courtesy Bruce Scates.*

BELOW **Buried in the south of England:** Arthur Parkes lies alongside the graves of other Australians in Sutton Veny graveyard. *Courtesy Bruce Scates.*

The heart of a lion

ROWLEY LORDING

BELOW **Towards the barbed wire:** Lording's story featured on the front cover of the RSL's journal. Reveille, *1 October 1935 courtesy State Library of Victoria.*

On the morning of his sixteenth birthday, Rowley Lording carried a steaming cup of tea to his mother's bedroom. She stretched, smiled and kissed him warmly. And then he raised the topic his mother had always feared: 'You know there's only one present worthwhile you can give me today . . . your consent to go.' [1]

Rowley Lording had already tried to enlist four times. Each time the recruiting officers had turned him away. But with his parents' consent, the military authorities turned a blind eye to his age. They made Rowley a signaller and his mother hoped that would keep him far from the front line. She was wrong.

In November 1915, Rowley sailed to Egypt. A few months later he saw action in the desert. And then, the following June, he sailed on to France.

Barely 17, Rowley Lording found himself in the trenches at Fromelles. He volunteered to cross no-man's-land, enter the German lines and set up a signal position. Rowley went in to battle 'on the heels of the men with the bayonets, racing with the infantry towards the Hun'.[2] He recounted the experience:

> *I was getting towards the barbed wire entanglements when shrapnel got me. My right arm got it and my elbow was shattered . . . I managed to get to a shell hole. There I found a badly wounded chap smoking . . . as if nothing were going on. I cadged a cigarette.*[3]

Rowley was hit a second time as the wounded were dragged back to the lines. An explosive bullet ploughed through his chest, punctured a lung and left a hole in his body the size of a man's hand.

For weeks, Rowley hovered between life and death. In the space of two months he was operated on eight separate times.

He was evacuated to England, and the King's surgeon was called in to build Rowley an artificial lung. He had to remove six ribs to do this. The operation lasted hour after hour. The surgical team watched the boy's heart beating through a hole in his side.

They set a silver plate in what was left of his rib cage. It was stamped with the name and date of the bungled battle: 'Fleurbaix, July 19, 1916.'

In November 1919, the boy soldier came home to Australia, where the operations continued. Over the next fifteen years, Rowley underwent fifty surgical procedures. They had to tip his broken body on its side to drain the pus away. His right arm was amputated above the elbow. Rowley was in constant pain.

'An undaunted spirit in a battered body,' the papers wrote, 'a boy with a heart of the lion,' he carried on 'with characteristic grit'.

But the pain paid no heed to newspaper headlines. By the time he was 20, Rowley Lording was addicted to morphine:

> *The military hospital [proved] a good market for the war profiteer whose nefarious business was the selling of drugs. Morphia, heroin, atropine, barbatone, cocaine 'snow' and even opium, found their way into the hospital unsuspected, while the attention of the authorities was directed towards suppressing the lesser and only apparent evil – drink. A hollow bedpost, a cake of soap, and many other things provided suitable hiding places, and a cunningly contrived fountain-pen, more than once lent to an unsuspecting sister to write her report or mark a chart, concealed a hypodermic syringe.*[4]

Like many returned soldiers, Rowley struggled with pain, addiction, and the costs of raising a family. He also founded the 30th Battalion Association, and worked for the welfare of limbless soldiers, placing their needs above his own.

But the experience of war broke the heart of that young lion. Rowley Lording died in a mental hospital in 1944.

Before he died, Rowley Lording wrote his memoirs. 'An epic of human suffering', they were published by the RSL. The men who served alongside Rowley believed his story deserved to be told.

ABOVE **An epic of human suffering:** Rowley Lording's confronting autobiography. Lording claimed his purpose was to 'draw a picture of the war and its aftermath'. In publishing this account L.A. Robb, State President of the New South Wales RSL, claimed it was a truthful account of men 'torn and hacked in the ghastliness of war'. *A. Tiveychoc (Rowland Lording) and decorations by Frank Dunne,* There and Back: The Story of an Australian Soldier 1915–1935 *(Sydney: Halstead Press, 1935).*

SOURCES AND FURTHER READING: This story draws on the work written by A. Tiveychoc (the pen name of Rowland Lording), *There and Back: The Story of an Australian Soldier 1915–1935* (Sydney: Halstead Publishing, 1935); Rowland Lording's service dossier NAA: B2455, LORDING RE; and his repatriation file NAA: PP645/1, LORDING Rowland Edward. The achievements and battles of Rowland Lording were reported in the press throughout his life and this story has drawn on many of the contemporary newspaper articles, including items from the NSW's RSL periodical, *Reveille*. For further reading on the history of repatriation see Stephen Garton, *The Cost of War: Australians Return* (Melbourne: Oxford University Press, 1996).

Never to love again

OLIVE PINK

ABOVE **I worship trees and flowers:** Olive's sensitive rendering of native flora. She made the sketches in Tasmania before trekking across the desert of central Australia. *Olive Pink Collection, Rare and Special Collections, courtesy University of Tasmania Library.*

Olive Pink was the kind of woman who stood out in a crowd. Tall, stern, with a sharp wit and a sharper tongue, she was one of the few white women to settle in Alice Springs in the 1930s. And in that dusty frontier town she quickly became known for a series of causes. Long before it became fashionable, Olive Pink championed the environment. Founder of the town's Botanic Gardens, she nurtured seedlings in the desert and found the dry heart of Australia a 'place of peace and beauty'. 'I worship trees and flowers,' she wrote, 'and especially the gallant ones of our arid regions.'

Olive was gallant herself and certainly something of a feminist. It was not just that she attended university, studying for a doctorate in the virtually all-male field of anthropology, or that she made an independent living for herself in an age when most women married. Olive Pink loved adventure. In the 1930s, 'she rolled up her swag, and travelled alone from Port Augusta to Darwin', pioneering fieldwork amongst the Aboriginal communities of central Australia. 'I like talking about "things",' she declared, 'ideas and beliefs, not babies, ornaments and love affairs and all the things a really womanly woman should.'[1]

Olive Pink was a tireless campaigner for those same Aboriginal communities she studied. At the height of the assimilationist era, she condemned the forced removal of Indigenous children from their families, demanded land for those 'shamefully' dispossessed, and called for equal wages at a time when most Aboriginal men and women worked for just a pittance in rations.

She was also an advocate of what today we would call cultural autonomy. 'All fair-minded Australians, with any real sense of justice, will support a sanctuary', she declared; a place far from the grog and exploitation of white townships, where 'the old tribal ways' were beyond the reach of missionaries and policemen, where Aboriginal communities could thrive on Aboriginal country.[2]

Fearlessly principled, outspoken and unorthodox, Olive Pink was in many ways exceptional. And yet she shared one thing in common with a generation of women in interwar Australia: Olive lost the man she loved at Gallipoli. And she never loved again.

Captain Harold Alfred Southern fell leading his men in a night attack on the Turkish front line. One of the few to survive the battle, William Hart, a Private in B Company, described his death in intimate detail:

> *We advanced up the Gully and rushed the ridge on the right of it . . . Southern was next to me. All of a sudden he was hit and fell backwards. It must have been in the throat or chest as he made a gurgling sound . . . I have not seen him since.*[3]

Captain Harold Southern died just ten days after the Landing. Like thousands of others, his body was never recovered from the battlefield. Nor were his parents the first to hear of his loss. Harold's mother only learned of her son's death when she received a consolation letter from a friend in Britain. The military authorities had failed to contact her.

BELOW LEFT **My reason for living:** Harold Southern on the eve of his departure for war. Harold, like Olive, was an accomplished artist. He was 26 years old when he died. *Olive Pink Collection, Rare and Special Collections courtesy University of Tasmania Library.*

BELOW **The kind of woman who stood out:** Olive Pink at the beginning of her career. *PH0091/0058 NTGP Collection courtesy Northern Territory Library.*

All her life, Olive treasured Harold's photograph and the pictures he painted as an art student in Hobart. These, she explained, were all she had left of him. As she confided to a friend 'her reason for living died at Gallipoli'.[4]

Every Anzac Day, Olive, like thousands of other women across Australia, would turn to the task of remembrance. She would climb Anzac Hill in the early hours of the morning and place a bunch of native flowers at the foot of the town's war memorial. Olive always came alone, long before the service commenced: her grief was something she bore alone, needing no words, nursed in reverent silence. For many years, locals wondered how the flowers came to be there, propped up in the cold night air beside the obelisk, waiting, it seemed, for a community to gather around them. Then, by chance, an old veteran came across Olive on her lonely vigil. 'She stood with head bowed for several minutes', then slipped away in the darkness.

BELOW TOP **Needing no words:** Floral tributes placed on the Alice Springs War Memorial. *PH0034-0048 Anzac Memorial courtesy Northern Territory Library.*

BELOW BOTTOM **Different to the end:** Olive's tombstone looks out over her 'beloved MacDonnell Ranges'. All the other graves face the opposite direction. *Olive Pink Collection, Rare and Special Collections courtesy University of Tasmania Library.*

Olive Pink died in Alice Springs aged 91, and her body was buried in the cemetery on the fringes of town. She wanted a photograph of Harold Southern placed in her coffin. Her plot faces the opposite direction to every other grave and looks out towards her 'beloved MacDonnell Ranges'. The authorities denied her last request, that she be buried in ground set aside for Aboriginal people.[5]

SOURCES AND FURTHER READING: This story draws on Harold Southern's service dossier NAA: B2455 SOUTHERN HAROLD ALFRED; Michael Jackson, *At Home in the World* (Durham: Duke University Press, 1995); Alison Holland, 'Feminism, Colonialism and Aboriginal Workers: An Anti-Slavery Crusade', *Labour History*, 1 November 1995, no. 69, November 1995, pp. 52–64; the works of Russell McGregor, 'The Clear Categories of Olive Pink, *Oceania*, vol 65, no 1, September 1994, pp.4–17; Julie Marcus, *The Indomitable Miss Pink: A Life in Anthropology* (Sydney: UNSW Press, 2001); Reg Harris, 'Olive Muriel Pink [Recollections of Miss Pink's personal life]', *Bulletin* (Olive Pink Society), vol. 6, no. 2, 1994, pp. 7–16. The authors gratefully acknowledge the assistance of Alison Holland. For a rich visual record of Olive's life see the Olive Pink Collection at the University of Tasmania.

Gone to pieces
WILLIAM BROWN

Beatrice Brown cleared a space at her kitchen table and set down a piece of paper. Her pen scratched across the page, and the flashing nib left a stream of ink blots behind it. She glanced up anxiously towards the window. Her husband might appear any moment; then again, he might not.

'He has been in a queer mental state of late,' she wrote, 'is always away and I never know his whereabouts.' And so she hurried to finish her letter. The first of many she would write to the authorities. Beatrice was alone, having left her only family back in South Africa. She needed help and she needed reassurance.

'Sir,' she continued, hoping that some office clerk would sense the urgency in her tone:

> *my husband, WCA Brown, a returned man on a pension came home for a few hours . . . He told me he was going to China . . . He took my pension card saying it was necessary . . . I dare not refuse him as he had been violent in temper and menacing in attitude, stuttering as when he first returned from war.*

People had often told Beatrice she was one of the lucky ones. Her man had come home and they could build a new life for themselves in Australia. But now she wasn't so sure of that. This was not the same man she'd married.

Beatrice's heart was racing. She plunged the nib into the ink bottle again:

> *He looked quite mad and talked about thrashing me and 'kicking my brains out' . . . Four years ago he was a very gentle man but he has reverted to the 'brutal'. He has gone to pieces physically, mentally and morally and looks unshaven – unclean – awful.*

Beatrice put her pen to one side and drew a deep breath. Fear was one thing to confess to a stranger, shame and dependency quite another:

> *I am in debt for rent and other necessaries. My husband has given me no support since his return and will not live in the home that I have provided . . . He prefers to pass himself off as a single man . . . Two days after his visit here a love letter arrived from a young lady who apparently he has got into trouble.*

Beatrice was at her wit's end now, her life and her marriage were collapsing around her. 'Right or wrong he is my husband,' she wrote, 'but duty, truth, kindness he has lost all sense of.' Could the doctors be sent to help him, she asked. Her husband seemed 'mentally wrong'. The war had taken him from her.[1]

William Charles Angus Brown had enlisted at the age of 43. A veteran of the Boer War, the Army thought he showed potential and selected him for officer training. Sergeant Brown was demoted to Private by the time he was sent to France. Sent into the line, he suffered what they called 'shell concussion'. Brown was trapped in the trenches for days on end, forced to drink water contaminated with the bodies of men.

'Has a slight stammer,' the medical files noted, 'tremors of hands', and his wounded knees could barely support him. Brown was discharged as medically unfit on 16 January 1918. By then there was not much 'organically wrong'. It was the wounds you couldn't see that were the problem.

Beatrice Brown petitioned for divorce in December 1920. Her husband had deserted her and his mind was 'so disturbed' that she could no longer live with him anyway. For Beatrice, there were no fresh beginnings; all she could hope for was to return to her people in South Africa. William Brown, by contrast, married again – Miss Frances Suttor, a young woman from Bathurst who was more than twenty years his junior.

We will never know why Frances married this shell-shocked soldier. Sympathy, perhaps, desperation probably – war had claimed the best young men of the district. Perhaps Frances had lost someone herself, and taking William on might have been a kind of compensation. More than likely she was that young lady he had got into trouble.

Whatever the reason, Frances believed William loved her. 'He married the girl of his heart,' people said, and they would build a future together. But the war had not treated William kindly – nor would the peace.

William and his new bride settled in the far west of New South Wales, in dry scrubby country bordering the desert. He'd taken up a Crown lease of about four thousand acres, and despite his 'trouble with nerves' believed they could make a go of it farming sheep. But there was no water on the block, and the government refused to sink a bore. Every day, the new bride carted buckets of water two miles from the nearest dam, just to meet the basic needs of her household.

The government also failed to provide an access road to the property. When William went to see the doctors in town, Frances was left 'alone in the wilderness', marooned and isolated on that block in the bush, 'hawkers and stray rabbiters . . . the only human beings seen for weeks'.[2]

Without reliable water, the holding was bound to fail; and William Brown's health was failing also. Like Beatrice before her, Frances took to writing to the authorities. '[H]is nerves … make him really ill,' she wrote to the pension department in 1923, '[h]e still suffers from sleeplessness and nervousness and horror.' Sometimes her husband went away to the city, for a spell in what he called the 'nerve home'. In 1923 he was laid up for three months in Mudgee Hospital, 'so nervous and broken down from lack of food and worry that [he] could not stand longer than half an hour at a time'.[3]

In 1925, William Brown made one last trip to Sydney. That March he went missing. Police found his body on a park bench in the Bennelong Point Reserve. He had swallowed a bottle of poison.

The death of yet another war-wrecked man wasn't likely to make the headlines in interwar Australia. Nor, as we've seen, were the victims of domestic violence, the casualties of men deranged or brutalised by their experiences overseas. But the pathetic plight of a widow, left alone to care for the babes of a 'nervy' soldier – that was another matter entirely. At last, the authorities took up the cause of Mrs Brown: 'It is one of the most shocking cases ever I heard of,' J.W. Percival MLA wrote to the Undersecretary. '[Brown] was a shell shocked wreck, mentally deficient and in a fit of madness committed suicide.' He left a 'bereaved widow … and two War babies', a debt she could barely cope with, and a pathetic pension of less than three pounds per week.[4]

Frances Brown was described as a frail woman, unable to take work 'because the two tiny tots need her attention'. This was deemed a 'deserving case', and one quick to merit the assistance of the state. Frances was given permission to sell her husband's desert property, and much of his debt on the same was written off. But no such concessions could be offered to the first Mrs Brown – or hundreds of others like her, whose men returned damaged by war.

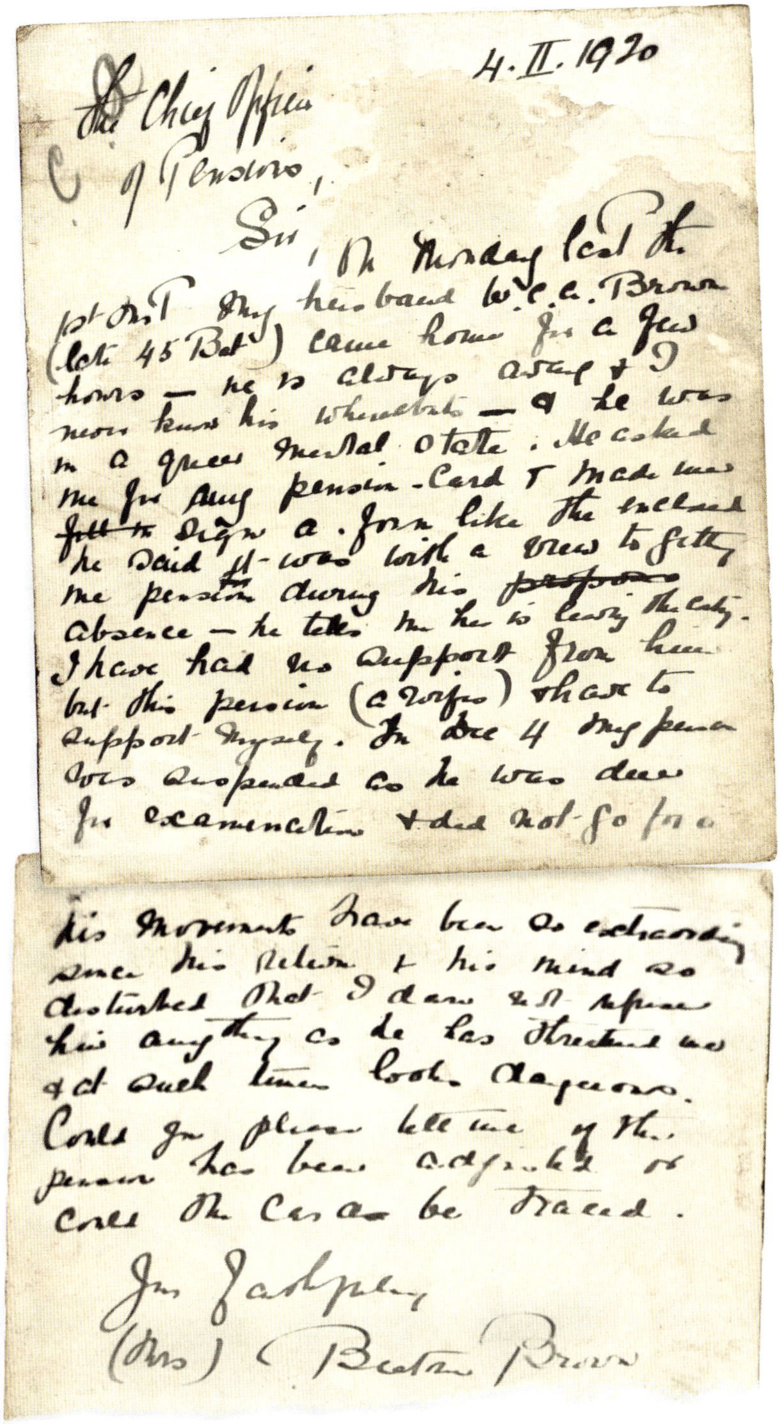
4. II. 1920

The Chief Officer of Pensions,

Sir, On Monday last the 1st inst my husband W.C.A. Brown (late 45 Batt) came home for a few hours – he is always away & I never know his whereabouts – & he was in a queer mental state. He asked me for my pension card & made me sign a form like the enclosed; he said it was with a view to getting me pension during his absence – he talks of leaving the city. I have had no support from him but this pension ([illegible]) & have to support myself. In Dec 4 my pension was suspended as he was due for examination & did not go for [illegible] his movements have been so extraordinary since his return & his mind so disturbed that I dare not refuse him anything as he has threatened me & at such times looks dangerous. Could you please tell me if the pension has been adjusted or could the case be traced.

Yours faithfully
(Mrs) Beatrice Brown

ABOVE **Her pen scratched quickly across the page:** Beatrice Brown's desperate letter to the authorities. Here she pleads for protection from a disturbed and violent husband. The ongoing trauma of war cast a shadow across domestic life in postwar Australia. *NAA: C138/4, C29645 courtesy National Archives of Australia.*

SOURCES AND FURTHER READING: This story draws on William Brown's service dossier NAA: B2455, BROWN WCA; his repatriation file NAA: C138/4, C29645, BROWN WCA; his soldier settlement file State Records NSW: 12/7274/07902. For further reading on the soldier settlement scheme see Bruce Scates and Melanie Oppenheimer, *The Last Battle of the Great War: Soldier Settlement in Australia* (Cambridge: Cambridge University Press, forthcoming).

Whatever time they had left

ADAM WARDROP

Adam Gladstone Wardrop was a horse driver from Mackay in Queensland. In 1916, he saddled up one last time, rode to Rockhampton and enlisted to serve in the Great War. Wardrop left his young wife, Minnie, behind in Australia. She lived on a property on Nebo Road bordering cane fields and farm land. She would never see her husband again.

Wardrop sailed from Sydney in September 1916. He was over fifty days at sea and was unwell enough to be hospitalised the week he arrived in England.

Barely recovered from his illness, Driver Wardrop joined the 7th Australian Field Artillery and was sent on to France. In September 1917, almost a year to the day after leaving Australia, he was wounded. Driver Wardrop, the medical report tells us, suffered 'severe exposure to mustard gas'. There were dozens of different kinds of poisonous gas used in the Great War, each designed to maim, kill or blind the enemy. Mustard gas burnt skin from a man's body; it corroded lungs, damaged eyes, left lips and tongue swollen and blistered. Severe exposure to mustard gas meant a man would probably die. Eventually. Decades after the war, exposed men coughed up blood and phlegm and choked on their own fluids.

Adam Wardrop never returned to active service. Weakened by the effects of being gassed, he succumbed to one illness after another and was moved from hospital to hospital. But there was nothing anyone could do to help him. Fourteen months after being gassed in France, the young man complained he could barely breathe. The doctors described 'an asthmatic condition', a 'pain in the chest' and shortness of breath at even the slightest exertion. Wardrop's pulse was weak, his skin discoloured and he had suffered 'intermittent attacks of vomiting, diarrhea since admission'. In late 1918, he'd also contracted Addison's Disease – Wardrop's kidneys were failing.

ABOVE **Carved in stone:** Adam Wardrop's name appears on the Australian National Memorial in Villers-Bretonneux. The memorial commemorates over ten thousand Australians who died in France and have no known grave. It also honours men like Wardrop buried at sea enroute home to Australia. *Courtesy Bruce Scates.*

Back home in Mackay, Minnie Wardrop received a series of telegrams delivered to her door in Nebo Road, each detailing Adam's changing condition. But all she could do was wait. There were 12 000 miles of water between her and her husband.

Meanwhile, in England, the doctors made a decision. They doubted a man as badly gassed as Wardrop could survive a northern winter. Perhaps he'd breathe a little easier in the warm, humid air of Queensland; surely there, he'd have family and friends to support him. And his wife would want to be near him for whatever time they had left together. So despite the dangers of a long ocean voyage, Wardrop was carried onto the hospital ship *Wandilla* in March 1919 and was sent home to Australia.

In the makeshift ward between decks, a new cast of doctors were worried. In rolling seas, they scrawled unsteadily in Wardrop's casebook:

> *29 April 1919 – vomiting, headache, discoloration of urine*
>
> *4 May 1919 – condition much worse, epistaxis, general weakness, twitching and vomiting'*

And in the early hours of the morning on 8 May, a doctor recorded the final entry:

> *3.26 a.m. – life extinct*[1]

Adam Wardrop died at sea just a few days' sailing time from Australia.

Later, Winnie received a letter from *Wandilla*'s Troop Commander. She must have sped through each line, reading each word hungrily, anxious for any news of her husband. 'Everything possible in the way of medical attention was done for him ... His end being peaceful & without pain ... He was buried at sea, with full military honours.'[2] So many words to say so little.

Like all Australian soldiers who died at sea coming home, Adam Wardrop's name was cast in bronze and raised on the cloistered walls of the Australian national memorial. It was carved in stone on the cenotaph at Mackay, published proudly in the local press, and printed – in archaic hand – on the King's expression of regret and gratitude. We don't know if Minnie found much comfort in a name. We know she lost her husband barely three years into their marriage, that she had no children and that she never remarried.

Wilhelmina Amelia Wardrop died in Mackay in 1936, seventeen years after the body of her husband was committed to the deep.

SOURCES AND FURTHER READING: This story draws on Adam Wardrop's service dossier NAA: B2455, WARDROP ADAM GLADSTONE. The authors acknowledge the assistance of Mike and Roz Goodwin and the school students of Mackay North State High School who have carried out regular commemorations at the Australian National Memorial, Villers-Bretonneux, where Wardrop's name is inscribed.

IN
MEMORY
OF
CAPT · N · GIBBINS.
55th
A.I.F.
KILLED
With my soul's homage and my heart's utmost love to my beloved and deeply mourned Brother
Violet Gibbins"

Inexpressibly dear to me

NORMAN GIBBINS

Norman Gibbins enlisted in August 1914, the month Australia went to war. He'd fought before, in South Africa, and rose to the rank of captain in one of the colonial contingents. In 1914, he enlisted as a private – such was his haste to serve again. Gibbins was amongst the first ashore at Gallipoli, and there he was commissioned for bravery in the field. He then went on to fight at Fromelles, Australia's first major engagement in France.

Fromelles was a pointless diversion during the battle of the Somme; a case study of the Great War's callous incompetence. Over 5000 Australians (and a comparable number of British troops) were killed, wounded or taken prisoner in less than twenty-four hours. The Australian casualties in a single day exceeded the combined Australian tolls for the Boer War, the Korean War and the Vietnam War – and the attack failed in all its objectives.

The battle plan for Fromelles was bungled from the outset. A preliminary bombardment failed to destroy enemy machine guns or artillery, but gave every notice an attack was imminent. Men were told to advance across open ground under heavy fire and take the third line of the German defences. But there was no 'third line' at Fromelles, just a series of drainage ditches cut through the sodden fields of Flanders. The men under Norman Gibbins' command were stranded in no-man's-land, cut to pieces by 'grazing fire' sweeping over the wheat fields. To this day every spring rain brings their bones to the surface.

In the frenzied heat of battle, Australian engineers dug a new trench towards the German lines, hoping to support the attack or at least bring back the wounded. Soon the trench was battered by shells, awash with mud, and choked with the dead and wounded. Men called it 'the butcher's shop'.

Gibbins held this trench to the very end, waiting until the last hopeless minute

OPPOSITE **No one had greater claim than her:** Violet insisted that her relationship with Norman was much closer than that of her mother. Usually the 'privilege' of choosing an epitaph would fall to the mother as next of kin. *P03788.003 courtesy Australian War Memorial.*

before retiring. 'There was no braver man in the action that day,' one report reads, 'Capt. Gibbins fought his way back with a pistol in one hand and a bomb in the other.'[1] Norman Gibbins refused to leave his wounded men behind. He was shot through the forehead on reaching the Australian parapet.

ABOVE **An iron code of discipline:** Violet Gibbins dressed in naval style uniform. She governed her schools according to a military code of conduct. *P04253.001 courtesy Australian War Memorial.*

Norman's sister Violet learned of his death several days later. 'He was inexpressibly dear to me,' she wrote, 'and made me his next-of-kin solely and absolutely.' She pleaded for his letters, his medals, and 'all the precious personal belongings which may have been removed from his dear body on the battlefield'. No one, and certainly not a mother, 'estranged' from him, had greater claim than her:

> *These and all the honour and glory of his supreme sacrifice are mine by my brother's oft-expressed wishes and as a recognition of the part I have played in his life. We have been all-in-all to each other, since the earliest childhood. My brother was the noblest and most just of men.*[2]

Violet continued to honour her brother all her life. She chose the inscription for his grave: 'With my soul's homage and my heart's utmost love to my beloved and deeply mourned brother'; she entrusted his letters to the Australian War Memorial so the nation would never forget his sacrifice; and she took it upon herself to decorate the graves of soldiers every Anzac Day.

Like many women of her generation, Violet Gibbins took up teaching in the 1920s – the war had emptied the classrooms of many young men who might well have taught in them. At Epping, just outside Sydney, and then at Leura, in the foothills of the Blue Mountains, Violet established private boarding schools, offering 'moral, physical and intellectual training'[3] to ladies of a certain class.

Every Anzac Day eve, Principal Gibbins and her charges would work into the night fashioning beautiful wreaths, a yard in diameter, to pile high on soldiers' graves and memorials. 'Well!' she wrote to Dr Mary Booth, founder of the Anzac Fellowship of Women,

> *The girls overwhelmed me with their choice of flowers. The School was full of them. Mothers sent all the flowers they could pick and people visited the School to see them. [We] sat up until 2 and 3 o'clock in the mornings of April 24th and 25th. I was making large wreaths of flowers each night . . . I hope you did not mind the laurel wreath being sent to the Soldiers' Club. The girls begged me to make it and place it where my brother's comrades might see it. Anzac Memorial was quite covered in flowers so there was no room for it there.*[4]

She did this for over a decade after her brother's death. And then she established a scholarship, which she called 'a living memorial', bearing Norman's name.

Miss Gibbins continued to teach young ladies until her death in 1958. Osborne College, a boarding school, was named after Osborne Naval College in England and run along naval lines, imbued with naval traditions and naval discipline. The girls dressed every day in bright blue uniforms; they marched, drilled and saluted. Teaching rooms were named after ships in the Royal Navy – *Sirius*, *Sydney* and *Nelson*. The school's bathroom was dubbed *Neptune* and the sickbay *Dreadnought*. Miss Gibbins was addressed as the Admiral.

Violet Gibbins educated her young women to be 'fine, strong, sensible types'.[5] And one must pity any spirited young lady who defied her iron code of discipline. Miss Gibbins believed in King and Country, Australia and Empire, and raised three generations of a nation's youth with those ideals in mind. They must be 'willing', she said, 'to serve their country in any capacity'. As had that brother of hers, 'the noblest and most just of men', buried in the cold earth of Flanders.

BELOW TOP **So the nation would never forget:** Violet Gibbins with C.E.W. Bean, the first Director of the Australian War Memorial. Both Gibbins and Bean were in the business of remembrance. The two worked together in the interwar period, Bean's daughter, Joyce, was sent to Miss Gibbins' school and Norman's papers were bequeathed to the Memorial. *P03788.002 courtesy Australian War Memorial.*

BELOW BOTTOM **Anzac Memorial was quite covered in flowers:** Some of the tributes laid at Sydney's Cenotaph would have been fashioned by Miss Gibbins' 'girls'. Sydney Morning Herald, *26 April 1928 courtesy National Library of Australia.*

SOURCES AND FURTHER READING: This story draws on Norman Gibbins' service dossier NAA: B2455, GIBBINS N; his Red Cross Wounded and Missing file AWM 1DRL/0428; and the Gibbins Papers AWM PR02053. For further reading on Violet Gibbins (or Gibbons, as she often went by), see Robyn Hanstock '"In the Spirit of the Navy": Violet Gibbons and Osborne Ladies' College, Blackheath', *Journal of the Royal Australian Historical Society,* vol. 91, no. 1, June 2005, pp. 29–47. We also gratefully acknowledge the research of John Low on the life of Violet Gibbins. For a perceptive study of women's experience of bereavement see Joy Damousi, *The Labour of Loss: Mourning, Memory and Wartime Bereavement in Australia* (Cambridge: Cambridge University Press, 1999).

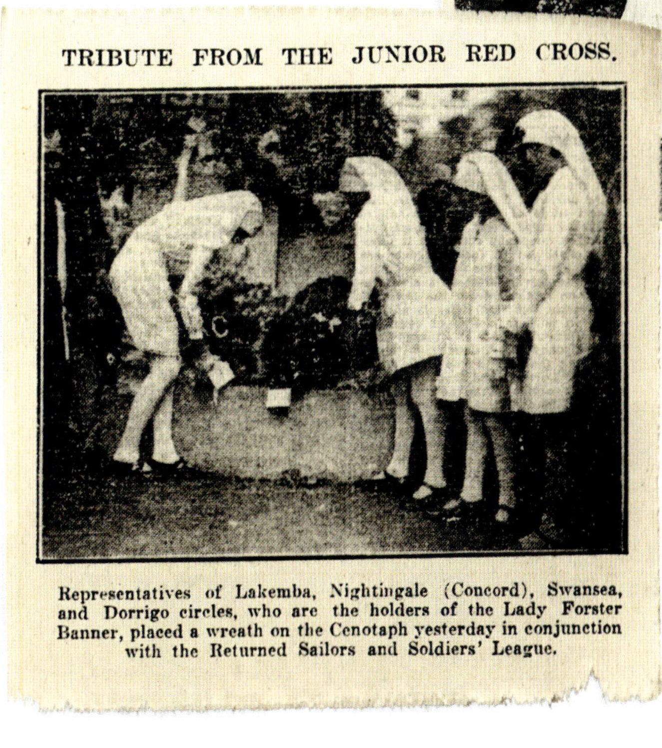

TRIBUTE FROM THE JUNIOR RED CROSS.

Representatives of Lakemba, Nightingale (Concord), Swansea, and Dorrigo circles, who are the holders of the Lady Forster Banner, placed a wreath on the Cenotaph yesterday in conjunction with the Returned Sailors and Soldiers' League.

The boy soldier
BERNARD HAINES

25 APRIL 1919

They wheeled poor Bernie Haines into the sunlight today. I say wheeled because he's one of our cot cases – paralysed from the waist down. Bernie caught a piece of high explosive shell in France. Every day his spine seems to weaken. It seems unlikely he'll ever walk again.

Some of the nurses call him 'Babe' and he doesn't seem to mind. The soldiers he served with called him that, and you can see why. Bernie Haines enlisted at just 14 years of age, Victoria's brave little boy soldier. And just a year later that stunt at Bapaume left him a cripple. You wonder what his mother must've thought. To send a boy to war like that, and know he might never grow to manhood.

Today's little outing seemed a success, though Bernie doesn't say much and it's hard to know what he's thinking. The Young Ladies' Auxiliary was there and heaven knows they made a fuss of him. One silly young thing planted a kiss on his forehead, another lass held a parasol over his face, so the bright light wouldn't trouble him. Bernie smiled bravely through all the commotion. The doctor had increased the dose of morphine, so that must have quelled the pain a little. Even so, I'm sure I saw a tear roll down that dear boy's face. Little wonder. The girl who kissed him must have been about his age. Young and strong and pretty, with her whole life ahead of her. Unlike Bernie.

None of those young women went anywhere near the bottom of the cot. Though I saw them looking time and time again at that telltale hollow. That shell blast shattered Bernie's left leg. They hacked off most of it in the casualty clearing station in France and tried to save what was left back in some hospital in England. But all there is now is a tiny stump. Sometimes Bernie says he can still feel his toes – once he even asked if I could scratch them. We call them 'phantom limbs' on the ward. It's the kindest way of describing all the horrors beneath those blankets.

OPPOSITE **Just the iron rails of his cot:** Although bedridden and in great pain, returned men like Haines were encouraged to take up 'useful pursuits'. Learning a trade like woodwork could generate an income. As the exquisite pieces above Bernie's bed suggest, it brought something of great beauty back into their lives. *H84.258/5 courtesy State Library of Victoria.*

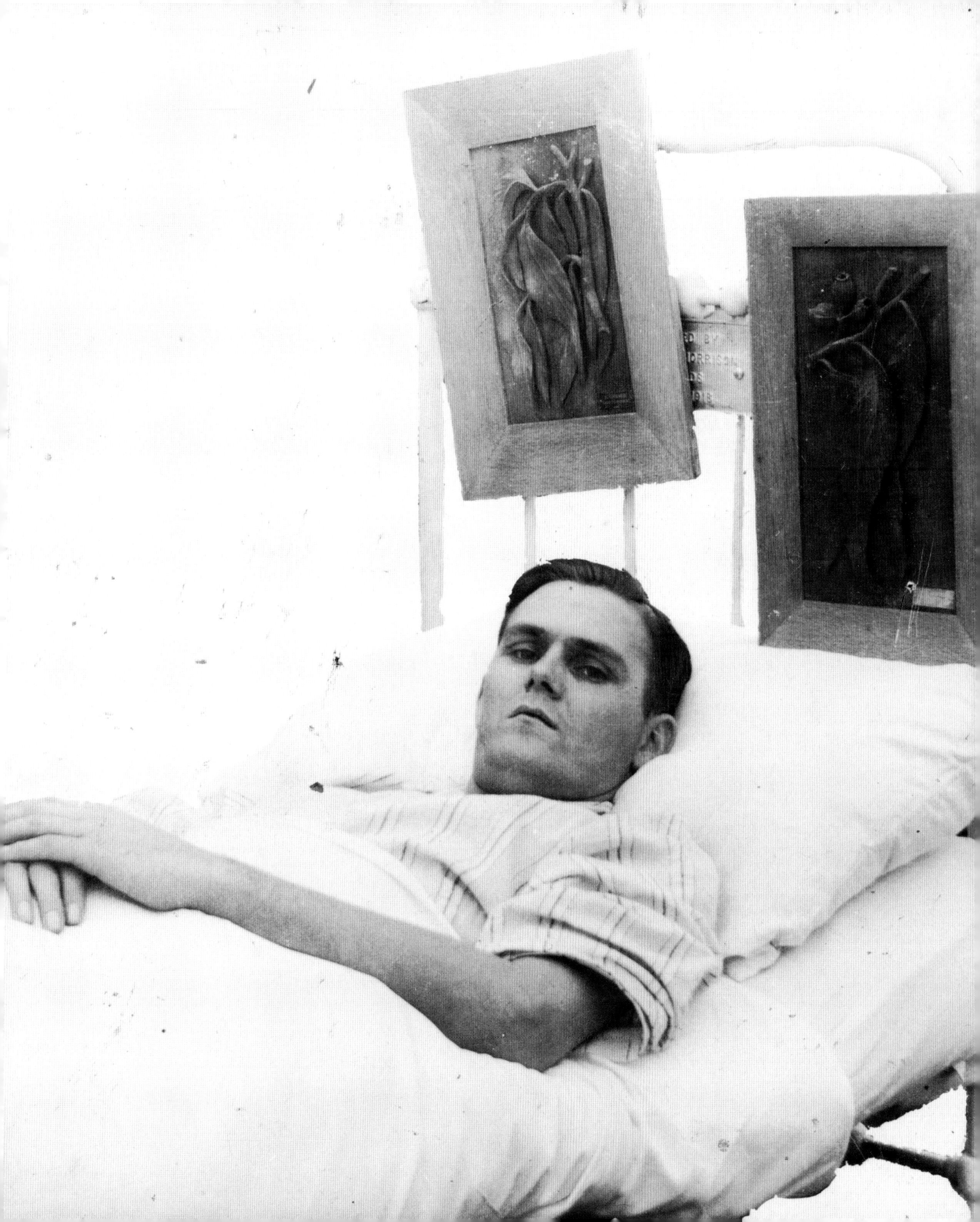

15 JUNE 1921

Another operation for Bernie tomorrow. I've lost count of how many he's been through. But the boy is in a terrible state and the doctors say we have to do something.

'Faecal fistula' someone scribbled in the case notes. Bernie's lost so much of his bowel and intestines that the waste has nowhere to go and it's seeping through his body. I listened to his lungs today, you can hear those foul fluids washing round his diaphragm – bubbling rales on both sides, a dull metallic thudding. So now we have to cut into the colon again and drain away what we can of the waste. And Bernie will be conscious when we do that. 'Colostomy under local anesthetic' it says quite clearly. I dread to think of the look in that boy's eyes. I've never seen worse things, not even in France.

15 OCTOBER 1924

They took Bernie out of the ward today and placed him in a room alone at the far end of the building. Matron said it had to be done. Bernie's been sulky, disruptive, upsetting the others. He says some terrible things now – even to us nurses. And yesterday he refused to let me dress him, said he'd had enough of everything.

It wasn't always like that. Not in the early days, anyway. When Bernie first came home he could still manage to get about on his crutches. He thought that with the help of his sisters he might even open a sweet shop. But the Repat said they wouldn't help him out with a loan. They said 'vocational training' was a much better use of departmental resources. I've seen quite a bit of vocational training here: blind men weaving baskets, men without hands painting with brushes clenched in their teeth, cot cases like Bernie whittling away at their woodwork. But Bernie is too sick to carve anymore. There's nothing much left now, no purpose, no beauty – just the iron rails of his cot and the filth welling up beneath the blankets. The girls draw lots to change the sheets. None of us can bear the smell of him.

ABOVE **Victoria's little boy soldier:** Bernard Haines enlisted at the age of 14 and served under the false name, Charlie Haines. His spine was shattered at Bapaume just a year later. *H84.258/2 courtesy State Library of Victoria.*

17 MARCH 1926

Babe Haines died last night and everyone agrees he was a hero. The papers say he kept smiling to the end but somehow I doubt that. Unless, of course, the doctors gave him more morphine than they should have, that would have been the kindest thing. Pulling the screen around the bed and smothering that dreadful pain forever. Some of the girls say that's what happens on the ward, but I've never seen it. Matron tells us only God can take a life away – not that I've seen much of God in the Repat.

In our new national capital, they're building Australia's War Memorial – a great stone building at the foot of Mt Ainslie. I hear there'll be an Honour Roll for all the nation's dead – all those 60 000 men killed in France and Gallipoli, Palestine and Belgium. But Bernie's name won't be on it. Bernie died eight years after the fighting was over, so the officials say he's not really one of our war dead. It's strange to think if Bernie had suffered less rather than more, if that short life had been even shorter, his name too would be gleaming in bronze, honoured by all who walk down those cloisters. But I imagine people will forget Bernie soon enough. No one – not even here – wants to remember the cot cases.

I've heard those young girls from the Ladies' Auxiliary won't visit us again, not after what one of our 'nervy cases' told them. I'm not surprised by that. It's so much easier to stay at home and read about boy heroes giving their lives for their country. But I'm not sure that Bernie really gave his life away. Someone stole it from him.[1]

SOURCES AND FURTHER READING: The authors warmly acknowledge the family of Bernard Haines and the assistance of Dr Amshuman Rao in reading and interpreting the extensive medical case notes relevant to this story. This story draws on Bernard Haines' service dossier NAA: B2455, HAINES C; and his repatriation file NAA: B73, R14400. This imagined narrative is based on a close reading of these official records. The story of 'Babe Haines' and his long painful death were reported on in the press and this story has drawn on many of the contemporary newspaper articles. For further reading on repatriation see Marina Larsson, *Shattered Anzacs: Living with the Scars of War* (Sydney: UNSW Press, 2009).

BELOW LEFT **One of our cot cases:** Bernard Haines in the grounds of Caulfield Repatriation Hospital. *H84.258/6 courtesy State Library of Victoria.*

BELOW **Everyone agrees he's a hero:** *The Maitland Weekly Mercury* announces the death of Bernard Haines. The Maitland Weekly Mercury, *27 Mar 1926 courtesy National Library of Australia.*

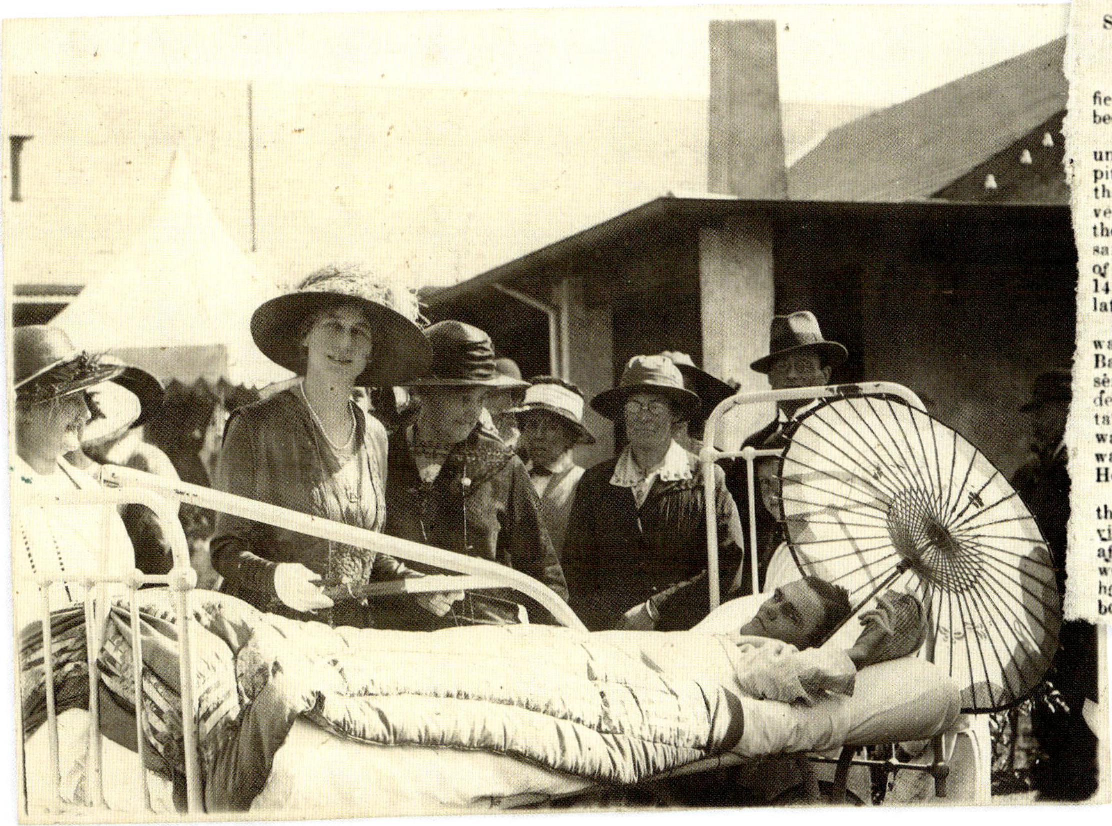

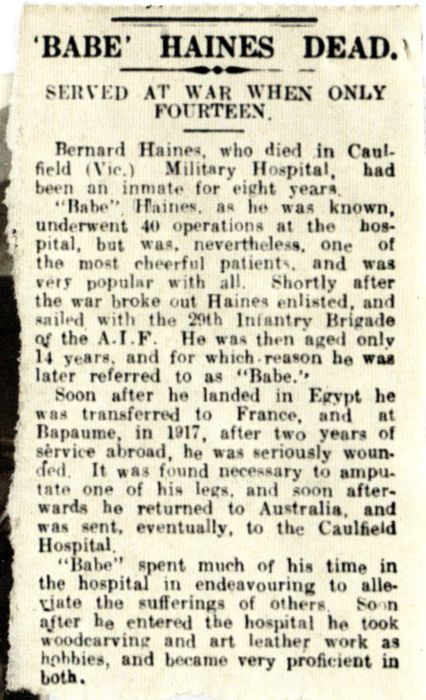

'BABE' HAINES DEAD.

SERVED AT WAR WHEN ONLY FOURTEEN.

Bernard Haines, who died in Caulfield (Vic.) Military Hospital, had been an inmate for eight years.

"Babe" Haines, as he was known, underwent 40 operations at the hospital, but was, nevertheless, one of the most cheerful patients, and was very popular with all. Shortly after the war broke out Haines enlisted, and sailed with the 29th Infantry Brigade of the A.I.F. He was then aged only 14 years, and for which reason he was later referred to as "Babe."

Soon after he landed in Egypt he was transferred to France, and at Bapaume, in 1917, after two years of service abroad, he was seriously wounded. It was found necessary to amputate one of his legs, and soon afterwards he returned to Australia, and was sent, eventually, to the Caulfield Hospital.

"Babe" spent much of his time in the hospital in endeavouring to alleviate the sufferings of others. Soon after he entered the hospital he took woodcarving and art leather work as hobbies, and became very proficient in both.

H.F. CROWTHER SMITH 17

My grief condemns me

HENRY HIGGINS

From the day his son Mervyn was killed on the Sinai Peninsula, to the moment of his own death twelve years later, Justice H B Higgins set out to remember. He erected an ornate Celtic cross over the family tomb at Dromana in Victoria, typed and bound all Mervyn's letters, framed his photographs and assembled his officer's kit like a shrine in the family home. And between 1916, the year of Mervyn's death, and 1924, when Henry Higgins at last stood by his son's distant grave, the High Court judge also wrote one letter of inquiry, complaint or outright reprimand after another. Usually a soldier's service dossier runs to a few dozen pages; the bare details of postings and promotions – Mervyn's record swells to one hundred and forty-two pages.

For the father who loved him, Mervyn's death was insurmountable. The letters of condolence, the caress of family and friends, even the sympathy of his King, all counted for nothing. 'My grief has condemned me to hard labour for the rest of my life,' Henry wrote, and that servitude of sorrow lessened little as one year folded into another.[1]

Reading Mervyn's letters (as Higgins must have read and reread them) it is not hard to see why this boy was so treasured. The correspondence from Gallipoli, where Mervyn watched one mate after another die, conveys courage, compassion and dignity. 'We are dug in like rabbits,' the young man wrote, 'the Turkish trenches [are] pretty close . . . with only a sandbag barricade between us.' But every letter home made light of the hardship and danger: 'The climate suits me very well [though] our wardrobes are of course limited'; 'The flies are very troublesome but on the whole we are very comfortable'; 'We are having splendid weather and feeling quite pleased with life in general'. Reading between the lines reveals another story: days without a break from fighting in the line, 'incessant' bomb duels, poor food, little water, lives snatched away in an instant by snipers.

Lieutenant Higgins survived the suicidal charge at the Nek. He was one of the

OPPOSITE **To the memory of a boy buried a world away:** This portrait of Mervyn Higgins was completed in the year after his death. It shows the young Mervyn resting on his oars having rowed the length of the Yarra. The portrait, like the cross raised at Dromana, was part of the memorialisation process – a way of ensuring this young man would always be remembered. In the 1920s the Mervyn B. Higgins Trophy was established and awarded annually in the inter-varsity rowing championships. Mervyn himself had rowed number 3 in the Ormond crew. *Portrait of Captain M B Higgins by H F Crowther Smith courtesy National Library of Australia.*

few officers to do so. Posted next to a bitter desert war in Palestine, his bravery earned him the admiration of his men and a mention in despatches. The correspondence ends abruptly in 1916. Mervyn's last letter home is as tender and loving as his first, selflessly consoling a friend 'cut up' over the death of his brother. Then the voice of that 'ever loving son' was covered over by 'the heavy sands' of the Eastern desert.[2]

The death of a son is always tragic, but it was the waste of this war that most outraged Higgins. Mervyn was killed in brief but savage action against the Turks at El Magdhaba. The battle had limited strategic significance and Mervyn was shot whilst taking prisoners. It should have been a consolation that the young soldier died almost instantly. He felt 'absolutely no pain', a comrade wrote, and the body was guarded by his men until the time came for burial. They lowered their captain into the earth on Christmas Eve, burying him 'right where he fell'. A rough wooden cross was raised and the padre read a service. But for the family back home, this swift death and hasty burial meant no last message, no final farewell. And everything done in the wake of Mervyn's death – from the epitaph chosen for the makeshift cross, to the return of his belongings to wet, windswept Dromana – served to prolong and sharpen the grief of his father. The whole process of public memorialisation went seriously wrong in the case of Mervyn Higgins.

The first failings were easy to forgive. The family knew that weeks, sometimes months, would pass between the first cable confirming death and some 'greater detail' from the chaplain and fellow officers. But the wait was torturous and in the meantime Higgins wrote to the authorities, extracting every possible detail of his son's service. And he longed for some token of his boy. Mervyn might not be coming home, but every day the family waited for the arrival of his kit.

When four boxes of belongings finally arrived in Melbourne, two were railed and carted all the way to distant Dromana (a holiday residence, closed out of season) and two were mislaid in the railway station at Mornington (the line stopped well short of Dromana). Higgins' distress still howls from his hastily scribbled handwriting: first his son and then these 'precious things' had been lost in a kind of limbo. And all the authorities seemed capable of was 'wooden inaction':

> *The records people say that Dromana is my 'registered address'; but it is not . . . By a little care, the officials could have found that my proper address is Malvern. I learn that two of the four cases have reached my home in Dromana; but what of the other two? And why should I have the painful duty of carting about any of the boxes!*[3]

But a little care seemed too much to ask of the authorities. Mervyn's body was exhumed and re-interred on two different occasions; the cross that came to mark his grave denied him a soldier's death ('died of wounds' was not quite the same as 'killed in action'); absurd and rigid rules prevented the sending of Mervyn's photograph to friends and family in England, and the Australian War Memorial even incorrectly recorded the action in which his life was taken.[4]

Seven years after his son's death, Higgins finally secured permission to visit the grave. It was a journey of over 8000 miles and one an old, sick man was scarcely capable of undertaking. Arriving in that lonely corner of the Sinai Peninsula must have been a terrible moment. The cemetery at El Magdhaba was still a wasteland; water could not be had, the plots were stark and windswept and all the plants had perished. Higgins found no memorial to his son, the marble for the tombstone had still not arrived and the grave was marked only with a rough wooden cross. Mervyn lay buried in the ever-shifting sands of the desert – a grave forsaken at the corners of Empire.

Higgins' story reads like a claimant's appeal against his grief: the picking, nagging correspondence; the weighing of evidence; the questioning of procedure – all that might be expected from a lifetime in the courtroom. But to read it as such would blind us to its true significance. The Higgins correspondence reminds us of an unfathomable loss – the separation of an only son from a father who will always love him. And Higgins is as unforgiving of himself as he is of those overworked and ill-resourced authorities, the clerks and officers who had to deal with anger and disbelief, who tried (however hopelessly) to offer comfort to the grieving.

But Henry Higgins did find some comfort in pilgrimage and poetry. 'The Grave at El Magdabha' was written after that long trek through the Middle East. Penned to

ABOVE **The ever-shifting sands of the desert:** Kantara War Memorial Cemetery where Captain Mervyn Higgins lies buried. Kantara is a concentration cemetery and relatives were distressed to hear that the bodies of their loved ones were moved several times in the postwar period. Kantara contains the graves of more than 1500 servicemen from the Great War. The Second World War saw a further 110 men buried there. *Courtesy the Commonwealth War Graves Commission.*

the memory of a boy buried a world away, it enables us to stand alongside not just one broken father but all those of his generation who journeyed across the oceans to find the grave of a loved one:

Ah, there he lies – moveless, in desert drear;
His broad breast weighted with the sullen sand;
The sword of the crusader marks him here,
A parting tribute from that gallant band . . .

He lies, in plenitude of rest, serene,
He rooks not now of welter, horrors, grime;
To him all was as if it had not been,
For us – his death divides the course of time.

. . . This, at the least, we know – in coming years
Nothing shall do his honour stain;
The test is over and the world with tears
Will cherish those for whom the world were slain.[5]

BELOW **The family tomb at Dromana:** Higgins had this Celtic cross raised in memory of his son. Mervyn's body is buried oceans away. This is a surrogate tomb for an absent body, but a place a family could come to grieve. *Courtesy Ross McMullin.*

Higgins would always cherish those 'for whom the world were slain'. And the first debt to that lost generation was to honour the promise made to them. Justice Higgins became the President of the World Disarmament Movement and devoted the rest of his life to the cause of peace. For him, the Great War had been the war to end all wars, otherwise how could he possibly justify the loss of his only son? Justice Higgins died in 1929, well before the outbreak of another world war. He was buried in Dromana beneath a cross bearing Mervyn's name.

SOURCES AND FURTHER READING: This story draws on Captain Higgins' service dossier NAA: B2455, HIGGINS M B CAPTAIN; and his Red Cross Wounded and Missing file AWM 1DRL/0428. This story also draws on the extensive archival collections held by the National Library of Australia and Australian War Memorial, Higgins Papers NLA MS 2525; Higgins Papers NLA MS1057; Higgins, Mervyn Bournes AWM 3DRL/0421. For further reading on Henry Higgins, his bereavement and his pilgrimage see Bruce Scates, *Return to Gallipoli: Walking the Battlefields of the Great War* (Cambridge: Cambridge University Press, 2006). There are also a number of outstanding biographies including Nettie Palmer, *Henry Bournes Higgins: A Memoir* (London: Harrap, 1931) and John Rickard, *Henry Higgins: The Rebel as Judge* (Sydney: Allen & Unwin, 1984).

A very different childhood

JOYCE McGRATH

Joyce swirled her brush through the paint on her palette. Each of the colours evoked memories of her childhood: reds and oranges of dry Mildura, the lightest to the darkest blues of bayside skies that she had stared at for so many hours, even the whites and creams of her plasters, at first pristine but so quickly stained.

Joyce still paints in her Ivanhoe studio, a few of her paintings hang on the walls of her home, but many more are hung in collections around the country. At 90 years of age, Joyce continues to be generous with her time, energy and talents. A stalwart of Victoria's artistic community and State Library, Joyce has lived a rich and rewarding life, despite the shadow of war that has always loomed over her.

Jack McGrath, Joyce's father, was 18 when he enlisted to fight in the war alongside his brother, Frank. Right from the beginning of his service at Gallipoli, Jack was plagued by illness and injury. It seemed that just as he recovered from one complaint, he was struck down with another – pleurisy, pneumonia, malaria. Eventually Jack was medically discharged. He sailed home to Australia in 1917, only to learn that Frank had been killed in the assault on Beersheba.

But coming home wouldn't cure Jack. Doctors were hopeful for his recovery; after all, he had 'youth on his side.' But Jack's body was irreversibly damaged. From 1917 until his death in 1933, he suffered years of debility and his medical records are an inventory of sickness: wheezing, continually 'hawking', creamy phlegm, vomiting, headaches, 'pale green clear fluid' in his lungs, 'inflamed eyes', swollen throat, 'gurgling chest', sharp pains throughout his body.[1]

Amongst his other illnesses, Jack was diagnosed with tuberculosis in 1918; well after his repatriation to Australia. He told the Repat that he had 'never suffered any sickness

ABOVE **A fortunate life:** Joyce McGrath feels like a blessed woman. She is eternally grateful for her loving and devoted mother. Joyce has had an incredibly rewarding life; she has enjoyed successful and impressive careers as both an artist and a librarian; she has travelled the world, exploring fascinating cultures and living abroad; she has been recognised for her service and her skills, in 1968 she was awarded a Churchill Fellowship, and travelled through Europe and North America. In 2000, Joyce was awarded the Medal of the Order of Australia. Throughout her life Joyce has moved in fascinating social circles and developed countless dear friendships. Joyce believes she has lived 'a fortunate life'. *Courtesy Joyce McGrath.*

prior to enlisting' so claimed that 'whatever the trouble may be, it is a result of war service'.[2]

Jack tried to overcome his ever-worsening health. In 1925 he married Nellie and soon after they welcomed their baby girl, Joyce. Together, the family embarked on a life on the land. Growing grapes on a soldier settlement block in Red Cliffs seemed a good idea; perhaps the drier, hotter climate might relieve Jack's tired lungs. But the reality was, unsurprisingly, that the hard labour of agriculture tired a weakened man.

When she was four years old Joyce began to feel pain in her right hip. At first it just hurt when she walked, but soon the ache would throb even when she was standing still. She began to limp, unable to place any weight on the leg, and was a visibly 'miserable little girl'.[3] In 1930 Joyce's pains were diagnosed as tuberculosis of the hip. Jack had passed his war illness on to his daughter.

Treatment was extreme. The little girl was laid still, and cotton wool was placed on her, from her lower ribs down to her toes. Then, her right leg was encased in smooth, white plaster. Each day, Joyce and the other children in her ward were wheeled outside to absorb the effects of sunshine and fresh air; these were still considered the most effective means to treat the disease. And this is how Joyce lived at Frankston Children's Hospital.

Of course the progression of little Joyce's tubercular hip is not noted in her father's medical records. The knowledge that he'd transmitted this disease to his daughter was surely devastating for Jack. He only saw Joyce once in Frankston. Visitors were discouraged but, always thinking of her, Jack would send his daughter sketches of little stick figures and jokes about hospitals.

Finally fed up with the hospitals and the sanatoriums, Jack discharged himself from Caulfield Repat. He hired a small boat and sailed up past the Frankston Hospital. From the water, Jack looked up at the building where Joyce lay. Father and daughter wouldn't see one another again. In 1933, after sixteen long years of fighting the effects of war, Jack's body relented and he died from cardiac failure.

But Joyce's fight continued. In her plaster shell, she had a very different childhood from other girls in her age group. Joyce did not experience human touch like most children do. Like the other young patients on the ward, Joyce was trapped within a sterile, unfeeling institution. But there, children developed a spirit beyond their years, an unwillingness to rely on others, a resilient independence and a certain unease with affection.[4]

In 1934, Joyce was finally able to leave the hospital, although it was certainly not the end of her treatment. Each month Nellie and Joyce would embark on the cumbersome journey to the Children's Hosptial in Carlton. Finally, Joyce was released from the plasters. But neither Nellie nor Joyce ever slowed down. The little girl was enrolled in piano, singing, elocution and dressmaking lessons. Nellie hoped that after such a difficult beginning, her daughter would make up for lost time and opportunities.

As Joyce grew up she began to think about her professional options. Although she had the skills and aptitude for many a potential position – radio actress, musician, nurse, teacher, dress designer – she always came back to the cross she bore, the remnants of the tuberculosis in her hip, the legacy of the Great War. And she doubted that matrimony was ever an option.

Never in question though was Joyce's creativity. With a love of the arts, Joyce took up drawing classes at Royal Melbourne Institute of Technology in her early twenties. Not long after, as she wandered through the city one afternoon, Joyce stumbled on the Colquhoun School of Painting. She eagerly enrolled and went on to study under the brother and sister team, Archie and Amalie Colquhoun, in their Bourke Street studio. Their style was inspired by the work of Max Meldrum, one of 'tonal impressionism'.

When Joyce was 27, she began working at the State Library of Victoria. Initially, she worked on the floor as a cadet attendant, carefully re-shelving books in their rightful place and helping patrons with their enquiries. But her artistic skill set equipped her for a far more demanding vocation. After a decade of service and further study, Joyce took on the role of Arts Librarian. Over her long and distinguished career, Joyce helped to create the largest art collection of any Australian public library.

In 2000, Joyce was awarded the Medal of the Order of Australia for her service 'to the collection and preservation of historical documentation relating to art and music, particularly through the establishment of the Australian Art Archives'. She remains an important figure in Victoria's artistic and library communities.

Joyce McGrath reminds us that the war came home to Australia. Although Joyce's life has been shaped by her own and her father's illness, she has lived a life of achievement and generous service. And through all the adversity and all the success, Joyce has always sensed that Jack was looking after her.

ABOVE **Father and daughter:** A proud Jack McGrath holds his baby girl. Joyce has always felt that her father and mother, Jack and Nellie, looked after her – in life and in spirit. *Courtesy Joyce McGrath.*

SOURCES AND FURTHER READING: The story draws on an interview with Joyce McGrath with the authors in October 2013; the biography of Joyce and her surgeon, John Colquhoun, Jan Harper, *Plaster and Paint: John Colquhoun, Orthopaedic Surgeon and His Patient, Joyce McGrath, Portrait Painter* (North Melbourne: Arcadia, 2007); Jack McGrath's service dossier NAA: B2455, MCGRATH J; and his repatriation file NAA: B73, H12398. The authors also drew on further reading in Peter Yule, *The Royal Children's : A History of Faith, Science and Love* (Rushcutters Bay: Halstead Press, 1999); Ken Mackenzie Wright, *A Land Fit for Heroes: The Story of the Soldier Settlement of Red Cliffs after World War 1* (Mildrua: Ken Mackenzie Wright, 1995) and Joyce McGrath, *Joyce McGrath Survey Exhibition 1949–1997* (Melbourne: Linden Press, 1998).

With due care?
ALEXANDER McKINNON

The centre of Australia is the oldest land on Earth. So old, the MacDonnell Ranges once stood as tall as the mighty Rockies. Now just stunted hills on the horizon, they have been eroded away by millennia of wind, sun and rain. So old, an inland sea once lapped at the heart of the continent. Now that vast dry seabed is desert as far as the eye can see. So old, the most ancient waterway on earth, the Finke River, cuts its weary way through the landscape. The centre of Australia is ancient beyond belief.

This country, now, then and always, is Aboriginal land. Tales of the Dreaming marked meaning in this place.

Whites came to the centre of Australia in the late nineteenth century. A man named McKinnon ran a cattle station at Charlotte Waters, midway between Alice Springs and Adelaide, not much more than a hut and a fence line. The whites took the land; and the water, and the women.

We do not know much about the relationship between Alexander McKinnon and Cobb, the name given to 'his' Aboriginal woman. We don't know if it was established in love and intimacy or based on coercion, dependency, and lust. What we do know is that Cobb gave birth to a so-called 'half-caste', a boy of mixed Indigenous and European descent. McKinnon gave the boy his own name and taught him the ways of the pastoral industry. Together they rode the length and breadth of the station, driving cattle through the desert country and mustering stock far to the north.

In the early years of the twentieth century, Alexander McKinnon Sr abandoned his Aboriginal partner, married a white woman named Mary and went to live in Adelaide. His son, Alex, stayed on at the station and his relationship with his mother grew stronger and stronger. In 1916, Alex – by then in his mid-twenties – 'answered the call' and volunteered to fight for the Empire. Technically, Aboriginal people were not permitted to enlist. Volunteers for the First AIF were supposed to be British subjects,

of 'predominantly European descent'. But Alex lived in a limbo between white and black Australia. His attestation papers note his Indigenous descent – 'dark brown eyes', 'black hair' and 'aboriginal half caste' are scrawled in the description column.

Before leaving for war, Alex made a will. Its intention was crystal clear:

> *I give devise and bequeath unto 'Cobb' . . . Northern Territory Aboriginal my mother all my good[s] and chattels real and personal to and for her own use and benefit absolutely.*[1]

Alex was killed at Passchendaele in 1917 in the advance on Broodseinde Ridge. All his possessions, and there were not many of them, were packed in a tiny parcel and sent home to Australia. In due course, Cobb received her son's pipe, his inkwell, a wallet, some books, and his Bible. But not his medals.

Not long after the war, Major J.W. Pugh, Base Commandant at Keswick Barracks, South Australia, considered the entitlements due to Aboriginal people. What did Australia owe to Indigenous mothers whose sons had died for the Empire?

> *I am of the opinion that the war medals would not be valued by 'Cobb', and would suggest they be awarded to Mrs Mary McKinnon, stepmother [in Adelaide].*[2]

ABOVE **Answering the call:** The memorial to Aboriginal and Torres Strait Islander servicemen and women. This sculpture raised in Adelaide commemorates 'black diggers' from the Northern Territory. When Australia went to war, the Territory was governed from South Australia. *Courtesy Bruce Scates.*

Nor did Cobb receive Alex's war gratuity – even though she applied for it. The military authorities thought that that sum of money, based on a soldier's period of service, would be better paid to the Chief Protector of Aborigines.

In 1922, a woman Alex McKinnon had never met received all his medals, the medallion struck in his name and the commemorative scroll bearing a message of consolation from the King.

Even then, perhaps, the authorities suspected an injustice had been done. The accompanying letter reserved the right to retrieve the medals if they were not treated 'with due care as memorials' or if some closer next-of-kin could be found.[3] But the central truth remains: in the eyes of white Australia in the early twentieth century, Alex's mother was not considered his next-of-kin.

Alexander McKinnon's remains were never found. Like many other Indigenous servicemen, his body blends with the mud of Flanders. Alexander McKinnon's name appears on the Menin Gate alongside 55 000 others who have no known grave.

In 2012, historians from Monash University reported this case to the Anzac Centenary Advisory Board. It was recommended that the government acknowledge the service and sacrifice of Indigenous Australians, make every effort to find Alex McKinnon's relatives and restore the medals that were surely due to them. The Centenary of the Great War is now upon us. And nothing has been done.

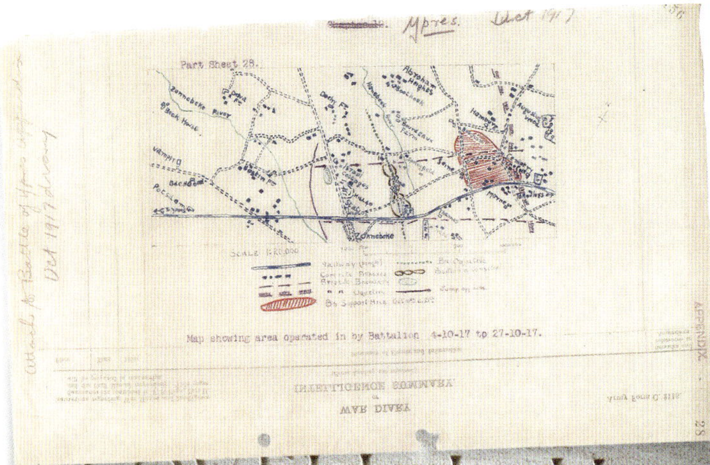

BEOW TOP **Ypres:** A map of the area of Belgium where Alex was killed on 4 October 1917. *43rd Battalion diary courtesy Australian War Memorial.*

BELOW BOTTOM **Memorial to the Missing:** Alex's name is listed on the Menin Gate Memorial along with thousands of other Australians who have no known grave. *Courtesy Rebecca Wheatley.*

SOURCES AND FURTHER READING: The authors respectfully acknowledge the Arrente people of central Australia and their elders, past and present. This story draws on Alexander McKinnon's service dossier NAA: B2455, MCKINNON ALEXANDER and contemporary newspaper reports. For further reading on the family see Marcelle Edwards, *MacKinnon Family: Scotland to Australia 1840* (Adelaide: np, 2010.) For general studies of Aboriginal people in the First AIF see Philippa Scarlett, *Aboriginal and Torres Strait Island Volunteers for the AIF: The Indigenous Response to World War One* (Canberra: Indigenous Histories, 2013); David Huggonson, *Too Dark for the Light Horse: An Exhibition of Photographs & Documents Depicting Aboriginal Involvement in the Australian Army at the Albury Regional Museum, August 11th–September 27th* compiled by David Huggonson, Albury, 1988; Alick Jackomos and Derek Fowell, *Forgotten Heroes: Aborigines at War from the Somme to Vietnam* (Melbourne: Victoria Press, 1993). The authors eagerly await the important work of Mick Dodson, John Maynard and Jack Pearson into Indigenous service.

Marked 'secret'

SAMUEL MELLOR

The officer in charge of AIF records in Melbourne looked at the pile of letters in his in-tray. He wondered if there would ever be any end to it. Thirty years since the signing of the Armistice, families still kept writing – hoping for news of a son or a husband or a brother taken by the war. Sometimes they'd heard that a man without a memory had been admitted to an asylum. Sometimes they'd seen a photograph that answered their boy's description. Many had spoken to the men he'd served with, desperate for some detail the authorities may have overlooked. All believed that the missing might one day be found.

The Major sighed and pulled the first of the envelopes towards him. The families of the missing lived in a kind of limbo. There was no definite news of their boy's death; no actual sighting of the body; not the cold, conclusive evidence of a grave. For the bereaved he could offer something – they had the right to choose an epitaph, or carve a name on a memorial, they could find the words to say goodbye. But there were no words for the families of the missing. And many were simply not ready to grieve.

The Major sighed again. He recognised the writing on the next envelope, the stilted, shaking hand pleading for his attention. This letter he knew was special, it was different. No one but himself would be permitted to read it, and soon it would be locked away in a steel cabinet marked 'secret' in his office.

Elizabeth Mellor had first written to Base Records in 1917. She had heard nothing from her son Samuel in years and feared 'something must have happened to him'. She wondered if the Army could tell her anything. 'This lad kept the home together and supported me . . . He was always such a good lad and very proud of being a soldier.'

But the Major knew otherwise. Samuel Mellor had not been a good lad at all. Barely 17 years old when he enlisted, the boy fell into bad company. He went AWOL in Egypt and deserted from the Army not long after arriving in England. In 1917, his

mother had been told that her son was 'illegally absent'. And that was something she couldn't believe.

At the end of the war, Mellor's official status was still 'absent'. The Major flicked through the file a busy clerk had brought him. In June 1919, Mrs Mellor sent him a photograph and asked it be forwarded on to London:

> *My son has a very faint scar at the corner of one eye . . . brown moles on his neck and body . . . it is now over three years since I've had a letter from him.*

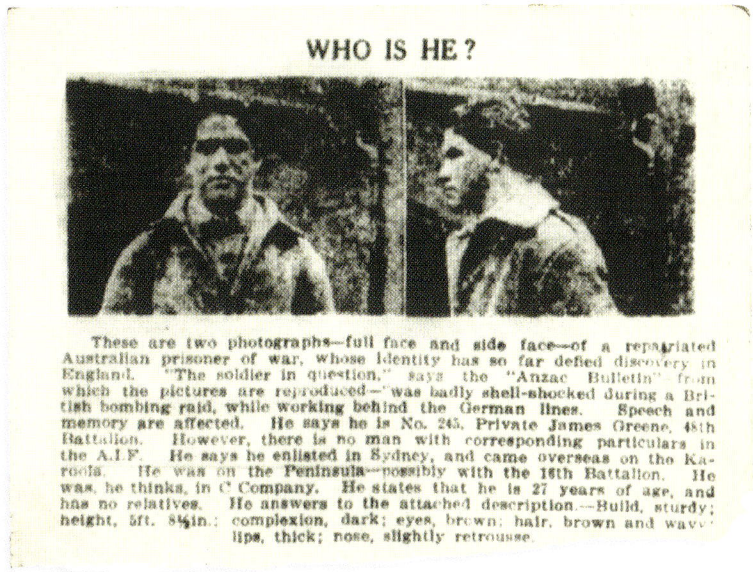

WHO IS HE?

These are two photographs—full face and side face—of a repatriated Australian prisoner of war, whose identity has so far defied discovery in England. "The soldier in question," says the "Anzac Bulletin" from which the pictures are reproduced—"was badly shell-shocked during a British bombing raid, while working behind the German lines. Speech and memory are affected. He says he is No. 245, Private James Greene, 48th Battalion. However, there is no man with corresponding particulars in the A.I.F. He says he enlisted in Sydney, and came overseas on the Karoola. He was on the Peninsula—possibly with the 16th Battalion. He was, he thinks, in C Company. He states that he is 27 years of age, and has no relatives. He answers to the attached description.—Build, sturdy; height, 5ft. 8½in.; complexion, dark; eyes, brown; hair, brown and wavy; lips, thick; nose, slightly retrousse.

ABOVE **Who is he?:** This photo appeared in a number of Sydney newspapers. Elizabeth Mellor claimed it was her son Samuel. The authorities denied that it was Mellor, insisting it was some other soldier. There is a note however in the margins of her letter. A clerk at Base Records has scrawled 'photo probably was of her son'. Evening Sun, *13 June 1919*.

The next year she thought she recognised her son in the picture published in the evening papers headed 'Who is He?' – one of a legion of nameless men who surfaced in the wake of war. And in 1921, she drew her own conclusion:

> *It has come to my knowledge that he is in an asylum badly shell-shocked and [suffering from] loss of speech. He is in a place 100 miles from London called Leicester, it is the one on a hill near the cemetery. Would you kindly investigate this matter for me.*

'The anxiety is terrible,' she went on, 'sometimes unbearable. Trusting you will do your best for me.'

But what was the best thing for Mrs Mellor, the Major wondered? He looked down at the letters again, page after page of them: 'My kind and loving boy', 'one of the best lads', 'my darling'. And now this latest letter, surely the last he would place in that file, dated 3 March 1939, as the world prepared for another war:

> *I had a son named Samuel Rowley Mellor. He joined up with the first light horse, 11th reinforcements, he left Sydney 1915 on 23 October . . . Now it is a long time ago, though my tears don't dry when I think of him. He joined up under the name of Richard Rowley Mellor, that was his older brother's name, he gave his age as 22 but my darling was only 17 years . . . I am now nearing the closing of life I am 80, I would feel very grateful to you for a reply.*

The Major knew the reply the official channels would send her. But he also knew the truth and the reason this file must remain locked away. Having deserted the First AIF, Mellor had adopted yet another name and joined the British Army. He had served out the war as Gunner Frank Oswald Wills of the Royal Field Artillery. In 1919, the young man was arrested in Paris. In a drunken brawl, he had killed a military policeman. Gunner Frank Wills was sentenced to death by firing squad; his last request was to speak to an Australian officer.

OPPOSITE **Shot at dawn:** Herbert Burden was one of over three hundred British soldiers executed by their own side during the Great War. Burden was 17 when he was put to death for cowardice and desertion, the same age Samuel Mellor was when he first enlisted. Burden was posthumously pardoned in 2006. *Shot at Dawn memorial at the National Memorial Arboretum courtesy NMA guide, Creative Commons.*

Samuel Mellor made no attempt to save his life. But he did ask that his mother in Australia be told what happened to him. Without delay, the officer cabled London for instructions. What action – if any – should be taken regarding the fate of Gunner Wills? London wired back several days later: 'message not understood'.

The Major sighed again, this sigh much deeper than the last. By the time AIF Headquarters in London had replied, it was too late anyway. Samuel Mellor had been shot at dawn on 27 May 1919. He was buried under the name he'd adopted, and the truth was buried with him.

The Major placed Mrs Mellor's last letter in the file and turned to face his typewriter. He wound a crisp white sheet of parchment into the Remington and thumped out the first letters on the keyboard. 'Dear Madam', he began . . .[1]

SOURCES AND FURTHER READING: This semi-fictionalised account is based on a close reading of Samuel Mellor's service dossier NAA: B2455 MELLOR RICHARD. See also Tim Lycett and Sandra Playle, 'A Mother's Son: The World War I Mystery of Private Richard Mellor', *Inside History*, June 2013. For further reading on military executions see Julian Putkowski and Julian Sykes, *Shot at Dawn: Executions in World War One by Authority of the British Army Act* (London: Pen & Sword, 1998).

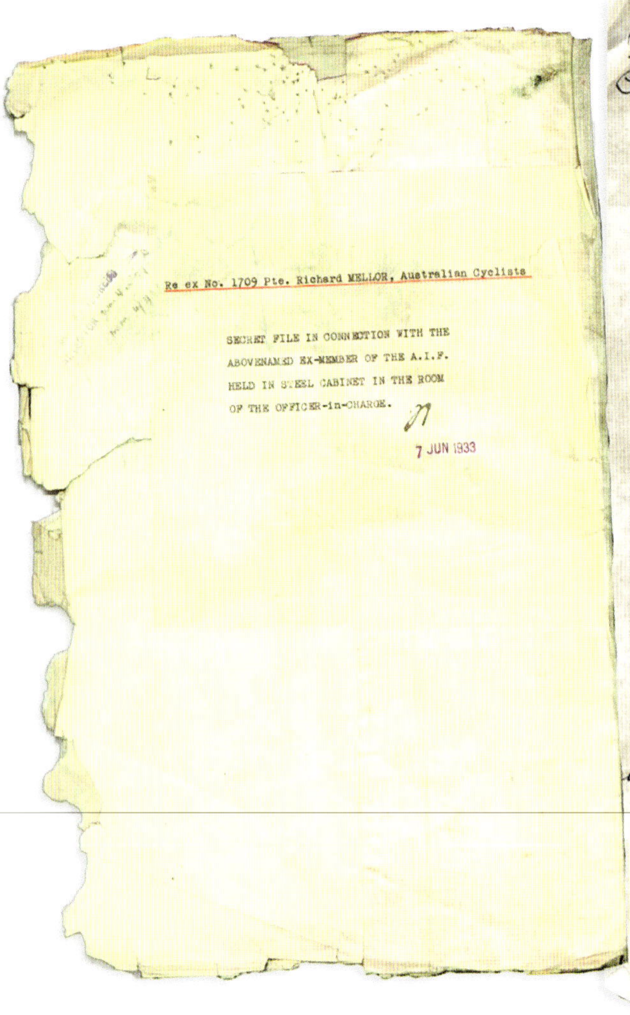

Re ex No. 1709 Pte. Richard MELLOR, Australian Cyclists

SECRET FILE IN CONNECTION WITH THE ABOVENAMED EX-MEMBER OF THE A.I.F. HELD IN STEEL CABINET IN THE ROOM OF THE OFFICER-in-CHARGE.

7 JUN 1933

BELOW LEFT **Locked away in a steel cabinet:** The secret files pertaining to Samuel Mellor were held at Victoria Barracks for decades, guarded by an army of officials and strong bluestone walls. *NAA: B2455, MELLOR RICHARD courtesy National Archives of Australia.*

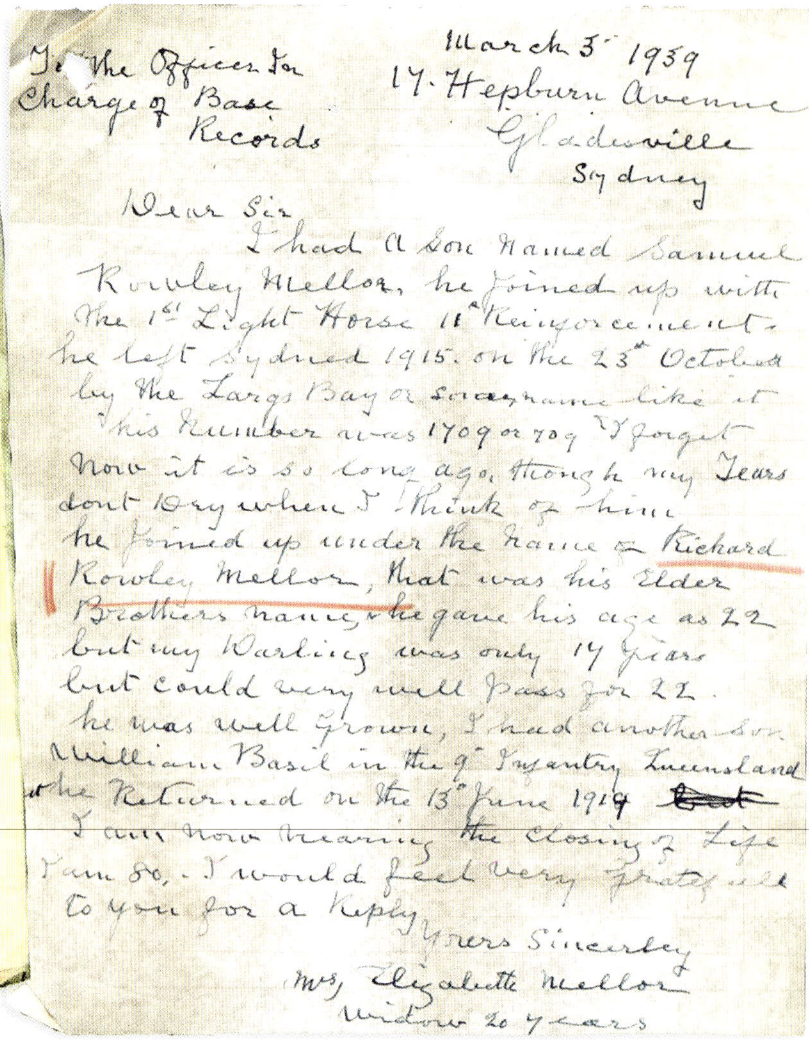

To the Officer for Charge of Base Records

March 5 1939
17 Hepburn Avenue
Gladesville
Sydney

Dear Sir

I had a Son named Samuel Rowley Mellor, he joined up with the 1st Light Horse 11th Reinforcement. he left Sydney 1915. on the 23rd October by the Largs Bay or some name like it his Number was 1709 or 709 I forget now it is so long ago, though my Tears dont Dry when I Think of him he joined up under the name of Richard Rowley Mellor, that was his Elder Brothers name, he gave his age as 22 but my Darling was only 17 years but could very well pass for 22. he was well grown, I had another Son William Basil in the 9th Infantry Queensland who Returned on the 13th June 1919 I am now nearing the closing of Life I am 80, I would feel very grateful to you for a Reply

Yours Sincerely
Mrs, Elizabeth Mellor
Widow 20 years

BELOW RIGHT **My tears don't dry:** Mrs Mellor's last letter to the authorities. Mrs Mellor wrote on the eve of World War Two. Her grief had already spanned three decades. *NAA: B2455, MELLOR RICHARD courtesy National Archives of Australia.*

The little digger

HENRI TOVELL

Australians aren't accustomed to a white Christmas, but in 1918 the No. 4 Squadron of the Australian Flying Corps celebrated the holiday, as well as the recent Armistice, in snowy Bickendorf. Amid the festivities, the bright decorations, a delicious roast dinner and a lively band, Air Mechanic Tim Tovell noticed an unexpected guest sneaking through the crowd. The inviting smells and sounds of the mess hall had tempted a ragged little waif in from the night.

Cold and hungry, this uninvited visitor quickly charmed the squadron. He appreciated the Australian flare for celebration, particularly in comparison to the more humble merriment hosted by the British troops. Tim Tovell had young children of his own at home in Queensland and immediately took on guardianship of Henri. Soon the boy was like his own son.

Henri's story mirrored that of a generation in war-torn Europe. His father was killed in Flanders and not long after, his mother died during a German bombardment. 'I don't know a lot about my past,' he confessed. Even so, he couldn't escape the memory of his mother's lifeless body amongst the rubble of their home. Since then, Henri had attached himself to British units, but the chaos of battle and deaths of newly made friends eventually led him to the Australian airmen that Christmas Eve.

Tim decided to take Henri back to Australia with him. He wrote home to tell his wife, Gertie, 'that really, one extra in the family wouldn't make that much of a difference.'[1] But sadly Henri would not mean 'one extra' for the Tovell family. Tim was told his young son at home had died from meningitis. Tim's grief made him more determined to provide Henri with a home.

Uncertain of Henri's age, he guessed the boy was perhaps eleven. But who really knew? Years of fear, hunger and loneliness had had a drastic effect on Henri's size and development. The squadron decided that his new date of birth would be 25 December;

ABOVE **A hundred-pound oat bag:** Henri was packed into a hundred-pound oat bag for the journey to England. *A03056 courtesy Australian War Memorial.*

after all, that date marked a new beginning for Henri. When the time came to return home, Tim knew there would be many obstacles on the voyage to Australia. He could hardly abandon Henri, but there would be a great deal of creativity required to ship the boy to Queensland.

Little Henri was packed inside a hundred-pound oat bag, slung over Tim's shoulder and smuggled aboard a troopship to England. They were sent to a camp on Salisbury Plain where Tim dressed the boy in a tailor-made replica of an AIF uniform and 'the little digger' was adored by everyone. He soon got up to mischief and adventure, trapping the rats that rummaged through the camp and joining the men in games of two-up.

For the next leg of his journey, Henri was put inside a hamper, covered with sporting equipment and smuggled into Tim's cabin. Their troopship stopped in Port Said and Henri, trying to keep up with the men, dived overboard to swim in the cool waters. Like his fellow leave-breakers, he returned to the ship horribly sunburned and in so much pain that Tim was forced to take him to the ship's doctor. Henri was hardly a secret stowaway now.

Luckily, one of their fellow travellers was Thomas Joseph Ryan, the Premier of Queensland. The moment he learned of Henri's story he contacted the Minister for Home Affairs and organised permission 'to land the mascot'.[2]

Difficult as it was to get Henri to Australia, arriving home wasn't easy for Tim either. He returned to a son's grave and to a daughter who had been just a baby when he'd left. When Henri arrived in his new home, he walked straight up to Gertie and said 'Hullo, Mum!'[3] He wrapped his little arms around her and gave her a small gold brooch he'd bought with the money he'd earned in camp. From that moment on Henri was part of the Tovell family.

BELOW **A French orphan:** Henri in his tailor-made replica AIF uniform. The cost of this outfit would have been considerable. *H13592 courtesy Australian War Memorial.*

In 1926, now a young man, Henri left for Melbourne to train with the RAAF as a motor mechanic. Although homesick for Gertie and Tim, Henri still made the most of the new city. He bought a flash motorcycle and found himself a sweetheart.

Late one night, Henri was riding home from visiting his girlfriend's house. He collided with a taxi and died not long after the accident.

Henri Tovell was buried in Fawkner Cemetery. Point Cook airmen were the pallbearers and an Air Force wagon his hearse. Some men from the No. 4 Squadron were there, as well as his girlfriend. She sobbed quietly by the gravesite. Before the dirt was shoveled over the coffin, a French flag was tossed down into his grave.

The story of the little mascot appealed to the hearts of many Melburnians, so much so that the *Argus* launched an appeal for a statue to commemorate him. Subscriptions rolled in and a small, stone figure of a boy was erected over Henri's grave. The memorial looked over his resting place for decades, until the 1950s when the plot was vandalised and the 'little digger' went missing. Tim and Gertie were never told about the desecration. It was thought it would be too much for them.

Mourning the loss of another son, the Tovells were comforted by the thought that Henri had been reunited with his French mother and father. And they hoped they had played a part in healing the wounds of war. It was their 'privilege to rescue him when

he might have become just a piece of human driftwood without hope and without happiness in the world.' The Tovells had offered the French orphan at least 'a few years of comfort and joy.'[4]

SOURCES AND FURTHER READING: This story draws on Tim Tovell's account of adopting Henri in Norman Ellison, *Flying Matilda* (Sydney: Angus and Robertson, 1957); Henri Tovell Papers at the Australian War Memorial AWM, PR87/199; the Coroner's Inquest for Henri Trovell PROV VPRS24, 1928/675; Tim Tovell's service dossier NAA: B2455, TOVELL TIMOTHY WILLIAM; and Henri H Tovell – Memorial, NAA: A705, 202/3/334. The story of the 'little digger', his death and the memorial erected at his gravesite were reported on widely in the press and this story has drawn on many of the contemporary newspaper articles. For an extended account of Henri Tovell's story see Anthony Hill, *Young Digger* (Camberwell: Penguin, 2002).

ABOVE LEFT **The little digger:** No. 4 Squadron mascot, Henri Tovell, dressed smartly in a replica AIF uniform made for him in London. Beside him are his adoptive uncle and father. *P00867.001 courtesy Australian War Memorial.*

ABOVE RIGHT **'Who plucked this flower?' said the gardener. 'I,' said the Master, and the gardener held his peace:** These words were a great comfort to the Tovell family as they mourned a second son. Inscribed on their son Timmy's headstone, Henri thought they were 'nice words' and Tim and Gertie hoped they might also be inscribed on his memorial. Sadly, those wishes were not met. In 2009 the RAAF Association in Victoria and the Department of Veterans' Affairs organised for a new headstone at Henri's grave – this time inscribed with the words that Tim and Gertie had wanted. *A03681 courtesy Australian War Memorial.*

At breaking point
FRANK WILKINSON

In 1996, a small group gathered in Rushworth Cemetery to honour a man they'd never known. Frank Wilkinson's story had long been suppressed or forgotten but nearly seventy years after his death, his relatives gathered around the new memorial installed at his grave. Though they had discovered a terrible family secret, they all grieved for Frank – they now knew what the war had cost him.

Although he wasn't a big man, Frank had a toughness about him, a ruddy complexion, his face hardened by a scar on his lip. He'd eagerly enlisted, leaving Australia months before three of his brothers, Arthur, Gus and Eric, would join him in Europe.

Frank took part in the Third Battle of Ypres. At 'great personal risk', and under heavy shelling, he helped extinguish a blaze threatening four ammunition dumps.[1] Frank was considered a war hero and awarded the Military Medal for his efforts. His family back home hoped he'd be 'spared to wear it'.[2]

Frank survived the war, but not all the Wilkinsons returned to their home town of Donald in Victoria. The eldest of the four brothers, Arthur, was killed at Polygon Wood; his body was never recovered from the battlefield.

After the Armistice, Frank travelled through the United Kingdom. In the long wait for repatriation he trained as a sheep shearer in the verdant hills of Galashiels, where he met his wife-to-be, Elizabeth.

Frank, Elizabeth and their baby girl, Isabella, settled on a block of land in Stanhope, Victoria. Frank's recommendations in his application to the soldier settlement scheme were glowing: 'steady', 'industrious', 'he is one that will make good'. He seemed the ideal man for the land. Few suspected the disaster to follow.[3]

In spite of his training, experience and hard work, the bleak and barren holding

ABOVE **Decorated for bravery:** Frank Wilkinson never recovered from his experiences overseas. *Courtesy Jill Fradd.*

yielded nothing but debt. By 1927 Frank owed more than a thousand pounds and he was having trouble breathing, a result of being gassed in the war. Frank's body was failing him and he was getting more 'nervy' by the day.

Elizabeth sensed her husband was at breaking point. 'I'm glad we're getting out of this,' she confided to a friend, 'I'm satisfied that Frank is going to go off his head.' The family had packed up their lives, ready to abandon their farm, move in with Frank's brother and build a new life for themselves in Seymour. But things went terribly wrong.[4]

The morning of their planned departure, as the Wilkinsons' possessions waited for them at the railway station, their worried neighbours discovered a gruesome scene. In the kitchen, Frank lay on the floor, face down in a pool of blood and a stained razor by his hand. There was a tremendous gash across his throat. It was so deep it cut to the bone.

Little Isabella, just four years old, lay lifeless on the bed, her tiny skull beaten and crushed.

The only signs of life were the quiet cries of Frank's wife. Cowering beneath the bed, Elizabeth, cold and dazed, whimpered, 'I never thought it would come to this.' Frank had strangled his wife and smashed her head in with a hammer. The records of the inquest are brutally explicit. Fragments of Elizabeth's skull littered the floor, the walls were 'splashed with blood'.[5]

Elizabeth's life ended a few days later in Mooroopna Hospital. But she had lived long enough to forgive what her husband had done. 'He couldn't help it, he couldn't help it,' was all she could say time and again.

Frank was buried with his 'loving wife' and 'beloved daughter'. All of them were victims of the Great War and the trauma that lingered on a decade after the Armistice. 'Peace' is their shared family epitaph. It was a plea both for Frank and those he loved.

SOURCES AND FURTHER READING: This story draws on the Wilkinson Papers courtesy Jill Fradd and her assistance is gratefully acknowledged. Other sources used include the Coroner's Inquest of the deaths of Frank, Elizabeth and Isabella Wilkinson PROV VPRS24, 1927/1017; Frank Wilkinson's service dossier NAA: B2455, WILKINSON FRANCIS EDELBERT; his repatriation record NAA: B73, R87683; and his soldier settlement file PROV VPRS5714, unit 1473, file 4147/12. The Wilkinson tragedy was reported on widely in the press and this story has drawn on many of the contemporary newspaper articles. The authors would like to thank George Gemmill, Secretary of the Stanhope RSL, for his generous assistance with this story. For further reading on postwar trauma see Jay Winter, 'Shell shock' in Jay Winter (ed), *The Cambridge History of the First World War*, vol. III (Cambridge: Cambridge University Press, 2014), pp. 310–333 and Tanja Lukins, *The Gates of Memory: Australian People's Experiences and Memories of Loss and the Great War* (Perth: Curtin University Press, 2004) and Richard Lindstrom, 'The Australian Experience of Psychological Casualties in War 1915–1939' (PhD thesis, Victoria University of Technology, 1997).

BELOW **A terrible secret:** The Wilkinson family headstone was replaced in 1996. Nearly seventy years after the tragedy, the Department of Veterans' Affairs made this acknowledgement that Frank's death was war related. *Courtesy George Gemmill.*

A guardian angel of the Anzacs
ETTIE ROUT

Few characters caused as much controversy as Ettie Rout. In pubs and teashops, schools and churches, the mere mention of her name could cause a fierce argument. To some, she was a wicked woman, her ideas as confronting as her appearance; to others she was a guardian angel, the saviour of the Anzacs.

Ettie was born in Launceston, Tasmania and as a girl moved to Wellington, New Zealand with her family. Always exceptional, this young woman shunned convention and often stood out from the crowd. Her tall, fit figure was known for sporting short skirts, men's boots, even trousers. Miss Rout was many things: an enthusiastic cyclist, skilled typist, bold journalist, committed socialist and a radical thinker. But it was her ideas on sex reform that caused a storm of controversy on both sides of the Tasman.

After the Landing at Gallipoli, Ettie established the New Zealand Volunteer Sisterhood, organising a small contingent of her fellow countrywomen to travel to Egypt and care for their Anzac men. At first, the work of the Sisterhood seemed unexceptional. Like most patriotic leagues, Ettie's association arranged outings for the men, organised social events and distributed comforts. But in Cairo, Ettie confronted what her contemporaries called the 'social evil'. Australian and New Zealand troops frequented bars and brothels, many visited prostitutes in the notorious Wasser district, and a large number contracted venereal diseases. By 1915, alarmed officials noted that Anzac forces had a higher rate of sexually transmitted diseases than any other fighting force in the British Empire. But their policy was one of pious denial – the authorities did little to address the problem.

Ettie was bewildered and outraged by the official reaction to VD. The blurring of the medical and the moral incensed her. To her mind, this was a health issue first and foremost, not a question of virtue or vice. Ever the realist, Ettie knew that abstinence was an impractical strategy. So with advice from medical professionals and the soldiers

OPPOSITE **A guardian angel of the Anzacs:** This is how Dr Jean Tissot, a French venereal disease doctor, described Ettie. Here she sits with some of the New Zealand, South African and Australian soldiers she looked out for in Paris, 1918. *H03654 courtesy Australian War Memorial.*

themselves, she put together a prophylactic kit. It contained calomel ointment, Condy's Crystals (potassium permanganate) and condoms, and was distributed to troops on leave. The authorities turned a blind eye. Mindful of public opinion back home, the Army could not be seen to condone 'immorality'.

But whilst Ettie's kits were not officially sanctioned, the generals knew all too well their value. Keeping fit men in the line was their first concern and in the land of 'sun, sex and syphilis', sexually transmitted diseases posed almost as great a threat as Ottoman artillery. In 1917, the New Zealand Government would quietly 'adopt' Ettie's kit, albeit without any kind of acknowledgement.

After Egypt, Ettie spent most of the war years in London and Paris. Anzac troops visited both places on leave; their three-day binges in the *Folies Bergère* and the red light districts a desperate attempt to forget the horrors of the trenches. In Paris, Ettie set up a sexual welfare service. Waiting on the platform at the Gare du Nord, she would greet men arriving in the City of Love, knowing full well what they were after. Some troops were equipped with Ettie's kit and left to their own devices. But most were directed to one of the 'clean' brothels Ettie had identified, where regular medical checks of the women and visual inspection of their clients helped stem the spread of infection.

It was never easy work. In light of what they'd been through, few soldiers feared 'the clap'. Some even sought infection – a self-inflicted wound that might spare them from the trenches. And Ettie knew her strategies would only work if both parties – men and women – adopted preventative measures. In hurried encounters in the alleys of London, safe sex wasn't always an option.

It wasn't just the sexual health of soldiers or sex workers that concerned Ettie Rout. She feared as much for the safety of the women back home. The long-term consequences of venereal disease – sterility, insanity and death – were ghastly, and before the discovery of penicillin there was no safe or lasting cure. In the early twentieth century, gonorrhoea and syphilis marred lives, broke marriages and destroyed the healthy, companionate home life idealised by feminist campaigners. Ettie was determined to protect her sex from what many called 'the red plague'. She was fighting for those 'weeping women who have done no wrong: the cry of innocent babes too young to know how they suffer – and why.'[1]

In such a campaign, she observed, 'the Good Women do more damage than the Bad Women'.[2] Holier-than-thou puritans who denied the extent of the problem or refused to take effective measures only aided the spread of disease. At the heart of this lay a feminist commitment to women's personal agency. We must not allow ourselves to become the victims of men's carelessness, selfishness and lust, Ettie Rout told her fellow campaigners, our bodies are ours and ours alone.

Thousands of lives were saved by the work of sex reformers like Ettie. Her enlightened approach to sexual health

BELOW **The Good Women do more damage than the Bad Women:** Ettie believed that fretful puritans were more culpable on the issue of VD than the supposedly immoral men and women. This is a card that Ettie distributed to the troops on their arrival in Paris. Madame Yvonne's was a regularly inspected brothel that adhered to Ettie's sexual health protocols. *3 DRL 6487 (55) courtesy Australian War Memorial.*

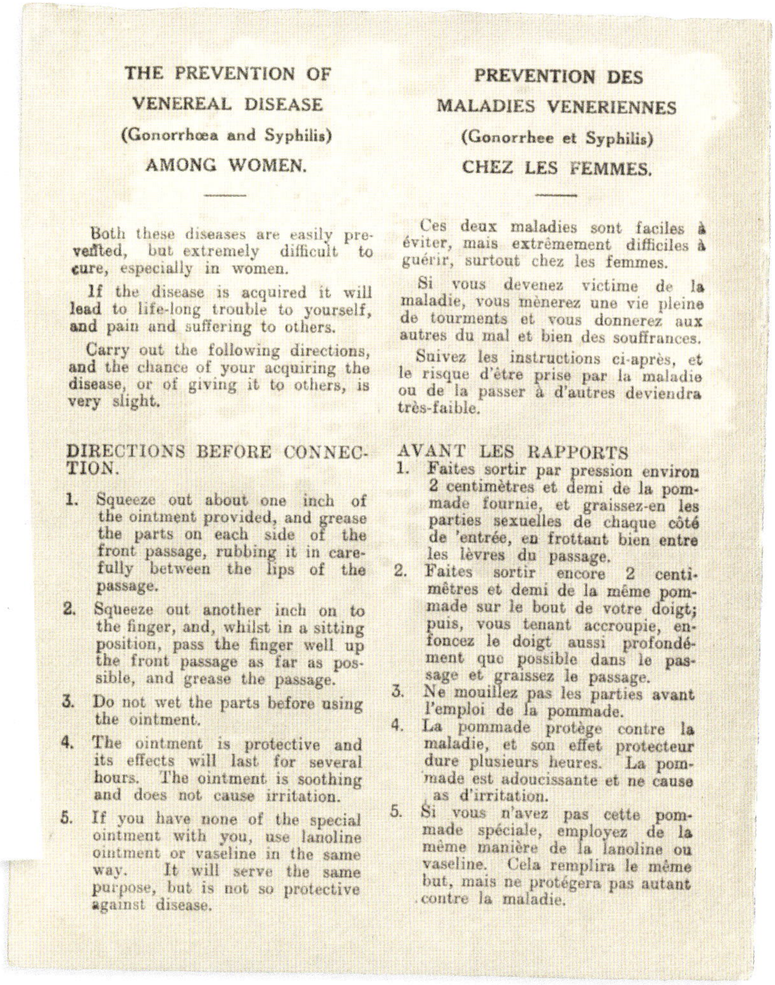

THE PREVENTION OF VENEREAL DISEASE (Gonorrhœa and Syphilis) AMONG WOMEN.

Both these diseases are easily prevented, but extremely difficult to cure, especially in women.

If the disease is acquired it will lead to life-long trouble to yourself, and pain and suffering to others.

Carry out the following directions, and the chance of your acquiring the disease, or of giving it to others, is very slight.

DIRECTIONS BEFORE CONNECTION.

1. Squeeze out about one inch of the ointment provided, and grease the parts on each side of the front passage, rubbing it in carefully between the lips of the passage.
2. Squeeze out another inch on to the finger, and, whilst in a sitting position, pass the finger well up the front passage as far as possible, and grease the passage.
3. Do not wet the parts before using the ointment.
4. The ointment is protective and its effects will last for several hours. The ointment is soothing and does not cause irritation.
5. If you have none of the special ointment with you, use lanoline ointment or vaseline in the same way. It will serve the same purpose, but is not so protective against disease.

PREVENTION DES MALADIES VENERIENNES (Gonorrhee et Syphilis) CHEZ LES FEMMES.

Ces deux maladies sont faciles à éviter, mais extrêmement difficiles à guérir, surtout chez les femmes.

Si vous devenez victime de la maladie, vous mènerez une vie pleine de tourments et vous donnerez aux autres du mal et bien des souffrances.

Suivez les instructions ci-après, et le risque d'être prise par la maladie ou de la passer à d'autres deviendra très-faible.

AVANT LES RAPPORTS

1. Faites sortir par pression environ 2 centimètres et demi de la pommade fournie, et graissez-en les parties sexuelles de chaque côté de 'entrée, en frottant bien entre les lèvres du passage.
2. Faites sortir encore 2 centimêtres et demi de la même pommade sur le bout de votre doigt; puis, vous tenant accroupie, enfoncez le doigt aussi profondément que possible dans le passage et graissez le passage.
3. Ne mouillez pas les parties avant l'emploi de la pommade.
4. La pommade protège contre la maladie, et son effet protecteur dure plusieurs heures. La pommade est adoucissante et ne cause as d'irritation.
5. Si vous n'avez pas cette pommade spéciale, employez de la même manière de la lanoline ou vaseline. Cela remplira le même but, mais ne protégera pas autant contre la maladie.

education anticipated later approaches to epidemics like AIDS. In France, her work was venerated – she was praised by politicians, celebrated by the media and awarded the Médaille de la Reconnaissance Française. But at home she met with a frosty reception. New Zealand authorities campaigned actively against her and imposed a hundred pound fine for the mere mention of her name. In Australia, certain organisations fought to bar her entry into the country, fearful of the influence this 'sexual pervert' and her 'pernicious doctrine' would have.[3]

Ettie Rout died in 1936 from a quinine overdose. Maligned and misunderstood, she wrote to her friend H.G. Wells, 'It's a mixed blessing to be born too soon.'

SOURCES AND FURTHER READING: This story draws on Ettie Rout's written work, *Two Years in Paris* (London: E Hornibrook, 1923); Ettie Rout - Question of admission to Australia NAA: A1, 1920/3508; Jane Tolerton, *Ettie: A life of Ettie Rout* (Auckland: Penguin, 1992); Judith Binney, Judith Bassett, Erik Olssen, *The People and the Land = Te Tangata me Te Whenua: An Illustrated History of New Zealand 1820–1920* (Wellington: Allen & Unwin, 1990). For further reading about the issue of venereal disease in the Australian and New Zealand forces see Raden Dunbar, *The Secrets of the Anzacs: The Untold Story of Venereal Disease in the Australian Army, 1914–1919* (Brunswick: Scribe Publications, 2014).

ABOVE **It's a mixed blessing to be born too soon:** Ettie wrote this line to her friend H.G. Wells in 1922 – she always recognised the challenges she faced with her progressive ideas. Here, she introduces her advice on sexual health practices to Anzac troops and French women. *Ettie Rout,* Two Years in Paris *(London: E Hornibrook, 1923).*

ABOVE LEFT **The City of Love:** The sylish dress of Parisian women (and their sexual sophistication) took many young diggers by surprise. *The Prodigal Sun: Homeward Ho! on H.M.A.T 'Mahia' in Chronicle and Caricature.*

All that is left of him

GEORGE IRWIN

Private George Irwin went missing at Gallipoli in August 1915. We will never find him. Last seen plunging into the Turkish trenches near Lone Pine, George's body vanished in the carnage. Without a body to mourn, his mother could not begin to accept his death. She began writing to the Red Cross in 1916:

> *I have interviewed so many boys who were with mine in the enemy trench and were blown up that I have . . . come to think that he might have been in one of these explosions, and been carried to some hospital in England suffering from loss of memory . . . [I've been] told . . . there were a number of cases like this . . .*

Sarah Irwin continued to hope, pray and imagine until the very end of the war:

> *I have never been able to think of him as dead. I feel he is still living somewhere. I write regularly to Turkey, but hardly expect a reply, still something urges me to write and I will keep on trusting and hoping, until this dreadful war is over and all the prisoners are exchanged.*[1]

Eleven years after his death, Private Irwin's parents made their way to Gallipoli. Their journey took them 12 000 miles from Australia; first to Britain, then to Italy and finally across the Mediterranean to Turkey. They travelled in the company of three hundred others, a 'mixed party' of grieving parents and returning soldiers determined to walk 'the hallowed ground' of the Peninsula. All were united in a common quest, 'all were connected with the precious dead of Gallipoli.'[2] In the heat of September, the Irwins climbed to the summit of Lone Pine and Australia's Memorial to the Missing. Unable

OPPOSITE **Doom-laden eyes:** The only surviving photograph of Sarah and her son. *Courtesy David Champion.*

ABOVE **Plunging into the Turkish trenches:** Ellis Silas' powerful depiction of face-to-face fighting at Anzac. *Ellis Silas, 'Capture of Turkish Trenches', Crusading at Anzac anon domini 1915 (British Australasian: London, 1916) courtesy State Library of Victoria.*

to lay the body of their son to rest, they took a rubbing of all that is left of him, his name.

Photographs published in the Sydney press captured that moment for many a mourning family back home in Australia. Mrs Irwin, whose long search for her son had finally ended, is crumpled at the base of the memorial. Her face is hidden from view, her hands limp and motionless, her eyes fixed on George's name as it is traced out before her. Beside her rests a formal wreath of paper poppies (carried there by the pilgrimage party) and her own ragged posy of freshly picked flowers. Mr Irwin kneels level with his son's name, a firm hand holding the paper in place – stoic, solemn, reverent.

Nearly a hundred years after his death, a photograph of George finally came to light. It had been passed down through the family, treasured by an ageing woman who never spoke of her son's death, then hidden away in the dusty attics of family memory. It's a studio portrait taken in Katoomba the very day before George sailed off to war. Father, mother and their soldier son were assembled in their Sunday best, the picturesque image of a cascading waterfall artistically positioned behind them. George stands to the back of the party – he barely looks his 18 years of age. He seems gauche and innocent, a boy dressed up in a soldier's uniform. George Sr stands resolutely at the front, shiny black shoes resting on a firm stone footing. It is Sarah who seems the most fragile of all. Already her face seems lined with grief and worry; those doom-laden eyes stare right back at you.

George Irwin, one of thousands missing from the Great War, has not been forgotten by his family. In 2012, George's cousin, David Champion, travelled to North Mackay on the coast of Queensland. There he presented the Irwin studio photograph to a young student researching the life and his death of that particular soldier. Jessie had chanced across Irwin's file, one of over 32 000 Red Cross files held by the Australian War Memorial, and was fascinated by its mystery. She found the Champion's family tree on the internet and quickly established David was one of the few surviving relatives. A long email conversation followed, a man of 82 sharing family stories with a teenager.

His aunt's house, David recalled, 'was full of things about Gallipoli', and the loss of her only son seemed to be a shadow all around her. And he knew 'poor old Auntie Sarah' had tried to find her boy, meeting the troopships to interview soldiers, writing letters to anyone in authority who might know something of his fate, even travelling to England to work for the Red Cross towards the end of the war. Jessie and David exchanged what they called 'discoveries' in the archives: a clipping from an ageing newspaper, a picture of a brooch issued to the mothers who offered up their sons to Empire, shipping lists from a journey across the oceans. And as with Sarah's story, this one ends with a pilgrimage. In 2012, a party of Jessie's classmates carried messages from both Jessie and David to the memorial at Lone Pine. They stood where Sarah Irwin had knelt eighty-six years earlier. And they too took a rubbing of that name in stone, something of George to bring home to Australia.

BELOW **All that is left of him:** Sarah Irwin watches as her son's name is traced from the stone of his memorial. Sydney Mail, *20 October 1926 courtesy State Library of Victoria.*

BOTTOM **The story ended in a pilgrimage:** Students at Mackay North State High School wander at Lone Pine near where George Irwin lost his life. Mackay North runs biannual pilgrimages to the battlefields of the First World War. Each of these students researched the life and death of a soldier, building what Jessie called 'personal connection' to history. *Courtesy Chris Albertson.*

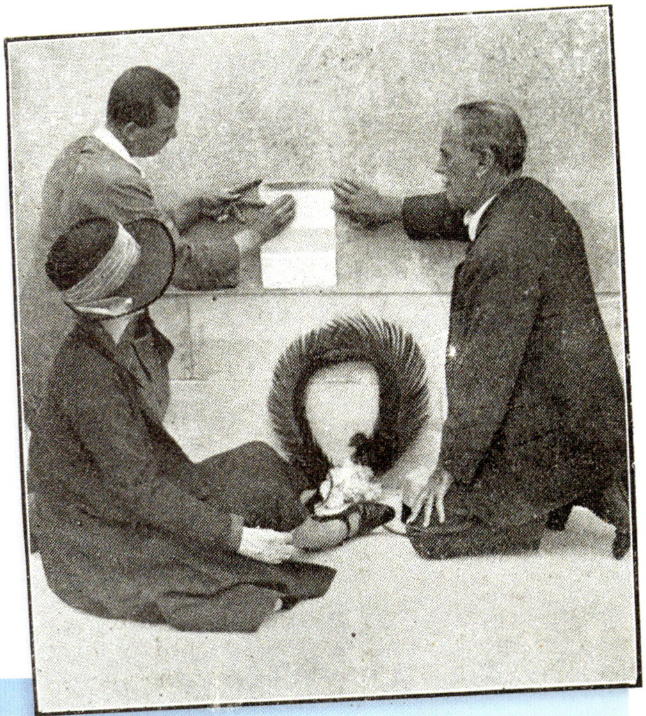

Sources and further reading: This story draws on George Irwin's service dossier NAA: B2455, IRWIN GEORGE ROY; and his Red Cross Wounded and Missing file AWM 1DRL/0428. The Irwins' pilgrimage in 1926 was reported in the press and this story has drawn on those contemporary articles. For further reading on the Irwin story and early Australian pilgrimages to battlefields overseas see Bruce Scates, *Return to Gallipoli: Walking the Battlefields of the Great War* (Cambridge: Cambridge University Press, 2006) and Bart Ziino, *A Distant Grief: Australians, War Graves and the Great War* (Perth: University of Western Australia Press, 2007). The authors thank Mike and Roz Goodwin, the students of Mackay North State High School and David Champion for sharing their story and their research into the Irwin family.

THE LORD KNOWETH THEM THAT ARE HIS
BENEATH THIS STONE RESTS THE BODY
OF A BRITISH WARRIOR
UNKNOWN BY NAME OR RANK
BROUGHT FROM FRANCE TO LIE AMONG
THE MOST ILLUSTRIOUS OF THE LAND
AND BURIED HERE ON ARMISTICE DAY
11 NOV: 1920, IN THE PRESENCE OF
HIS MAJESTY KING GEORGE V
HIS MINISTERS OF STATE
THE CHIEFS OF HIS FORCES
AND A VAST CONCOURSE OF THE NATION
THUS ARE COMMEMORATED THE MANY
MULTITUDES WHO DURING THE GREAT
WAR OF 1914-1918 GAVE THE MOST THAT
MAN CAN GIVE LIFE ITSELF
FOR GOD
FOR KING AND COUNTRY
FOR LOVED ONES HOME AND EMPIRE
FOR THE SACRED CAUSE OF JUSTICE AND
THE FREEDOM OF THE WORLD
THEY BURIED HIM AMONG THE KINGS BECAUSE HE
HAD DONE GOOD TOWARD GOD AND TOWARD
HIS HOUSE
IN CHRIST SHALL ALL BE MADE ALIVE
GREATER LOVE HATH NO MAN THAN THIS
UNKNOWN AND YET WELL KNOWN DYING AND BEHOLD WE LIVE

Denouncing a gruesome trade in the dead

W.A. WINDEYER

In the autumn of 1921, Mr W.A. Windeyer of Hunter's Hill made ready for his journey. We can imagine him assembling all the things a man of his age and status was likely to need for many months abroad – a sturdy suitcase, a hat box, an umbrella, camera and notebook. We can imagine him looking sceptically at the dark woollen overcoat, sagging beneath the weight of itself. It was much too warm for Sydney, even in the darkest days of winter. This was a garment fashioned for another place and another climate, made to cheat the icy winds of the Somme and the drenching rain of Flanders.

William Archibald Windeyer was a man born to privilege; only the elite of Sydney society could afford that first class passage to England. The son of a Supreme Court judge, his family included politicians and pastoralists, university men and senior civil servants. Windeyer himself had invested wisely in the buoyant property market in Sydney. In the years before the war, this canny young solicitor had bought and sold over a dozen residential properties. But privilege, Windeyer believed, carried with it the burden of responsibility. Civic minded to the core, he worked as an alderman of Hunter's Hill municipal council for twenty-three years and served as the mayor for nine. He was also deputy chairman, then chairman of the Boy Scout Association; secretary and treasurer of the Suburban and Country Golf Association; and an avid supporter of any number of charities.

When hostilities broke out, Windeyer took up patriotic work. He was a driving force behind the Belgian Relief Fund, the War Chest Fund and one public appeal after another to help repatriate wounded soldiers. An ardent imperialist, Windeyer believed the war was just, and he campaigned for conscription of the nation's young men to fight it.

In February 1921, Windeyer prepared for yet another patriotic gesture. He and his wife would sail on RMS *Narkunda* for Britain. His destinations included the

OPPOSITE **A pilgrimage by proxy:** The grave of the Unknown Warrior in Westminster Abbey. Mrs Ruby Millicent Windeyer laid a wreath here on Armistice Day in 1921. It was on behalf of the mothers of Hunter's Hill who had lost sons during the war. Lost quite literally. Twelve of Hunter's Hill's war dead were never recovered from the battlefield. The grave of the Unknown Warrior acted as their surrogate tomb. *Courtesy © Dean and Chapter of Westminster.*

war cemeteries of Belgium and France. That warm Sunday afternoon there was just one task remaining

Windeyer took a sheet of paper from his desk and dipped his pen into an inkwell. Cursive writing curled across the page. Soon forty-four names were assembled in a column, much like the lists of names lined up on honour boards across the country.

These were the boys from Hunter's Hill who didn't come home: a fireman from Paul Street, a mechanic from Woolwich Road, a bricklayer from Madeline Street. Lads who once kicked footballs in the grounds of Boronia Park, buried now in the cold mud of Flanders.

Windeyer's journey was a pilgrimage by proxy. He went not just for himself but for mothers who had lost an only boy, fathers bottled up with grief, wives who barely knew their husbands. One woman who wrote to him had lost three sons in a single day. And twelve of the suburb's forty-four dead were still officially listed as 'missing'. Windeyer promised to seek out every grave he could. And he would bring an image of that grave home to Australia, photographing a cross and a name, offering some kind of closure.

And that wasn't all. In his time abroad, the Mayor of Hunter's Hill (himself an avid gardener) 'systematically collected seeds of different flowers which [he found] growing freely in most of the cemeteries': golden coreopsis and blood-coloured poppies, asters, nasturtiums and antirrhinums. On returning to Australia, photographs and seeds were dispatched to dead men's relatives, proof that life sprang anew even in a battered wasteland.[1]

ABOVE **Patriotic work:** Notice of the Grand Patriotic Concert in Hunter's Hill, in aid of the Belgian Relief Fund. The handsome invitation wove together local, national and imperial loyalties, the flags of Great Britain and its allies draped around floral emblems of Australia. The Rising Sun of Japan unfurls beneath the Australian flag – in the First World War Japan was Britain's ally. Patriotic events like these were largely a preserve of the well-to-do. The same significant citizens (Windeyer included) hosted pro-conscription rallies, hoping to force young men to fight the war in Europe. *Courtesy the Windeyer/Bragg families.*

Windeyer hoped his journey would heal. He saw himself as an agent of hope and consolation. But the horrors of the killing fields soon came to haunt him.

In October 1921, this well-connected, Empire-minded man carried his protest to Australia House in London at the head of a deputation of concerned Australians. He claimed thousands of bodies were still left 'uncovered' on the battlefields. That 'unsystematic' searches by indifferent authorities had failed to find them. That 'Belgian peasants' eager to reclaim their farmlands ploughed bodies into the earth: no reward was offered for the recovery of Australian or British dead so there was simply no incentive to bury them. There were rumours the French practice of demanding a body to authorise pension payments had led to a 'gruesome' trade in the dead and reports of corpses being dissected to claim double rewards. 'I know from personal knowledge of a British body from which the tunic and pocket buttons were removed in order to destroy its identity,' Windeyer told the Australian High Commissioner. The deputation demanded that each and every battlefield be searched again 'by Britishers' and made to yield up its harvest of dead for formal burial. And they suggested that 'rewards should be paid to the Belgians and the French for the discovery of Australian bodies, as other nationalities paid for such information'. Cost should be no obstacle to the decent burial of 'our dead'. The High Commissioner promised to put the concerns to the Government and within a fortnight Prime Minister Billy Hughes, still 'the Little Digger', announced that the Commonwealth would authorise 'whatever expenditure may be necessary' to resume the search for Australia's missing.[2]

Windeyer returned to Australia in December 1921, carrying with him a folio of photographs and packets of seeds. He supported efforts to build a local memorial. A proud stone obelisk pointing to the sky, it helped heal the memory of battered bodies scattered across killing fields. Its simple inscription: 'For the Brave 1914–1918.'

In 1936, the NSW Congress of the RSL presented W.A. Windeyer with a certificate of appreciation on behalf of returned men and their families. Four years later, Windeyer's own boy Frank went to war. Frank would die of wounds received at the siege of Tobruk. Windeyer – who died in 1943 – would never see the grave of his son.

SOURCES AND FURTHER READING: This story draws on the biography by Windeyer's grandson, J.B. Windeyer, *W.A. Windeyer: Not Idle but Useless? Not he!* (Canberra: J.B. Windeyer, 2011); J. M. Bennett, 'Windeyer, William Archibald (1871–1943)', *Australian Dictionary of Biography*, National Centre of Biography, Australian National University, adb.anu.edu.au/biography/windeyer-william-archibald-1063/text16157, published first in hardcopy 1990, accessed online 15 March 2015. This story also draws on contemporary newspaper accounts including a detailed survey of the *British Australasian*. For further information see the entry for Windeyer in *Who's Who in Australia*, 1922 & 1938. The authors thank J.B. Windeyer for his detailed comments on this piece. The opinions expressed in this account are the authors' alone.

BELOW **The search for Australia's missing:** A newspaper report in Adelaide details Windeyer's 'unwelcome allegations' in London. News that the bodies of the dead were left exposed on the battleground caused great distress amongst relatives, as did even more sensational claims (relayed in newspaper columns across the country) about the dissection and trade in bodies. The report highlights the diplomatic sensitivities in recovering the war dead; note the High Commissioner's claim that Australia could not act independently in the matter. Adelaide Register, *15 October 1921 courtesy National Library of Australia.*

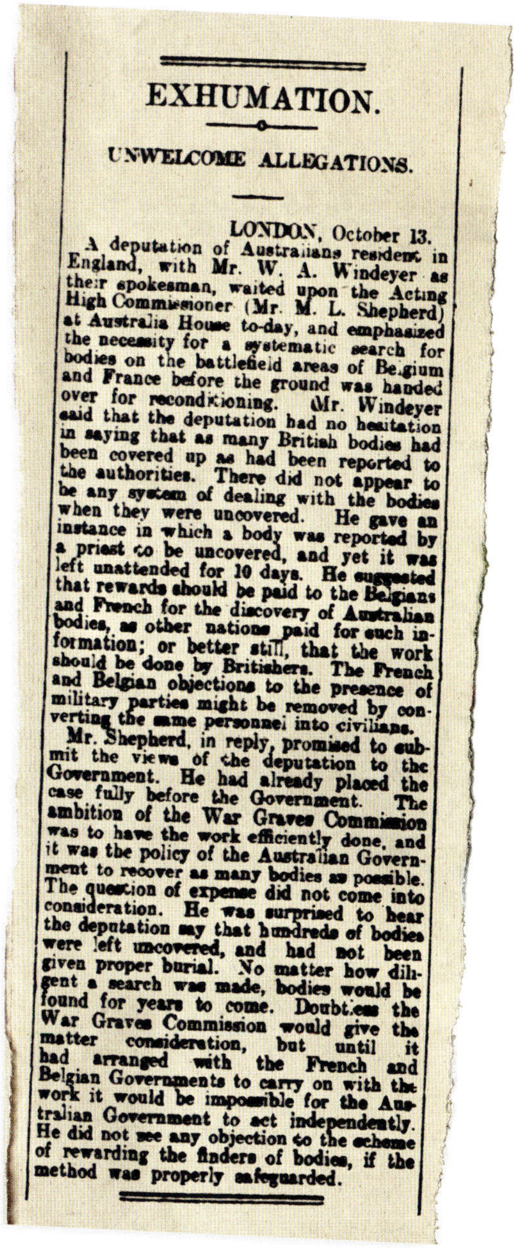

EXHUMATION.

UNWELCOME ALLEGATIONS.

LONDON, October 13.

A deputation of Australians resident in England, with Mr. W. A. Windeyer as their spokesman, waited upon the Acting High Commissioner (Mr. M. L. Shepherd) at Australia House to-day, and emphasized the necessity for a systematic search for bodies on the battlefield areas of Belgium and France before the ground was handed over for reconditioning. Mr. Windeyer said that the deputation had no hesitation in saying that as many British bodies had been covered up as had been reported to the authorities. There did not appear to be any system of dealing with the bodies when they were uncovered. He gave an instance in which a body was reported by a priest to be uncovered, and yet it was left unattended for 10 days. He suggested that rewards should be paid to the Belgians and French for the discovery of Australian bodies, as other nations paid for such information; or better still, that the work should be done by Britishers. The French and Belgian objections to the presence of military parties might be removed by converting the same personnel into civilians.

Mr. Shepherd, in reply, promised to submit the views of the deputation to the Government. He had already placed the case fully before the Government. The ambition of the War Graves Commission was to have the work efficiently done, and it was the policy of the Australian Government to recover as many bodies as possible. The question of expense did not come into consideration. He was surprised to hear the deputation say that hundreds of bodies were left uncovered, and had not been given proper burial. No matter how diligent a search was made, bodies would be found for years to come. Doubtless the War Graves Commission would give the matter consideration, but until it had arranged with the French and Belgian Governments to carry on with the work it would be impossible for the Australian Government to act independently. He did not see any objection to the scheme of rewarding the finders of bodies, if the method was properly safeguarded.

Died of shell shock

ROYCE BAESJOU

On Anzac Day, 1921, Albany honoured her dead. Around two thousand people assembled on York Street, within sight of St John's Anglican Church, to witness the dedication of the Fallen Soldiers' Memorial. A party of school children, led by their head teacher, neatly lined the footpath. A host of dignitaries, the chaplain of St John's and the relatives of the dead were seated beside the town band. They all watched as a squadron of navy cadets marched into position.

Proceedings began with the singing of the national anthem; the young, faint voices of the schoolgirls straining against the bugles of the band. The president of the local RSL branch presented the mayor with a silver trowel and asked him to lay the foundation stone. Then the mayor invited all in attendance to imagine their memorial – a proud granite obelisk bearing its burden of names.

It would be fashioned of stone, he said, 'indigenous to this town', the same grey, granite boulders that line the shores of King George's Sound. These great rocks 'had stood sentinel [over Albany] for ages'; they were the last sight of Australia 'our departed heroes' saw as they sailed off to war. And this memorial too, the mayor promised, would be here for eternity: 'as it stands now it should stand a thousand years hence, proclaiming to the world the . . . valour of the men who fought in the great world war'. Australia had lost 60 000 of 'her finest' and her 'bravest', he continued, and Albany paid 'her share of the toll':

> *Their graves are scattered far and wide – on the rugged hills of Gallipoli, the sandy plains of Palestine and the fields of France – and though the hand of kindred may never tend them, their memories will be kept green by a grateful people in their native land.*[1]

OPPOSITE **A southern son of Empire:** Royce Baesjou in the uniform of a West Australian artillery militia unit. Baesjou subscribed to the values of many middle class families in Australia. He was fiercely patriotic, believed in the British Empire and was a deeply religious man. Baesjou was a lay reader in St Barnabas Church in Greenbushes, Western Australia. His faith helped to sustain him through his long ordeal. *P08953.001 courtesy Australian War Memorial.*

But not all of Albany's war dead were buried quite so far away. Amongst the men to be named on that memorial was Royce Baesjou, a parishioner of the very church in which the monument would stand. Royce had belonged to one of the first white families to settle on the Great Southern – shipping agents, medical men, farmers and pastoralists; the Baesjou name was one of the most important in the district. Royce had worked as a bank clerk and served part-time in the West Australian Artillery Militia prior to joining up. A southern son of Empire, he believed passionately in England's cause.

Royce Baesjou fought with the 28th Battalion at Gallipoli, endured heavy artillery bombardment on Russell's Top and was evacuated 'shell-shocked' from the peninsula. Private Baesjou would suffer shell shock a second time in France. What doctors diagnosed as 'Myalgia/Neurasthenia' took him out of the line. It was hell, he wrote home to his family:

> *That is the only word for it. It is quite impossible to describe . . . My mate and I were manning our machine gun when a shell fell in the position . . . We were blown yards away. The first thing I can recall is the doctor at the casualty clearing station. My nerves are shaky and my eyes not too good but a rest will put everything right.*[2]

It didn't. With nerves shot to pieces, and suffering from debility and rheumatism, the young soldier was invalided home in 1916.

Despite a brave attempt to return to civilian life, Royce Baesjou never recovered from his injuries. The shell blasts that had killed the men around him, and blown his body yards from where he stood, had damaged his brain. Shell shock was not just a psychological disposition – a kind of emotional trauma. Doctors at the time believed it also sprang from physical causes: the 'shock waves' that attended the explosion of a shell. In Baesjou's case, concussion – or what the doctors called 'commotional shock' – had caused irreparable harm.[3]

Royce Baesjou died of a cerebral haemorrhage at the 8th Australian General Hospital in Fremantle on 19 May 1918. It was just a few months before the fighting in Europe ended and almost two years after Baesjou had come home. He was buried on 21 May 1918 in the Church of England section of Fremantle Cemetery. Former comrades acted as pallbearers, representatives of the Returned Soldiers Association and the Returned Soldiers Relatives Association joined the mourners, as did Baesjou's family and 'many friends'. The funeral of this former soldier reminds us that not all of Australia's war dead lie in the soil of distant countries. Men died in the midst of their 'kindred' as well.[4]

BELOW **In the midst of kindred:** The private memorial raised to Royce Baesjou. Note the regulation Imperial War Graves headstone in the background. Many returned men died at Fremantle Base Hospital in the aftermath of the war. *Courtesy Bruce Scates.*

BELOW RIGHT **Albany's second memorial:** The town's Avenue of Honour on Mount Clarence. The memorial was originally located along Middleton Road, and was known by the locals as 'Memory Mile'. Most of the trees were as ill-fated as the soldiers they honoured. Some twenty-five of the red gums (a tree not indigenous to the district) had died by 1949, and the plaques were relocated. *Courtesy Bruce Scates.*

In July 1921, the citizens of Albany raised a second memorial, an Avenue of Honour stretching a mile along Middleton Road. A red gum was planted for each of the 'brave men' of the township who had 'made the supreme sacrifice', and a plaque set at the base of each tree reverently recorded their rank, battalion and age.[5] But the family of Royce Baesjou added another unique epitaph:

> *DIED FROM SHELL SHOCK*
> *BASE HOSPITAL FREMANTLE*
> *MAY 19 1918*

SOURCES AND FURTHER READING: This story draws on Royce Baesjou's service dossier NAA: B2455 BAESJOU, R C; his repatriation file NAA: PP18/1, R3317; and contemporary newspaper reports. The authors acknowledge Claire Gregory's website roadtowarandback.blogspot.com.au which first alerted them to this case and thank Claire and Bev Taylor for assistance in accessing family papers, including Royce Baesjou's journal. The literature surrounding shell shock is extensive and ranges from historical studies such as Peter Leese, *Traumatic Neurosis and the British Soldiers of the First World War* (London: Palgrave Macmillan, 2002) and for an Australian context, Bruce Scates and Melanie Oppenheimer, *The Last Battle of the Great War: Soldier Settlement in Australia*, (Cambridge: Cambridge University Press, forthcoming) and Alistair Thomson, *Anzac Memories: Living With the Legend* (Melbourne: Monash University Publishing, new edition, 2013); as well as fictional accounts like Pat Barker, *The Regeneration Trilogy* (London: Viking Books, 1996).

A shot fired by a fellow Australian

ALLAN WHITTAKER

Allan Whittaker sailed to war in October 1914. Hundreds turned out to farewell the troopships, the very first contingent to sail out from Sydney. They gathered in a bustling throng by the wharves at Woolloomooloo and sang songs, waved flags and flung streamers to the men high above them on the transports.

Leaning over the railing, Allan Whittaker may well have caught one. As HMAT *Afric* pulled away from Finger Wharf, the thin paper ribbons were broken and the soldiers' last physical link with Australia fell into the sea.

Whittaker was a Victorian by birth, even though he enlisted in Sydney. He had lived around Yarraville for most of his life and worked as a waiter in Port Melbourne. Perhaps it was a love of travel and adventure that took him north. Perhaps the same restless spirit persuaded him to sign on for war service. Whatever the reason, almost a year would pass before Whittaker saw home again. The *Afric* slipped past the entrance to Port Philip Bay in the early hours of the morning, crossed the Great Australian Bight and steamed on towards Albany. There it joined a great armada – thirty-six transports and three escorting cruisers destined for the battlefields of Europe.

It wasn't long before Private Whittaker saw action. After a few months of training in Egypt, the 1st Battalion was dispatched to Lemnos, the staging base for the invasion of the Dardanelles. Whittaker landed at Gallipoli around eight o'clock in the morning on 25 April 1915, just as the Ottoman troops were rallying to drive the Anzacs into the sea. Within half an hour he'd been wounded. A Turkish bullet ploughed into his left foot, leaving behind a gaping wound. Whittaker struggled back down to the beach and was evacuated to a hospital ship crammed with dying men. He'd survived Gallipoli but would never fight again.

Allan Whittaker arrived back in Port Melbourne in August 1915. A man who had sailed with the first contingent and fought on the first day of the Landing was also on one of the first ships of wounded to be repatriated to Australia. The 'Heroes of the Dardanelles' were received with enthusiasm at the wharf. Some families had been gathered on the foreshore since early light, expectant mothers gazing out to sea, their 'shining eyes' hungry for the *Hororata*'s arrival.

As the ship approached the shore, one of the first things Whittaker would have seen was a sign reading 'Australia is Proud of You' displayed on the pier gates. A 'welcoming arch' of gum leaves and wattle blossom festooned the wharf entrance beside it.

Unloading the vessel was a lengthy business. 'Many of the [sick and wounded] looked pale and thin,' *The Argus* reported, 'some of them limped on sticks or crutches; one or two showed empty sleeves.' An ambulance whisked the stretcher cases away quickly, the authorities were concerned the sight of badly damaged men might prejudice recruitment. Whittaker himself limped ashore with the other walking wounded. A few in the boisterous crowd unwittingly cheered for the 'venereal cases' dishonourably discharged from Egypt.[1]

BELOW **Heroes of the Dardanelles:** A cross for Allan Whittaker planted beside Port Melbourne's war memorial. Whittaker was also remembered in a commemorative service marking the 85th anniversary of the 1928 Dock Strike. *Courtesy Bruce Scates.*

Australia may have been proud of its returning veterans, but men like Whittaker found the return to civilian life far from easy. The pension he was paid was never enough to support him. At first he received less than half the basic wage. Then, as his wound healed, his 'incapacity allowance' was reduced accordingly. By 1917, Whittaker's pension was just fifteen shillings a fortnight at a time when an unskilled labourer in regular work could expect seven shillings a day.

The restaurant trade had suffered during the war so he took on work at the wharves. It was a challenge for a fit man, let alone an injured one: wrestling with the great weights tangled down from ships' cranes; lugging loads into the hulls of steamers; and buckling beneath crates of produce, blackened sacks of coal, and greasy bales of wool.

Work on the wharves in early twentieth century Australia was heavy, dirty and dangerous. It was also poorly paid. In busy times, Allan Whittaker could barely scrape a living for himself, let alone his extended family. Like most who lived in the port, the young man struggled with debt, hardship and poverty. Every week, the landlord, the storekeeper, the gas man and the grocer claimed what little money he had made.

And work at the wharf was day labour. As each ship came in, Whittaker queued up with hundreds of others hoping he'd be 'taken on'. By the late 1920s the export markets were failing, Australia faced the Great

Depression, and every day the lines of hungry idle men grew longer and longer.

An injury at the wharf would mean that Whittaker couldn't work at all. The union would do what it could to support him: sickness pay, a bag of groceries, sometimes even a loan. But there was no such thing as workers' compensation. Men broken by the weights they carried were left to live off charity, and men injured – even crippled – on the wharves would have been far better off having lost a leg on the Somme. When he came back from war, Allan Whittaker had been promised a land fit for heroes. Now he laboured for a pittance through a fourteen-hour day.

In 1928, the wharfies went on strike. Allan Whittaker joined them. Men prepared to work at non-union rates ('scabs' as they were called by the unionists) were brought in to take the place of the strikers. As the Depression deepened, employers hoped to break the union and pay a desperate, casualised workforce a fraction of a living wage. Police, armed with guns and brandishing batons, lined the wharf to protect the strike-breakers. Tempers rose, fighting broke out, and police fired their revolvers once into the air and then into the crowd.

'There were a number of shots fired,' one witness reported, 'it was like a machine gun.'[2] Several claimed police had fired as protestors fled the scene. Many men were seriously wounded, Allan Whittaker amongst them. More might have died had some constables not disobeyed their panicking commander and fired away from the crowd.

Allan Whittaker had survived the withering fire of Gallipoli. But a shot fired by a fellow Australian would end up killing him. That, and the conditions he'd endured in the trenches and then back in Australia. When Whittaker was taken to hospital, his teeth were described as 'filthy'. Some were broken and the stumps of those that remained were riddled with decay.

Whittaker's teeth reflected the poor diet of soldiers: monotonous meals of hard tack biscuits, bully beef and jam. A similar diet was the lot of most men working the wharves, and doctors described Whittaker as a weak, malnourished man. Filthy teeth quickly infected the wound at the back of Whittaker's neck – five teeth were extracted in the hope of saving him. But three months after his admission to hospital, Whittaker died of toxemia and an abscess on the brain. Chief Commissioner Thomas Blamey rejected public calls for a full parliamentary inquiry.

'The shooting was fully justified,' he declared. 'There must be no half measures.'[3] Blamey was a vehement anti-unionist and a supporter of paramilitary movements plotting the overthrow of Labor governments. Not everyone who 'fought for freedom' during the Great War really believed in democracy.

The remains of Allan Whittaker were interred in Fawkner Cemetery. The union turned out to bury its own. Amongst the mourners were the family and friends who had welcomed Allan home to Port Melbourne. They lowered the coffin slowly, gently into the grave and pulled the ropes away. The eulogy that day reminded onlookers that Allan Whittaker had fought for his country. But the debt owed to a veteran didn't extend to the right to work, or to provide for a family, or to a decent living wage.

By the height of the Great Depression, around one third of Australia's returned men had joined the dole queues. The 'lucky ones' eked out a living from their war pensions. Some were sent to lousy blocks of land as soldier settlers. Some survived on

ABOVE **The union turned out to bury its own:** Allan Whittaker's grave in Fawkner Cemetery. The Whittaker family tomb also serves as the memorial for Allan's younger brother Cecil, killed aged 19 in France. As Cecil was underage, his mother signed his enlistment papers. Note the regulation Commonwealth War Graves Commission tombstones behind Whittaker's grave. The authorities accepted that these veterans had died as a result of their war service and subsidised both their funeral expenses and the cost of the grave. This privilege was not accorded to the Whittaker family. *Courtesy Greg Whiddon.*

charity. And some – in the city Whittaker was born in – laboured for rations building Melbourne's Shrine of Remembrance. The men who dug the trenches of Flanders and the Somme were dressed in their old army greatcoats, given a pick and shovel, and put to work levelling the site of Victoria's war memorial. Returning home, Whittaker had been told Australia was proud of him. His story suggests otherwise.

SOURCES AND FURTHER READING: This story draws on Allan Whittaker's service dossier NAA: B2455 WHITTAKER ALLAN; his repatriation record NAA: B73 R44423; and the Coroner's Inquest into the death of Allan Whittaker, PROV VPRS24, 1929: 428. The authors gratefully acknowledge the fine eulogies delivered in memory of Allan Whittaker by historian Chris McConville, retired Supreme Court judge Frank Vincent and Martin Foley, MLA, (Member for Albert Park). Thanks are also due to Paddy Garrity, Perce White and Kevin Bracken of the Maritime Union of Australia. For more information on the life of dock workers in Port Melbourne see Wendy Lowenstein and Tom Hills, *Under The Hook* (Melbourne: Melbourne Bookworkers in association with the Australian Society for the Study of Labour History, 1982); Rhonda Wilson and Sue Formby, *Good Talk* (Melbourne: McPhee Gribble, 1985). Further background on the Dockers' strike is provided by David Baker, '"You Dirty Bastards, Are You Fair Dinkum?": Police And Union Confrontation On The Wharf', *New Zealand Journal Of Industrial Relations*, vol. 27, no. 1, 2002, pp. 33–48. For differing assessments of Blamey's fascist sympathies see Michael Cathcart, *Defending The National Tuckshop* (Melbourne: McPhee Gribble/Penguin Books, 1989); and D. M Horner, *Blamey* (St. Leonards: Allen & Unwin, 1998).

The angel of Durban
ETHEL CAMPBELL

Standing at the edge of the wharf, a young woman dressed in a sailor suit reached repeatedly into the sky. Her hands shot up and down in a stiff and steady rhythm. The bright flags flashed against the blue sky, calling to the troopships in semaphore across the sea – 'Welcome diggers!'

Ethel Campbell was born in her mother's homeland, Scotland, but her father's home, South Africa, was her country. He was a doctor, descended from a line of wealthy sugar planters and, like many of their class and race, Ethel's family enjoyed power and privilege in South Africa. Their every need was attended to by a host of so-called black and coloured servants. But come the war, Ethel tired of the leisured life of a Durban socialite. From 1915 until the last of the transports departed, she dedicated herself to the welfare of travelling soldiers.

BELOW **The girl with the flags:** Ethel brought her flags with her on her travels around Australia. Although worn out over the years, she semaphored messages to huge waiting crowds around the country. Here, Ethel greets Launceston during the Tasmanian leg of her journey. *Source Mercury 15 October 1923 courtesy National Library of Australia.*

Her semaphored messages, one soldier remembered, 'brought the sparkle of youth and adventure [back] into our eyes'. Some soldiers were setting forth on their first great adventure, others limping home, their health and often their spirits broken by years in the trenches. But whatever direction they travelled, Australian and New Zealand troops who passed through Durban all knew to keep a look out for Miss Campbell.

As every troopship sailed into port, the young woman, sporting a handsome hat, would greet them. She carried baskets brimming with oranges, jams, books, magazines and tobacco. The gifts were thrown up onto the decks of the transports and men made sport of catching them. Those permitted to land were treated to a tour of the town, the sociable Miss Campbell their lively companion.

All through the war the Campbell family home was open to tired, lonely and homesick soldiers. Ethel had two brothers serving with the

ABOVE **Worthy sister to brother Anzacs[6]:** Ethel Campbell arrives in Sydney to a crowd of diggers. In cities and towns across Australia, countless thousands turned out to see her. This enthusiastic welcome by returned men suggests that she was one of their happier memories of wartime. Adelaide Chronicle *28 July 1923 courtesy National Library of Australia.*

Royal Flying Corp and another training with the British Army. For the Campbells, caring for these men was rather like looking after their own. Hundreds called at their grand homestead; they took tea on the verandah or enjoyed a cool drink in the shade of the jacarandas. And when they left Durban for Australia or the Front, Ethel was there to farewell them. They heard her 'sweet voice' and hearty 'cooee' amidst the roar of ship engines, and watched those flags flash 'good luck and safe journey' in the distance.

They called her 'Angel Ettie' and her kindness was not forgotten after the last troops sailed home. In 1923, Ethel embarked on a voyage to Australia accompanied by her parents. Not far from the coast of Western Australia, lights from the shoreline flashed a message, 'A digger welcomes Miss Campbell'. Ethel and her father were permitted to disembark briefly at Albany. They set foot on the ground where many of her boys said goodbye forever to Australia.

Ethel spent four months travelling the length and breadth of the continent. Hundreds, sometimes thousands, of troops would gather at wharves and train stations hoping to catch a glimpse of her. The newspapers compared her welcomes with that of the Prince of Wales – everywhere she went 'the girl with the flags' caused a sensation. Ethel was received by politicians, authors, poets. But most of her time she spent with her 'digger pals'.

During her tour of Australia, Ethel Campbell visited military hospitals, convalescent homes and asylums; those sparkling eyes smiled again for those she called her 'battered, and worn, and war scarred' diggers. Ethel travelled from Devonport to Toowoomba, Castlemaine to Orange, Broken Hill to Fremantle. She was the guest of honour at concerts, dances, receptions and dinners. But the Angel of Durban also turned to the solemn task of remembrance. Ethel unveiled Port Augusta's memorial rotunda, laid the foundation stone at Bundaberg's memorial baths, and planted commemorative trees in Balwyn.

Australian cities, suburbs and towns bestowed their gifts upon her: a Tasmanian blackwood writing desk from Hobart, emu eggs from the centre of Australia, even a stuffed koala from the eastern coast. These mementos of Australia she would treasure all her life. But her most precious gift of all was a lifetime membership granted by the RSL. Durban's girl had been claimed by the diggers.

Miss Campbell, the newspapers declared, was 'the best loved woman in Australia', the 'fairest in the land', every digger's 'sweetheart'. Not once on her tour did the enthusiasm wane or the crowds dwindle. Why did she cause such a sensation? Most who greeted Ethel had met her before. She was the girl on the wharf who threw them fruit or cigarettes. Some had shared her wit and conversation; many appreciated her willing ear and 'cheery smile'; a few, no doubt, admired her handsome figure.

'[It] was her constancy' that won our hearts, one returned digger explained. Ethel greeted 'every boat', 'never failing or faltering . . . regardless of the weather.'[1]

Another said she had the common touch. She saw the individual in that mass of khaki, reminded the boys they did not belong to the Army. One lovestruck digger wrote to her:

> *You made a man feel like a man – you appealed to his self-respect – that counted, and you don't know how hard it is for a man – not an officer – to keep his self respect in the army . . . And it is because you treated the men and officers alike as men that there are thousands of ex-soldiers all over*

BELOW **Durban's hospitality:** A sketch in *The Natal Licensed Victuallers Journal*, December 1919, highlighting the special bond between Miss Campbell and Australian visitors. *3DRL/2110 courtesy Austalian War Memorial.*

Australia – men of every type and condition – who are all united one way – everyone has a warm spot in his heart for the girl in Durban who made him feel like a man, even among a mob of damned 'Brass Hats'.[2]

Australian women also had a 'warm spot' for the girl from Durban. And Ethel understood why:

I was the last individual that many of their men had mentioned in their home-letters, they felt that I was the last link with their loved ones. Bereaved mothers, wives, sisters, and sweethearts, read me extracts from letters they had received after the ships called at Durban (some of these were 'last letters' written before their men had been killed in France) in which they had been told about me, and with which my verses had been enclosed. Meeting me seemed to bring everything back to them, and it made me realise more than ever how little I had done compared to all that they had sacrificed. It seemed to be a solace, even though a sad one, to them to talk to me about their men.[3]

What did this war work mean for Ethel? No doubt it was a chance to feel needed, an opportunity for a woman to engage with events shaping the world, a welcome distraction from a life of petty diversions. Ethel was certainly a product of Empire, she believed passionately in Britain's cause and played the part of a dutiful daughter of the dominions. As was the case for thousands of other women across the globe, this was no abstract sense of patriotism – the war had cost Ethel dearly. Her fiancé had been killed at the beginning of the conflict. Perhaps honouring these men was a way of holding on to the man the war had taken from her.

During Ethel's Australian tour, many hoped romance would blossom with an Anzac. 'Aren't you going to take an Aussie back with you?' someone yelled from one of the crowds. Ethel laughed off the suggestion, 'There are too many. I love you all.'[4] Like many women of her generation whose sweethearts were killed in the war, Ethel never married.

BELOW **Taking tea on the veranda:** Australian and New Zealand troops gather at the Campbell family home on Anzac Day. This was one of the first Anzac Day observances in Durban, and one initiated by Miss Campbell and her band of willing helpers. Ethel continued to host Anzac Day gatherings after the war, a chance to stay connected to the memories of her digger pals. *3DRL/2110 courtesy Australian War Memorial.*

Home in South Africa, in her little patch of Empire, Ethel never forgot Australia. When another world war erupted she welcomed another generation of men through her port town. At her home in Pietermaritzberg, amid a forest of Australian and South African flora, stood a bluestone hut, a Zulu dronga called 'Little Australia'. Photographs covered every inch of its walls and cupboards, and shelves were stacked high with mementos. In 1942, a soldier from the Second AIF told his family of his visit:

We all felt we were in some sacred place where one should tread softly, and we told her so. She replied that she had it built as a memory of the wonderful men whom she had met in the last

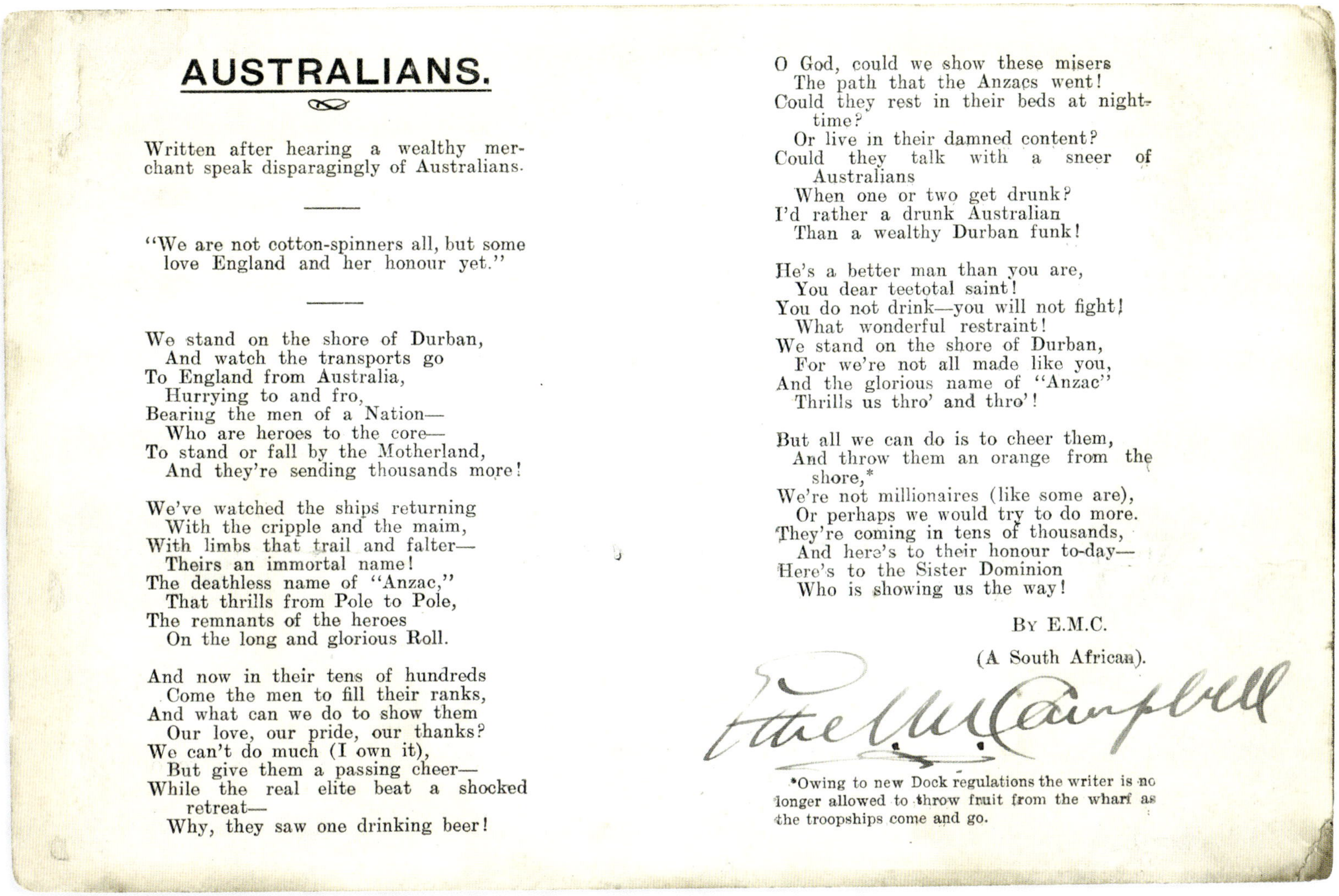

AUSTRALIANS.

Written after hearing a wealthy merchant speak disparagingly of Australians.

"We are not cotton-spinners all, but some
love England and her honour yet."

We stand on the shore of Durban,
And watch the transports go
To England from Australia,
Hurrying to and fro,
Bearing the men of a Nation—
Who are heroes to the core—
To stand or fall by the Motherland,
And they're sending thousands more!

We've watched the ships returning
With the cripple and the maim,
With limbs that trail and falter—
Theirs an immortal name!
The deathless name of "Anzac,"
That thrills from Pole to Pole,
The remnants of the heroes
On the long and glorious Roll.

And now in their tens of hundreds
Come the men to fill their ranks,
And what can we do to show them
Our love, our pride, our thanks?
We can't do much (I own it),
But give them a passing cheer—
While the real elite beat a shocked
retreat—
Why, they saw one drinking beer!

O God, could we show these misers
The path that the Anzacs went!
Could they rest in their beds at night-
time?
Or live in their damned content?
Could they talk with a sneer of
Australians
When one or two get drunk?
I'd rather a drunk Australian
Than a wealthy Durban funk!

He's a better man than you are,
You dear teetotal saint!
You do not drink—you will not fight!
What wonderful restraint!
We stand on the shore of Durban,
For we're not all made like you,
And the glorious name of "Anzac"
Thrills us thro' and thro'!

But all we can do is to cheer them,
And throw them an orange from the
shore,*
We're not millionaires (like some are),
Or perhaps we would try to do more.
They're coming in tens of thousands,
And here's to their honour to-day—
Here's to the Sister Dominion
Who is showing us the way!

By E.M.C.

(A South African).

Ethel M. Campbell

*Owing to new Dock regulations the writer is no longer allowed to throw fruit from the wharf as the troopships come and go.

war . . . and in what more fitting place could she entertain the sons of these men? . . . the 'Angel of Durban' is at work again.[5]

Today very few remember Ethel Campbell. A celebrity during and after the war, she has slipped almost entirely from memory. Ships no longer call in at Durban to take on coal and supplies. Today, crossings from Australasia to Europe are mostly made by air and not all that many visit a country where thousands of Australians and New Zealanders once settled. In her day Ethel represented the links that bound the Empire together; the common cause of Britain and the dominions; and the way a woman's welcome rescued men, however briefly, from the rough world of soldiering.

SOURCES AND FURTHER READING: This story is based on the Ethel Campbell collection at the Australian War Memorial 3DRL/2110. There is a collection of her poetry at the same, 2DRL/6701. Ethel Campbell's work during the war and her tour of Australia were widely documented in Australian and South African newspapers at the time, and in Ethel's own book, *The Life of Sam Campbell* (Durban: Singleton & Williams, 1938).

ABOVE **The deathless name of Anzac:** Ethel Campbell penned many poems celebrating the Australian soldier. Her poetry is a model of strident Empire patriotism but also affords space for the larrikin qualities of the digger. Ethel's verse often questioned authority, condemned needless rules and baulked at military hierarchy. This particular poem lampoons dock regulations preventing her from throwing fruit to passing troopships. Never one with much time for 'red tape, ridiculous restrictions and insulting treatment', Ethel openly defied these restrictions.[7] *Ethel Campbell,* The Life of Sam Campbell *(Durban: Singleton & Williams, 1938) courtesy Rare Book Collection, Monash University.*

Quite a decent type of man
CORNELIUS DANSWAN

It was late in the morning when Dr Benjafield, a medical officer assigned to the Repatriation Department in Sydney, finished his examination of Cornelius Danswan. In many ways that day's appointment was like so many others. Another sick man, burnt out by his war experience, battling to support his family on a pension. But there was one important point of difference, and Dr Benjafield thought it best to record it. He reached across his desk and jotted a quick note on the bottom of a departmental memo. 'A half caste Chinaman', it read, 'father Chinese, mother English'. 'Quite a decent type of man', Benjafield added, as if naming a patient's ethnic descent somehow defined his character, 'though very miserable'. Dr Benjafield almost certainly embraced eugenicist ideals commonplace in medical circles. And that helped shape his diagnosis:

> *Teeth shew the gingivitis etc., which is almost universal in this type of Chinese (at any rate those seen in Australia) from which he is descended.*[1]

Cornelius Danswan was seen as something of an oddity by Benjafield and other doctors from the Repatriation Department. He was certainly exceptional. In 1914, technically only those of predominantly 'British stock' were permitted to serve in the First AIF. But by the third year of the war, to feed the carnage raging on the Western Front, the military authorities would take almost anyone.

Danswan, a shearer from north-western New South Wales, enlisted in 1916. His mother, Sarah, had emigrated from Ireland and his father, Thomas, left Amoy, China, in 1852, as an indentured labourer assigned to the Australian Agricultural Company. Bound by his contract, Thomas Danswan would be forced to work for half the wages of whites. At the end of his service he did not return home – unlike thousands of Chinese gold seekers who came before him. Thomas Danswan's marriage to Flora, a white woman, may well have reflected his desire to assimilate into the white community. More likely, a poor Irishwoman was his only chance of matrimony as so few Chinese women joined their countrymen in Australia. Together the couple had ten children, Cornelius King Danswan amongst them.

Hundreds of Australians of Chinese descent served the country they had adopted during the Great War. No doubt they joined up for any number of reasons. Perhaps it was patriotism and a hope they might 'earn' a place in the British Empire – can we read anything into the middle name, King, that Thomas gave his son? Perhaps it was the hope that soldiering abroad might offer a more interesting life than shearing on the Liverpool Plains. What we do know about Cornelius is that he was something of a lad – convicted, like many a digger larrikin, of 'riotous behaviour' in one of the hotels he frequented. He also had a more respectable side, walking his sister down the aisle at her wedding at Murrundindi. Cornelius's sister Tilly, the local paper tells us:

> *looked charming in white silk, trimmed with Valenciennes lace and insertion, with transparent yoke, and wore a coronet of orange blossom, and bridal veil, and carried a shower bouquet, the gift of the bridegroom.*

This was a far cry from the penury of an agricultural labourer from Amoy, a signal that in some ways at least this immigrant family had succeeded. Cornelius Danswan was also fond of shooting – membership of the local rifle club confirms that.[2]

If Cornelius hoped for adventure abroad he was sorely disappointed. Sapper Danswan served in France, through one of the worst winters on record. In the freezing conditions of the trenches he succumbed to bronchitis, debility and exhaustion. He was also subjected to severe artillery bombardment and eventually taken out of the line with shell shock. They sent Sapper Danswan back to Australia in 1919. Seven years later he still wrestled with the trauma: 'He has been nervy and shaky ever since the war,' one of Benjafield's colleagues noted, 'fits start with twitching of the lips and he stutters'; 'complains of general weakness and chronic cough and attacks of precordial pain'; 'has to lie down, and then becomes unconscious'.[3]

BELOW **A departmental memo:** Dr Benjafield notes Cornelius Danswan's Chinese descent. Eugenics was much in currency in medical circles during the 1920s. This memo suggests medical officers working for the Repatriation Department were concerned to classify racial types. *NAA: C138, R54054 courtesy National Archives of Australia.*

28.7.26. Dr. V. Benjafield, D.M.O. -

"A half caste Chinaman, father Chinese, mother English.
Quite a decent type of man though very miserable.
Has had a poultry farm for the last 6 yrs. but has been unable to make it pay and has had to take outside work.
Has four children, the oldest 10 years. Wife has Asthma.
Deafness is so slight that he hears very low conversation even when the speakers face is turned away from him.
Teeth shew the gingivitis, etc., which is almost universal in this type of Chinese (at any rate those seen in Australia)from which he is descended, in middle life."

The doctors diagnosed 'neurasthenia' and debated whether Danswan's nerves were due to his war service, 'mild encephalitis' or 'business worry and anxiety'.[4]

Cornelius had every reason to be anxious. After the war, he struggled to provide for a wife and young family on a pension of a few shillings a week. That, and irregular earnings from his poultry farm outside Sydney, offered not much more than a bare existence. In May 1920, though still an outpatient at Prince of Wales Hospital, Danswan had his pension withdrawn. Still unable to make the poultry farm pay, he took on outside work.

By the mid 1920s, the Danswans had six children, only one of them old enough to help much on the farm. Flora's health was also deteriorating, serious asthma attacks making it all the more difficult to work with poultry. By that time, Flora had had enough and took it upon herself to write to the authorities. Within weeks of that first assessment by Dr Benjafield, she pleaded the case of her family and her husband:

> *The absence of any income so preyed in his mind that he is now much worse than ever before and appears to be losing his self balance. As he is unable to speak or write for himself, I appeal on his behalf for a pension until such time as he is able to work. I trust you will expedite this matter and thus relieve him of a worry that is practically killing him and also relieve my natural anxiety as to where I am to obtain the necessities of life for my children.*[5]

Cornelius Danswan's pension was reinstated (at 50 per cent) in May 1926. He died in Randwick Military Hospital just five months later.

Left without any breadwinner , Flora Danswan applied for a war widow's pension. That too was refused. Her husband's death – at the age of 50 – was deemed 'not due to War Service'. She was also unable to manage on the farm. 'I have been trying to carry on,' she wrote in March 1928, 'but . . . I have found it an impossibility and the fowls are [just] running me into debt.'

Flora Danswan's last correspondence with the Repatriation authorities was in March 1929, a defiant letter rejecting the 'ridiculous' suggestion that she should repay her husband's debt on the farm. Perhaps she believed Cornelius had already given enough to his country.[6]

SOURCES AND FURTHER READING: This story draws on Cornelius Danswan's service dossier NAA: B2455 DANSWAN C K; his repatriation record NAA: C138, R54054; and his soldier settlement file State Records NSW: 12/7052/4948. In addition to these sources contemporary newspaper reports have also been consulted. The authors thank Keir Reeves for his insights into Australia's Chinese community in wartime. For further reading on soldier settlement see Bruce Scates and Melanie Oppenheimer, *The Last Battle of the Great War: Soldier Settlement in Australia* (Cambridge: Cambridge University Press, forthcoming)

A Duntroon man
TOM ELLIOTT

Tom Elliott's name is one of more than a thousand chiselled into the memorial wall at VC Corner Cemetery in Fromelles. Etched in cold, white stone the names upon layered names cry out a nation's loss. Amongst those names were Australia's brightest and bravest – Tom Elliott included.

Tom was one of eleven children. Thomas and Mary Elliott raised seven sons and four daughters and Tom was the eldest boy. His mother was bright, capable and had the courage of her convictions. Although she had trained as a midwife, was well informed and politically aware, she had never had the opportunity of any formal education. Mary was determined her children would not suffer the same limitations she had. Least of all the most promising of her children, Tom.

Tom enrolled as a cadet at the Royal Military College, Duntroon in 1912. The college was a very different establishment then to what it is today. Then, in just its second year, Duntroon was a remote institution, marooned in a vast bush landscape waiting on a city.

Duntroon offered Tom the kind of quality education he could not have otherwise had. Whatever its failings, the Australian Army was a young institution, unencumbered by ancient regimental traditions and determined to be something of a meritocracy. Tom may not have been born to power and privilege, but he placed first amongst more than one hundred entrants' application tests. He secured a place at the college, and moved to Canberra from Sydney to attend.

Tom's potential impressed his superiors. He was 'methodical, brainy, plucky and resolute', the kind of young man destined to succeed.[1] After two years of academic and sporting achievement, Tom graduated third in his class. But term ended early: war had broken out in Europe and the freshly minted graduates of Duntroon were needed overseas.

Tom sailed off to war with the second contingent in December 1914. He fought at Gallipoli with the 7th Light Horse and was evacuated to Malta in September with

ABOVE **A man likely to become a second Kitchener or Lord Roberts:** Tom's enrolment at Duntroon bound him to twelve years' service in the military forces. Tragically his commitment went far beyond that. *Courtesy Ross McMullin.*

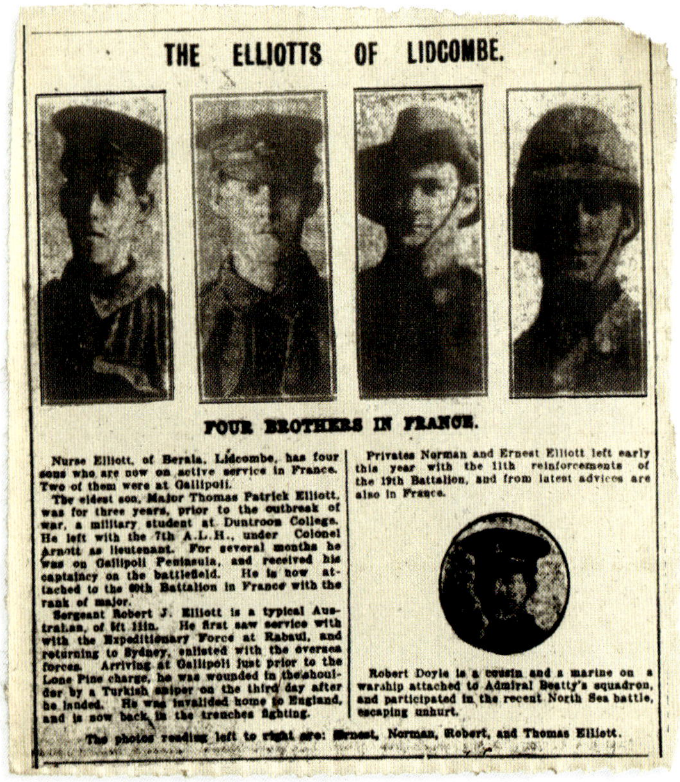

THE ELLIOTTS OF LIDCOMBE.

FOUR BROTHERS IN FRANCE.

Nurse Elliott, of Berala, Lidcombe, has four sons who are now on active service in France. Two of them were at Gallipoli.

The eldest son, Major Thomas Patrick Elliott, was for three years, prior to the outbreak of war, a military student at Duntroon College. He left with the 7th A.L.H., under Colonel Arnott as lieutenant. For several months he was on Gallipoli Peninsula, and received his captaincy on the battlefield. He is now attached to the 60th Battalion in France with the rank of major.

Sergeant Robert J. Elliott is a typical Australian, of 5ft 11in. He first saw service with with the Expeditionary Force at Rabaul, and returning to Sydney, enlisted with the oversea forces. Arriving at Gallipoli just prior to the Lone Pine charge, he was wounded in the shoulder by a Turkish sniper on the third day after he landed. He was invalided home to England, and is now back in the trenches fighting.

Privates Norman and Ernest Elliott left early this year with the 11th reinforcements of the 19th Battalion, and from latest advices are also in France.

Robert Doyle is a cousin and a marine on a warship attached to Admiral Beatty's squadron, and participated in the recent North Sea battle, escaping unhurt.

The photos reading left to right are: Ernest, Norman, Robert, and Thomas Elliott.

ABOVE **Not content with killing my good noble son in your rotten commercial war and cheating me and his helpless brothers and sisters, my other three sons have been maimed for life in the wretched slaughter[7]:** The Great War tore the Elliott family apart beyond the sad deaths of Tom (far right) and Mary. Norm Elliott (second from the left) died of tuberculosis not long after his repatriation home. Ernie Elliott (far left) suffered from nerves after the war and would often beat his brothers. Evening News, *21 July 1916 courtesy National Library of Australia.*

severe enteritis. By June 1916, at just 22 years of age, Tom had achieved the rank of Major. He was sent to the Western Front to join Pompey Elliott's 15th Brigade.

On July 16, 1916, just before six o'clock in the evening, Tom Elliott led his men out of the trenches at Fromelles. It was a fine summer night and, although the artillery barrage had scarred the landscape, enough of a wheat crop remained to glow gold in the sunset. That night the wheat was cut down by concentrated fire from the German trenches. Men fell in what was called 'grazing fire', Tom Elliott amongst them.

As with hundreds of men lost that night, Tom's body was never recovered. A comrade had seen him falling in the mud with a 'big gash in his back' and bleeding profusely.[2] But no one had seen him killed, and so technically Tom was missing. In the carnage at Fromelles, there was very little hope of survival. His commander, Brigadier General Pompey Elliott wrote a long and intimate letter to Tom's family:

> *[His] personality and force of character impressed itself very forcibly on all he came in contact with . . . He was looked upon just before his death as a man likely to become a second Kitchener or Lord Roberts.*[3]

He hoped they could accept their loss and offered what comfort he could in their grief.

But Mary refused to accept that her darling boy was dead. Accounts of the battle were confused and contradictory, and what did that awful word 'missing' really mean?

> *It is an awful thing to leave a mother in dought [sic] . . . I have heard things here and there that made me dought [sic] he was killed, if you [k]now anything about what happened to him in mercy let me know the suspense is awful . . . I can't make anything of the war but that it is wrong, wrong, wrong, from beginning to end.*[4]

It wasn't long before the sadness turned to anger:

> *I was a fool [to send] all my bread winners of the family [to the war] . . . when it is all over King George of England and the Kaiser will be kissin' one another and wondering what it was all about.*[5]

Bitter and disillusioned, Mary Elliott found no comfort in patriotic platitudes. Instead, she turned to drink. Beer was her 'crutch', she confessed. 'I have no love for it, but it saved me from going mad when I was terribly depressed and worried.'[6] Alcohol offered Mary a few hours of oblivion, for a time at least it pushed the demons away.

But not for long. Struggling with her grief and her addiction, Mary became known as a public nuisance. She was brought before the courts to enter charges of violent behaviour and threatening language. In August 1918, she was committed to Callan Park Mental Hospital. Discharged after inadequate treatment, her delusions, mania and drinking only worsened. By November she had been admitted to Parramatta Mental Hospital. She died there in June 1919 of Spanish influenza.

The war took everything from Mary Elliott: the boy she loved, her sanity, her purpose for living. In her time in hospital she was troubled by visions of Tom returning.

In a sense his loss was the first of many. Three more of her boys had served in the First AIF. Though all returned, they were, she insisted, 'maimed by this wretched slaughter'. All Mary's sons suffered multiple wounds, and Norman, Tom's younger brother, died of tuberculosis at 21 years of age.

The Memorial to the Missing at Fromelles honours the name of Major Tom Elliott. Every year, Australian pilgrims visit the site, patriotic speeches are made, flags raised in the air and the white stone piled high with flowers. But few remember Mary Elliott, or the price that 'rotten commercial war' exacted on her generation.

SOURCES AND FURTHER READING: This story draws on the service dossier of Major Thomas Patrick Elliott NAA B2455, ELLIOTT TP; his Red Cross Missing and Wounded file AWM 1DRL/0428; and contemporary newspaper reports. The story of Tom Elliott also features in Ross McMullin, *Farewell Dear People: Biographies of Australia's Lost Generation* (Brunswick: Scribe Publishing, 2012); and Jennifer Roberts, 'Bereft: War, Grief and Experiences of the Asylum, 1915–1935' (PhD thesis, University of Wollongong, 2013).

BELOW **Etched in cold, white stone:** Tom Elliott's name is on the Memorial to the Missing at Fromelles. There are over four hundred men buried in this graveyard – all 'Unknowns'. The authorities opted for two mass graves rather than row after row of tombstones reading only 'An Australian Soldier Known Unto God'. *Courtesy Bruce Scates.*

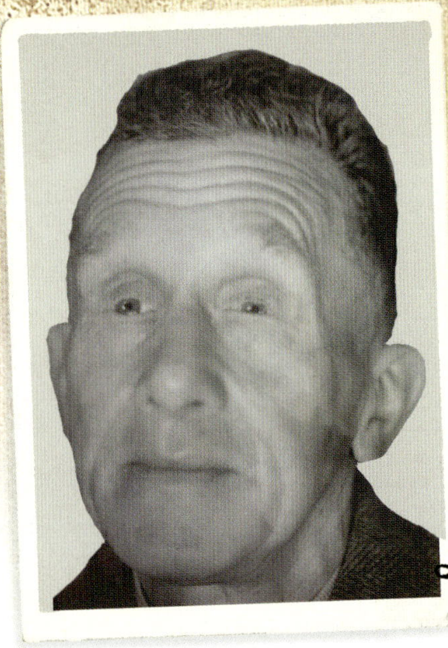

Despite the darkness

VERNON MULLIN

ABOVE **Acrylic eyes:** Throughout his life Vernon enjoyed interests that could have been considered unconventional or too difficult for a blind man. His stamp collections were awarded national philatelic prizes, he built wireless sets and he loved to garden at his Malvern home. *NAA: B73, M27111 courtsey National Archives of Australia.*

OPPOSITE **Hazel eyes:** Vernon's discharge form differs greatly from his enlistment papers. Where previously he had noted hazel eyes, the detail later recorded 'sockets only' and his signature slants downward, written without the familiarity of vision. *DA08630 courtesy Australian War Memorial.*

Tracing his fingers across the ridges of the scrapbook, Vernon could imagine the colours of his stamp collection: dark empire reds, soft violets and bold, vibrant blues. All these were unchanged from the colours he knew from before the war. Or so his wife, Adelaide, assured him.

Some evenings the couple would sit together in the parlour of their Malvern cottage. Adelaide would describe the newly printed stamps he'd bought, and guide his hands to paste them carefully on the clean pages. People thought it odd that a blind man collected stamps. How could he manage, they asked, and what possible joy could those intricate patterns bring him? Vernon didn't care though. He had learned to deny his disability, defy its limitations.

Some blind men gave in to the darkness. They sat in the shadows, learnt by heart the contours of their homes, accepted their lives of confinement. Not Vernon. With his wife, he travelled the length and breadth of Australia. Vernon couldn't see the landscape, but he could smell, hear and touch all the places they visited. Adelaide described each sight to him, all the beautiful photographs she took could not compete with the visions formed in Vernon's blindness. 'Even though he has no sight,' she explained, 'he forms pictures in his own mind – better ones than I can produce on paper.'[1]

But just as vivid in Vernon's mind were the final moments he saw the world, the last sharp flash of battle that plunged everything around him into darkness.

Vernon was 21 when he sailed for Gallipoli. He arrived on the peninsula in the blistering heat of the August Offensive. He was shot and wounded during the Battle of Lone Pine. But for young Vernon, much worse was to come. Barely recovered, he was ordered to return to his unit and take up the fight in France.

63

August 1916, Pozières: shrapnel rained down from the sky. Amid the chaos of battle, Vernon saw a grenade hurtling towards a nearby officer. Instinctively he leapt at it and tried to hurl the ripe explosive back towards the enemy trenches. He was too late. Metal tore into a thousand pieces, blasting hot shards into his eyes. Vernon crawled into a nearby shell hole and drifted in and out of delirium.

The Germans found him. He was taken prisoner, sent to a field hospital and operated on by German surgeons. His eyes could not be saved, so they were completely excised. His head was bound with thin bandages and there was little post-surgery care. Vernon's weeping sockets soaked their dressings and the empty holes went uncleaned. The smell of wounds was sickening, and Vernon and the other prisoners went hungry and cold. The Australian captives could hardly have expected more. Strangled of supplies by the Allied blockade, the German Army could not care for its own, let alone the mangled ranks of prisoners.

After months of captivity, Vernon was amongst the first Australian prisoners exchanged with Germany. Weak and blind, he was sent straight to England for further treatment.

BELOW **Memories and When night sets in, the sun is down:** Although Pearson garnered much support from other wealthy philanthropists, the hostel also appealed for public support. In 1916, St Dunstan's issued fundraising postcards, these were part of a series of six. The charitable organisation St Dunstan's, now known as Blind Veterans UK, continues to help vision impaired servicemen and women lead independent lives. *Postcards by Richard Caton-Woodville courtesy State Library of Victoria.*

Vernon's new home was the blinded soldiers' hostel, St Dunstan's. Its founder, Sir Arthur Pearson, was a newspaper magnate whose own sight had been lost to glaucoma. He established St Dunstan's to offer men a chance at a full life. Blind men could be taught to manage for themselves without demeaning charity. Here, Vernon was to be retrained and reskilled; learn to live with disability. Here, he would learn how to be blind.

Caring and patient tutors instructed Vernon in braille. Words conjured up worlds otherwise lost to blindness. And St Dunstan's offered the blind practical, even professional, skills. Vernon was trained in typing, shorthand and telephoning. A switchboard was set up within the hostel, allowing the young apprentices to transfer calls between the estate's rooms, practicing for the grand buildings they might one day work at in London, Melbourne, Auckland or Toronto. Other St Dunstaners chose to train in massage, basketry, mat and net making, or joinery. Each man sought the vocation that best suited him.

Arthur Pearson wrote to Mrs Mullin, as he did to all his men's kin. He reassured a fretful mother that her Vernon was:

> *bearing the burden which has been placed upon him with great courage and fortitude, and has, I am pleased to say, already recognised the fact that there are many worse things that can befall a man than blindness.*[2]

He convinced Mrs Mullin that her son could have a happy and useful life despite that fateful shrapnel.

When he was ready to go home, ready for his new life, Vernon travelled back to Australia with the gifts of a braille machine and a Remington typewriter – tokens of hope from St Dunstan's.

St Dunstan's trained men for work. It also equipped them for matrimony. Sir Arthur strongly believed that 'marriage was clearly the happiest fate that could befall these young blinded soldiers'[3] and acted as a kind of matchmaker for these surrogate sons, his sightless soldiers. Residents of St Dunstan's (Pearson did not consider them patients) were introduced to a pool of eligible women. Some, no doubt, were lonely, some filled with pity for the blind, others yearned to give themselves – in an almost literal way – to the war effort. But Vernon met his Adelaide quite independently of St Dunstan's. And when they married it was he that would support her. Not long after his return to Australia, Vernon secured a post as an operator in Melbourne's Repatriation Department.

The couple had a happy married life. Though Vernon never actually saw his wife, he was convinced of her faultless beauty. Adelaide died almost twenty years before Vernon but he would always remember her as his inner light. She had revealed a beauty in life that many with the clearest vision would never see.

BLIND SOLDIER AS TELEPHONE OPERATOR

Although Vernon Mullin, a young Australian soldier, was robbed of his eyesight as a result of war service, he is a skilled telephone exchange operator, an ardent stamp collector, a successful builder of wireless sets, and a keen gardener. The picture shows Mr. Mullin on the switchboard at the Repatriation Department Building in Melbourne.

ABOVE **An ideal vocation:** Sir Arthur Pearson explained, 'the memory of the trained blind operator for numbers becomes astonishing, and I imagine is seldom equaled by those who can see.'[4] Here Vernon works the switchboard at the Repatriation Commission office in Melbourne. Vernon was praised as an efficient and skilful operator. Mercury, *30 May 1928 courtesy National Library of Australia.*

SOURCES AND FURTHER READING: This story draws on Vernon Mullin's service dossier NAA: B2455, MULLIN VERNON ISAAC; his repatriation file NAA: B73, M27111; his Red Cross Missing and Wounded file AWM 1DRL/0428; and contemporary newspaper reports. For further reading on blind soldiers see Sir Arthur Pearson, *Victory over Blindness: How it Was Won by the Men of St Dunstan's and How Others May Win it* (New York: George H. Doran Company, 1919); and David Costello, *The Mind's Eye: The Blinded Veterans of St Dunstan's* (London: Pen and Sword, 2014).

The Empire's bidding

JAMES FERGUSON

In October 1918, Turkey finally sued for peace. For centuries, the Ottoman Empire had controlled a large swathe of Northern Africa, part of the Balkans and much of the Mediterranean. Now it was in ruins. The victorious Allied Powers occupied Constantinople. Then they proceeded to carve up the Middle East. In the postwar period, politicians in London and Paris effectively redrew the maps of Mesopotamia, Iraq and Palestine. The borders they created would be disputed for generations and remain a flashpoint for conflict today.

By the end of the war, the Australian Light Horse had fought against Ottoman forces throughout much of that empire's territory – in Egypt, Sinai and Palestine. Anzac troops had charged the wells of Beersheba, stormed the forts of Damascus, and taken the ancient city of Jerusalem. They expected to be sent home when the war was over. Instead they were ordered to stay on and charged with the 'unhappy work' of suppressing an Arab uprising in Egypt.[1]

Even before the war, Egypt had been declared a British protectorate. At the gateway of the Suez Canal, it held the shipping lines that linked Empire and the dominions. Cairo had been occupied by thousands of troops, Egyptian assets had been seized, Egyptian industry mobilised for the war effort. By 1919, most of the local population had tired of England's war. Arab nationalists now demanded their independence.

The Egyptian uprising began in Cairo and spread quickly through the countryside. All across the Middle East, nationalist movements vowed to end foreign rule and cast aside the shackles of colonialism.

James Ferguson of the 8th Light Horse was one of the Australian troops ordered to put down the rebellion. A Gallipoli veteran, he'd been hardened by years in the desert and seen much of the worst fighting in Palestine.

We don't know what this farmer from the outskirts of Perth thought of Egyptian

nationalism. We don't know if he believed that this country, or his own, was ready for independence. Nor can we assume his belief in the British Empire – once strong enough that he enlisted – survived the brutal campaigns of the desert.

We do know he was ill. James Ferguson was suffering from malaria when he was deployed to Tel-el-Kebir, and his isolated sentry post stood little chance against a sea of angry protestors.

On the night of 19 March 1919, several hundred rebels cut telegraph lines and burnt British flags. They tore railway lines from the ground and heaved them into the canal, attacking anyone who opposed them.

James Ferguson was one of four men stationed on a hill overlooking the railway line and canal. Their vulnerable position blocked the rebels' way into the town. Trooper Ferguson and his comrades fled as the protesters advanced – four men had no chance of stopping such a large and determined force. A few escaped, but James was not so lucky. He was found 'terribly battered about' the next morning and died without regaining consciousness.[2]

Trooper Ferguson's death was avenged with ferocious resolution. Assembled like riot troops, British, Indian, New Zealand and Australian infantry quickly 'taught the natives a lesson'. The rebellion was suppressed, its leaders imprisoned, and hundreds of protestors lost their lives. Egypt was taken back by its colonial rulers.

Like a generation of the bereaved, James' parents were told their son died for democracy, for freedom, even for the rights of small nations. But Trooper Ferguson really died to safeguard the Empire's interests – and decades more of colonial rule in Egypt.

ABOVE LEFT **Ordered to stay:** James Ferguson's body on the verandah of the 3rd Light Horse Field Hospital, adorned with wreaths from the local British population in Zagazig. *P01668.011 courtesy Australian War Memorial.*

ABOVE **Unhappy work:** James was buried in the European Cemetery in Zagazig and later reinterred in the Tel-el-Kebir Commonwealth War Memorial Cemetery. The cemetery is pictured here in the interwar years. *Courtesy the Commonwealth War Graves Commission.*

SOURCES AND FURTHER READING: This story draws on the service dossier of James Ferguson NAA: B2455 FERGUSON J M; 10th Australian Light Horse Regiment diary AWM 4/10/15; and contemporary newspaper reports. For further reading on the Egyptian uprising of 1919, see Harry Gullett, 'Appendix – The Egyptian Rebellion in 1919, Volume VII – The Australian Imperial Force in Sinai and Palestine, 1914–1918', *Official History of Australia in the War of 1914–1918, 10th edition* (Sydney: Angus & Robertson, 1941); and Michael Hough, *Gallipoli to Tripoli: History of the Tenth Light Horse Regiment 1914–1918* (Victoria Park: Hesperia Press, 2012); and the Australian History-International Explorer Guide for Egypt and Lebanon, ahieg.com.au.

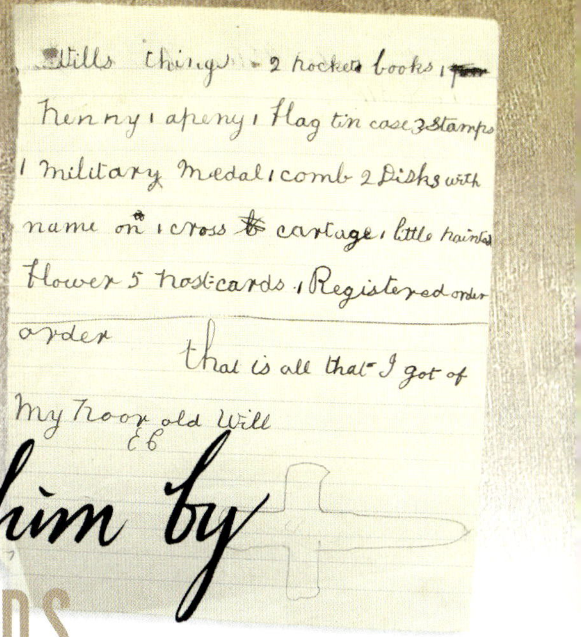

Wills things – 2 hockets books, 1 henny 1 apeny 1 Flag tin case 3 stamps
1 military medal 1 comb 2 Dishs with name on 1 cross & cartage, little hainted
Flower 5 host-cards, 1 Registered order
order
That is all that I got of
My hoor old Will
E6

Something to remember him by

THE MAYNARDS

Cape Barren Island is a high, rocky outcrop off Tasmania's north-east coast. Thirty kilometres long and twelve kilometres at its widest point, it sits in the wild waters of Bass Strait. Little of the land is arable, and much of it – as the name suggests – is desolate and windswept. This was the land whites set aside as an Aboriginal reserve in the 1880s, long after most Aboriginal people had been displaced from their traditional homelands.

At the outbreak of war, around one hundred and seventy Palawa people lived on Cape Barren Island Reserve. Few qualified for a ninety-nine year lease, and fewer still wanted to farm the land after the fashion of Europeans. Islanders earned a living from fishing, sealing, whaling and snaring animals. From February to May each year, much of the community was absent mutton birding, working with the sea and the seasons as generations had before them. White authorities viewed the Island population with suspicion, labelled them lazy 'half-castes', and bemoaned their 'communistic tendencies'.[1]

Twenty-seven Islander men were deemed eligible to serve in 1914. Of these, twenty-one signed up; an enlistment rate around four times the national average. Palawa men would fight at Gallipoli, in Flanders and on the Somme. Several were wounded, several died, all were honoured on a simple granite cairn that still serves as the island's war memorial. 'For King and Country' reads an inscription above their names.

The records don't tell us why Private James Maynard went to war. Perhaps, as with many Indigenous Australian servicemen, it was a quest to secure full citizenship; perhaps like many white diggers, it was the hope of travel and adventure; he may have listened to the island's schoolmaster who 'exhorted the Islanders to prove themselves equal to . . . white settlers by making great sacrifices'. More than likely it was just the chance of earning a regular wage.[2] James Maynard was wounded twice in action – 1917 at Passchendaele and 1918 during the attack on the Hindenburg Line. He was sent home to Australia a deeply damaged man.

ABOVE **That is all I got of my poor old Will:** Eva Maynard's tally of her lost son's possessions. *NAA: B2455 MANYARD WILLIAM SAMUEL courtesy National Archives of Australia.*

OPPOSITE **A deeply damaged man:** James Maynard on the eve of his departure for war. His daughter Mary remembered her father's body 'bloated' with gas. Towards the end of his life he 'could feel the hot air coming out of him'. She always remembered her father's love of the accordion and the 'music [he] played to us kids when we were growing up'. *P00889.014 courtesy Australian War Memorial.*

His cousins William and Frank went to war as well, but they never returned to Cape Barren Island. Frank was killed in 1916 and is buried at Pozières. William went missing during the Battle of Bullecourt and is missing still – his body was never recovered from the killing fields.

From the end of the war and right through the 1920s, their mother wrote to the military authorities time and time again. She was hoping to learn something of William's fate, longing for a photograph of his final resting place, craving something to remember him by. An unsteady hand wrote many of these letters and the sentences often jolt with pain:

> *2 pocketbooks, 1 penny, 1 apeny, two disks with name on, 1 cross, 1 little painted flower, 5 postcards . . . That is all that I got of my poor old Will.*

Eva Maynard's correspondence has much in common with the letters thousands of other parents wrote. Grief laid low a generation, as young and old, rich and poor, Aboriginal and white Australians endured their terrible loss. But of course war wasn't the only way that Aboriginal people – Islander people – lost their children.

From the 1930s to the 1960s, this small, already devastated community was devastated once again as white authorities relocated children (including the children of returned servicemen) to white families and white institutions on the mainland. The Cape Barren Island community was shattered by assimilationist policies adopted in the aftermath of war.

The Tasmanian Government forced Aboriginal people off the island once set aside for them; welfare intruded on their lives, and missionaries demanded the 'dispersal of the half-castes and their absorption into the general community'.[3] Islanders survived the assimilationist policies that marred Australia in the 1950s – though many still bear the scars of the Stolen Generations.

Today, Palawa people proudly assert their distinctive identity; their resilience in the face of cultural genocide is testimony to the strength and courage of Aboriginal communities. Perhaps that courage is not so unlike that of Islander men who went to war, fighting for a country that denied them citizenship, and a British King who dispossessed them of their land.

BELOW **Something to remember him by:** An embroidered postcard Jim sent from France to his 'loving mother.' 'Hoping you are all well at home,' he wrote, 'as I am myself.' Eva hoped for a similar memento of her eldest boy and wrote insistently to the military authorities for a photograph of his grave. *Molly Mallett,* My Past – Their Future: Stories from Cape Barren Island *(Sandy Bay: Blubber Head Press, 2001).*

SOURCES AND FURTHER READING: The authors respectfully acknowledge the Palawa people of Tasmania and their elders, past and present. This story draws on the service dossiers of James, William, and Frank Maynard NAA: B2455 MAYNARD JAMES HENRY PAUL; NAA: B2455 MAYNARD WILLIAM SAMUEL; NAA: B2455 MAYNARD FRANK; James Maynard's repatriation file NAA: P130, R9386 MAYNARD JAMES HENRY PAUL; and contemporary newspaper accounts. This account is further informed by Molly Mallet, *My Past – Their Future: Stories from Cape Barren Island* (Sandy Bay: Blubber Head Press, 2001) and Amanda Jane Reynolds (ed), *Keeping Culture: Aboriginal Tasmanians* (Canberra: National Museum of Australia Press, 2006).

She prefers the khaki uniform to the feminine mode of dress

MAUD BUTLER

In December 1915, Miss Maud Butler, a waitress working in Pyrmont, Sydney, cut her long brown hair, donned the prickly woollen uniform of an Australian soldier and walked down to the transport ships moored at Woolloomooloo. Barely 17 years of age, her slight and boyish figure easily passed for that of a soldier. She lingered awhile on the wharf, carefully observing movement on and off the ships. The moment night fell, she slipped aboard HMAT *Suevic*, a vessel of 12 531 tons, bound for Egypt.

Entering the ship was the first of Miss Butler's many adventures. Evading sentries guarding the gangplank, Maud spied a halyard hanging from the bows. 'The girl seized the rope,' an admiring journalist reported, 'and with an agility which nine boys out of ten would have envied, went up hand over hand and got on board.'[1]

Once on deck, Miss Butler took shelter in a small covered boat and remained there until the ship was well out at sea. For two days, she mingled in the company of soldiers, yarning, playing cards and 'picking up all the points about soldiering she could'. Then she was discovered. An officer noted her dainty black shoes, 'not at all fit for campaigning' and asked to see her identity disc. Even then, her sex 'was not suspected'. Surprising as it may seem, Miss Butler still passed as a boy. The officer asked if his young stowaway 'wanted to go on' with the troops and suggested 'he' see the medical officer and pass the required physical exam. Only then did Maud reveal her true identity.[2]

'My object is to do what I could to help,' she explained to her astonished captors. Rejected by the Red Cross for service as a nurse, the young woman was determined to make her way to Egypt and offer herself for service at the Front.[3]

Though Maud Butler risked punishment as a stowaway or a spy, the authorities treated her leniently. She was offloaded in Melbourne, interviewed at Victoria Barracks and permitted to go free. The captain of the *Suevic* reassured Military Intelligence that 'the girl was of good moral character', but added she was 'venturesome and had a very strong will'.[4] As it turns out, Maud was also the kind of girl not easily discouraged. In March 1916, she tried to stow away again. Forewarned by her former attempt, she acquired a pair of sturdy tan boots and manufactured her own set of identity discs, stamped with a likely name. This time there was no rope hanging from the troopship, so the quick thinking Maud Butler devised a cunning plan. A group of drunken soldiers coming back from final leave was boarding the vessel:

> *Miss Butler noticed that the sentries grew tired of asking these individuals for names, numbers, and other particulars because in most cases the men were too drunk to tell them. So just as a particularly unsteady group of soldiers passed her she stepped in behind them. Walking with heavy lurches to either side, and making rough verbal imitations of the noises uttered by the men, Miss Butler essayed a few possible hiccups and eluded the wearied sentries.*[5]

Eluding the ship's officers proved more difficult this time, and she was marched from the ship long before it sailed.

Miss Butler's story is intriguing enough, but even more interesting is the response of male authorities. Journalists, public figures, and even the magistrates who tried her expressed their admiration for the young girl's 'pluck' and 'determination'. Maud was portrayed as the kind of youth the Army would do well to recruit – 'spirited', 'healthy', and 'used to a free life in the country' (Maud had moved from Kurri Kurri to Sydney seeking work on the outbreak of war). 'The girl has grit as well as love of adventure,' one columnist continued:

> *She evidently prefers the khaki uniform and its puttees to the feminine mode of dress, for she crept into the forbidden garments on Anzac Day [again], and made a big sum [fundraising] for the Anzac Committee.*[6]

Normally, the authorities would not countenance this kind of cross-dressing. In this case it was tolerated, even tacitly condoned. Why? Although Maud's attire seemed to cross the gender lines, it actually reinforced them. Journalists pointed out that despite that masculine haircut, she was actually quite 'good looking' – 'a clear skinned, rosy cheeked, bright eyed type of healthy country girl'. And they emphasised that she sought to serve not as a soldier but as a nurse. This was a temporary rather than a permanent transgression of gender roles and a limited transgression at that. In a way, cutting her hair and donning those rough tanned boots symbolised the kind of sacrifice Australia would expect of its womenfolk. War was not a time for feminine artifice. It was a time for the gentler sex to be strong.

But there was another reason the authorities praised the example of this 'girl soldier' and again it tells us much about the construction of male and female identities in early twentieth century Australia. The real breach in the world between the masculine and feminine was not this pretty girl dressing in the rough garb of a soldier, but young

OPPOSITE **Playing at being soldiers:** Here, women join reinforcements on a march through the streets of Sydney in 1915. Parades like this one were as close as women came to actually shouldering arms in the Great War. Nonetheless, several paramilitary organisations, including the Australian Women's Service Corps, readily offered their services at the Front. For women like these, knitting socks on the sidelines was simply not enough. *H11568 courtesy Australian War Memorial.*

ABOVE **Forbidden garments:** Maud Butler in the uniform of an Australian soldier. This photograph was one of dozens taken on board HMAT *Suevic*; news of the female stowaway determined to get to the Front spread like wildfire through the ship. Maud's boyish figure explains in part how she passed for a soldier but note the dainty boots that gave her away. On her second attempt at enlisting, Maud had acquired regulation boots, identity discs and even a revolver. *P04683.010 courtesy Australian War Memorial.*

men fit to fight for their country who simply refused to go:

> *Her example should be held up to the shirker, especially the perfumed, manicured species that affects coloured silk socks and fur collared and cuffed overcoats, and is in such demand at tea parties, theatres, and bridge.*[7]

Whether she intended to or not, Maud Butler became a cause célèbre amongst the pro-conscription movement in Australia. She was a means of shaming the shirker and showing men what should be done. But her example also highlighted women's limited opportunities for war service. Maud Butler was not alone in her attempt to join the Army. Throughout the war, hundreds of Australian women wrote to the military authorities offering their services in Europe. They volunteered to work in any capacity: as ambulance drivers, cooks, hospital orderlies or office workers. In almost every instance, the authorities declined the services of these patriotic women. The Front was seen as a male domain and even nurses were supposed to serve well behind the lines.

Some women actually offered their services as soldiers. By January 1917, the Australian Women's Service Corps boasted seven hundred members. The most eager recruits fashioned their own (stylish) uniforms and called for the formation of a women's battalion. They hoped to shoulder arms for their country and show those shirkers at home how 'real men' might fight. Members of the Women's Corps continued to play at being soldiers until the very end of hostilities. Meeting twice a week, they paraded, exercised and studied military manuals. But the closest they came to war was to march alongside junior cadets in a naval and military tattoo held in the streets of Sydney. Although the Russian and Serbian armies found a place for female combatants, the Australian Army, then at least, did not.

And what of Maud Butler? A stiff fine in the Magistrate's Court discouraged any further acts of impersonating a soldier. 'I can't go to the Front,' she told a reporter, 'but perhaps I can do a little good here attending to the boys.' Maud Butler served out the war in the YMCA rooms in Sydney, 'a very smart waitress', serving tea and cakes to soldiers. But they never looked quite as good in that uniform as she did.[8]

SOURCES AND FURTHER READING: The case of Maud Butler was first examined in Bruce Scates and Raelene Frances, *Women and the Great War* (Cambridge: Cambridge University Press, 1997). This story extends that narrative using contemporary newspaper reports and a World War I intelligence case file on Maud Butler NAA: MP/16/1 1915/3/1785. For further discussion of how war challenges gender roles see Joy Damousi and Marilyn Lake (eds), *Gender and War: Australians at War in the Twentieth Century* (Cambridge: Cambridge University Press, 1995); and Margeret Higonnet et al. (eds) *Behind the Lines: Gender and the Two World Wars* (New Haven: Yale University Press, 1987).

No more to send

CAROLINE GILBERT

Caroline Gilbert sent three of her sons to war. None of them returned to her.

Robert died from multiple wounds in France. 'I was quite near the lad when a shell exploded,' the battalion chaplain wrote. 'Both legs were shattered and I carried him to the dressing station.'

'Had the boy lived he would have been maimed,' Father Devine explained, and of course all the officers and men offered their sympathy. Devine clutched for the words that might lessen 'a great sorrow'. Your son was 'very brave', he said. He was 'quite cheerful' as he bled to death, 'and told me to write to his mother'.

'Excuse this scribble,' the letter ended, 'as I can scarcely hold a pen at present. Anyhow there is little more to add . . . he died a soldier's death.'[1]

Father William Devine MC wrote many such letters – hoping 'some gallant lie' might blunt the pain a little.[2]

News of Charlie's death came to Caroline next, in a cablegram. Charlie had served in the 10th Light Horse at Anzac, survived the slaughter at the Nek and was killed in southern Palestine. He was shot through the head near Beersheba.

Albert's death was probably the hardest to deal with. Her youngest son was 'blown to pieces' in Belgium. His comrades 'gathered up different parts of him' and buried what they could in the mud. She was told that one day, perhaps after the war, someone might find his final resting place.[3] So she wrote one letter after another to the authorities:

> *I have waited for years hoping that I would receive the photo of my third beloved son's grave, but it has never come. No 3924. Private Albert Henry Gilbert, 28th Battalion who was killed in action Oct 4th, 1917. The Graves Committee promised to send me a photo of his grave. Dear Sir, I will be most sincerely grateful to you if you can obtain any information.*[4]

ABOVE **Their names immortal:** Three plaques side by side in Kings Park Avenue of Honour record a family's sacrifice. *Courtesy Phillip Marshall.*

No such information ever came. Private Gilbert's name is carved on the Menin Gate amongst the legion of the missing.

Never able to visit her sons' graves, Mrs Gilbert raised her own memorial: a photograph on a mantelpiece, a letter folded in a Bible, the treasured 'personal effects' eventually shipped home to her.

On the fifth anniversary of the declaration of war, she attended the dedication of Perth's Avenue of Honour. Two rows of royal oak trees were planted in the bushlands of Kings Park, all raised from seeds sent from Windsor Castle. Although she was old and partly deaf, Mrs Gilbert heard something in the speeches, muffled by a downpour of rain. These 'sons of Empire', it was said, 'gave their lives in the cause of justice, freedom, and right'. Their names have become 'immortal'. But Mrs Gilbert knew better than most the cost of that war. 'I have given my three sons for the Empire,' she wrote in 1918, 'and have no more to send.'[5]

ABOVE **I have given all my three sons and have no more to send:** Mrs Gilbert's boys stare back out to eternity from the pages of a Perth newspaper. For a time it seemed Charlie (far left) might have come home to her. He was invalided back to Australia after being shot in the left lung at Gallipoli. Within a year he had returned overseas and would die in the desert in Palestine. *Source* Australia's Fighting Son's of Empire: Portraits and Biographies of Australians in the Great War *(Sydney: Palmer and Ashworth, 1920) courtesy Doreen Scarlet.*

Caroline Gilbert would mourn her sons for the rest of her life. The plaques on those trees in Kings Park are still a place of pilgrimage for her family. To this day, Caroline's granddaughter Ivy visits them with her own grandchildren, keen to keep the memory of those young men alive. In doing so, she retraces the steps of the grandmother before her.

Ivy herself was born on Anzac Day the year the Great War ended, and due to the solemn nature the day has always held for the family, has never celebrated her birthday. Caroline's great-great-granddaughter Doreen explains:

> *Aunty Ivy remembers going often with her grandmother to Kings park to place flowers on her uncles' memorials. Caroline held the flowers and wee Ivy held the jam tins of water . . . Aunty Ivy did not meet any of her uncles but . . . grew to love them . . . listening to stories . . . of these lovely young men.*

A hundred years after the death of those 'lovely young men' their loss is still felt by their family. The same is true for other families the world over.

SOURCES AND FURTHER READINGS: This story draws on the service dossiers of Albert, Charles and Robert Gilbert NAA: B2455 GILBERT ALBERT HENRY; NAA: B2455 GILBERT CHARLES; NAA: B2455 GILBERT R W; and Charles' Red Cross Wounded and Missing files AWM 1DRL/0428; and contemporary newspaper reports. The authors would also like to gratefully acknowledge the assistance of Doreen Scarlett for providing us with a number of compelling family stories about Caroline Gilbert.

Captain Charlie's Boozer
CHARLES KINGSTON

In 1918, the bodies of Australian dead lay scattered over the battlefields, half buried in unmarked graves, the rest heaped together in shell holes, rotting in the mud. Major Alfred Allen, Inspector of the Australian War Graves Service on the Western Front, was sent out to find them. They called him the 'discoverer of missing men'.

Contemporary accounts emphasise Allen's care and diligence, in language intended to comfort the bereaved. Determined to recover the dead, and use any clue he could to identify them, the Major promised closure to 'many an aching heart':

> *A Quaker, a non-drinker, non-smoker, non-swearer . . . [Allen] is in every respects a big man – bodily, mentally, spiritually, and he does his grim and gruesome work in a spirit of reverence and devotion to his fellows alive and dead, which is a tonic to his own soul and the souls of all he meets . . . His parish . . . is everywhere north of a line drawn from St. Valery on the French coast through Arras to the German frontier.*

Allen and his men divided this vast area into thousands of squares and coordinates. Armed with information from battalion diaries, soldiers and families, he searched and re-searched the fields of Flanders and the Somme:

> *Are there any indications of bodies still below? [Major Allen's] trained sense leads him here, there . . . He carries with him a specially made slender steel rod with an oblong slot in its sharp point, and with it he delicately probes the soil . . . and in a manner little short of magical the earth yields up its secrets.*[1]

But not all the members of the war graves detachments had the Christian zeal of Alfred Allen, and not all found their work quite so 'magical'.

For the first two years after the Armistice, the Australian War Graves Service at Villers-Bretonneux was commanded by Captain Charles Kingston. A Gallipoli veteran, Kingston had seen four years of war and supervised the recovery of hundreds of bodies. Most had proved impossible to identify. The corpses were ravaged by battle and the elements, and the passage of time had destroyed most, if not all, of their personal effects. Identity discs issued at the beginning of the war were made of compressed cardboard; they rotted as quickly as the bodies they were made to name. Then there was one of the Great War's more pitiable ironies: intent on sending grieving families some memento of their loved ones, soldiers often stripped corpses bare of papers, personal effects and identity discs, needlessly swelling the ranks of the unknown.

Perhaps it is little wonder Captain Kingston took to drink. During his service with the War Graves Service in France, he was said to have been intoxicated much of the time. He frequented an *estaminet* in Amiens, known by the locals as 'Captain Charlie's boozer'. There he perfected what he liked to call the 'Villers-Bretonneux cocktail', a potent blend of rum, whisky and sauce mixed in a half-pint glass.[2]

Tired of military discipline, Captain Kingston invited his men to call him 'Charlie the Bastard'. He often shouted them a drink, and treated German prisoners deployed to the War Graves Service to joyrides about the town. Captain Kingston also allowed his men to visit 'houses of ill fame' in Amiens and authorised the use of government vehicles for transport to them. Sex and alcohol offered these men an easy escape, and no doubt that was needed after days and weeks sifting through the remains of the dead.

Allegations of 'impropriety' in the Australian War Graves Service eventually reached the Australian Government. The military authorities convened a court of inquiry in March 1920. The court confirmed serious breaches of military discipline at Villers-Bretonneux and listed a series of 'scandalous' irregularities. It found that 'drunkenness was common and frequent' amongst the men and that 'loose women' were permitted to visit them in the compound. These ladies had been breakfasted in the sergeants' mess, French girls had been seen 'half naked' in the huts, the Mayor of Villers-Bretonneux had written an official letter of complaint. One witness described the Australian camp as not much better than 'a drunken brothel'.[3]

The court of inquiry forwarded its recommendations on to Melbourne. The camp at Villers-Bretonneux was to be disbanded and the headquarters of the Australian War Graves Service shifted to Poperinge. There it would come under the capable control of the clean living Major Allen. Captain Charles Kingston was deemed 'wholly unqualified and unfit for command' and packed off home to Australia. This was the same Charles Kingston who had been awarded the Distinguished Conduct Medal for 'remarkable gallantry and devotion to duty' in the attack on the Hindenburg Line and a Meritorious Service Medal for outstanding work in the field.[4]

ABOVE **The price of that duty:** A studio portrait of Staff Sergeant Frank Carr. Like Kingston, Carr served in Gallipoli and was decorated for gallantry in France. A chemist before the war, he volunteered to stay on with the War Graves Service and photograph war cemeteries. The court of inquiry made no criticism of Carr and he was one of many whose conduct was beyond reproach. But the emotionally taxing work of the Graves Service may well have affected him. Having failed to readjust to civilian life back in Australia, Carr suicided by taking poison. *P05039.0001 courtesy Australian War Memorial.*

OPPOSITE **Some memento of their loved ones:** A painting by Frank Crozier of a soldier searching a corpse. Objects found on a body were precious to grieving relatives but the common practice of removing all personal possessions – including both sets of identity disks – swelled the ranks of the unknown. This man is a recent casualty. The work of the War Graves Service in the early 1920s was even more 'gruesome'. *ART00221 courtesy Australian War Memorial.*

Six months after Kingston's dismissal, General Birdwood himself visited the War Graves detachments in France and Belgium. Mindful of the 'not too creditable' performance of the service in the past, he cabled reassurance to the Minister for Defence in Melbourne:

> *I think you and the people of Australia will be glad to hear that all ranks are working most willingly and contentedly on what is naturally a very trying duty . . . I fear it must be a considerable time before work is completed.*[5]

It was. Over one thousand Australians volunteered to stay on in France and search for the bodies of their comrades. The Australian Government had assumed that Australian troops, and many of them veterans of Gallipoli, would be best suited to the 'sacred work' of recovering the dead. It had overlooked the strain this 'gruesome work' entailed, the shock of examining sacks of grey-green slime clinging to a rotting uniform and the cost of prolonging that already long exile from Australia. Charles Kingston and his men paid the price of that 'very trying duty'. And for all the undoubted zeal and dedication of Major Allen, 18 000 Australians lost on Flanders and the Somme still have no known grave.

SOURCES AND FURTHER READING: This story draws on the service dossier of Charles Kingston NAA: B2455, KINGSTON ALLEN CHARLES WATERS; the court of inquiry into the Graves Detachment at Villers-Bretonneux NAA: MP376/1, 446/10/1840; and contemporary newspaper reports, both in Australia and Britain.

BELOW **Scandalous irregularities:** Unidentified members of the Australian War Graves Service pose in front of a ruined building at Villers-Bretonneux. The woman in the centre is Miss Ettie Rout. Miss Rout established a Red Cross Depot and YMCA Club in the devastated township, facilities much appreciated by the men. But the attractions of Amien's Red Light District proved hard to compete with. Like Charlie Kingston, Rout took a practical approach to behaviour many condemned as 'immoral'. Determined to check the spread of venereal diseases, she distributed condoms to the troops. *E05467 courtesy Australian War Memorial.*

The man with half a face
GORDON WALLACE

Gordon stumbled along in the dark. He'd drunk more than he should have. Most of them did on Anzac Day, and people made allowances. That one day, anyway.

The route down St Kilda Road became more tiring each year, but Gordon wouldn't miss it for the world. He felt a part of something marching in that parade. It was the only day of the year that he didn't need to hide his face away; the day a mangled mess became a badge of honour. It was the pity Gordon hated most. That day he felt proud again.

His wife thought he was brave to join the march, told him he deserved the crowd's cheers more than anyone else, said he was a hero. Today was the day she forgot the whimpering in the night, the cruel things he sometimes said and did. Being married to a damaged man wasn't easy. All that anger, all that regret – turned in on himself and out at others.

Gordon glanced at his watch and tried to read the time through the shadows. It was late, much later than he'd intended to stay out. Evelyn would be worried he wasn't home by now. For all their troubles, she was always fretting about him.

After the march, Gordon had gone on to the reunion. The old battalion – what was left of it – had headed to the Richmond Rowing Club, a rambling wooden shed fronting onto the Yarra. Things went well at first. The stories seemed to get bigger with every pint, the voices louder, the jokes more raucous. Gordon had enjoyed their boozy companionship, that special bond that came from fighting together. It was a secretive fellowship only

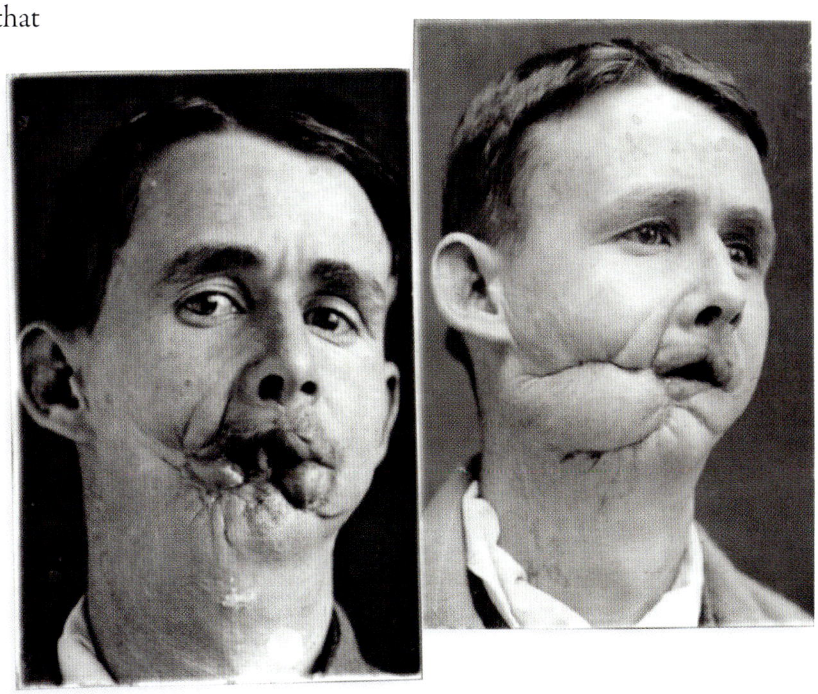

BELOW **His face used to get him down:** These photographs show Gordon's progress over three months as surgeons attempted to mend his broken face at Queen's Hospital, Sidcup. When Gordon returned to Australia he endured more years of treatment. *Gordon Wallace Photographs courtesy Royal Australasian College of Surgeons.*

men who had been to war could understand; here he belonged, here he was accepted.

But as the evening went on, Gordon noticed one or two staring that little too long in his direction, trying to decipher his fractured face and thanking God it wasn't them that shell had butchered. They turned away the moment he caught their eyes, burying their faces in their drinks like guilty children. It was then that Gordon had downed his last drink, pulled on his overcoat and walked down towards the river.

Private Gordon Wallace was one of more than five thousand Australian casualties at Menin Road. That first day of the battle, hot metal exploded in his face. Shrapnel stripped away his skin, tore off his lips, smashed in his jaw and shattered his teeth. He was lucky to survive a wound like that. At least that's what the nurses told him.

Private Wallace was evacuated from the Belgian battlefields to England. There, he would spend as much of his war in hospital as he had in the field. Gordon lost count of the number of times the surgeons worked on him, trying to mould the remnants of his face into some semblance of a man again.

Coming home didn't change anything: more hospitals, more operations, months of confinement to bed and the torture they called 'therapy'. He came to be known as a difficult patient. '[F]requently intoxicated,' one doctor complained, 'a great nuisance in the ward interfering with others and sick patients and keeping [the] hospital awake at night.'[1]

Gordon was discharged in 1921, but men like him never really recovered. The wounds to his face seemed to affect his whole body. Eating was a challenge – every meal was mashed to a pulp as there were too few teeth in his mouth to chew anything. Raw ulcers sent stabbing pains around his tongue, a cough rattled in his throat and the last of his teeth ached constantly. Digesting anything he could get down was difficult as well. He suffered searing pains in his gut as the food went through him, then he might just throw up what he'd eaten.[2]

All that pain went away on Anzac Day, 1954, when Gordon Wallace drowned in the river. No one really knew how he came to be there. Some said he'd simply had too much to drink and stumbled insensible into the Yarra. Perhaps it was the darkness of the night or another of those dizzy spells he complained of. Others wondered if the man with half a face had simply had enough. Water poured into a mouth that couldn't close and drowned him quickly.

What we do know is that Evelyn was left to mourn him and to manage without his pension. She pleaded with the Premier to acknowledge the true cause of her husband's death:

> *I have been to a tribunal, and the Repatriation won't accept his death as war, but the background of it all was due to war service, war was the guilty element and I think I am entitled to a war widows pensions.*

She demanded the indifferent authorities listen:

> *Gordon gave his life for his country and what is the country doing for his? It is all very well to say, Greater love has no man . . .* [3]

OPPOSITE **War was the guilty element:** Daryl Lindsay was the official medical artist at Queen's Hospital, Sidcup. Lindsay's watercolours are soft and sympathetic paintings of men whose faces have been ravaged by war. After a year and a half of treatment at Queen's Hospital, Gordon was left with a tiny disfigured mouth. Here Gordon is in his 'blues', the hospital's trademark uniform. His face appears tired and wracked with worry and pain. *Portrait of Gordon Wallace by Daryl Lindsay, Se 96/184 courtesy Royal Australasian College of Surgeons.*

DARYL LINDSAY
18.

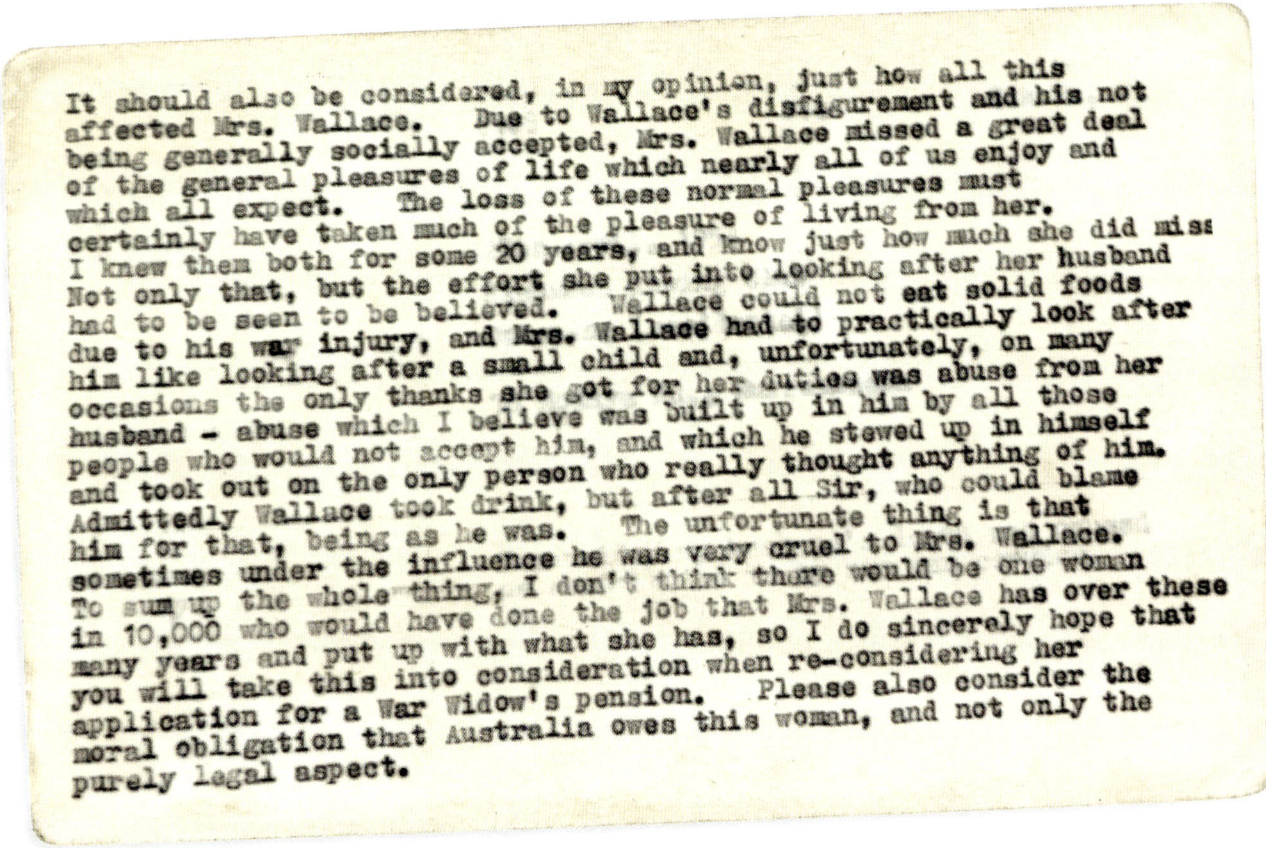

It should also be considered, in my opinion, just how all this affected Mrs. Wallace. Due to Wallace's disfigurement and his not being generally socially accepted, Mrs. Wallace missed a great deal of the general pleasures of life which nearly all of us enjoy and which all expect. The loss of these normal pleasures must certainly have taken much of the pleasure of living from her. I knew them both for some 20 years, and know just how much she did miss Not only that, but the effort she put into looking after her husband had to be seen to be believed. Wallace could not eat solid foods due to his war injury, and Mrs. Wallace had to practically look after him like looking after a small child and, unfortunately, on many occasions the only thanks she got for her duties was abuse from her husband - abuse which I believe was built up in him by all those people who would not accept him, and which he stewed up in himself and took out on the only person who really thought anything of him. Admittedly Wallace took drink, but after all Sir, who could blame him for that, being as he was. The unfortunate thing is that sometimes under the influence he was very cruel to Mrs. Wallace. To sum up the whole thing, I don't think there would be one woman in 10,000 who would have done the job that Mrs. Wallace has over these many years and put up with what she has, so I do sincerely hope that you will take this into consideration when re-considering her application for a War Widow's pension. Please also consider the moral obligation that Australia owes this woman, and not only the purely legal aspect.

ABOVE **Being married to a damaged man wasn't easy:** Close friends rallied behind Evelyn and they tried to explain to the Repatriation Department what life had been like for her. This letter describes Wallace as 'like a small child'. That sense he had lost his manhood – and the drink – fuelled domestic violence. *NAA: B73, M61609 courtesy National Archives of Australia.*

But they stood firm. They declared Gordon Wallace's death was due to his own drunkenness. But Evelyn, and the men who had gathered that day in the Richmond Rowing Club, knew otherwise. They knew why old soldiers like Gordon took to drink. They knew the kinds of demons he had to hide from. They knew they couldn't blame him. Yes, Private Gordon Wallace was a drunkard, but even a letter of support from H.B. Gullett, Evelyn's local Federal member and decorated veteran of the Second World War admitted, 'a man who, as a result of his service, was so shockingly disfigured, may reasonably attribute a weakness for alcohol to his war service.'[4]

Evelyn Wallace died in 1956, two years after they dragged the body of her husband from the river. She was denied a pension.

SOURCES AND FURTHER READING: This story draws on the service dossier of Gordon Wallace NAA: B2455, WALLACE GORDON JOHN; and his repatriation file NAA: B73, H61609; as well as Gordon Wallace's file at the Royal Australasian College of Surgeons. The authors would like to acknowledge Peter Thornton for highlighting Gordon Wallace's case amongst his work on repatriation files at the National Archives of Australia. For further reading on facial injuries of the Great War see Kerry Neale 'Without the Faces of Men: Disfigured Great War Veterans of Britain and the Dominions' (PhD thesis, Univeristy of New South Wales, 2015).

Like a spring wound up

THOMAS DOWELL

Bessie watched her husband glaring into the distance. She knew he was on the edge. For years now Bessie had been able to sense when Thomas was going to have one of his turns. She knew what was coming.

Bessie had married Thomas not long after the war ended and just a few months after he was discharged from Mont Park Hospital for the Insane. The repatriation doctors said he was ready to leave their care. In some ways, her husband was better off than most. In the early years of their marriage, Thomas had few health complaints, fewer than one would have expected for a man who'd spent four years imprisoned in Turkey. Even so, he still had that stare, as if he could still see all the horrors he had left behind him.

Private Thomas Dowell had sailed to war with the second contingent, just before Christmas 1914. Most of the troops thought they'd be home within a year, in time perhaps to spend the next Christmas with their families. They were sadly mistaken.

Thomas served at Gallipoli from the very beginning of the campaign. He'd survived the Landing and months of attrition in static trench warfare. Then came the August Offensive. Private Dowell was part of a night attack on the summit of Sari Bair. Like most attacks at Gallipoli it was poorly planned and far too ambitious. Thomas and his unit were soon lost in the scrub, their left flank was hopelessly exposed, and they were hemmed in by the gullies.

Then the Turks counterattacked. Thomas was very nearly killed: a Turk lunged towards him with a bayonet, but an Australian officer blocked the charge and pushed the young soldier to safety. Even so, Thomas was badly injured. The fall had broken his leg and he lay in a clump of bushes for hours, unable to move to safety.

The following day, the Turks captured Thomas. He was loaded onto a ship that sailed

ABOVE **In the sordid, straggling town/asleep, with minarets among the brown/of squalid huts, like candles set/in vigil on the sea of sand:** Captain T. W. White describes in verse Afion Kara Hissar, where he, Thomas Dowell and the majority of the Allied prisoners of war were held. Throughout the war, more than two hundred Australians were captured by the Turkish. *A02254 courtesy Australian War Memorial.*

up the Dardanelles to Constantinople. The Ottoman Army had few medical facilities for their own men, let alone for prisoners. Morphia was in short supply and operations were often performed without anaesthetic, Thomas Dowell remembered:

> *Four Turks put me on the table and held me while the Doctor used his knife, after each cut he would ask 'Good, Australia' then go on some more and do the same again . . . I was again held down while the doctor opened the abscess and cut it out then the bone was scrubbed with a wire brush.*[1]

Brutal it may have been but that primitive procedure saved Thomas' leg and probably his life. Months later, Thomas was moved from the hospital to the prison camp at Afion Kara Hissar. Thomas and the other captives lived in an Armenian church turned jail, surrounded by fields of white opium poppies. The Allied prisoners suffered many hardships. In a war fought on so many fronts, Turkey could scarcely afford to feed its prisoners. Irregular comfort parcels delivered by the Red Cross kept Thomas and his fellow prisoners alive. He also lived in a constant state of fear. It was not just the occasional beatings or the torrent of abuse from long-suffering Turkish soldiers – unable to properly man the camps, the Ottoman authorities sought to cow their prisoners into submission. Thomas reported that he and his fellow inmates were marched past the hanging bodies of executed criminals and told that could happen to them. As gaolers passed by the cells, they signalled the cutting of throats. Vague promises of a prisoner exchange raised men's hopes, but these never eventuated. Instead, frequent movement from one camp to another, hours of confinement in primitive cells, loneliness, hunger and fear took a huge emotional toll.

Thomas Dowell, prisoner 4161, was not released until the end of the war. Thomas returned to Australia that same Christmas, but he brought the war home with him.

'I feel just like a spring wound up,' he wrote years later, 'and can't unwind.'[2] The memories of imprisonment never faded. Twenty years later, Thomas still complained of nerves, nightmares, even hallucinations: 'Even at this distant time, I can mentally see the whole scene as clearly as possible.'[3] Repatriation doctors noted his 'fears of some impending disaster of an unknown nature'.[4]

Bessie knew that trauma better than most. Despite the Department's scepticism, she attributed her husband's strange behaviour directly to his war service:

> *I do earnestly and sincerely believe that his trouble is due to his experiences while held a prisoner of war in Turkey . . . [he was] subject to extreme mental aggravation by the Turks; and the strain of being surrounded by wounded and dead; cut off from all his own, and all contact with the outside world; his long confinement among strange people in foreign land, unable to understand speech*

or custom without difficulty, nor they him; his increased suffering from neglect and unskilful treatment of his war wounds . . . scanty rations of improper and unsuitable food [ruined his] health. His body, he declares was covered with scurf and large sores, jaundice and stomach trouble set in and he has never really been well of the latter, [so there is physical illness] to accompany the nervous trouble.[5]

It was the 'nervous trouble' rather than the physical ailments that burdened Bessie the most. Thomas would switch from indifferently mute to erratically violent. He shot their farm animals on a whim and threatened to do away with the family. He sharpened razors and knives in front of them all, climbed atop their roof and shot into the sky and built explosives to 'bomb the place'. Thomas would stalk the halls of their house throughout the night, follow his wife in fits of irrational jealousy and was strangely cruel to the children. Bessie believed her husband had an 'impulse to kill'. And she had other fears as well. She would never want to leave her children alone with him.[6]

Her husband's mind, she concluded, was in a great 'state of unrest'. The same fear that characterised life in Turkish prisons 'is still present in our home'.[7] Thomas would pack up their belongings and place all their possessions in the yard, ready to move at the command of some unseen authority. He denied his family food, imposing a strict regime of rations. Bessie herself lived as a virtual recluse, 'I kept to myself' she explained, knowing it was impossible to explain her husband's behaviour to her neighbours.

Explaining her plight to the authorities proved no easier. In the Depression of the 1930s, the Repatriation Department was overwhelmed by claims from sick and needy veterans. Thomas Dowell's case was viewed as 'doubtful' and his need for medical assistance described as 'transient'.[8]

As with many other cases, a returned man's determination to manage on his own at first, and do without a pension, now counted against him. Bessie's fears were also dismissed as exaggerated. The doctors saw no evidence of actual physical beating, and wondered if all that worry was really warranted.

After several appeals, the Repatriation Department finally granted Thomas a partial pension. By that time he was a physical wreck, suffering from stomach ulcers, adhesions on his bowel and a displaced colon. That leg broken at Gallipoli had never truly healed. Thomas limped badly and was often in great pain. As the scars broke down, pieces of bone protruded from his body.

The psychological damage Thomas suffered was far less obvious, at least to the Department. Most of the time, Bessie lived in terror, fearful for her safety and that of the children, knowing if she tried to escape she 'would need an Undertaker and sheet', as Thomas threatened.[9]

Then, sometimes for days on end, Thomas would fall back into silence, staring blankly out on nowhere. Thomas Dowell had endured four long years as a prisoner of war. Bessie Dowell's imprisonment lasted every moment of her marriage.

BELOW **Every moment of her marriage:** Bessie lived in fear of her troubled husband for most of her married life, and didn't want to leave their children alone with him. The children's names are inscribed on Thomas' headstone, but Bessie's name is not. *Courtesy Melissa Wheatley.*

SOURCES AND FURTHER READING: This story draws on Thomas Dowell's service dossier NAA: B2455, DOWELL T H; his repatriation file NAA: B73, M41646; and prisoner of war repatriation statement, AWM30, B1.10. The authors thank Jennifer Lawless, Kate Ariotti and Chelsie Cunneen.

This striking case of courage and devotion

HILDA WILLIAMS

In October 1918, HMAT *Boonah* sailed out of Fremantle harbor. She carried a cargo of over a thousand soldiers, all destined for the battlefields of Europe. The *Boonah* was the last such troopship to leave from Australia. Hers would prove an ill-fated journey.

Three days from Durban, the ship's wireless received a message: The fighting was over – the armistice had been signed. It is difficult to imagine the wave of emotion that must have swept over the ship. Spared injury or death in war, many men must have felt relief, some were moved to tears by the enormity of their country's loss, others brimmed with joyous excitement. And not a few felt disappointment. They had joined up to make their own small mark on history, to be part of the largest conflict known to humankind. In a few words of a telex, their destinies seemed somehow diminished and their old lives rushed back on them.

The *Boonah* was ordered to proceed to Durban, take on coal, and return directly to Australia. But the deadly Spanish flu got to Durban before her.

It was probably Durban's stevedores who carried the virus onto the ship. The men noted the 'natives' looked weak and unwell, that some had collapsed beneath the sacks of coal they were carrying. Whatever the source, infection spread like wildfire through the cramped conditions of the ship. Within a few days, men complained of sore throats, constricted chests and difficulties breathing.

The commander of the *Boonah* knew he faced a crisis. The Spanish flu had already been dubbed 'the plague of the twentieth century'. There was no known cure. More than likely, most of the ship's company would succumb to the disease; some might be nursed to health but, in all probability, many would die.

At around the same time the *Boonah* arrived in port, a contingent of Australian nurses landed in South Africa. All forty women on the *Wyreema* were bound for hospital camps in Salonika. Now the war had ended they could return safely home.

ABOVE **None of the rights, pay or entitlements:** Hilda Williams in the uniform of a civilian nurse. Throughout the war, Hilda had worked in public hospitals and private nursing homes. Her work was as arduous as that of her military counterparts and inspired by much the same ideals of patriotism, service and humanity. *Courtesy Earle Seubert and the Friends of Woodman Point Recreation Camp (Inc).*

The *Wyreema*'s commander appealed for twenty volunteers to nurse the sick and dying. Despite the danger to themselves, none of the nurses hesitated for an instant. So many women stepped forward that they had to draw twenty names from a hat. They marched aboard the flu-stricken vessel knowing they were needed. And from the moment they stepped aboard the ship their lives were in peril.

The *Boonah* limped back to Fremantle in December 1918, a slow and staggered voyage across the baking heat of the Indian Ocean. At least twenty of the passengers were dangerously ill, hundreds more showed signs of infection. The authorities panicked. Fearing the arrival of a pandemic, they denied the *Boonah* permission to dock. For weeks the vessel was diverted from one Australian port to another. One newspaper described the ship as 'a floating hell'[1]. Doctors pleaded the case of men left to die without comfort. Returned servicemen threatened to rescue their sick and incarcerated comrades.

After a public outcry, the *Boonah* was finally ordered back to Fremantle. Men touched by the 'plague' were ferried ashore to the Quarantine Station at Woodman Point. There they would be kept in strict isolation. Over the next twelve months, no fewer than thirty-one patients would die. And their nurses died with them. Despite every precaution, three nurses were carried off by the disease. Others fell seriously ill, victims to infection or primitive attempts at inoculation. An army chaplain quickly likened their sacrifice to that of the battlefield.

ABOVE **The arrival of a pandemic:** Voluntary Aid Detachment nurses in protective masks and clothing at the height of the flu epidemic. Measures like these proved hopelessly inadequate. It's estimated that 13 000 Australians were killed by the virus, almost twice the number lost at Gallipoli. Hilda was amongst the first of many victims. *P01102.021 courtesy Australian War Memorial.*

To me, this striking case of courage and devotion to duty equals the action of a body of soldiers ordered to go over the top in trench warfare, the casualties being equivalent to those sustained in such an action, viz. three killed and twelve wounded out of a detachment of 20.[2]

But it wasn't just army nurses who risked their lives. Hilda Williams, a civilian nurse from the comfortable Perth suburb of Claremont, was one of several women who volunteered to work at Woodman Point. She wrote a hasty note to her mother before she left, stating it was her duty to do what she could, and promising to be home soon. Ten days later her mother received a telegram to say her daughter was dead. It was the second such cable that Mrs Williams had received. Hilda's brother Arthur had been killed at Pozières in 1916.

All four of the nurses who died of flu were buried in the bushlands of Woodman Point. Their bodies were taken out from the mortuary in the cool of the evening and sunk deep in the sand near the graves of the men they cared for. In time, the remains of the flu victims were reverently relocated to military cemeteries in Perth.

As with every military casualty, the families of nurses were entitled to choose an epitaph and told their daughters' graves would be cared for in perpetuity. But Hilda Williams was not considered a military casualty. She had served as a civilian so had none of the rights, pay or entitlements of a regular army nurse. Her grave still lies in the scrub, marked by a simple wooden cross. She was 25 years old at the time of her death.

We will never know how many lives the Spanish flu claimed. Estimates range between 20 and 100 million, many times more than all the military casualties of war put together. The pandemic was the worst the world had seen in several hundred years. It brought the war home to Australia in a way no one had expected.

Our dominant memory of the Great War honours the sacrifice of soldiers – men who fell on distant battlefields. But the Spanish flu visited pain and loss on civilian populations far from the fighting. The dying and the sadness continued long after the big guns fell silent.

BELOW **Sunk deep in the sand:** A simple wooden cross marks Hilda Williams' grave in the bushlands of Woodman Point. In recent years, this has been a site of Anzac Day pilgrimage as the communities acknowledge civilian fatalities of war. *Courtesy Earle Seubert and the Friends of Woodman Point Recreation Camp (Inc).*

SOURCES AND FURTHER READING: This story draws on an extensive survey of contemporary newspaper reports. The authors have also drawn on a forum discussion published by the ABC and information from Earle Seubert and the Friends of Woodman Point Recreation Camp (Inc). We thank Kirsty Harris for her informed reading of the Williams' case. For a study of the Boonah's ill-fated voyage see Ian Darroch, *The Boonah Tragedy* (Bassebdean: Access Press, 2004). For more details on civilian nursing and the largely unacknowledged contribution of the Voluntary Aids Detachments see Rupert Goodman, *Voluntary Aids Detachments in Peace and War* (Brisbane: Boolarong Publications, 1991). For further reading on the Spanish Flu, see Anne Rasmussen, 'The Spanish Flu' in Jay Winter (ed) *The Cambridge History of the First World War*, vol. III (Cambridge: Cambridge University Press, 2014), pp. 334–357.

Amongst the first ashore at Anzac

BERNHARDT WALTHER

Bernhardt Hermann Walther enlisted in Perth at the outbreak of the war. His grandfather had immigrated to Australia from Germany in the 1840s. Bernie looked a good deal like him. He was blond, blue-eyed, and shared his grandfather's love of music and chess. His family had been farmers, first in the Wimmera, and then in Western Australia. Bernie's father, Johann, devoted all he could to his only son's education. A bright boy, full of promise, the lad attended Perth Boys' State School, trained as an accountant and secured a government job. Like the grandchild of many an immigrant, Bernie had made good.

Private Bernhardt Walther sailed to war with the first contingent to leave Australia. He was just 19 when he boarded the ship. Normally HMAT *Ascanius* had accommodation for two hundred passengers, but when she sailed from Fremantle there were over two thousand men crammed between her decks, along with four nurses, supplies, munitions, horses, three kangaroos and a cockatoo.[1]

It wasn't long before Bernie saw action. Private Walther was amongst the first ashore at Anzac. Eight months later he was amongst the last to leave. The diary he kept during those first days of the Landing captured the carnage and confusion:

> *April 25th Sunday*
> *Boarded the destroyer and landed on Galipoli Pinninsula [sic] at 4 am under heavy fire. Left Pack on beach & advanced about 2 miles with. M. Guns over heavy country. Entrenched on top of hill & got guns in position under exceptionally heavy fire . . . The bullets were whistling round us in thousands & raising the head a few inches meant stopping one of the Turks Pills. It's a marvel how we got . . . through . . .'*[2]

April 26th Monday
. . . The enemy were plonking away all night & we had a cold miserable time, every minute expecting a charge.[3]

April 27th Tuesday
. . . their snipers are getting a lot of our chaps . . . we had to advance under murderous schapnel fire & it was a terrible sight to see the wounded patiently waiting their removal to the hospital station. The men are all showing wonderful spirit . . . stretcher bearers are working right in the firing line.[4]

ABOVE **Good luck to you and best love:** Boyce's postcard from France. Bernie sent this memento to Mavis in 1916. He was killed at Pozières a few weeks later. *Courtesy David Walker.*

OPPOSITE **Blond and blue-eyed:** Young Bernie on his departure from Australia. *Courtesy David Walker.*

And in the terror of the fighting Bernie found a moment to be lighthearted:

April 28th Wednesday
Scrambled over to the gun trench, made a couple of 'comfortable' dugouts & settled down in earnest with a good supply of tucker & a big tin of jam. Some silly ass just scrambled into our trench & knowcked [sic] over the jam . . . It has been a fairly quiet day but their machine guns gave us a murderous fire . . . I made 3 wild rushes but only succeeded in getting a bullet through the left boot. Close shaves are as common as dirt.[5]

In the seven months he served at Gallipoli, Bernie fought in all the major offensives. At the beginning of August, a Turkish shell exploded in his gun emplacement: '[it] killed and wounded four men who were with me,' he scribbled in his diary, 'it was horrible.' That same day Bernie noted that he was 'the only one of the original section who had not been killed, wounded, or [evacuated] sick'. 'The reactions on the nerves,' he wrote, 'was awful.' 'Much needed quiet day,' the next entry reads, 'had a glorious sleep last night and a swim after dinner.'[6]

The diary Bernhardt Walther kept at Gallipoli oscillates between extremes. On one page, graphic descriptions of the bloodshed in battle, on the next, an almost tender account of the men beside him. Bernie played cricket at Shell Green on 16 December and the next day he evacuated Anzac, dodging a last burst of machine-gun fire. Then he went on to France.

In eighteen months of war, Bernie Walther had risen through the ranks from private to captain. He climbed the pyramids in Egypt, toured the countryside of England, walked the palaces of Westminster and drank red wine in the *estaminets* of France.

But what they called 'the charmed life' of Captain Walther could not last forever. Bernie was shot in the abdomen at Pozières in July 1916. It took him three days to die. He was 21 years of age.[7]

It was not until November that the family learned of Bernie's death. Vera Deakin of

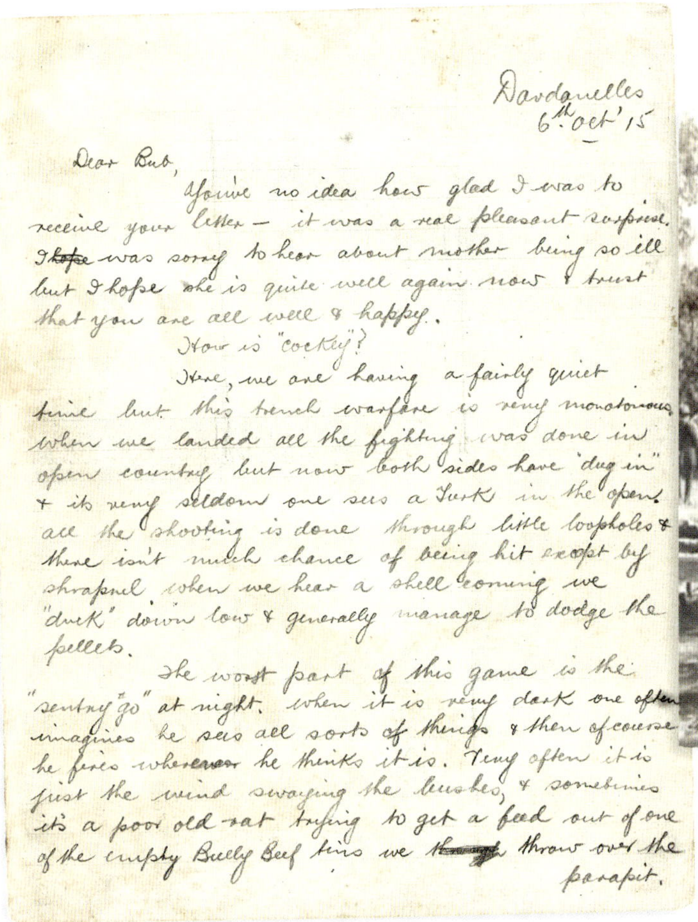

Dardanelles
6th Oct '15

Dear Bub,

You've no idea how glad I was to receive your letter – it was a real pleasant surprise. I ~~hope~~ was sorry to hear about mother being so ill but I hope she is quite well again now & trust that you are all well & happy.

How is "Cocky"?

Here, we are having a fairly quiet time but this trench warfare is very monotonous. When we landed all the fighting was done in open country but now both sides have "dug in" & its very seldom one sees a Turk in the open. All the shooting is done through little loopholes & there isn't much chance of being hit except by shrapnel when we hear a shell coming we "duck" down low & generally manage to dodge the pellets.

The worst part of this game is the "sentry go" at night. When it is very dark one often imagines he sees all sorts of things & then of course he fires wherever he thinks it is. Very often it is just the wind swaying the bushes, & sometimes it's a poor old rat trying to get a feed out of one of the empty Bully Beef tins we ~~throug~~ throw over the parapit.

ABOVE **Having a fairly quiet time:** Bernie's letter from the Dardanelles. Whatever the authorities thought, few of the Walther's neighbours thought them disloyal. Throughout the war, young Mavis corresponded tirelessly with Bernie, or Boyce, as she called him, her childhood friend. Bernie, in return, dubbed Mavis 'Bubbles' – Bub for short. He treasured the mittens she'd knitted for him, and wrote 'in good spirits' from the Front whenever he could. Bub would learn of Boyce's death when she was barely 11 years old. She kept his letters and the announcement of his death in the Perth press for the rest of her life. *Courtesy David Walker.*

ABOVE RIGHT **Just 19:** Bernie outside his 'villa' in Black Boy Camp, Western Australia. *Courtesy David Walker.*

the Red Cross wrote to them. She promised them that Bernie 'had not suffered much', and described a grave marked by a sturdy wooden cross. We don't know what Johann thought when he read that letter, but he knew his son had served with distinction in the First AIF. He knew Bernie, his only boy, had given his life for his native land. But Johann himself was of 'German parentage'. The father of this celebrated soldier was considered an enemy alien. Along with thousands of other German-Australians, he faced persecution and rejection throughout the war.

SOURCES AND FURTHER READING: This story draws on the service dossier of Bernhardt Walther NAA: B2455, WALTHER BERNHARDT HERMAN; his Red Cross Wounded and Missing file AWM 1DRL/0428; the war diaries of Captain Bernhardt Hermann Walther AWM PR00937; Walker Family Papers; and contemporary newspaper reports. The authors would like to thank David Walker for bringing this story to our attention and for generously sharing his research with us.

He still owes something to his country and his manhood

CHARLES BYRNE

Gunnedah in central New South Wales is a place of extremes. In summer, the wide brown plains bake in their own heat, in winter, an icy wind blows down from the mountains. The soil of Gunnedah is rich and robust, fed by a flooding river that has flowed through that valley for millennia. But even the most fertile land can be scorched by months without rain, and crops blighted bare when the valley freezes over.

After he returned from the war, Private Charles Byrne settled at Gunnedah. Something of a larrikin, the Gallipoli veteran renamed his wheat farm 'Bugralong'. Like thousands of other soldier settlers, Byrne had been promised 'land fit for heroes'. But the reality proved very different:

> *I have 90 acres ploughed & with wheat. It is up and no fence. It is at the mercy of rabbits and sheep. I have no money. It has been drought ever since my advent here and I am £300 to the bad in the last 4 months . . . it breaks a man's heart to see his wheat destroyed.*[1]

Byrne pleaded with the New South Wales Lands Department to use some of his soldier settlement loan to raise fencing. He was weakened by his war injuries, and fencing was a task 'impossible' to manage on his own. In 1923, Byrne took his case directly to the Minister. 'This soldier settlement business is a grim affair,' he wrote, and good men like himself asked only for the chance to 'make a go of it':

> *We are grafters, stickers and won't be licked . . . We gave . . . the best part of our life to our country . . . we went through something akin to hell.*[2]

But the Secretary for Lands and Minister for Forests, W.E. Wearne, refused to grant any concessions to a man described as a 'persistent complainant'. [3] 'This settler will not make good,' he scribbled at the bottom of the memo. 'I am of the opinion he will fail . . . He must be made to understand that he is not privileged to . . . dictate terms.'

Byrne, the minister concluded, was not much better than a troublemaker, inclined to 'trade on his war service':

> *Although I am perfectly aware the great service rendered to the Empire by the true blue Digger, I want each soldier to realise he still owes something to his country and his manhood.*[4]

It is hard to say what exactly Charlie Byrne still owed his country. He enlisted with the 6th Light Horse in 1914 and was wounded within weeks of landing at Gallipoli. He relayed his experience to a doctor with the Repatriation Department and the resulting medical report suggests something of what he went through:

> *A shell burst on top of me, just picked me up and bashed me down. The others with me were either killed or wounded. There was little known of shell shock or anything like that and no-one was game to go on sick parade unless he had his guts hanging out. His mates saw to that, for no man likes the appellation of a malingerer.*[5]

Byrne was evacuated off the peninsula 'rotten with rheumatism', plagued by 'maddening headaches' and with his nerves shot to pieces.[6] He never recovered, was discharged as medically unfit and sent home to Australia. The man the minister dismissed as a troublemaker 'inclined to trade on his war service' refused the offer of a pension. He had worked the land all his life and was keen to return to it.

But Byrne's war injuries worsened, almost at the same pace as the value of his property declined. By the 1930s, the doctors described him as 'highly neurotic', afflicted by sleeplessness, heart trouble, 'pains in hips, shoulders and elbows', and 'shortness of breath'. The ex-soldier was deemed 'incapable of doing any solid or continuous work' and recommended again for a pension. But by that time, as Byrne tersely put it, 'my block "Bugralong" has gone Bug-herd and me along with it'. Drought, debt, disability and an inflexible bureaucracy had forced Charlie off his land.[7]

Charlie Byrne described his life on a soldier settlement block as 'living on a precipice'. He wrote that '[w]ar, sickness, accidents and debts [was] not a very good diet with which to face the world.' By the end of his time at 'Bugralong', this man who 'wouldn't be licked' was truly at the end of his tether: 'God knows, I would give a lot for a decent nights sleep and a day spent with a free mind.'[8]

Even so, it would be wrong to see Charlie Byrne or the thousands of other failed soldier settlers like him simply as victims. That was an 'appellation' that generation of battlers would surely decline. When Charles Byrne walked off his property in 1932, he'd not repaid a penny of the £625 loan originally granted by the Crown. The sheep, the only thing of value on the place, were 'stolen' not long before Byrne abandoned the holding. A number of sheep were coincidentally auctioned off by his brother (also a

LEFT **A land fit for heroes:** Harold Cazneaux's striking photograph of rural labour. Entitled 'Peace after War and Memories', it was intended to convey the promise of postwar reconstruction. But settlers like Bryne were sent to work unviable blocks, and even the most experienced men found life on the land a struggle. *Courtesy Cazneaux family and the National Library of Australia.*

veteran, and a man who lost a leg in the war), not long after. In 1932, a final memo from the Department recommended:

> *Charles Bryne be requested to call at Head Office and explain the discrepancy or account for the lost or missing sheep – otherwise an officer at the Department be sent to call on him at his address "Dun moving", Anzac Avenue, Coloroy and demand a full explanation.*

For once, Charlie Byrne, that most persistent of correspondents, failed to reply.[9]

SOURCES AND FURTHER READING: This story is based on Charles Byrne's service dossier NAA: B2455, BYRNE C R; his soldier settlement file State Records NSW: 12/7305/8440; and his repatriation record NAA: C138/4, M3444. To date, published studies of soldier settlement have focused on Victoria rather than New South Wales, but a general introduction to the scheme is provided by Marilyn Lake, *The Limits of Hope: Soldier Settlement in Victoria 1915–1938* (Melbourne: Oxford University Press, 1987); Kent Fedorowich, *Unfit for Heroes: Reconstruction and Soldier Settlement in the Empire Between the Wars* (Manchester: Manchester University Press, 1995); and Richard Waterhouse, *The Vision Splendid: A Social and Cultural History of Rural Australia* (Fremantle: Curtin University Books, 2005). For further discussion of that strong sense of entitlement shared by men promised 'a land fit for heroes' see Bruce Scates and Melanie Oppenheimer, '"I intend to get justice": The moral economy of soldier settlement', *Labour History*, no. 106, June 2014, pp. 229–253.

His own brand of broken men

WALTER BAGENAL

Mr Walter Beauchamp Bagenal was not a man to do anything by halves. His was a life dedicated to the interests of two very different parties.

As a young man Walter was apprenticed in Bordeaux, the wine capital of the world. There, the Irishman from County Carlow was schooled in the techniques of viticulture. In 1894, Walter ventured to the other side of the world to the newly planted vineyards of the Emu Wine Company in Victoria. A decade later, he married Marion, the daughter of a pastoralist family in Adelaide. Another decade passed, then the outbreak of war drew Walter back to Europe.

At the beginning of the war the AIF accepted men aged between 18 and 35. But enlistment levels fell as the casualty lists grew longer, and by 1915 the upper age limit had increased to 45. Walter Bagenal enlisted in 1916, the same month the first conscription referendum was held. At nearly 44 years of age, he was one of the older Anzacs.

Sapper Bagenal and the 10th Field Company Engineers were stationed on the Somme in 1918. On 24 April, more than two thousand shells blasted their position. Mustard gas and high explosives rained down from above. Several men were killed and Walter was severely wounded.

Walter was sent to the 3rd Southern General Hospital in England. A hasty operation saved his life but not his leg. A mangled toe on his right foot was cut away and his left leg was amputated just below the knee. Walter's days as a soldier were well and truly over.

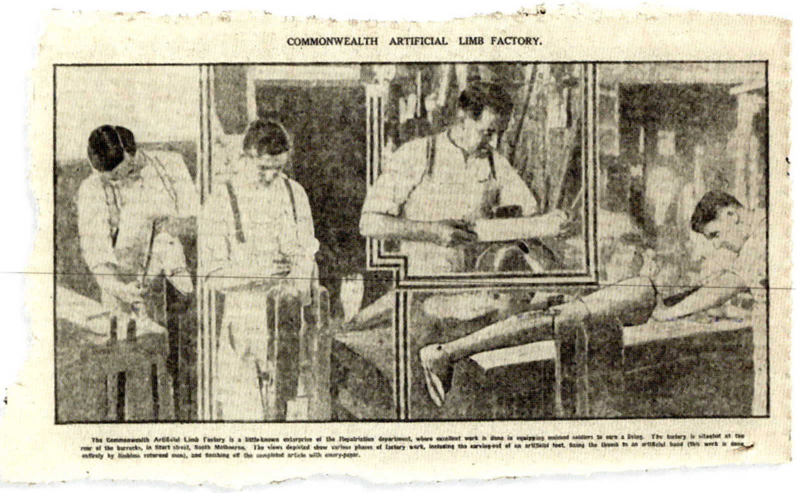

COMMONWEALTH ARTIFICIAL LIMB FACTORY.

The Commonwealth Artificial Limb Factory is a little-known enterprise of the Repatriation department, where excellent work is done in equipping maimed soldiers to earn a living. The factory is situated at the rear of the barracks, in Sturt street, South Melbourne. The views depicted show various phases of factory work, including the carving-out of an artificial foot, fixing the thumb to an artificial hand (this work is done entirely by limbless returned men), and finishing off the completed article with emery-paper.

BELOW **A leg of his own invention:** Former soldiers at work in the Artificial Limb Factory, South Melbourne. Workers can be seen carving an artificial foot and attaching a thumb to a prosthetic hand. Duralumin was introduced to the factory thanks to Walter's research and development. The Argus, *24 January 1923 courtesy National Library of Australia.*

ABOVE **Their own brand of broken men:** Walter Bagenal (far left) with delegates from the state branches of Limbless Soldiers' Associations at a national meeting. *The Chronicle* noted there were only 'five real legs between them'. The Chronicle, *16 September 1922 courtesy National Library of Australia.*

Walter Bagenal returned to Australia and became a founding member of the Victorian Limbless Soldiers' Association. Rather than being subsumed by the RSL, the Association prized their independence and battled for their own brand of broken men. Walter was the Association's first president and held that post for much of the 1920s. Many saw him as the limbless soldiers' strongest advocate – a formidable committee man and zealous campaigner.

Walter and his executive threw themselves into fundraising. They assisted over 750 crippled men, finding them work, distributing relief, even establishing school scholarships.

Alongside that voluntary service, Walter worked tirelessly to promote the burgeoning wine industry in Victoria. The Emu Wine Company went from strength to strength under his management and by the 1920s, Walter was earning a wage many Australians would have envied. That suited Walter perfectly: he had the time and the money to improve the lot of limbless men.

Walter was never a man to settle for second best. The artificial legs issued by the Repatriation Department were heavy, crude and clumsy. In his own time and at his own expense, Walter experimented – fashioning a prosthetic limb from duralumin, an alloy of aluminum, copper, manganese and magnesium. The piece he produced was two pounds lighter than any apparatus issued by the Department, sparing much fatigue for the wearer.

At first the Department was skeptical – how could a wine-drinking Irishman know better than the experts? But success was a hard thing to ignore, and the Repatriation Department eventually entered into partnership with Walter. They began using his innovations at the Artificial Limb Factory in South Melbourne.

For much of his later life, Walter Bagenal lived in his wife's home state of South Australia. No sooner had he arrived in Adelaide, he became a force in that state's Limbless Soldiers' Association. He also travelled the world over, refusing to accept the confinement and immobility that afflicted so many of the disabled.

In South Australia, as in Victoria, Walter divided his time between the men and the vines. He fought for the retention of pensions and benefits through the dark years of the Depression, and helped strengthen quarantine laws to protect a struggling industry. Walter was described as a 'veritable apostle' in the fight against phylloxera – a tiny, yellow pest that then threatened to destroy Australia's youthful vineyards.

None of this was easy. Like all limbless men, Walter struggled every day against his injury. In 1927, he had a terrible fall, as his 'bad leg' gave way navigating down a flight of stairs. And then there were the pains: his stump swelled up each morning, circulation was a problem, there was a 'progressive shortening' of his good leg, and his skin was broken and tender where his 'peg' was attached. Walter's weeping ulcers also refused to heal. But he never gave into them.

When Walter Bagenal died in 1952, the Department accepted his death was due to war service. Although he was nearly eighty, sympathetic doctors acknowledged the 'mental stress [caused by] the difficulties and frustrations associated with the amputated leg'. He had lived too long in a 'good deal of pains' and the 'sepsis associated with the stump' had reached a dangerous level. In a sense, the war had killed Walter thirty-four years after his leg had been severed from his body.[1]

BELOW **When governments needed badgering into action, it was Mr Bagenal who badgered them:** Walter was a prominent figure in the Australian wine industry. He was a leader in the fight against phylloxera, a pest that devastates vineyards. Walter loyally worked for the Emu Wine Company for close to six decades; the company was one of the largest and most internationally recognisable brands of Australian wine. Here, Walter is judging the wines at the Wayville Showgrounds in 1929. According to the newspaper report, Walter 'liked the bouquet on this one.' The Register-News Pictorial, *29 October 1929 courtesy National Library of Australia.*

RIGHT **Their unique needs:** A Limbless Soldiers' Association of South Australia badge from their 1925 appeal. Fundraising was a major part of these associations' work. *Courtesy Laura James.*

SOURCES AND FURTHER READING: This story draws on Walter Bagenal's repatriation file NAA: D63, H029717; his service dossier NAA: B2455, BAGENAL BW; 10th Field Company, Australian Engineers diary, AWM 14/29/15; 3rd Australian Pioneer Battalion diary AWM 14/15/18; and contemporary newspaper reports. For further reading on the Limbless Soldiers' Association see Charles Henry Stevens, *Limbless Soldiers' Association of Victoria: Official History, 1921–1971* (Melbourne: Limbless Soldiers' Association, 1971) and Joy Damousi, *The Labour of Loss: Mourning, Memory and Wartime Bereavment in Australia* (Cambridge: Cambridge University Press, 1999).

A man who stood out

BERT CROWLE

Bert Crowle was a man who stood out, the kind of bloke everyone expected to succeed. At 30 years of age, he'd already made a name for himself in his profession. An architect and master builder, Crowle trained first in Melbourne and then moved to Adelaide. Some of the most beautiful homes in those two cities are the product of his innovative designs.

Outside of work, there was plenty to keep him busy: cricket, football and, of course, the motorcycle club. Bert Crowle was the proud owner of a Triumph 3.5 hp motorcycle, one of the fastest and best engineered machines of its time, a sleek, black symbol of power and modernity. Riding his bike and keeping every inch of it in good working order was the fulfilment of a childhood dream.

From the moment motorcycles were first imported to Australia, Bert had taken a 'keen interest in them'. He was fascinated by the chugging purr of their engines, their power, their agility and their speed. Bert rode his Triumph to victory in speed trials and hill climbs, revving the engine to sixty miles per hour and overtaking all his rivals on their high-powered, smoke-belching machines. A 'much liked member of the South Australian Motor Cycle Club', he toured the hills around Adelaide and explored the hinterland and beyond. But first and foremost for Bert was his family – 'Dearest Beat', as he liked to call Beatrice, the girl he married in Melbourne, and Billy, their infant son.[1]

There was much to keep Bert in Australia, but once war broke out, a sense of duty to his country and to Empire overrode his deep attachment to club and colleagues, family and friends. And perhaps – as for many others – there was the lure of adventure. A fearless rider addicted to speed was all the better prepared to take his chances in war. Not long after hostilities broke out in Europe, Bert packed away his motorcycle goggles and made his way to the recruiting offices in Oaklands. He joined the colours in December 1914 and embarked for Egypt on HMAT *Runic* early the following year.

ABOVE **A man who stood out:** Bert Crowle on the eve of his departure to Europe. Like many men who joined the First AIF, he left a wife and child behind. His loss would be felt by the entire community. *Courtesy the Crowle Family.*

Private Crowle proved as competent at soldiering as he was at most things. He saw seven months service in the trenches at Gallipoli and six months in France. In that time, he steadily worked his way up the ranks and eventually gained a commission. But he also learnt that soldiering was not the adventure many had hoped for. When the Turks attacked the Anzac line in May 1915, Private Crowle was caught in the thick of the fighting – a bullet wound to his face almost took out an eye. He had a brief spell of rest on the island of Lemnos and then – after the evacuation from the Peninsula – Bert was sent on to France.

The carnage on the Somme made fighting at Gallipoli seem like a picnic. In July 1915, as the British offensive ground to a halt, Australian forces were ordered to attack at Pozières. The town was taken at a terrible human cost. Unable to retake it, the Germans pounded the position with shells. The bombardment of Pozières was one of the heaviest artillery barrages on the Somme. Men were driven mad by the deafening roar of it. After three days, the 1st Division suffered over five thousand casualties. Then the 2nd Division was thrown into the fighting. Bert Crowle, who had been made an officer after little more than a fortnight, was ordered to lead his men in an attack on a German stronghold, Mouquet Farm.

All of the officers in the 10th Battalion were hit. Lieutenant Crowle was caught by machine-gun fire in the early stages of the advance. Stretcher-bearers carried him to safety. It was a slow and agonising journey over four miles of battered open ground. An unarmed soldier waving a red flag walked at the head of the party. In a rare moment of compassion, amid the shocking brutality of that fighting, not a single German soldier fired on them.

The surgeons at the Casualty Clearing Station cut pounds of flesh away from the wounded man's buttocks. Bert knew that even if he survived his injury he would never ride again. Infection set in a few days later. With the aid of a chaplain, drifting in and out of consciousness, Bert composed a final letter to his wife and son:

> *Dearest Beat and Bill*
> *Just a line you must be prepared for the worst to happen any day.*
> *It is no use trying to hide things . . .*

Bert told his wife he was in terrible agony, that gangrene had taken hold, and that there was little chance they could save him:

> *Tomorrow I shall know the worst as the dressing was to be left on for three days and tomorrow is the third day . . . it smells rotten . . . Well dearest I have had a rest. The doctor gave me some morphia which eased me a little. But the pain is getting worse and worse.*
>
> *I am very sorry dear, but still you will be well provided for I am easy on that score. So cheer up dear I could write on a lot but I am nearly unconscious. Give my love to dear Bill and yourself, do take care of yourself and him.*
>
> *Your loving husband*
> *Bert.*[2]

OPPOSITE **A sleek, black symbol of power and modernity:** An unidentified digger poses on his motorcycle. *DAOD0223 courtesy Austalian War Memorial.*

ABOVE **A monument stark and enduring:** The tribute raised to Bert Crowle. When it was first erected, this stone memorial towered over hastily erected battlefield crosses. Even today its bulk and size clashes with the modest tombstones raised by the Commission. *Courtesy Bruce Scates.*

Lieutenant Bert Crowle died the next day. He was buried in Puchevillers British Cemetery, not far from the ruined village, on the gentle hills of the Somme.

Beatrice received her husband's final letter several weeks after the curt telegram announcing his death. Obituaries to Bert were placed in the Adelaide press every August for years to come, grim milestones in a long journey of bereavement. At the end of the war, with considerable trouble and no small expense, Beatrice arranged for a sturdy stone monument to be set on the grave. The inscription she chose etched the distant grief of a family in Australia, and the longing of the community that felt the loss of one of its own.

Erected in loving memory by his
Wife and brother October 1919
From Adelaide Australia
He gave his all
That they should not pass

Most private memorials were removed after the war, and temporary wooden crosses replaced by the regulation Imperial War Graves Commission tombstones. Partly it was a way of ensuring uniformity. To this day, the neatly aligned headstones stand proudly on their manicured lawns, like so many soldiers marshalled on a parade ground. But replacing private memorials was also a way of ensuring all would be honoured equally. Between officer and private, rich and poor, no distinction would be made. It is an irony that the British Empire, steeped in age-old privilege, should preside over this democracy of the dead.

But Bert Crowle had always stood out, in life and now in death. For some reason that has escaped any record in the archives, the War Graves Services and then the War Graves Commission left the Crowle family's final tribute in its place. It stands there to this day, a grey granite outcrop stranded in a sea of white tombstones – a monument as stark and as enduring as Beatrice's grief.

SOURCES AND FURTHER READING: This story is based Bert Crowle's service dossier NAA: B24455, CROWLE H W; the Herbert Crowle Papers at the Australian War Memorial 1DRL/0227; contemporary newspaper reports; and 10th Infantry Battalion diary AWM 23/27/10. For further detail on Pozières and the attack at Mouquet Farm see Charles Bean, *Official History of Australia in the War 1914–1918*, vol. 3 (Sydney: Angus and Robertson, 12th edition, 1941); and Christopher Wray, *Pozières: Echoes of a Distant Battle* (Cambridge: Cambridge University Press, 2015).

The name he helped to make

ROBERT PENNINGTON

Robert Pennington was one of the first men from Western Australia to enlist. At 26 years of age, with a black swan tattooed on his upper arm, he farewelled his mother and sailed off to war. Robert arrived in Egypt in December 1914. Much of his time there was spent in hospital racked by rheumatism and all the ailments of the East. But he was deemed well enough to join the 3rd Field Artillery Brigade at Anzac in May 1915, discharged to his unit and sent on to Gallipoli.

BELOW **Her only son:** A studio portrait of Robert Pennington. He enlisted within a fortnight of Australia entering the war and died within a fortnight of landing at Gallipoli. *Courtesy State Library of Western Australia.*

Driver Robert Pennington was wounded on 10 July 1915 and died that same day on the hospital ship *Gascon*. They covered his body in a blanket, draped it with the Union Jack, and Chaplain Mayne read a brief service. Then they slipped Robert's body into the sea, three miles off the coast of Gabe Tepe.

Back home, a mother mourned the loss of her only son. She assembled the personal effects sent home from the battlefield; treasured a handsome portrait taken at Dease Studios, Barrack Street, on the eve of Robert's departure; and imagined that young, beautiful body decaying in the deep. Then, Mrs Alice Pennington devised her own memorial. Prior to her son's departure for war, she had built him a small shop in Como, South Perth. Intended as the means whereby Robert might earn his livelihood on his return from the Front, it now became the monument to commemorate his death.

Mrs Pennington wrote to the Australian Government asking to name her tea rooms 'Anzac' in honour of her only boy and of the place that had claimed him:

> *I feel as a Mother who has given her only son at 'Anzac' that none could be more entitled to use the name which he has helped to make – hence my request for this concession.*[1]

But the Anzac Tea Rooms in Coode Street were denied permission to operate. They were deemed a breach of legislation protecting the 'sacred' word 'Anzac' from commercial use. The Secretary to the Attorney-General tapped out a slight variation to the standard reply on his typewriter:

> *Referring to your letter . . . addressed to the Attorney General applying for permission to use the word 'Anzac' in connection with your business, I have the honour, by direction, to inform you that the Attorney General keenly appreciates the spirit with which you wish to use the name and the associations which 'Anzac' has for you, but regrets that he is unable to grant your application.*[2]

No further correspondence was entered into.

In the first two decades following the Gallipoli Landing, the Australian Government rejected hundreds of applications to use the name Anzac. Some requests were no doubt made with personal gain in mind – billiard rooms, mining syndicates, news agencies, even housing estates sought to use the word Anzac for purely trading purposes. But many applications also came from returned servicemen, many from grieving relatives and many from women like Mrs Pennington who were denied even the comfort of a grave. The Australian Government still claims the power to monopolise the memory of Anzac. In the lead-up to the Centenary, it even questioned projects launched for educational purposes, with no commercial use.

Today, Robert Pennington's name is inscribed on the Memorial to the Missing at Lone Pine – a white stone pylon perched on the crest of the peninsula, clearly visible from the sea off Gabe Tepe. It was not completed until 1926, eleven years after Robert died. Alice wrote her last letter to the government in 1922. She enclosed six standard stamps, more than enough to defray the postage of a sketchbook of Gallipoli's cemeteries. At that time she had no official memorial – only the thought of a watery grave in the deep.

BELOW **With personal gain in mind:** W.J. Perry's Anzac Billiard Palace in Wallaroo. This was precisely the kind of commercialisation the authorities feared. If Anzac could be used to market a billiard palace, one newspaper editorial mused, then an Anzac liver pill was only a matter of time. But even in this case the issues are not clear cut. 'Anzac is very dear to me in more ways than one', Perry told the Attorney General's Department – he mourned the loss of neighbours lost overseas and he himself had served in the British Army. *NAA: A432, 1929/3484 PART 25 courtesy National Archives of Australia.*

SOURCES AND FURTHER READING: This story draws on Robert Pennington's service dossier NAA B2455 PENNINGTON ROBERT; Various papers re applications for permission to use the word Anzac, NAA: A432, 1929/3484 PART 25; and contemporary newspaper reports. The authors gratefully acknowledge the assistance of Gareth Knapman, who surveyed government files relating to the word Anzac for the ARC funded History of Anzac Day project. For recent work on the commodification of Anzac see Jo Hawkins, 'Anzac for Sale: consumer culture, regulation and the shaping of a legend, 1915–21', *Australian Historical Studies*, vol. 46, no. 1, March 2015, pp. 7–26.

The last wattle you sent

EVELYN (TEV) DAVIES

In November 1915, as a pitiless wind whipped across Lemnos, Tev Davies found a moment to write home to her mother in Australia. 'I'm sending some snaps Mum,' she began:

> *I do not think they will keep from fading as the water is too scarce here to wash them sufficiently. I took the donkey one, to show you how they load the poor little beasts . . . [The baskets they carry] are laden with almost anything . . . stones, earth, wood, . . . iron bars, in fact almost anything in the carrying line.*

Tev paused a moment and considered an old man balancing a load of timber on the donkey's back. '[I]t is a wonder [he] is not perched on top,' she added. She had seen so many of those 'poor little beasts' worked till they dropped.[1]

It says much for Evelyn Davies that she could spare a thought for the donkeys of Lemnos. Rather like them, nurses on the island were worked to the point of exhaustion and, again not unlike those donkeys, Australian nurses were badly maltreated by those charged with their care.

Tev arrived on the island just as the August Offensive began at Gallipoli. She was part of the first contingent of nurses sent to staff No. 3 Australian General Hospital. However, hospital was hardly the right word for it. Medical equipment and even the most basic provisions had gone astray. Tev and her fellow sisters found 150 patients lying on the stony ground, their wounds dressed with filthy bandages and with almost no water to wash them. A week into the fighting another 400 'badly shattered men' arrived. Conditions were little short of chaotic. Tents were thrown up over the bodies of dying men, and nurses were forced to use their own clothing to bandage them.[2]

ABOVE **We get plenty of the air:** Tev perched on her own donkey negotiating the rocky ground of Lemnos. Note the line of tents in the background, the canvas city that was Tev Davies' home. Tev took few photographs during her time in England and France. '[N]othing appeals to me after life in the East,' she wrote to her mother, 'where one never tires of snapping.' *A05375 courtesy Australian War Memorial.*

Conditions on the island remained spartan for all the time that Tev nursed there. For most of her stay, the only accommodation was in the same rickety tents occupied by the soldiers. On one night alone, five tents were blown down, their canvas 'creaking, shaking, straining' to the point of collapse.[3] The food was poor and there was very little of it. Greek bread, baked on the island, sometimes gave the nurses dysentery. Lice filled their hair, and centipedes and scorpions crawled about their feet. Even so, Tev's only thought in her letters was the welfare of her patients. In the midst of all her discomfort she made light of the hardship. In September she wrote:

> *Am wonderfully well mum, . . . life . . . is tiring but full of interest and we get plenty of air, and the glorious sunsets would alone compensate for everything mum, they are quite different from ours at home and the mountains are deep purple . . . pale yellow [and] a delicate shade of salmon or rose.*[4]

Tev Davies stayed on at Lemnos right up to the Allied evacuation of Gallipoli in 1915. Through her eyes we can witness the moment that campaign ended. Again Tev's thoughts were first and foremost with the men: 'I shall never forget the suspense watching for boats to come in during the night,' she wrote from a hospital ship anchored in Mudros harbour:

> *[every hour we were] listening for [the] bombardment, it took in all about five days [to get all the men off the peninsula], it was quite a relief to see boats creeping stealthily about the harbour, and see the shadowy form of a barge laden with men.*[5]

After Lemnos, Tev Davies nursed in Egypt and Northern India, the last post 'in full view of the Himalayas' and 'only 23 miles' from the famous Khyber Pass. Shipped on to England, she nursed shell-shock cases, 'poor, poor boys', as she curtly put it, 'all smashed up'.[6]

Like most nurses, Tev also served in France, sometimes too close to the firing line for comfort. In all four years of Sister Davies' service, the tone of the letters to her mother never alters. She is reassuring, loving, eager always to hear the news from home. But something does alter in her attitude. When Tev Davies enlisted in 1914 she was a loyal subject of the British Empire, apt to idealise all things English. The incompetence and cruelty of British command changed all of that. In India, the inequalities of British rule appalled her:

> *The class distinction . . . is most marked . . . in this [hill] station, [you] notice the different circles of friends each class depending on the height of rank . . . English people are not free or natural like we are, you have no idea how awful it is to have to be straight laced always still I'll make up for it when I go home.*[7]

OPPOSITE **Am weary of war and tragedies:** A studio portrait of Evelyn Davies. This photograph was taken long before the war had taken its full toll. *A05376 courtesy Australian War Memorial.*

Tev told her mother the English Tommy 'was not free at all'. 'Poor things even when they are fearfully ill they stiffen at the sight of an officer and it's "Yes Sir, or no Sir".' Unlike her 'Australian boys', she added. How she missed their broad accents, wide smiles and that easy demeanour that reminded her of home.[8]

Tev moved to London. Yet another futile push was coming to its close, and her hospital was overwhelmed with the wounded. 'I wish I could be as brave as you are,' she confided to her mother, 'but I can't help getting absolutely down, beautiful lives being lost and so little to show for it.'[9]

The longer Tev stayed in England the more she seemed to tire of it. The land she had once idealised became a place of 'food famine, red tape and artificiality' and even the English countryside seemed 'small' and 'bounded'. Instead, Tev pined for the ragged bush and open spaces of home:

> *Mum you have no idea what a cramped country it is, I long for space, freedom, and Nature in its wild state, not make-believe like the woods are here . . . if only Man hadn't a hand in everything, the people then would be broader minded and less pompous.* [10]

Of course, there were plenty of 'chirping' little birds in the 'placid' woods of England, but Tev missed the 'definite song' of a whip bird or 'old Jappy', riotous and raucous, singing the praises of the Australian bush.[11]

For this nostalgic traveller, English folk – all 'gush and outside show' – proved a poor match for loved ones left back home in Australia. 'I'm not keen on England, Mum,' she wrote in the midst of yet another lingering winter, 'all [the] people annoy me, I'm sure you would feel the same, there is no freedom of either thought or action, they hang on to tradition and do as their fore-fathers did in many ways.'[12]

Tev Davies' letters are a remarkable testimony of a woman's experience of war. It is not just the humanity that pervades all her correspondence, or her sharp, biting insight into character. Australian nationalism is often said to have been born on the cliffs of Gallipoli, and mateship, egalitarianism and a healthy contempt for 'humbug' and authority seen somehow as the monopoly of men. Tev's letters suggest otherwise. War also widened women's horizons – as much, if not more, than the men who served abroad. After the 'glorious' sunsets of Lemnos and the 'wondrous' sights of Luxor and the Nile, some 'humdrum life' of suburban matrimony was no longer an option for Tev.[13]

Finally, and perhaps most importantly, Tev Davies' letters show how the memory of home sustained women as well as men through the long dark years of fighting: 'am weary of war and tragedies mum dear,' Tev wrote. '[M]y word, Mum the last wattle you sent was wonderfully fresh and the scent so strong, I love it, so did the others.'[14]

SOURCES AND FURTHER READING: Along with extensive secondary sources, this story draws on Evelyn Davies' service dossier NAA:B2455 DAVIES E; contemporary newspaper reports; the Papers of Sister Evelyn Davies, AANS, AIF at the Australian War Memorial 3DRL/3398(B); and the papers of Matron Grace Wilson at the Australian War Memorial 3DRL 7819.

Hearts broken for what

ARTHUR RAE

ABOVE **Gazing homeward:** A studio portrait of Donald and William Rae on the eve of their departure for Europe. Donald Rae combined support for the war effort with stalwart trade unionism. He also held the distinction of being the youngest trade unionist in the world, having been presented at birth with an AWU membership card. Most soldiers who served in the First AIF came from working-class backgrounds and many, like Donald himself, believed the war was fought to defend democracy and save the world from Prussian militarism. The Australian Worker, *25 May 1916 courtesy National Library of Australia.*

Soldiers say you see all kinds of courage in war: bravery under fire, fearless resolution, stoic endurance. But to oppose a war requires a courage all of its own. When Australia marched to war in 1914, and the world plunged into madness, Arthur Rae – unionist, Labor Party leader, feminist and socialist – pleaded for peace.

He believed a new nation should not fight for old empires, that war profited a few at the cost of many, and that the violence that tore Europe apart might have been avoided. In parliament, the pages of the press and stormy meetings of the peace movement, Arthur Rae spoke out against conscription and was called a traitor. He called for diplomacy and was dubbed pro-German. He faced ridicule, isolation and contempt.

Rae was unusual amongst Labor leaders in that he opposed Australia's participation in the war from the outset. Most of his party rallied to the flag. It was a Labor Prime Minister, Andrew Fisher, who uttered that famous phrase vowing to support the Empire to 'the last man and the last shilling'.[1]

Rae, by contrast, remained true to the internationalism that shaped his long career as a radical. A union organiser in Aotearoa/New Zealand, Rae crossed the Tasman in 1889 and helped to found the first Labor Party in Sydney. He went to prison during the Maritime Strike and continued to organise the bush unions through the long, bitter years of the 1890s' depression.

It was Rae who helped commit the infant Labor Party to a socialist objective in 1896; twenty years later he moved the motion opposing conscription at the NSW State Conference. At the 1918 Federal Labor Conference, Arthur Rae argued against the departure of further enforcements overseas. His motion to that effect was only narrowly defeated. Rae hoped that by 'the end of the twentieth century', Australia would become 'a free and independent Republic'. 'Every Empire', he declared, 'has been founded on force and fraud', and it was the Empire that drove the nation's 'heroic youth' to slaughter in Europe.[2]

Arthur Rae may have opposed the Great War, but he also had three sons who served overseas. Donald and William were the first to enlist, joining up together in December 1915. Donald, a union organiser himself, served in Belgium and France until he was taken prisoner in the German offensive of 1918.

Poor William's war took a different track. He was wounded in the right arm in 1916 and spent almost as long in hospital as he did in the field. William's twin, Charlie, followed his brothers to war in 1917 and served in France with the 10th Field Artillery Brigade.

Of the three boys, only Charlie would survive the war. William died on the Somme on the first day of the Australian offensive that marked the beginning of the end for the German Army. Donald survived captivity and was repatriated to England in 1919. He died that same year of enteric fever whilst on leave in Scotland.

In 1922, Arthur Rae was asked to compose an epitaph for both his departed boys' graves. It must have been a heartbreaking task, honouring the memory of young men who died in a conflict he believed to be wrong.

Donald's body rests in Dumfries Cemetery, lying just outside the small market town in the south west of Scotland. The words Rae chose evoke the sadness of his loss; his boy 'taken by the war' when the conflict was all but over:

Through Fire, Wounds, Prison
Came Safely
Then Gazing Homeward Died

William was first buried at Marcelcave, a battlefield cemetery near Amiens. Some years after the war, his body was exhumed and taken to the Australian National Memorial at Villers-Bretonneux. It lies there to this day, on a gentle slope leading to a shining white tower, flanked by the names of the missing. And to this day a father's words challenge the sense of war that swallowed up a generation:

Another Life Lost
Hearts Broken
For what

BELOW **The sadness of his loss:** William Rae's epitaph on the slopes of Villers-Bretonneux. Headstones nearby evoke manhood and sacrifice, King and Country, 'big words' that ennobled the carnage. Rae's inscription offers no such consolation. Bitter and uncompromising, it confronts both the futility of war and its horrendous human cost. *Courtesy Bruce Scates.*

SOURCES AND FURTHER READING: This story was informed by the service dossiers of Arthur Rae's three sons, NAA: B2455, RAE WILLIAM LINCOLN; NAA: B2455, RAE DONALD MAC and NAA: B2455, RAE CHARLES JOSEPH. In addition to these, contemporary newspaper reports were also used. For studies of labour dissent during the Great War see Frank Bongiorno, Raelene Frances and Bruce Scates, *Labour and the Great War: The Australian Working Class and the Making of Anzac* (Sydney: Australian Society for the Study of Labour History, 2014).

Born on the wings of high adventure

CHARLES CAMPBELL

Charles Bruce Campbell was born in 1890 at Yarralumla homestead, now the site of Australia's Government House but then the seat of the Campbell family's pastoral empire. Doted on by his parents, he had the carefree childhood of the wealthy elite, and divided his time between his family's sprawling properties and a leading Sydney boys' school. The firstborn son, and heir to the Campbell fortune, Charlie was a product of his time and his class: assertive, self-confident and full of a boyish enthusiasm for Empire. And, like many young men, he had a love of risk and adventure.

When war came to Australia, Charlie was the manager of Cooinbil, a 60 000-acre sheep station in the New South Wales Riverina. Like many Australian lads, Charlie was keen to enlist – but not necessarily in the ranks of the Australian Army. Old families like his were accustomed to serving in a British regiment, and a number of Charlie's peers had been successful in applying for a commission in the Royal Flying Corps. War in the air had an appeal to Charlie that ordinary soldiering did not. It promised glamour and adventure. Charlie set his sights on becoming a pilot and paid his own way to England. Using family connections Charlie secured a commission within weeks of arriving in London. Flight was still in its infancy and the planes he would train in were flimsy, primitive and mechanically unreliable. But Charlie knew the Flying Corps would change the face of modern warfare, and he wanted to be a part of it.

But the life of a pilot was not all that Charlie had hoped for. Much of the training was dull and uneventful, and the weather tested the Australian lad, used to sunshine and warmth. Writing to his brother Walter, Charlie complained:

> *This climate is only fit for ducks and [Eskimos] we usually drill here in a sea of mud or snow . . . what use all this is teaching one to fly I don't quite know . . . I haven't seen a plane . . . yet.*[1]

That same weather plagued Charlie's squadron, even once they'd learnt to fly. The 'beast of a climate' ensured that the men of the 49th had little time to train as a unit before being sent on to France.[2] Some of the men in Charlie's squadron had only fifteen hours in the air solo, and they didn't even have the chance to practice battle formations before they were sent into the action.[3]

Poor training wasn't the only disadvantage pilots faced. The new two-seater De Havillands were faster and more powerful than anything the Flying Corps had used before, yet still they came up short against the formidable German Albatrosses. In 1917 alone, over two thousand men of the RFC were shot down. In what they called 'Bloody April', the life expectancy of a new pilot was between three and eight weeks.[4]

Charlie and his men took off for their 'first show' at the end of November 1917. Although they were keen to 'do something useful in the way of annoying the Hun', adrenaline and terror sent blood pumping through their chests.[5] At first the flight went well enough. The weather had recently turned and the French countryside was covered in a thin blanket of snow, eerily calm and peaceful from above, it seemed to almost veil the fury taking place below. The men of the 49th swerved their way across the sky, dodging the German guns as the Battle of Cambrai rumbled on beneath them. With their observation mission a success, and seemingly unopposed, they turned for home.

ABOVE **She clung to the belief her son would come home:** Christie Campbell gazes out from the verandah of the family home, Yarralumla. Many parents left the rooms of their sons unaltered in the hope they would return to them. *Courtesy Walter Campbell Memorial Trust, Charles Sturt University, Regional Archives and University Art Collection, Wagga Wagga.*

Just as their hearts began to settle in their chests, a distant roar alerted the men to danger. Scores of brightly coloured machines came swiftly through the mist, outnumbering Charlie and his men three to one. Charlie recognised the markings of those aircraft instantly. The Red Baron's Flying Circus were closing in on them.

The 49th panicked and the lead plane swung left, throwing the formation into chaos and confusion. Charlie's plane was the very last in the squadron, and the very first to be isolated. Elite German pilots swooped down from above and peppered his machine with bullets. The fuel tank was hit and Charlie's hapless aircraft was engulfed in flames. The De Havilland plunged towards the earth – ablaze and out of control.

Back in Australia, Charlie's parents, Christie and Fred, were told that their boy was 'missing'. Despite the numerous reports that his plane had been seen going down in flames, they still held out hope that he had survived. Perhaps Charlie had managed to land his crippled aircraft? Perhaps he was a prisoner of war in Germany? Christie, unable to imagine a life without her son began to write him letters:

> *Dear Charlie, on Thursday last since the news came that you were missing and no further news since.*
>
> *Your machine was seen in flames & this awful nightmare still haunts me,*

oh Charlie Boy, surely this suspense cannot go on much longer.[6]
I get through the days hoping and hoping on news that you have been saved.[7]
. . . perhaps some news will come through this week.[8]

In time, the men of Charlie's squadron wrote to the Campbells. Their letters offered sympathy but also finality. Several of Charlie's comrades were able to provide first-hand accounts of his death. But still, for Christie, the loss of 'Charlie boy' was unimaginable. Despite all the brutal evidence, she clung to the belief her son would come home.

In 1918, Christie and her daughter Kate travelled to Egypt. There they met up with Charlie's brother Walter, then in camp with the Australian Light Horse. As soon as peace was declared, the three Campbells travelled through France in search of Charlie. They questioned his comrades, sought out German records, and – on finding a grave near Cambrai marked C.B. Campbell RFC – demanded it be opened. Not finding the answers she wanted to hear, Christie visited the mother of Charlie's observer, William Samways, in England. There, two women bereft of their sons comforted one another and shared the burden of their grief.

Returning to Australia, Christie began to come to terms with her loss. Like many grieving parents, she turned to the task of remembrance, memorialising Charlie's life in every way she could. Christie began a scholarship in his name at his old school; had a window commissioned in his honour at their local church; and sent ornately framed photographs of her handsome boy to friends and family, urging them to remember him. As late as the 1920s, a generous provision was made in Fred Campbell's will for a son who would never return home.

Despite the enormous physical distance between them, the bond Christie had formed with Flora Samways grew stronger over the years. The two women often corresponded, nurturing the memories of their sons, forging a kind of kinship in their grief. 'It's comforting to know that they are not divided,' Flora wrote to Christie. Their 'two heroes' were 'born on the wings of high adventure to the presence of god where they now rest'.[9] And one day – soon, she hoped – they would join them on 'that shining shore'.[10]

SOURCES AND FURTHER READING: This story draws on the Walter Campbell Memorial Trust, Charles Sturt University Regional Archives and University Art Collection, Wagga Wagga and contemporary newspaper reports. The authors would like to thank the Reverand Paul Black and St John's congregation. For more information on the Campbell family and the Yarralumla estate, see Charles Newman, *The Spirit of Wharf House: Campbell Enterprise from Calcutta to Canberra, 1788–1930* (Sydney: Angus and Robertson, 1987); and C D Coulthard-Clark, *Gables, Ghosts and Governers-General: The Historic House at Yarralumla, Canberra* (Sydney: Allen & Unwin in association with the Canberra and District Historical Society, 1988). The authors would like to thank Chris Clark for directing us to the Campbell story.

BELOW TOP **A window in his honour:** Charlie Campbell's memorial window in St John's Church, Canberra. The window bears the motto of the Royal Flying Corp, *Par Ardua ad Astra*, Through Adversity to the Stars. *Courtesy Bruce Scates.*

BELOW BOTTTOM **Charlie Boy:** A portrait of Charles Campbell. *Courtesy Walter Campbell Memorial Trust, Charles Sturt University, Regional Archives and University Art Collection, Wagga Wagga.*

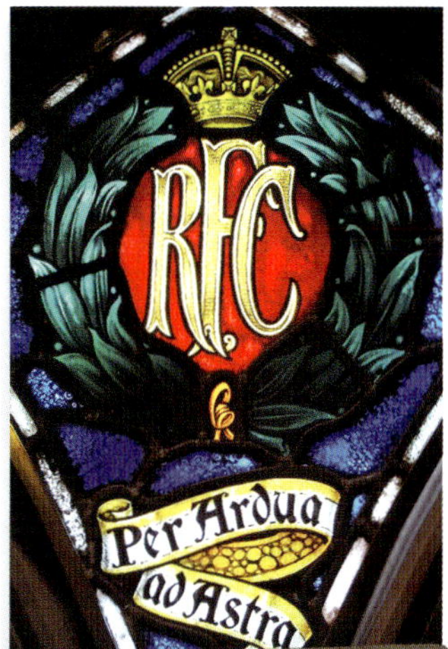

She hath done what she could

EDITH MOORHOUSE

OPPOSITE **Ennobling the women of our Land and the Empire:** The soft filtered light of York Minster's memorial window. The campaign to restore the Five Sisters Window began in 1923, an initiative of Helen Little of York. 'I had a vision', she explained in a letter to the London *Times* published after her death, 'On entering York Minster for evensong I saw two white clad figures, one beckoning to me and the other pointing to the 'Five Sisters' window. I recognised them as my sisters who died in childhood. I looked at the window, which opened, revealing to my gaze an exquisite garden with five women sitting in the shade of a great tree, and many girls and women, clad in grey-blue approaching. The vision faded . . . I woke crying 'The Five Sisters window for the Sisters'. *Creative Commons courtesy Mattana.*

York Minster Cathedral is one of the most ancient and beautiful in all of Christendom. Its cloistered halls and vaulted ceilings have long been the site of pomp and ceremony: investitures of the Archbishop, masses and requiems, splendid state visits of kings and queens. In June 1925, York Minster witnessed a very different kind of ritual, the first ever memorial service to 'the women of the British Empire who gave their lives in the Great War'.

That day the Cathedral was filled 'to the uttermost' and – for the first time – by 'hosts of uniformed women'. They represented 'all the branches of the services in which women took part during the war', a press report related:

> *Women doctors in their academic robes, hundreds of nurses in the various uniforms, V.A.D. workers in their blue-and-white with scarlet crosses on their apron. Wrens, munitions workers, and so on.*[1]

The great congregation heard the sound of triumphal music as the Archbishop marched in procession to the dais; watched the Duke and Duchess of York receive the Royal Salute; and smelt the sweet, ashen scent of incense drift through the air. Then, at a signal from the Archbishop, 'a great sheet', which covered the northern transept drifted down from its moorings, and the brilliant colour of a stained glass window flashed 'like rich jewels' in the sunlight. The 'assembled multitude', it was said, let out a single sigh.

The Five Sisters Window had stood in York Minster since the 13th century but it was fundraising efforts led by women that had it restored. That day, the windows were rededicated to women who many feared would be forgotten – those who had made the supreme sacrifice 'in the cause of King and Country'. Their contribution was no less than that of their menfolk, the Archbishop proclaimed from his pulpit. 'The light of this service and sacrifice . . . ennobled the women of our land and Empire in the dark days of the Great War.' It was a light more 'glorious', more 'pure' more 'delicate' than the filtered colour beamed through the great windows above him, and it would shine, he said, forevermore.[2]

Beneath the window, a wide oak screen had been erected. Like countless stone pillars raised across the Empire, it carried its burden of names – over one thousand from Great Britain, a single name from India, four from South Africa, thirty-nine from Canada, and thirty-nine names in all from Australia and Aotearoa/New Zealand. Included in the tally were women who died of sickness, were killed in air raids, drowned when their transports were torpedoed, lost their lives in munitions factories and – in the case of Edith Cavell – were executed by the Germans during the war.

The service at York Minster set a precedent across the British Empire. Synchronised ceremonies were organised by the National Council of Women throughout Australia, and the largest and most 'impressive' services took place in the Melbourne, Adelaide and Sydney Town Halls. His Excellency Lord Forster, Governor of New South Wales, presided over the last of these. 'I have taken part in many ceremonials to honour the memory of men,' he told an attentive (and, again, largely female) audience, 'but this is the first occasion I have had to participate in a ceremony devoted solely to women.' A soldier himself, he had seen those women at work in many theatres of war:

> *In the midst of the greatest danger [they] carried on, with unfailing courage and endurance, and gave of their love and strength to the battered remains of humanity that were in their care.*

On this occasion, the names of the Australian women who died in the conflict were read out to the audience, a way, as the Governor put it, 'to affirm their remembrance'. Amongst the first to be called out was Sister Edith Moorhouse.[3]

Edith was born in Undera, a small town outside Kyabram in country Victoria. Her mother died in 1891 at the age of 38, her father a year later. At the age of six, Edith was left an orphan – as were her four siblings. All of them moved to Echuca where they came under the care of their uncle, Henry Moorhouse. As for many women of her generation, nursing offered Edith a chance of self-reliance and independence. She trained at Mooroopna General Hospital for three years and was still a resident at Mooroopna when she enlisted as a staff nurse in 1915. She embarked from Melbourne on HMAT *Kyarra* that August.

In over three years of service, Edith Moorhouse nursed servicemen in Australia, Egypt and France. She also worked on hospital ships, freighting sick, wounded and sometimes dying men across the Mediterranean back to England and even home to Australia. She had two periods of leave in England, both to recover from bouts of illness, and may well have visited York Minster where her memorial would eventually be placed. In 1918, she returned to France, was posted to the 1st Australian Casualty Clearing Station.

Conditions in northern France were appalling. The hospitals around Lille swelled with the sick and wounded, and the site of the casualty clearing stations shifted hurriedly with every battle. And just like the steady stream of wounded, the weather gave no respite: '[We] were moved . . . [t]o a dreary spot called Fretin beyond Lille,' Sister Leila Brown recalled:

> *Here we were billeted in an old château about 20 minutes walk from the camp . . . My team went on night duty and filthy weather prevailed cold winds and rain for it was now late in October. We were cold and miserable long before we reached our ward for the night's work. It was during this night's duty that . . . Sister Moorhouse took ill.*[4]

Edith Moorhouse refused to leave her post. Despite illness and exhaustion, she continued to tend the 'battered remains of humanity' left in her care. 'She would not give in until she could not move,' Sister Brown remembered, 'and it was too late [then] to save her precious life.'

Edith survived long enough to see the end of fighting but died of pneumonia two weeks after the signing of the Armistice. She was 33 years of age.[5]

Edith Moorhouse was buried beside the men she nursed, in Lille Southern Cemetery. Her uncle Henry died in 1920, long before the permanent headstones were set in place, so it was almost certainly her brother Matthew who composed the epitaph for her grave. Matthew had inserted a series of obituary notices in the Melbourne *Argus*. The few words he chose were simpler and more eloquent than any archbishop's eulogy, or any grand speech the Governor might have made:

SHE HATH DONE WHAT SHE COULD

BELOW **A ceremony devoted wholly to honouring women:** Breanna Janson from Bairnsdale, Victoria, pays her respects at Edith Moorhouse's grave. Breanna represented Nagel College on the Victorian Premier's Spirit of Anzac Tour in 2014 and chose Edith Moorhouse to commemorate. In the ninth year of the Tour's operation, it was the first year the 'Adopt a Digger' program had been extended to include a nurse. *Courtesy Bruce Scates.*

SOURCES AND FURTHER READING: Along with extensive secondary sources, this story draws on the service dossier of Edith Moorhouse NAA: B2455 MOORHOUSE EDITH ANN; her Red Cross Wounded and Missing file AWM 1DRL/0428; the war diary of the Matron-in-Chief, The National Archives, Kew, W095/3991, November 1–30, 1918; the Papers of Matron Grace Wilson at the Australian War Memorial 3DRL 7819; and contemporary newspaper reports both in Australia and Britain.

The hardships of war
PETER RADOS

Private Peter Rados of the 3rd Battalion died the same day as John Simpson Kirkpatrick – the man with the donkey – as Turks attacked the Anzac line at Gallipoli. That June, a letter was sent to his parents. No doubt it read the way so many others did: 'I regret to inform you . . . Your son was Killed in Action . . . He was buried by his comrades in a grave beside the sea.'[1]

But the letter never reached his family.

Some months later, an officer attached to AIF Headquarters in London jotted down a memo to the Secretary for External Affairs in Melbourne. The standard letter had been sent to the next-of-kin recorded on this soldier's attestation papers. It was returned by the postal authorities some time later, marked with a blunt finality: 'Not Known.'

There was nothing so unusual in that. Families often travelled in search of work and some next-of-kin proved difficult to find, especially in remote parts of Australia. On some occasions the news of the death of a loved one was relayed from one forwarding address to another. Parents sometimes chanced across their son's name in a casualty list published by the major dailies long before they heard anything from the authorities. We can only imagine their horror as that print stared back from a morning paper.

But the route this particular file had travelled was even more circuitous. News of Peter Rados' death travelled by telex or ship from Gallipoli to Egypt, on to Britain, then back to the Mediterranean. Private Rados, it appears, had changed his identity to serve with Australian Forces. His real name was Santelis Pannagioty, a Greek veteran of the Balkan wars (from which he sported a scar on his chest) but keen to fight a second time. And his mother, father, and four sisters lived not in Athens – as his recruitment papers claimed – but in Smyrna (now Izmir) on the Aegean coast of Turkey.

Private Rados also had a brother. Like Peter, Nick Rados had emigrated from

Greece, both men had adopted the same anglicised surname, both had crossed the ocean to build new lives for themselves. As late as 1918, Nick knew nothing of his brother's fate. Just a few weeks before the war ended, he wrote to the Red Cross from Atlantic City, New Jersey:

> *My brother… has not been heard of since he enlisted at Sidney [sic] Australia during the early part of the war. Kindly write any information you know of him. His mother and brother are very anxious [to learn] his whereabouts.*[2]

Nick explained why his brother had kept his identity a secret:

> *Pvt P. Rados gave his parents address as Athens so that it would not interfere with his enlisting as his people were living under Turkish rule and [he] himself was a Turkish subject.*[3]

Santelis Pannagioty's parents never found out what became of their son. Both died before the war ended. As did at least three million other Ottoman civilians: victims of famine, disease, an Allied blockade that starved Turkish cities, the forced relocations of ethnic minorities, and genocide.

Private Rados was survived by four sisters, Marika aged 15, Atho aged 13, Smaro aged 11 and Georgina, the youngest, barely 10. Nick pleaded for any help Australia might offer them. His sisters were stranded in Erdik, a territory of Turkey ceded to the Allies, and he feared for their fate, as he had for that of his brother:

> *They are in very poor condition, as they have lost all during the war. You will be doing a great act of charity if you will go to their assistance… And what the late Private P. Rados left should be given to them.*[4]

The authorities never found Private Rados' sisters. Nor is there any evidence they searched for them. The protocols of the day defined the next-of-kin as the eldest male relative. Four sisters, living under Turkish rule, were really of little interest to them, and given the chaotic state of Turkey in the immediate aftermath of the Great War, it is unlikely that any inquiries would have been successful.

In 1921, Peter Rados' personal effects were sealed and mailed off to his brother in America, along with a commemorative medallion, a letter from the King, and a sketch of the cemetery where the Greek-Australian lay buried. Base Records, Melbourne, noted 'the gallant service rendered by Pte. Rados'. And perhaps, as the form letter was typed, someone noticed his service number. Rados had been one of the first to enlist and had died in the first month of the Gallipoli campaign.[5]

Directly and indirectly, 'the hardships of … war' had claimed his life, that of his parents, and quite probably his four young sisters. In 1923, after another Greco-Turkish war, Greece and Turkey agreed to population exchanges that would tear families and communities apart, depopulate towns and cities, and leave a legacy of bitterness and confusion. The hardships of the Rados family were shared by many.[6]

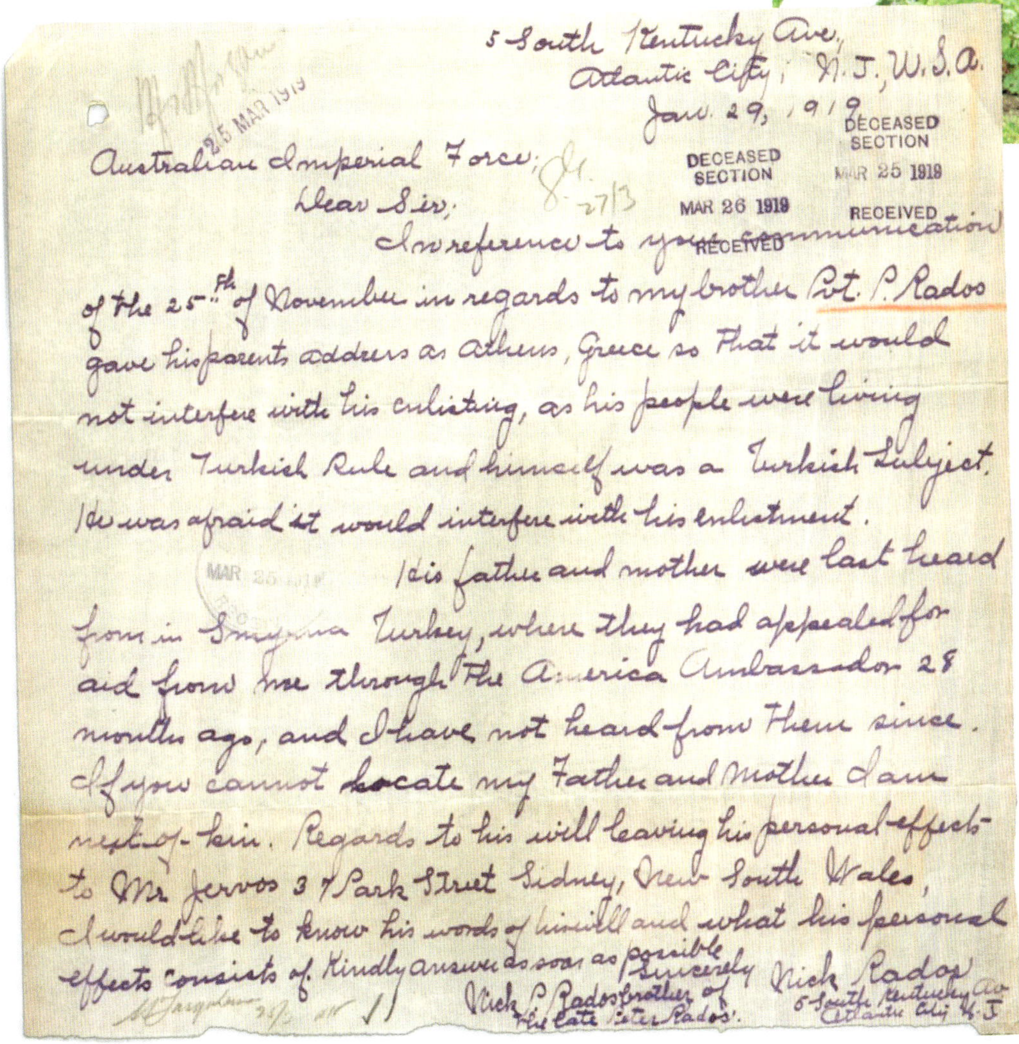

5 South Kentucky Ave,
Atlantic City, N.J., U.S.A.
Jan. 29, 1919

DECEASED SECTION MAR 26 1919 RECEIVED

DECEASED SECTION MAR 25 1919 RECEIVED

Australian Imperial Force;
Dear Sir;
In reference to your communication of the 25th of November in regards to my brother Pvt. P. Rados gave his parents address as Athens, Greece so that it would not interfere with his enlisting, as his people were living under Turkish Rule and himself was a Turkish Subject. He was afraid it would interfere with his enlistment.

His father and mother were last heard from in Smyrna Turkey, where they had appealed for aid from me through the America Ambassador 28 months ago, and I have not heard from them since. If you cannot locate my Father and Mother I am next-of-kin. Regards to his will leaving his personal effects to Mr Jervos 37 Park Street Sidney, New South Wales, I would like to know his words of his will and what his personal effects consists of. Kindly answer as soon as possible

Sincerely Nick Rados
Nick P Rados brother of the late Peter Rados.
5 South Kentucky Ave Atlantic City N.J.

ABOVE **The cemetery where a Greek-Australian lay buried:** Michael Manoussakis kneels by the grave of Peter Rados at Ari Burnu Cemetery in Gallipoli. Michael 'adopted' Rados' grave in a government sponsored study tour of Turkey. His own family had emigrated to Australia in the 1950s and he met his great aunt for the first time at an airport hotel in Athens. Waves of migration followed the Second World War as they did the First. Generations later, its effects are still felt by Greek, Turkish and Australian families. *Courtesy Bruce Scates.*

LEFT **In very poor condition:** Private Rados's brother struggles to reunite a family torn asunder by the fighting. Note the attempt to recruit the aid of the American ambassador. Nick Rados appealed to his adopted country for assistance – just as he hoped for help from Australia. America was no longer neutral by 1918, entering the war on the side of the Allies. None of these entreaties were successful. *NAA: B2455, RADOS PETER courtesy National Archives of Australia.*

Sources and further reading: This story draws on Peter Rados' service dossier NAA:B2455 RADOS PETER; and his immigration records NAA: A1 1914/15312. The authors gratefully acknowledge Michael Manoussakis for his assistance in bringing these records to light. One of the best and most recent books on the dispersal of the Greek diaspora and the rise of Greek and Turkish nationalism is by Nicolas Doumanis, *Before the Nation,* (Oxford: Oxford University Press, 2012) and for the debate surrounding the Armenians, see Eugene Rogan, *The Fall of the Ottomans: The Great War in the Middle East* (New York: Basic Books, 2015).

Their war never ended

JOHN AND EDWARD SADLER

Rodney Smith's generation lived with the memory of war. His mother lost two of her brothers. Edward Sadler was killed on 27 January 1917 in France, and four months later her older brother John died at the Second Battle of Bullecourt.

'My mother's family did not forget,' Rodney remembers. 'The feeling of sorrow and loss was obvious to me even as a small child. There were two large portraits of John and Ed where everyone could see them in my grandfather's house in Warrnambool.' Rodney's mother would mourn the loss of those two boys to the very end of her life. Both were in their early twenties when they died.

The two portraits of long dead soldiers were not the only reminders of the war to young Rodney. The maimed and the crippled were a frequent sight all throughout Rodney's childhood, blokes hobbling on 'crutches with one of his trousers pinned up' or 'the sleeve of a shirt pinned because the arm was missing'. Rodney remembered the gassed men wheezing for breath, and the blind who stumbled about in their darkness. But he also remembered a rare kind of courage:

> I was about 12 at the time when I stopped to watch a game of bowls. One of the players appeared to be a dwarf but I soon saw that he had lost both legs at about the knees. His legs ended in what looked like rubber cushions and he used all four limbs to get from end to end. He protected his hands with wooden blocks which looked like black board dusters, which in those days were common.
>
> This chap saw me looking at him and in a cheery voice called out 'I have an advantage over the others, I am closer to the ball'. I still remember that – in quite fine detail – even after more than seventy years.

OPPOSITE **The feeling of sorrow and loss:** A portrait of Edward Sadler, a dairyman from Allansford who went to war. A portrait of Edward alongside his brother John hung in the family home in Warrnambool in Victoria and Rodney remembered the pictures vividly from when he was a child. Edward was buried in Péronne. A few personal effects – some photographs, cards, a watch, wallet and devotional books were sent home to the family. *DA15403 courtesy Australian War Memorial.*

Rodney started work straight after leaving school. It was 1948 and he came into contact with a number of old 'Digs' on an almost daily basis. He realises now that what he saw in their behaviour was the result of what we'd now call post-traumatic stress. Back then they were just called 'nervy'.

> 'M' was a sergeant in the First AIF in France and was wounded more than once. He wore evidence of one such wound on his face: a massive scar that extended across his face from almost ear to ear. He said something which shocked me at the time – the subject of suicide had come up when he said that he had been buried in a trench collapse, a result of a shell burst nearby, 'I had a side arm and if I had been able to get at it I would have shot myself'. He did not want to suffocate but a couple of his mates dug him out. 'M' drank during the day – every working day it seemed. His job allowed him to move around the city so he made a few 'calls' as he referred to them. He did his job reasonably. He fathered a family and seemed to be on good terms with them.
>
> 'H' was another case altogether. He was able to function for much of the day but lost it sometimes. He was a bad alcoholic who secreted his bottles of booze in hiding places, which became known to the boss 'F', who took them into his office to be returned at knock-off time. 'H' had lost most of his teeth when hit in the face by a sniper's bullet.
>
> 'F' protected 'M' and 'H' from the powers and understood their suffering. 'F' had served in the RAN in the First World War and was typical of how the 'Returned Men' looked out for one another.

Rodney began to work with the Department of Veterans' Affairs in the 1970s. He can still remember many of the cases he dealt with. His job was to help veterans in a broad sense to cope with their injuries. And it wasn't the physical wounds that were the hardest to deal with.

> 'P' was the eldest of a large family who showed great promise before the war. He was commissioned in France but failed to 'settle' back in Australia. He retreated to a bush shack and lived the life of a hermit, except for weekly visits by members of his family who kept him supplied with the necessities of life. He was one of the sad cases, one of the men whose remembering overwhelmed them.

There were men who 'just couldn't cope'. What they had seen and what they had done was simply too much for them. And there were some, he continued, whose memories were so 'stark' that society came to fear them.

> These were the ones who we kept out of sight and out of mind. Most were institutionalised, at Mont Park, for example. While at Veterans' Affairs, I stumbled across a number of cases involving men in institutions

overseas who never came home. We forgot these men completely.
And their war never ended.

Rodney left Veterans' Affairs in 1981. By that time he had worked his way through the ranks of the public service and gained a wealth of experience. Early in his career he went on a cycling tour of France, and journeyed across the same land many of those 'old Digs' had fought on. 'My conversion to pacifism happened then,' he told us, 'when I rode my bike through the mile upon mile of cemeteries that surround Verdun and read the words on headstone after headstone.'

Now in his eighties, Rodney Smith can still visualise those portraits of John and Ed hanging in his grandfather's hallway, two bright young lives full of hope and promise snuffed out on the battlefields of France. And for Rodney there's still a purpose in remembering:

> I fear that 'Lest we Forget' has taken on a very different meaning than when it first entered our consciousness. As we hurry towards 2015 it seems it is being used to promote commercial ventures . . . My concern is that the awfulness of war and its aftermath are slipping away and even conflict is becoming glamorous again. The men of 1914 deserve better than that. At the very least we owe them honesty.[1]

SOURCES AND FURTHER READING: This story is based on a letter written by Rodney Smith to Bruce Scates in response to the One Hundred Stories Project. It also draws on the service dossiers of John and Edward Sadler NAA: B2455, SADLER EDWARD JOHN and NAA: B2455, SADLER JOHN WILLIAM; and their Red Cross Wounded and Missing files, AWM 1DRL/0428.

LEFT **We forgot these men completely:** Amongst the cases Rodney dealt with were the physical and psychological casualties of war; men who lived in repat hospitals, were incarcerated in asylums, or spent years confined to iron beds like this one. Cases that, as Rodney puts it, became almost too painful for society to remember. By exhibiting items like these, Melbourne Museum's 'Love and Sorrow' exhibition invites visitors to grapple with the difficult memories of war. *Courtesy Bruce Scates.*

I have only spoke for my rights

JAMES ARDEN

James Arden volunteered twice for service in the First AIF. On the first occasion, in 1916, he was 43 years of age, a labourer, and described himself as a 'Natural Born British Subject'. The authorities were more explicit the next time: in 1918 a recruiting officer didn't bother to record Arden's height or his weight but bluntly described his complexion as 'Aboriginal'.[1]

Arden and his family had been 'removed' to Lake Condah Mission Station in June 1912. Lake Condah was a government reserve situated on the traditional lands of the Gunditjmara people of western Victoria. Here, so-called 'half-caste' Aboriginal people were provided with rations, clothing and accommodation – if they were well behaved. Defiance of the station manager could lead to expulsion from the settlement, and allowances for 'the natives' were never enough. In 1916 (in the face of a wartime economy), the Victorian Government made the decision to replace clothing only when 'absolutely necessary'. Aboriginal people like James Arden endured the Western District's freezing winter in bare feet, light cotton trousers and threadbare clothing.[2]

Perhaps it was the attraction of regular meals and a decent woollen coat that persuaded Arden to enlist. Perhaps a white man's wage would enable him to provide for his wife and six children. James Arden also belonged to a proud warrior tradition. Gunditjmara people had bravely resisted white incursions on their traditional lands since the mid-nineteenth century.

What was clear from the outset was that James Arden was deeply dissatisfied with the treatment meted out on the station. When he arrived in 1912, there was no furniture or bedding in the small timber hut his family were allocated. Arden was told he was not permitted to wander about the place 'at will', receive visitors from outside, or neglect to send his children to religious services. James Arden protested that these restrictions were a breach of his rights:

[He] announced in a loud voice that he intended writing . . . about the way the Board and Constable Gleeson had treated them in sending them to a place like this without any comforts.

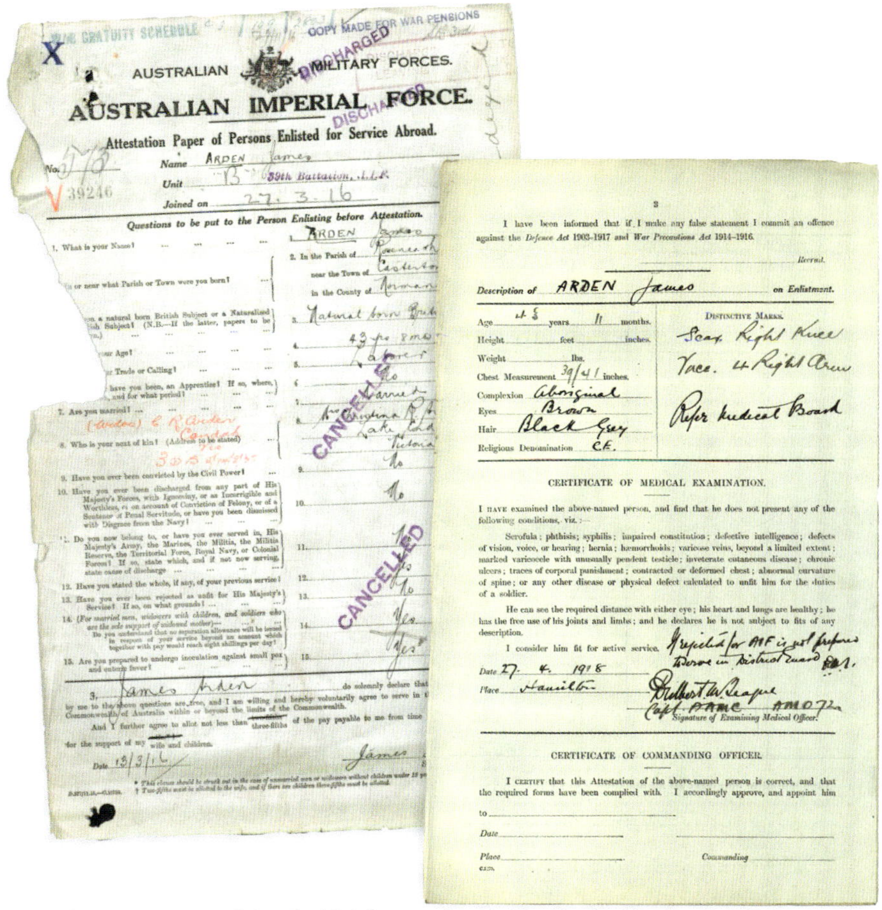

AUSTRALIAN MILITARY FORCES.

AUSTRALIAN IMPERIAL FORCE.

Attestation Paper of Persons Enlisted for Service Abroad.

Name ARDEN James

Joined on 27. 3. 16

Questions to be put to the Person Enlisting before Attestation.

CANCELLED

Description of ARDEN James on Enlistment.

Complexion Aboriginal

Eyes Brown

Hair Black Grey

Religious Denomination C.E.

CERTIFICATE OF MEDICAL EXAMINATION.

CERTIFICATE OF COMMANDING OFFICER.

Arden declared he would be 'frank' and 'straightforward': 'I think Sir I know my place as a man ought to' but 'I have only spoke for my rights' and no one has a right to 'interfere with my family' or 'keep them down under'.

White authorities at the station soon complained that Arden was a troublesome 'native', apt to complain, quick to defy and 'as rude and ruder than I have ever seen any Black'.[3]

It says much about the arbitrary authority of life on a station that James Arden hoped white army officers might be any more mindful of his rights than government-appointed missionaries and officials. Arden marched into Ballarat training camp in March 1916 but never went to war. No sooner had he arrived than he contracted meningitis. After 196 days service he was discharged medically unfit from the Army.

The authorities conceded that Arden contracted meningitis 'as a result of [his] war service'. Its effects were crippling: 'I am not the same man as I was before I left the Station,' he wrote in 1917, 'this sickness has left its marks on me.' Arden complained that he ached from 'head to foot', 'the [hurt] in my head is something awful when it starts to ache, the pains go all through my body'. The effects were mental as much as physical:

I feel tired of life since I got this sickness, I feel I don't care what becomes of me, I am what you call dead weary, the doctor says it will be a very long time before I ever recover and when I do I will never be fit for active service.[4]

With a condition as severe as this, Arden was granted a pension – a little over three pounds a fortnight for himself and his family. He had also accrued back pay – twenty-four pounds in all. It was a pittance for a man with seven dependents, but enough to cause resentment from the authorities. Within a few weeks of his release from hospital, W L Galbraith, Manager of Lake Condah Station, challenged Arden's entitlements:

Arden . . . must [be ordered to] leave the Station immediately, [and] no further rations [should] be supplied [to his family]. This man is strong enough for any class of work and only scheming underhand falsehoods gave him this money. The Ardens are always trying to cause mischief.[5]

ABOVE **Complexion Aboriginal:** The details from James Arden's service dossier. Note the way Arden describes himself as both natural born and a British subject, declaring his Indigenous descent but also claiming the entitlements of white citizenship. Lake Condah Mission (then Arden's place of residence) was officially closed after the First World War, and after the Second World War the land was broken up for soldier settlement. All applications for land from Gunditjmara veterans were refused. It was not until 1984, after a series of legal challenges against the mining company Alcoa, that the government intervened and returned fifty-three hectares of the original Lake Condah reserve to Gunditjmara people. This landmark decision was long overdue recognition of traditional ownership, connection to country and the importance of cultural heritage. *NAA: B2455, ARDEN JAMES courtesy National Archives of Australia.*

At the heart of all this 'mischief' was a challenge to white authority. It wasn't just that Galbraith insisted Arden was a 'healthy, strong native . . . able to earn his living', his idleness was seen as a bad example to others; it undermined the work ethic white authorities laboured to instil in the 'natives'. Galbraith went on:

> *Since Arden received the military pension, he does nothing but drive around the country . . . Arden's home at the present time is a camping ground for natives who will not work and these loafers give me a great deal of worry, annoyance and [come] to the station without [my] permission.*[6]

For her part, Mrs Galbraith, the manager's wife, dutifully compiled instances of that 'rude black's' wilful extravagance:

> *If the Board could daily see the way Ardens waste their £3-2-6 weekly. They would quickly come to the conclusion to move them from the place, Arden's wife's temper and language is intolerable, they come and go as they like, [and] are a curse to the peace of the place. He also intends buying a billiard table, is going to Hamilton to buy £65 piano [and] they have £58-50 in the bank. I have had no peace since he returned [and] their children are dressed in finery far above their station . . . [it] seems dreadful that great fat powerful man with such a income living on government food, meat, milk and butter.*[7]

With both the manager and his wife threatening resignation, the government decided to take action. In February 1917, James Arden received a curt letter from the Board:

> *Re the renewal of your Licence to reside at Lake Condah Station, I am directed by the Board to state that as you are in receipt of a pension from*

the Commonwealth Government in consequence of your being incapacitated in connection with warlike operations, such pension amounting to £3-5-0 per fortnight for your children, it is considered that as you and your family are being maintained by the State, the pension should be handed over to the Board to be utilised in the maintenance of yourself and family or to be held in trust.[8]

It took Arden less than forty-eight hours to respond to the Board's ultimatum. And just like that first day on the Station, he was resolved to 'speak for his rights':

[Y]ou . . . say that the pension I am receiving should be handed over to the Board to be utilised in the maintenance of myself and family or to be held in trust, Sir, I beg to say that I cannot see my way clear to hand my money over to the Board, I think I deserve the money I am getting, no one knows the pains and suffering I underwent with Meningitis and I furthermore state that I have started a banking account of my own, so rather than do what you have asked me to do and hand over my money to the Board, I have made my mind up to remove from here and to leave the Station, I have done all work which was to be done on the place here before I went and enlisted . . .[9]

James Arden found life outside the station was far from easy. Despite the Galbraith's allegations of an extravagant life on the pension, he struggled to provide for his own family, let alone others who came to depend on him. By June 1917, Arden had taken on care of his sister-in-law and her children, another family seeking refuge from the mission. 'I would not see anyone go hungry,' he explained. Nor did a man as weak and sick as James Arden find it easy to find work. Ploughing a field sent pain shooting down his back; his old life as a rural labourer was simply no longer tenable.

BELOW **On the traditional lands of the Gunditjmara people:** A view of the ruins of Lake Condah Mission. The church played a central but divided role on the reserve and elsewhere – an institution Arden's children were forced to attend was embraced by many other members of the community. Despite his earlier differences with white missionaries, Arden would be buried in the church graveyard, and 'Safe in the Arms of Jesus' was one of the hymns sung at the service. The church's restoration is an aim of the Lake Condah Sustainable Development Program, which hopes to promote healing and reconciliation in the community. The original steeple was demolished in the 1950s, long after the station had been resumed for white settlement. *Courtesy Michael Coleman.*

The Arden case tells us much about attitudes towards Indigenous Australians in the early twentieth century. On the one hand, the authorities told Aboriginal people to work hard to advance themselves; on the other, to dress their children 'in finery' or drive about the countryside like a white man was to put on airs 'above their station'. Frugality and independence were all very well, but a bank account of one's own challenged the paternalism on which the authority of the station depended. And whilst the Board was very quick to accept W. L. Galbraith's claim that James Arden was a drunken 'nuisance', there was never any investigation of Arden's claim that both the manager and his wife were all 'too fond of their drink' and 'not fit to manage an aboriginal station'.[10]

When James Arden tried to enlist a second time in 1918, he was rejected as medically unfit by the authorities. He returned to Lake Condah soon after the end of the war. By that time, the station had been disbanded and many Aboriginal families again uprooted and relocated to Lake Tyers Reserve on the other side of Victoria. James Arden died in June 1935 after a long illness related to his war service. By then, he was 68 years of age (one of the 'eldest residents'), still caring for country and occupying the buildings of the old mission. That July, his wife, Christine, wrote to the Repatriation Department asking for a contribution towards her husband's funeral and burial expenses. He was a serviceman, she explained, 'a private soldier ... in the 39th Battalion', and as entitled to that grant as any other veteran. In one last triumph for a man who had always spoken up for his rights, James Arden was buried at government expense.[11]

Gunditjmara Anzacs are still remembered by the community, and Dave Arden assisted by Paul Kelly has put the story of his grandfather to song. The refrain in the chorus of 'Freedom Called' would have met with James Arden's approval: 'When freedom called, Gunditj men and women stood tall.'

SOURCES AND FURTHER READING: The authors respectfully acknowledge the Gunditjmara people of western Victoria and their elders, past and present. This story draws on the service dossiers of James Arden NAA: B2455 ARDEN J; NAA: B2455 ARDEN JAMES; and the Arden family's Aboriginal case file NAA: B337, 28 Arden, James and Family; the Victorian Board for the Protection of Aborigines, Correspondence Files, VPRS1694 units 2, 3 and 4; and contemporary newspaper reports. The authors would like to thank Dave Arden, Damien Bell (CEO of the Gunditj Mirring Traditional Owners Aboriginal Corporation) who kindly facilitated Monash University visits to Budj Bim and the old Mission and Uncle Daryl Rose (of the Budj Bim Indigenous Tour Company) who ably led staff and students over the site. Thanks are also due to Damien Williams, who represented Monash University in this important cultural collaboration. For further reading on the management of the missions see Keith Cole, *The Lake Condah Aboriginal Mission* (Bendigo: Keith Cole Publications, 1984); Jan Critchett, *Untold Stories: Memories and Lives of Victorian Kooris* (Carlton: Melbourne University Press, 1998); Iris Lovett-Gardiner, *Lady of the Lake: Aunty Iris's Story* (Melbourne: Koorie Heritage Trust, 1997) and Aldo Massola, *Aboriginal Mission Stations in Victoria: Yelta, Ebenezer, Ramahyuck, Lake Condah* (Melbourne: Hawthorn Press, 1970). The best introduction to the Gunditjmara's ongoing connection to country is by Gunditjmara people themselves, see The Gunditjmara people with Gib Wettenhall, *The People of Budj Bim: Engineers of Aquaculture, Builders of Stone House Settlements and Warriors Defending Country* (Heywood: EM Press Publishing for the Gunditj Mirring Traditional Owners Aboriginal Corporation, 2010). The authors gratefully acknowledge Jessica Haughton whose work on the Lake Condah and Framlingham settlement suggests rewarding insights into the Indigenous politics of the era. We have also consulted the oral histories from Gunditjmara people available on Radio National Website abc.net.au/missionvoices/lake_condah/. For more information on Dave Arden or to hear 'Freedom Called' see daveaarden.com/.

The first to arrive, the last to leave

ROSE VENN BROWN

Rose Venn Brown was the first Australian woman to sign on for war work in France. She would also be the last to leave.

When war broke out, Rose was working as the Assistant Registrar at Sydney Hospital. Secretarial work was one of the few white-collar occupations open to women in the early twentieth century, even for a woman as well educated, articulate and capable as Rose. At ease with the smart set in Sydney, this woman from Lane Cove had a future. But Rose Venn Brown believed her duty lay elsewhere, and the war offered opportunities all of its own.

Rose procured a passage to London and was 'immediately appointed to the [AIF's] medical records [branch] at Horseferry road'.[1] A month later, she was working for the Red Cross and YMCA, and found herself in France long before the AIF was sent there. Rose was the only Australian woman appointed to the Red Cross staff at Le Havre.

Described as an 'ardent' and 'indefatigable' war worker, she would serve five years in France, acting as a YMCA organiser, a Red Cross Commissioner, and a representative of the war chest. All these voluntary bodies distributed what were called 'comforts' to Allied soldiers: fresh fruit, warm clothing, newspapers and messages from home. Rose knew that every parcel told a story: a mother knitting socks for some other mother's son, a housewife baking biscuits soaked in treacle, a school girl writing letters to a soldier she'd never meet. Every parcel was a package of love as much as it was a way of helping the war effort. They connected families with sons, husbands and lovers far from home.

Rose carried these parcels as close as she could to the battle zones. 'During hostilities,' one paper noted:

ABOVE **As close as she could to the battle zones:** Dressed in her war workers' uniform Rose worked in close proximity to the front line. No other woman (except nurses and ambulances workers) went as far. Note her masculine attire and demeanour. Rose breached conventional expectations of womanhood in more ways than one. Sunday Times, *30 May 1920 courtesy National Library of Australia.*

> *she went to areas where diggers were waiting to go into or coming out of action. These men were cut off from all possibility of comfort, and Miss Venn Brown [made] their conditions less distressful.*

For days and sometimes weeks on end, the young woman intercepted trains of wounded men en route to hospitals behind the lines. She distributed hot coffee to soldiers frozen from the trenches, shared a yarn and perhaps a smoke with men longing for a voice from home.[2]

The creation and distribution of comforts during the war was an enormous physical and emotional labour. In Rose's case, it was an act of courage and selflessness as well. Her willingness to share the dangers and discomforts of the Front won the hearts of Australians, New Zealanders and 'Tommies' alike. And, rather like the sex reformer Ettie Rout, who distributed prophylactic kits to soldiers, Rose 'understood the wants' of ordinary soldiers.

At a time when dry canteens were favoured by military authorities, Rose knew a little alcohol would not go astray. It blunted the memory of a brutal war and kept the cold at bay. In the midst of tragedy, she contrived at frivolity, organising films, acting troupes, and other lively entertainments, competing with the bars and brothels vying for the soldiers' trade.[3]

At war's end, Rose set up a digger's club at Abbeville. She gave it the unlikely title of 'Ye Old Gum Leaf' and encouraged soldiers, anxious for repatriation, to treat it as a home away from home. She also became the first woman to join the War Graves Commission and work in what were called the 'devastated areas'. Ever mindful of an opportunity to help, Rose set up her tent and marquee in the Australian cemetery at Villers-Bretonneux, dispensing tea and good cheer to the men who worked there. She must have been a welcome sight amidst the grim task of bringing in the war dead.

Rose stayed in a village that was not much more than a ruin, and daily walked through a landscape devastated by war. It was 'like living in a grave-yard', she wrote, 'the terrible silence' broken only by explosives 'bursting' deep beneath the earth. But her labours healed a grief even more desolate back in Australia. Miss Venn Brown, the *British Australasian* noted, 'collected photographs of the graves of hundreds of our men buried over there, and sent them home to Australia'. On the graves themselves she planted roses, daisies and forget-me-nots, spreading warmth and colour across the moonscape of the Somme.

Having provided comforts to soldiers at war, Rose Venn Brown now offered comfort to families mourning their loss. '[T]here is nothing I would cherish more,' one mother wrote, 'as the photo of my Darling boy's grave.'[4]

To this day, the Venn Brown's family papers bulge with letters from the grateful and the grieving: 'sorrowing aunts', 'sad lonely mothers', those whose lives 'can never be the same again'. A photo of the cemetery 'brought [them] nearer to [their] loved ones'; 'still as fresh in my mind as when he came to bid me goodbye':

OPPOSITE **Not much more than a ruin:** Evelyn Chapman paints the ruins of Villers-Bretonneux. Chapman arrived in the town some time after Rose Venn Brown had moved there. The town would not be rebuilt until the 1920s and was restored with funds raised in Australia. *E05495 courtesy Australian War Memorial.*

ABOVE **Connecting families with sons, husbands and lovers far from home:** The symbol of the Red Cross framed by a victory laurel. *Courtesy Melbourne Museum.*

> *It is such a great comfort for us to know that someone has cared for my boy's last resting place and . . . pleasant to think that [she] is an Australian.*[5]

Sadly, not all found comfort in Rose's kindness. Hanna Fenwick could not find her brother's name in the list Miss Venn Brown so carefully compiled:

> *[Does that mean] my darling brother is not killed and that he will return to us . . . do try and get some new[s] for me . . . I pray night and day.*[6]

Many of the accolades of Rose Venn Brown's work describe her as a dutiful daughter of Australia. But that description does not quite ring true. Rose had a sense of duty, yes, and a deep belief in the cause of the Empire. But she acted, as many Red Cross workers did, out of a sense of humanity. She provided comfort to anyone, certainly not just Australian or New Zealand troops, who suffered the deprivations of war.

Nor does 'dutiful' quite convey the vitality, independence and initiative of this remarkable woman. After peace was declared, she continued to travel, working for a petroleum company in China, exploring remote parts of Asia, and advocating the interests of Australian trade. She also organised a lecture tour by Captain Flora Sandes, a woman who served in the Serbian Army, was wounded in battle and decorated in the field.

Rose believed there was nothing a woman couldn't do. Miss Venn Brown would never marry but she would work again for soldiers' comforts throughout the Second World War. She died in 1950, back in the town she'd wandered so far from.

SOURCES AND FURTHER READING: This story draws on the Venn Brown Papers held by the Australian War Memorial 2DRL/0598; and a systematic search of the *British Australasian*, and other contemporary newspaper reports in Australia. For an earlier appreciation of Rose Venn Brown's work see Bruce Scates, *Return to Gallipoli: Walking the Battlefields of the Great War* (Cambridge: Cambridge University Press, 2006) and Bart Ziino, *A Distant Grief: Australians, War Graves and the Great War* (Crawley: University of Western Australia Press, 2007).

The man who died twice
DAVID BISSET

David Bisset went to fight the Great War on two separate occasions. In January 1915, the young ironmonger from Aberdeen joined up in Brisbane. Sporting a crop of red hair and bright blue eyes, he spoke with a thick Scottish brogue and gave his religion as Methodist. Bisset's family still lived in Scotland and perhaps David was hoping for a free passage home. If so, he was disappointed – HMAT *Ceramic* sailed via Colombo to Egypt. Private Bisset, or 'Jock' as most of his mates called him, was transferred to the 59th Battalion and sent to join the Australian forces at Tel-el-Kebir.

David Bisset's desert war did not last long. By July, the young man had contracted VD and was sent back to Australia in disgrace. Arriving in Melbourne, he was hurried away to an isolation camp at Langwarrin. The venereal camp was a primitive facility, a hastily assembled collection of huts and tents surrounded by swamps and barbed wire. Here, Bisset received crude medical treatment, but the authorities' main concern was to keep infected men well away from the civilian population. By 1915, Langwarrin's numbers had swelled to several hundred. Escapes were not uncommon.

Bisset left the camp in October and not long after that was posted as a deserter. But he joined up again, this time in Melbourne. Attached to the 57th Battalion, he embarked for a second time in 1915. He served out the rest of the war in France, was wounded by shrapnel in the face, took a few weeks leave in England and spent 108 days out of the line with yet another dose of 'the clap'.

Bisset went twice to war and, as far as his family was concerned, this was a man who died twice as well. In September 1918, he was sent out on patrol in no-man's-land. The party was 'surprised by [machine-gun] fire' and Bisset was cut down near the German wire. His company commander 'saw him fall' and was 'satisfied he was killed'.[1]

The news of Private David Bisset's death in the field was dutifully cabled overseas – one telegram to his sister in Scotland and a second to a fiancée back in

ABOVE **Thou sleepest with the brave:** Aberdeen's war memorial in Scotland. 'Jock' Bisset's name is listed here alongside five thousand others. The lion at the front of the building symbolised the Empire these Scotsman died for, and a memorial supplement, issued to mark the monument's dedication, notes that David Bisset from Hardgate served with the First AIF. *Creative Commons courtesy Bill Harrison.*

Queensland. In Gresham Cottage, Hardgate Street, Aberdeen, and Auchenpine Homestead, Petrie, Queensland, the women David Bisset had known and loved took up the task of mourning.

The authorities realised their mistake when Private Bisset's name turned up in a Red Cross hospital list just a few days before the war ended. It seems he had been taken prisoner by the Germans and sent on for treatment behind the lines. A new round of telegrams was duly sent out from London. 'Thank you for sending so promptly the good news,' a grateful Mary Bisset replied:

> *We have not had any letter or postcard from our brother so that we have no address [to write to him]. Perhaps, in view of the signing of the Armistice, that will not now be necessary. But we shall be very anxious to know to what extent he has been wounded and shall be grateful to have further particulars, should you receive such from Germany.*[2]

On the other side of the world Miss Agnes Gordon was also rejoicing:

> *[We] are engaged to be married that is why I am so anxious to get latest news. It takes so long for news to come through from his next of kin in Scotland [would you] be kind enough to notify me when you get word of his release.*[3]

The news, when it finally came, must have been devastating. The war may have ended, but not the dying or the suffering. Private Bottomley, also from the 57th Battalion, had been sent to the same German hospital in France. Bisset was in a bed not far from him. 'He had been shot in the back,' Bottomley told the Red Cross:

> *[A] bullet had travelled through [his] body and come out at [his] shoulder – His lower limbs were paralysed – when I left on 18th September 1918 they were injecting morphia 3 or 4 times a day. I asked the nurse what she thought. She did not have much hope – I do not think he could have lived.*[4]

Private Bisset's last request was to send a card to his sister in Scotland. It seems it never reached her. But there was another telegram, and two letters from the Red Cross in London. As late as March 1919, a voluntary secretary wrote to Miss Bisset:

> *With further reference to your enquiry for 4000 Pte. DAVID BISSETT [sic] 57th Battalion. A.I.F. We very much regret to inform you that we have received a report about him from our representative, who is now abroad investigating all matters concerning Prisoners of War, and he stated that your brother died on 19.9.18 [in German hands] at No 10 War Hospital.*[5]

A second secretary wrote again three months later. She corrected the spelling of the dead man's name, confirmed that he had died of 'catarrh of the bowels', gave the name of the cemetery in France where he lay, and provided the exact location of the grave. Her sparse prose and precise geography was no doubt intentional.[6] The man who had died twice would not be allowed to die a third time.

And what of his fiancée? On the first anniversary of David Bisset's death, Agnes Gordon placed an obituary in *The Brisbane Courier* along with a companion notice written by her parents, also Scottish. It pledged 'loving memory' to a man mostly known as 'Jock'. The words Agnes chose suggest she knew nothing of the disease David contracted while at war. Perhaps his hasty re-enlistment was a bid to avoid awkward questions in Australia.

Neither Agnes nor her parents alluded to hopes raised and shattered in the confusion of war. Memorial columns were not the place to harbour doubt or disappointment. 'Rest thou with honour', the entry in the *Courier*'s Honour Roll reads, 'For thou sleepest with the brave'.[7]

SOURCES AND FURTHER READING: This story draws on the service dossier of David Bisset NAA: B2455 BISSET D; his Red Cross Wounded and Missing file AWM 1DRL/0428; and contemporary newspaper reports. For conditions at Langwarrin Camp see Judith Smart, '"Sex, the State and the 'Scarlet Scourge": Gender, Citizenship and Venereal Diseases Regulation in Australia during the Great War', *Women's History Review*, vol. 7, no. 1, pp. 5–36; and Raden Dunbar, *Secrets of the Anzacs* (Melbourne: Scribe, 2014). The authors acknowledge Jo Kildea's 'Miss Chomley and her Prisoners: The Prisoner of War Experience and the Australian Red Cross in the Great War' (BA honours thesis, University of New South Wales, 2006).

Attempting the impossible
FREDERICK WEIR

Frederick Weir returned to Adelaide in 1918. He was just 22 when he joined the Army and much of his adult life had been spent at war. For almost four years he'd served with the 4th Field Ambulance in the Middle East, Belgium and France. Weir had nursed the injured of Fromelles, the Menin Road and Passchendaele, patching together pieces of men brought in from the battlefield. He'd also succumbed to enteric fever, contracted VD, and been jailed for drunkenness and insubordination.

Weir's service dossier suggests he was too ill-disciplined to take to the life of a soldier – or perhaps too badly damaged. His return to civilian life was never going to be easy. In January 1919, medical staff at Keswick Barracks in Adelaide reported that Frederick Weir had been drinking 'for a couple of days'. There was a tremor in his hands and he was 'restless, maniacal and had delusions'. The 'nervy' Weir complained of 'wireless affecting his head'. It may have been the DTs of course, but the doctors conceded that the young man's alcoholism was 'aggravated by war service'.[1]

Men like Weir were in need of a fresh start, and a place far from liquor. After a time in Adelaide's repatriation workshops, Frederick moved to New South Wales and took up a soldier settlement block in Tallong, forty kilometres from Goulburn. His young wife, Elizabeth, went with him.

Frederick Weir struck Inspector Albert Smith as a 'trier'. Here was a 'nerve stricken soldier' determined to make a go of it. The problem was that Weir had 'attempted . . . the impossible'. As an orchard, his land was absolutely worthless, 'not worth a shilling' in Smith's careful estimation. Given 'a fair chance' Weir might 'make good', but to imagine so poor a block could ever offer a living was yet another 'delusion'. 'He thinks of going in for cows and pigs,' Smith noted. 'I feel that the place would not support a rat.' Inspector Smith urged abandoning the property immediately – 'starvation is the only alternative'.[2]

We don't know why Weir stayed on in Tallong. But, having invested his gratuity in an overpriced and now unsaleable block, there was probably little option. For three years the debts mounted. Then, a man who'd survived the deserts of the Middle East and the killing fields of Flanders loaded his rifle and shot himself.

Inspector Smith returned to the block not long after Weir's suicide. He wrote to the Lands Department in Sydney:

> *I inspected this place three years ago. The orchard has improved since that date, but is still hopeless. Mr Weir has put a lot of work into the orchard since my first inspection and made an effort to succeed. Their chance of success from the outset was nil, and the financial embarrassment in which Mr Weir found himself was in no way due to his lack of effort to try . . .* [3]

But trying wasn't quite enough. 'The case generally is an unfortunate and distressing one,' Smith told his superiors. It seemed easier to blame a 'nerve stricken' soldier's 'bad business sense' than a system that put damaged men on land never fit for farming.[4]

Elizabeth Weir managed as best she could after her husband killed himself. A bit of a 'trier' herself, she wanted to carry on with the orchard 'and at the same time [run] a boarding house'. Mrs Weir had no children to help her, no capital and no prospects. Inspector Smith judged it 'a kindness' to write off her husband's debts and repossess the holding. There would be nothing to show for three years of labour.[5]

For decades to come Elizabeth Weir lived a life of penury on a pension, eking out a living from rooms she let in Randwick. In the midst of the Second World War, she wrote one last time to the Department. Still insistently polite, she apologised for trespassing on their 'valuable time'. But had her husband's Returned Soldier's Badge been found, she asked, as she longed to have it for 'purely sentimental' reasons. Mrs Weir signed herself 'Widow' – her identity still bound up with that of a man who had taken his own life thirty years earlier.[6]

Today, Frederick Weir's grave lies in a forgotten corner of Tallong Cemetery. His tombstone borders the bush, isolated from all the graves around it. There is no epitaph and even his name is now barely decipherable. In Tallong township, a marble plaque propped beside the memorial hall honours the men of the district who fought 'for human rights'.

SOURCES AND FURTHER READING: This story draws on the service dossier of Frederick Weir NAA: B2455, WEIR FREDERICK ROBERT; and his soldier settlement file State Records NSW: 12/7286 8093. Frederick Weir's repatriation record is not yet available. For a detailed account of the trials of soldier settlers in New South Wales see Bruce Scates and Melanie Oppenheimer, *The Last Battle of the Great War: Soldier Settlement in Australia* (Cambridge: Cambridge University Press, forthcoming) The authors would also like to thank Catherine Tiernan for her valuable assistance in compiling this piece.

ABOVE **Not worth a shilling:** Fred Weir's neglected grave in Tallong Cemetery. Much of the surrounding land – land Weir struggled to work – was described as worthless. This tombstone was raised at departmental expense. Its inscription has been weathered by the elements. *Courtesy Bruce Scates.*

OPPOSITE **Purely sentimental reasons:** The Returned Serviceman's Badge. Veterans of the Great War wore the badge for many reasons. It was a symbol of sacrifice, and identified them as men who had served overseas. It carried with it the promise of respect and preferential employment, and signalled a common affinity with other returned soldiers. The badge distinguished returned men from 'the shirkers' who had stayed behind. Mrs Weir's 'sentimental' attachment to the badge may have been a way of connecting to a defining period of her husband's troubled life, a world she could never truly be a part of. The widow of this returned man experienced battles all of her own. *REL34983 courtesy Australian War Memorial.*

The angel of the prison camps

MARY CHOMLEY

Nearly four thousand Australian troops were taken prisoner on the Western Front. Conditions differed in every camp, but by the end of the war the situation for all POWs was appalling.

Contrary to the Geneva Conventions, men were put to work at the Front. Across Germany, POWs were forced to work on 'commandos'. They felled forests, tilled fields and toiled in salt mines to aid the Central Powers' war effort. 'We are having a bad time just now,' Private George Anderson of the 47th Battalion wrote from a stone quarry in Friedrichsfeld:

> *[O]ur work is getting heavier. We used to load [rock onto] four wagons a day, but that has been increased . . . We work [everyday now] from 6 [in the morning] till we are done, that may mean any time between seven or eight o'clock at night. The work is killing the poor boys.*

OPPOSITE **Methodical and efficient:** Mary Chomley in her Red Cross uniform towards the end of the war. Although men described her as the 'Angel of the prison camps' this image adopts a masculine pose of power and control. Women like Miss Chomley challenged Edwardian conventions of femininity, claiming an authority and a purpose seldom seen before wartime. Note the Rising Sun badge pinned to her lapel. Mary Chomley was at once ardently imperialist and proudly Australian. *H2013.231/54 courtesy State Library of Victoria.*

Private Anderson believed the Germans were intent on 'getting the last drop of blood' out of them. That was the 'only reason' they took prisoners, he claimed, 'not for any act of humanity, but because, we are useful to them'.[1] George Anderson's boots were broken on the sharp stone of the quarry, his clothing was ragged, and he was 'gaunt, unwashed, unshaven, devoured by vermin'.[2]

Anderson complained that 'a matter of fact pigs are fed better at home' than they were.[3] The rations issued to prisoners at Strohen camp were fairly typical. Once a day men were given a meal of a thin soup – there was little nourishment in it. Their bread was adulterated with sawdust and they drank burnt barley as a coffee substitute or tea made of leaves and grass. The only meat prisoners tasted was horse flesh, from animals who had died of exhaustion or been 'badly blown about at the front'.[4]

ABOVE **Miss Chomley and 'her girls':** The Red Cross Prisoner of War Department assembled outside their headquarters in London. Fur stoles, handsome hats and smart uniforms remind us of the relatively privileged background of most Australian volunteers in London. The girls relegated to the back row are dressed more modestly. Perhaps they were part of the paid staff – but young ladies also donned working clothes and pitched into the war effort. Note the shadowy figures gazing out from the window – keen to be part of the picture. *H2013.234/7 courtesy State Library of Victoria.*

What comfort came to these men? Who kept them alive in such horrendous conditions?

In 1916, Mary Elizabeth Chomley established the Red Cross Prisoner of War Department in London. She had journeyed to Britain at the outbreak of war, determined to 'do her bit' for Australia and the Empire. Methodical, efficient and with an insatiable appetite for work, Miss Chomely managed a team of around thirty volunteers. Most, like her, were expatriate women from Australia; many had sons, brothers or husbands serving overseas.

The Red Cross Prisoner of War Department packed parcels of food, medicine and clothing and sent them to prisoners languishing in Germany. Though every package varied, each usually contained tea, tobacco, butter, biscuits, bread, sugar, condensed milk, cheese, camp pie and sometimes dripping.

Thousands of these parcels were dispatched every week to prisoner of war camps across Europe. They kept these hungry men alive and buoyed their spirits: 'You know dear Lady,' George Anderson wrote to Miss Chomley:

> *your parcels are the only link between the Motherland and despair, without them we should be mere human wrecks and many of the poor lads would be beneath the turf.*[5]

With 'the precision of a watch maker' Miss Chomley established eight separate card indexes, carefully tracking every parcel sent from London.[6] She helped process over twenty thousand letters every month, personally answering many herself. Miss Chomley made sure the medical needs and personal requests of every man were dealt with. 'Your choice and selection and packing of parcels leaves nothing to be desired,' Private Hubert Berning told Miss Chomley:

> *[It] speaks volumes for the care you take of us poor exiles. And I am pleased to note you are not sending us any Flemington Dripping. I've noticed that Victorian produce has not been up to the same standard as the other states. Baynes bros. Queensland Dripping tops the list . . .*

Quality dripping wasn't the only thing that took Private Berning's fancy:

> *Could you send me some Australian sporting news, very anxious to know who won last Melbourne Cup, also all other principal races of this year, any and all kinds of sporting news would be very welcome.*[7]

Men asked for books (Henry Lawson and Banjo Patterson the favourites), described tinned butter as a 'great treat' and pleaded for more tobacco. Gunner Roy McNeill, a student from Auckland, wondered if he was 'asking a little too much' to request a decent football.[8] 'I have to thank you for your kindness in writing to my people in New Zealand,' he added to his request, '[and] thank you for the splendid relief work done by your Society.'[9]

In more ways than one, Miss Chomley and her 'girls' built a lifeline to Australia. Chomley arranged for lonely prisoners to be 'adopted' by Australians back home, and restored men to families far away, resuming conversations cut short by captivity. Lance Corporal Angelo was one such case:

> *If I am not asking too much, could you drop a line to my dear mother and say you have heard from me, as I am afraid she is not getting my letters and is very anxious, she would think so much of it, getting a letter from you after all your kindness to me.*

Thanks to Miss Chomley's index cards, correspondence travelled both ways across the oceans. 'Letters from home!' Tommy Taylor, a farmer from Victoria declared:

> *You can't imagine what it meant to us. 15 weary months knowing practically nothing of what was going on behind . . . wire enclosures; seemingly dead to the world, and for all we know, mourned as dead; would we ever see our loved ones again? . . . And at last to see the old familiar handwriting; to be brought into touch with the outer world. At sight of those letters I broke down completely.*[10]

In the absence of mail from home, men were very grateful for a letter from Miss Chomley. 'I am glad to hear that you are from Victoria also,' Sapper Lawry wrote in the freezing winter of 1917:

> *I know all the places you mention . . . I was born at Daylesford but lately have lived in town at Albert Park and Middle Brighton and at the time of enlisting was on the staff at the St. Kilda to Brighton Electric Tramway Station. I shall be glad to get back again. Oh for an afternoon on 'the block' or a Saturday night at St. Kilda . . .* [11]

In the darkest of days, men sent their love to sunny Australia and longed for the day that 'this cruel war was over'.[12]

Men dubbed Miss Chomley 'the Angel of the prison camps'.[13] They called themselves her 'big family of boys' and addressed her as they would their mother.[14] Many sent their photographs. All longed to meet her: 'I know you take a great interest in all our doings here,' Wat Findlay declared:

> *especially your own boys – the 'Aussies'. One has to be a prisoner of war to realise and appreciate what [you] are to us. We do appreciate everything you do . . . especially as we know it is a labour of love. . . Ask any Australian here what he is going to do directly when he arrives in England – and what do you hear? – 'Go direct to the Red Cross and meet Miss Chomley' – 'I want to see her myself' – 'She's the goods' etc. and so Miss Chomley I hope before long to have that pleasure of 'seeing her myself'.* [15]

Miss Chomley saved these men from absolute privation and despair. But she couldn't help everyone.

The British Red Cross offered relief to 'British' troops alone. Disowned by the Bolshevik Government, Russian prisoners suffered in their thousands. Nor could Miss Chomley extend comfort to the enemy. By the end of the war, the German Army fought while on the verge of starvation – that was one of the reasons prisoners were treated so badly. Guards scavenged in bins for scraps from prisoners' parcels while, blockaded by the Allied navies, the country was starved into submission. It is estimated that over 700 000 women and children died of exhaustion and malnutrition during the Allied blockade.

Not all of Miss Chomley's 'boys' survived the war. Although 2682 prisoners of war returned to Australia, around 8 per cent died in captivity in Germany, most of wounds received in the fighting.

Miss Chomley was awarded an OBE for her war work, but not everyone was prepared to award a woman her fair share of recognition. Mary Chomley's name was somehow omitted in *The Official History of Australia in the War*, and management of the Red Cross Prisoner of War Department was attributed to a Mr Fairburn.

Even so, the parents of prisoners knew where the real credit lay. 'We Australians will never forget,' one mother wrote:

[We] will treasure you forever in our memories. [We had] five months of worry and anxious waiting until we heard [of our] son through your society. We were supported by the knowledge you would always keep him in sight, he would be taken care of and supplied to the utmost of your power. However can we thank you.[16]

ABOVE LEFT **A lifeline to Australia:** Red Cross workers pack parcels for the camps. Most found their way to their British prisoners – despite starving themselves towards the end of the war, German troops respected the work of the Red Cross and seldom pillaged the contents. *H07977 courtesy Australian War Memorial.*

ABOVE RIGHT **I hope I have the pleasure:** The Howard brothers from Norwood, South Australia send a signed studio portrait of themselves to Miss Chomley. Albert Howard (seated) was one of Miss Chomley's 'big family of boys'. He enlisted at the age of 22, served at Gallipoli and was wounded in both arms at Mouquet Farm in August 1916. It is unclear whether Albert actually met Miss Chomley but he certainly believed he had her to thank for surviving the war. *P03236.065 courtesy Australian War Memorial.*

SOURCES AND FURTHER READING: This entry is based on prisoners' letters sent to Miss Chomley and the Australian-British Red Cross in AWM: 1DRL615 [749/19/20]; statements by repatriated prisoners AWM 30; and the Chomley Papers held in the State Library of Victoria MS 11000 and in the Red Cross Archives in both London and Melbourne. The most extensive treatment of Miss Chomley's life and work can be found in Josephine Kildea's honours thesis, 'Miss Chomley and her Prisoners: the Prisoner of War Experience and the Australian Red Cross in the Great War (BA honours thesis, University of New South Wales, 2006). Other useful sources include Nola Anderson, 'Dear Miss Chomley', *Wartime*, no. 21, pp. 44–46; Joan Beaumont, 'Whatever Happened to Patriotic Women, 1914-1918?', *Australian Historical Studies*, vol. 31, no. 115, 2000, pp. 273–286 and Melanie Oppenheimer, *The Power of Humanity: 100 Years of the Australian Red Cross* (Sydney: HarperCollins Australia, 2014). The authors thank Jane High of the British Red Cross for her help in accessing records in London.

Asleep in the deep
GORDON CORBOULD

BELOW **Australia's first submarine:** The *AE1* cuts her way through the water. Gordon Corbould may well be one of the sailors standing on the deck. The submarine was lost with all hands within weeks of war being declared. *H91.250/1435 courtesy State Library of Victoria.*

Leading Seaman Gordon Corbould was the first and only son of Ernst and Alice Corbould of Epping, New South Wales. He served on the *AE1*, Australia's first submarine, and took part in the capture of German New Guinea in Australia's first military engagement of the Great War.

Gordon was not much more than a boy when he first went to sea. His baby cheeks, soft features and deep brown eyes look back at you from one surviving photograph. Gordon travelled in the company of thirty-four other submariners, some, like him, from humble backgrounds in Australia, eighteen from the United Kingdom (seconded by the British Navy) and two, Able Seamen Reardon and Woodland, from Aotearoa/New Zealand.

On 14 September 1914, the *AE1* went out on patrol and was never seen again. No trace has ever been found of her or any of her crew. The thirty-five men of the *AE1* left seventeen widows, and over thirty children fatherless. With the loss of a single vessel all these families lost their major means of support.

Many of the unmarried men had also provided for their families. James Fettes, a mechanic who worked in the ill-fated vessel's engine room, regularly sent his mother most of his pay. With a father who was 62 years of age and 'practically an invalid', three sisters (one 'an imbecile', another sickly and a third earning less than ten shillings a week), James was the family's principal breadwinner.[1]

Stoker John Bray's father had been killed in a

mining accident, and his mother, 'in failing health and poor circumstances', relied on him to feed four younger siblings.[2] And then there was Gordon. Charles Thomas, Rector of St Alban's Anglican Church, Epping, told the naval authorities that Gordon's father had deserted his mother and sent nothing towards the family's upkeep. '[Alice's] only son lost on the submarine was her sole support.'[3] The sinking of a submarine with the loss of all hands was not a tragedy confined to itself, it left a great surge of hardship and suffering in its wake.

In time, the families received some assistance. The men of HMAS *Australia* took up a collection (it was a naval tradition to do so) and the lost men's pensions were granted to their next-of-kin. But the money was rarely equal to the cost of raising a family; emotionally vulnerable, the young widows and aging mothers struggled with financial worry.

Not all the families of the *AE1*'s crew were left wanting, at least not in the material sense. The submarine's commander was a senior officer in the Royal Navy. His kit, left behind on the *AE1*'s storeship, included a riding crop and opera hat, golf clubs, camera, twenty-five volumes of books and a silver whisky flask. Lieutenant Commander Besant's kit, his frock coats and his Masonic regalia were shipped home in four separate cases to his family in England.

Only one parcel of clothing was sent to Alice Corbould, and it lay forgotten for weeks on a railway platform in Epping.

ABOVE **Not much more than a boy:** A studio portrait taken of Gordon not long before his ill-fated voyage. Sydney City Mission Herald, *1 December 1914 courtesy State Library of New South Wales.*

Gordon Corbould may have come from a poor and broken family, but even the most desperate families felt the need to grieve. Every September, despite the expense, the Corboulds placed an obituary for Gordon in *The Sydney Morning Herald*. The first appeared on the anniversary of the *AE1*'s loss: 'In loving memory of Gordon Corbould and his comrades . . . Asleep in the deep.'[4] The last was published in 1954, forty years after Gordon vanished.

SOURCES AND FURTHER READING: In the absence of a service dossier, this story draws on contemporary newspaper reports; the Australian War Memorial's file related to the loss of *AE1* AWM 50, 18/2; and a short biography on Gordon published in the *Sydney City Morning Herald*, 1 December 1914. For an introduction to the mystery surrounding the *AE1* see Benjamin Evans, 'The loss of the *AE1*', *Wartime*, vol. 16, 2001, pp. 10–13.

Conscription by stealth

GIOVANNI FERRANDO

Australians fought to defend democracy during the Great War. But the greatest triumph of democratic values wasn't on distant battlefields in Europe, it was in the polling booths back home. In 1916 and 1917, in two bitterly contested referenda, the Australian people voted against conscription. Great Britain introduced compulsory military service after the slaughter of the Somme, and most of her dominions did the same soon after. Australia would have the distinction of fielding one of the few volunteer armies in the world. No man would be forced to die or kill for his country.

Australian citizens may not have been forced to fight, but what of those born outside Australia? In 1914, the Italian community in Australia numbered several thousand. Most worked in the cane fields of Queensland and the remote minefields in Western Australia. It was poorly paid labour, work many Australians of British descent thought beneath them. But the Italian community made a crucial contribution to the national economy, and their clubs, restaurants, music schools and academies enlivened and diversified a largely Anglophile culture.

Italy entered the war in 1915. Italian citizens in Australia were immediately invited to join the colours. In 1916, the Australian Government offered space on AIF transports to take reservists to Europe. Then came conscription. As Rome faced one military disaster after another on a mountainous northern frontier, the Italian consulate in Melbourne called up male citizens aged between 18 and 43. They were to report for a medical assessment and, if deemed fit, they were dispatched to holding camps run by the Australian Army. Those who failed to comply, a sternly worded directive warned, 'will be considered guilty of desertion and coercive measures prescribed by law will be taken against them.'[1]

The Australian Government was to be the instrument of that coercion. And a willing instrument at that. Rebuked by defeat in the conscription referenda, the

Nationalist Government under Billy Hughes did all in its power to compel Italian citizens to serve. Some accepted their fate, answering 'with a heavy heart' the 'urgent call of their mother county'; others were persuaded by promises of support for the families they left behind; and some were forcibly deported, Giovanni Ferrando amongst them.[2]

Conscription in Australia

Italians Deported

Australians Next

Those people in Australia who believed that the issue of Conscription, having been twice voted upon and turned down by the people, was dead, and that no Government, purporting to represent a democracy, would dare enforce it until the people had had an opportunity of reversing their decision, and had actually reversed it, must receive a rude shock when they learn that the Cabinet, behind Parliament's back, and with the utmost secrecy, is **ENFORCING CONSCRIPTION AGAINST A SECTION OF THIS COMMUNITY**, and forcibly deporting those affected by their War Precaution Regulation, and ordering them to thereafter remain out of Australia.

Naturally, the Italians, who are the first victims, are protesting against this gross violation of the people's will, and of the Government's pledge to accept their verdict; but the Government, by means of the censorship, has **FORBIDDEN THE PUBLICATION IN THE PRESS AND ELSEWHERE** of any mention of this protest. True to its principles and solid in its opposition to the hateful system of conscription, the Labor party of Australia has taken up the issue, and in every State of the Commonwealth vast meetings of protest **ARE BEING HELD AND WILL BE HELD.**

It is believed that this secret action of the Government is a "TRY-ON," and if the people of Australia take it "LYING DOWN," then it will be an easy step to conscript Australians as well.

ABOVE **Coercive measures prescribed by law:** A leaflet produced by the radical press and distributed in Sydney. The War Precautions Act entailed a massive curtailment of the freedom of the press. Leaflets like this could be confiscated and those distributing them imprisoned, their actions deemed 'prejudicial to recruitment'. *NAA: MP367/1, 592/4/295 courtesy National Archives of Australia.*

Signor Ferrando was a former consul for the Kingdom of Italy, a successful businessman and twenty-two years an Australian resident. He had volunteered for service in the early days of the war, only to be classed as medically unfit, suited only for what was called 'sedentary service'. By 1918, his health had further deteriorated. Medical officers noted with concern a weak heart and a nervous condition, and at the time of the call-up Ferrando was recovering from a serious operation. But that did not lesson the resolve of either the Italian Consul, Signor Eles, or the Australian Minister for Defence, Senator George Pearce. The former was a professional rival of Giovanni Fernando's, 'activated', some said, 'by spite' and 'petty jealousies'. Eles was determined to support his beleaguered Italian allies and willing to make an example of this well-connected 'shirker'. Ferrando was told to leave Broadmeadows Military Hospital for service in Italy. He refused to do so. Pearce exercised executive powers under the War Precautions Act and ordered his immediate deportation.[3]

The Ferrando case made the headlines in Australia. He appealed to the High Court against the deportation order, protested at the curtailment of his liberty and claimed military authorities boasted of 'rounding up' all his countrymen.[4] Fernando was 41 at the time of his arrest – over the age limit for deportation under a treaty signed by the British and Italian governments. Even so, with one dissenting judgment, the High Court upheld the government's decision. Ferrando was sent under escort to a transport ship leaving for Europe.

The same labour movement that had rallied against conscription viewed the attack on the Italian community as an 'outrage'. 'This country has twice refused conscription,' Percy Brookfield, MLA, told a gathering in Sydney's Town Hall, 'it is up to us to see that none of us are deported against our will.'

Further to the left of the political spectrum, the Industrial Workers of the World and the Australian Socialist Party warned deportation orders were 'conscription by stealth' and that the same coercive measures would soon be turned against Australian workers. Within the Italian community there was a small subversive element. Intelligence officers described Felice Corro as a 'foreign agitator', whose language was as immoderate as his appearance. Subject is dressed in 'the revolutionary attire of the Italian Republicano' 'a red shirt, green sash and black handkerchief around the neck'.

Corro . . . addressed the meeting in both Italian and English language, and exhorted his hearers to make every effort to prevent the deportation of Italian citizens . . . and resist it to their last drop of blood. [He] would be willing to wear the revolutionary uniform and march in procession to the Domain on Sunday next, when the Anniversary of Garribaldi's(sic) birth would be celebrated with Garribaldian [sic] Songs and Music.[5]

The deportation of Giovanni Fernando is a stark illustration of how the political climate in Australia drifted to extremes in the final years of the war. The conscription referenda, the great strike of 1917, and the draconian exercise of government powers under the War Precautions Act, created an atmosphere of crisis and fostered bitter divisions. In this particular case it served no real purpose. On arrival in Italy, Giovanni Ferrando was again deemed unfit for service, decorated by the King for his services to Italy and duly returned to Australia.

At the end of the war, Ferrando sued both Senator Pearce and the (then) Italian Consul for damages. '[I]n applying deportation to all the Italians and especially to a man like me,' he explained, 'the Australian government . . . Committed the greatest blunder ever made amounting to cruelty . . . suffering [and] humiliation.'[6]

Deportation had damaged his reputation, ruined his health and caused considerable financial loss. But an even greater price was paid by those Italians deported to fight 'the white war' in the frozen heights of the mountains. A good many of those men never returned to their families. Seven hundred thousand Italian soldiers died during the Great War, over ten times the AIF's losses.

Giovanni Ferrando lost his case against the Australian Government. Many foreign nationals active in the labour movement were deported and in the wake of the Great War, nationalist governments encouraged renewed British immigration to Australia. Australia in the 1920s remained bitterly divided. We had emerged from the Great War a less tolerant and less inclusive society.

SOURCES AND FURTHER READING: This story draws on intelligence records held in the National Archives of Australia NAA MP367/1; and contemporary newspaper reports. For political divisions during the Great War see Ian Turner, *Industrial Labour and Politics: the Dynamics of the Labour Movement in Eastern Australia, 1900–1921* (Sydney: Hale and Iremonger, 1979); Robert Bolard, *In the Shadow of Gallipoli: The Hidden History of Australia in World War I* (Sydney: Newsouth, 2013) and Joan Beaumont, *Broken Nation:Australians in the Great War* (Sydney: Allen & Unwin, 2013). For an account of the fighting on the Italian front see Mark Thompson, *The White War: Life and Death on the Western Front* (London: Faber & Faber, 2008) and for further background on the Ferrando case see 'Captive Allies: Italian Immigrants in World War One Australia' Karen Agutter, Close NLA, 2009, nla.gov.au/openpublish/index.php/australian-studies/article/view/1558/1865.

Hard up against it

DENNIS (PADDY) HAUENSTEIN

Dennis Hauenstein never thought of himself as a hero. 'I am as ugly as they make them,' he'd written home during the war, 'and the makings of a rotten hero.'[1] In truth, Paddy (as he liked to be called) was rather handsome in a rugged kind of way. Six feet tall, a talented rower, wrestler and runner, he quickly gained renown as one of the 'crack athletes of the army'.[2] Out in the field, Hauenstein served with distinction. Attached to the 1st Field Ambulance, he worked as a stretcher-bearer on the Somme and found himself selected for officer training in England.

Even when they sent Paddy back to 'Blighty', wounded by shrapnel and stricken with rheumatic fever, the young man continued to excel, playing for the West of England XV. And Paddy's physical prowess was matched with equal courage. Far from being a 'rotten hero', one general thought, 'there were no braver man on God's earth'[3] than Paddy Hauenstein.

Lieutenant Hauenstein survived the war, but coping with the peace proved quite a different matter. On his return to Australia, Paddy found work wherever he could. Always 'a trier', he scratched out a living rabbiting, building and painting. But for Paddy, and many more like him, it was a case of one step forward and two back. Long before the Great Depression of the 1930s, jobs were hard to find in Australia. Drought, economic uncertainty, and a glut of returned men on the market meant getting ahead was pretty unlikely.[4]

By February 1923, Paddy had been six months without work. The banks had closed on him and people all around town were chasing him for money. Paddy couldn't provide for his wife, Grace, let alone

BELOW **Australia owes these bonny youngsters something:** Grace Hauenstein and her children pictured in an appeal for charity, 'the family of a man who never had a chance'.[7] Evening News, *23 February 1923 courtesy National Library of Australia.*

their four young children. It hurt his pride not to be able to pay the bills and it broke his heart to see the kiddies hungry. Paddy felt he had failed as a husband, a father, and a man. He decided to take drastic measures.

Late one Tuesday in February 1923, Paddy waited outside the Government Savings Bank in Hurlstone Park. It was a sunny afternoon, so he stood in the shadows, watching from the street, waiting for his chance. When the last customer left, Paddy moved quickly. Creeping through the building, he could see the manager counting that day's takings. That money seemed the answer to everything.

Paddy rushed at the counter and grabbed the manager by the throat. He hit him in the head, knocked him to the ground and punched the man repeatedly. Partly it was desperation, partly fear and panic, and partly his training. In a matter of moments, Paddy had overwhelmed the manager, clutched him firmly round the throat and planted his knees on the man's chest. The manager called out to his wife for help and in an all too familiar rush of adrenaline, Paddy broke away from the scuffle and fled from the building.

Paddy ran away from the town towards Canterbury Racecourse. It was a good stretch and all the way the police were gaining on him. At the racetrack the exhausted, starving man surrendered meekly to arresting officers.

'I am desperate and hard up against it,' he told them. 'That job looked easy, and I thought I would give it a go but . . . a woman came on the scene and that settled it.' Paddy panted loudly between each sentence, still struggling to catch his breath. 'It's not for myself that I care; it's for the wife and kids.'[5]

Soon after arriving at the police station, Paddy buckled over. His breathing was even more erratic now and he clutched at his stomach. 'It is all over,' he said, 'let me go, do not try to save me.' Paddy fell to the ground, lurching with convulsions, and died just a few minutes later. He'd swallowed poison as he watched the police close in on him – the only way out for a man unwilling to rot in prison. And as Paddy himself had said, the wife and children would probably be better off without him. His last wish was that someone say goodbye for him.

Paddy's crime and his death shocked the community. He was eulogised in the press, 'a good soldier, a good husband and father, and, until his fatal lapse . . . a good citizen.'[6] A public subscription was raised to help his family – Paddy's children were aged 15 months, 9, 11 and 13 years old. 'Australia,' the papers piously announced, 'owes these bonny youngsters something.' The money flooded in, over two hundred pounds, deferring, at least for a few years, absolute destitution for the widow and her children. But help had come far too late for Paddy Hauenstein.

SOURCES AND FURTHER READING: This account is based on contemporary newspaper reports and Paddy Hauenstein's service dossier NAA: B2455, HAUENSTEIN Dennis Dunbar. For further reading on readjusting to life after the war see Marina Larsson, *Shattered Anzacs: Living with the Scars of War* (Sydney: University of New South Wales Press, 2009).

In a special way
ELSIE TRANTER

Elsie Tranter's journal was the place she kept her secrets. By lamplight late at night, or in the quiet times in the ward, she recorded things that Matron or her parents would never chance to see.

Like many of the young women who went overseas as nurses, Elsie's service began as a great adventure. The girl from Geelong watched with wonder as sunsets splashed colour on the ocean; thrilled at the sight of new lands and ancient cultures; recorded, with not a little interest, handsome black men, 'finely built' and virtually naked, diving 'beautifully' into the sea.[1]

Elsie's journal is the place she dreamed of romance, confessed to thoughts a Baptist girl was bound to think a little 'wicked', and described 'all sorts of tricks' to 'steal a few minutes conversation with one of the "forbidden diggers"'.[2] Elsie was well aware the Army forbade fraternisation with enlisted men, 'but we don't take very much notice of that rule so perhaps they will send us home in disgrace'.[3]

The tempo of the diary changes when Elsie arrives in France. Her first posting was at Étaples, a base hospital for 'badly wounded cases' and the site of a large training camp for British and dominion troops. 'Thousands of men pass by each day,' she wrote:

> *Daily we sing 'Goodbye' and 'Goodluck' to them with their full kit on their way to that well known place just up the line.*

There was a continual 'thump thump' all day long. Within weeks the same men she flirted with would come back to her, convoys of wounded, 'all frightfully mutilated'. 'One Australian boy had twenty-two wounds' she noted in her diary, his body so badly damaged 'it would not be possible for one person to dress him'.[4] 'Can you form any idea of the work that goes on and the suffering?' she writes. 'It makes one's heart ache.'[5]

In the midst of the cruelty of war, Elsie's diary was a space for tenderness and compassion. The same hands that cleaned wounds and tightened dressings shake with feeling on the page:

> *I have in my huts some very young boys, (baby soldiers we call them) there's a Jock with his right arm gone and the muscles of his chest badly lacerated. He looks such a wee boy and when I ask him what is keeping him awake he tells me he is a wee bit too tired to sleep. Baby 2 is a little scrap of a boy named Hancock with a bad abdominal wound. He certainly doesn't look a day over 14 . . . Baby 3 is a Staffordshire kid named Dort with a tremendous wound on his back. When this wound has to be dressed Corporal holds him up in his arms. The poor little chap cries piteously when we go to do him . . . As soon as they are fit to move they are evacuated to Blighty to make room for others.*[6]

And others came in their droves. When a push was on, Elsie's work was virtually continuous. 'I used to see the long casualty lists,' she confided to her diary, 'but did not realise one thousandth part the full meaning of them. There is no doubt in our minds now'.

Even at the end of the day, there was little rest for Elsie. It was not just the shell-shock cases screaming down the camp, or the German biplanes releasing their bombs uncomfortably nearby:

> *Today I had to assist 10 amputations one after the other. It is frightfully nerve wracking work. I seem to hear that wretched saw at work whenever I try to sleep. We see the most ghastly wounds and all day long are inhaling the odour of gangrene. How these boys suffer! This war is absolute hell.*

'We can hear the guns quite plainly here', the entry continues. Then, suddenly and unexpectedly, the diary turns. Elsie's careful copperplate writing weaves a kind of sanity from the madness erupting around her:

> *Dame Nature is treating us to a feast of beauty in the outside world. Flowers are everywhere. Never have I seen such gorgeous tulips, all shades, brown, gold and green and such perfect blooms.*[7]

In the final year of the war, Elsie was posted to a casualty clearing station on the Somme. She was there when the German offensive buckled the Allied lines:

> *22 March 18.*
> *Such a noisy night. Barrage commenced at 1.15am. Shells were wizzing and screaming. We were watching the shrapnel bursting in the air. At 3am there was a terrific explosion and everything was lighted up. The dump at Baupaume was struck. We three Australians were wondering what would happen next – everything seemed so unreal . . . By 7am the wounded were pouring in . . . I went over to my tent and . . . received a sudden surprise – a fairly large*

OPPOSITE **Space for tenderness and compassion:** Elsie Tranter in her nurse's uniform. Note the Rising Sun brooch pinned to her neck, identifying her as an Australian. *P09173.001, courtesy Australian War Memorial.*

> *piece of shell ripped my tent, grazed past my face and passed right between my hands . . . All day long we worked under very trying conditions. We had four operating tables in constant use and poor fellows lying on stretchers on the theatre floor . . . One poor chap walked in with half his jaw blown away, walked in supported by two wounded comrades . . . I gave twenty anaesthetics finishing at 2.30 this morning. Then orders came for us to evacuate . . .*

Elsie was sent to the No. 3 Canadian Stationary Hospital near Doullens. It was a journey she would never forget. Again, she finds a moment to record the war's 'frightfulness' and this time she reflects on the cost it posed to civilians as much as soldiers:

> *As we passed through Albert the last of the civilians were leaving it – old people, tiny children all making their way to a safe place, taking with them what few belongings they could. One family we saw resting on the roadside, one tiny child asleep on the baggage and a little girl about 10 years of age standing with her hands on her hips looking back towards the home they had been forced to leave – a look of defiance and hatred on her face. Scenes like this will live forever.*

Elsie's work continued to mount as the German offensive gained momentum. By April, the well-equipped hospitals had given way to makeshift dressing stations in abandoned buildings. There were no minutes to 'spare in one long rush of work'. The diary entries that month are short but compelling. Truly it is a wonder she could manage to write at all:

> *Everything here is unutterably sad and awful. Thousands coming in day and night. We are in the theatre from 7am till 8pm, then work in the Chapel attending to the new admissions till any hour in the morning.*[8]

The physical labour was taxing enough. But for Elsie, the work of nursing was also emotionally exhausting. She regretted that she could no longer speak to her wounded and frightened charges: 'working among the gassed men [we] have lost our voices – and can just about manage to whisper.' And she knew each moment spent with one man was care stolen from another, those 'frightfully mutilated boys coming in all the time'.[9]

'Boys' was the term Elsie used most for her soldiers, particularly 'her boys'– those lads from Australia. 'They always seem to be the nicest, the bravest and the most humorous of all,' she confides in her diary. 'But then perhaps it is just because they belong in a special way to us.' But those boys also belonged to families far away. A few weeks from Anzac Day, Elsie noted she had many 'last letters' to write to mothers in Australia and New Zealand: 'Many of the boys have entrusted me with very precious messages. They are game to the end.'[10]

For Elsie, the end of that 'ghastly' war could not come soon enough. On 11 November 1918, she found herself in a field hospital on the edge of Amiens. And true to form she snatched a moment to record the excitement erupting all around her:

11 November 1918 Armistice
At 11am Church bells pealed out, bugles were blown, guns boomed and France went almost mad with joy. Pourquoi? Armistice has been signed. I was unable to go into the town, but those who went said that the joy of the people was beyond bounds. Little children and adults too were singing and dancing in the streets, flags were flying from all windows . . . The French children were well provided with crackers and other fireworks and the adults were so excited they danced around kissing almost everyone they met first on one cheek then on the other.

Elsie didn't go into the town. Rather she spent that day as she did almost every other, attending to the sick and the dying:

Here in the hut we have had a very busy day – such a number of delirious boys. One very young fair-haired boy who has been suitably nicknamed 'Sunny Jim' was practically dying when we went on duty in the morning. When the noise started at 11am he wanted to know the meaning of it – he thought it was the commencement of a barrage. When we told him that the war was over he seemed unable to realise it, and, during the few hours remaining to him called us frequently and asked 'Is it really over? Won't I have to go back?' He seemed so happy each time that we reassured him. This poor little lad finished his battle towards evening. He was barely 18 years and we were all so fond of him. He was a 'Sunny Jim' to the last.

'Our day in the hut was . . . rather a heartbreaking one,' the entry concluded, 'and when duty for the day was finished we did not feel able to enter fully into the meaning and joy of Armistice.'

Instead, Elsie scribbled those last words in her diary hoping perhaps that one day someone would read them. Elsie's diary began as her secret and ended as her testimony, one woman's account of the inhumanity of war.

BELOW **The long casualties lists:** The names of Australia's World War One dead piled high in the national memorial in Canberra. Elsie nursed many men such as these. *Courtesy Bruce Scates.*

SOURCES AND FURTHER READING: This story draws on the service dossier for Elsie Tranter NAA: B2455, TRANTER ELSIE MAY; her repatriation file NAA: B73, R45567 TRANTER ELSIE MAY, and NAA: P107, M16226; as well as the personal diary of Sister Elsie Tranter AWM DRL 4081A. For further reading on Australian nurses in the Great War see Jan Bassett, *Guns and Brooches: Australian Army Nursing from the Boer War to the Gulf War* (Melbourne: Oxford University Press, 1992); and Bruce Scates and Raelene Frances, *Women and the Great War* (Cambridge: Cambridge University Press, 1997).

An Anzac by any other name

THOMAS HENLEY MANNS

OPPOSITE **Civilian service overseas:** Munitions and war workers from the troop transport HMAT *Borda* land at Plymouth. The voyage out had been slow and dangerous, the ship only just evading German submarines. These are just some of over 700 civilian volunteers on the vessel. A wide demographic is present here and telling differences in dress (and headwear) suggest a range of professional, skilled and semi-skilled workers. *H02034 courtesy Australian War Memorial.*

The fortunes of war are fickle. They alter lives in a thousand different ways, and can take a life in different ways as well.

Thomas Henley Manns was one of the thousands of British immigrants who sought a new life in Australia. A boilermaker by trade, and a man prepared to travel to better himself, he worked in New South Wales, took a wife in Melbourne and moved to Western Australia a few years before the outbreak of war. In 1914, he was employed in one of the timber camps near Busselton, servicing the saws and machinery that felled the great forests of the South West.

In October of that year, Manns enlisted in the AIF; he was amongst the first six hundred West Australians to volunteer. He sailed from Fremantle with the 16th Battalion in December 1914, bound, he thought, for England but destined for the Dardanelles.

Manns landed at Gallipoli on 25 April. Almost six feet in height, he made an easier target than most. He was wounded in the leg by bullet and shrapnel fire and evacuated from the peninsula.

They took Manns to Harefield to recuperate. The country estate in southern England hosted the 1st Australian Auxiliary Hospital. Manns' leg healed soon enough, but his health remained fragile. 'Exposure and strain', the medical report reads, reminding us that even a few weeks at Gallipoli could exact a terrible toll.[1] With his constitution already weak, Manns showed the first signs of pulmonary tuberculosis. He suffered night sweats, broken sleep, and a hacking cough that woke the men around him. Thomas Henley Manns was discharged as permanently unfit and returned to Australia in 1916. But that wasn't the end of Thomas's war.

No longer able to serve in the First AIF, Thomas Manns signed on for the Australian Munitions Workers Scheme. With thousands of men serving on the front line, British

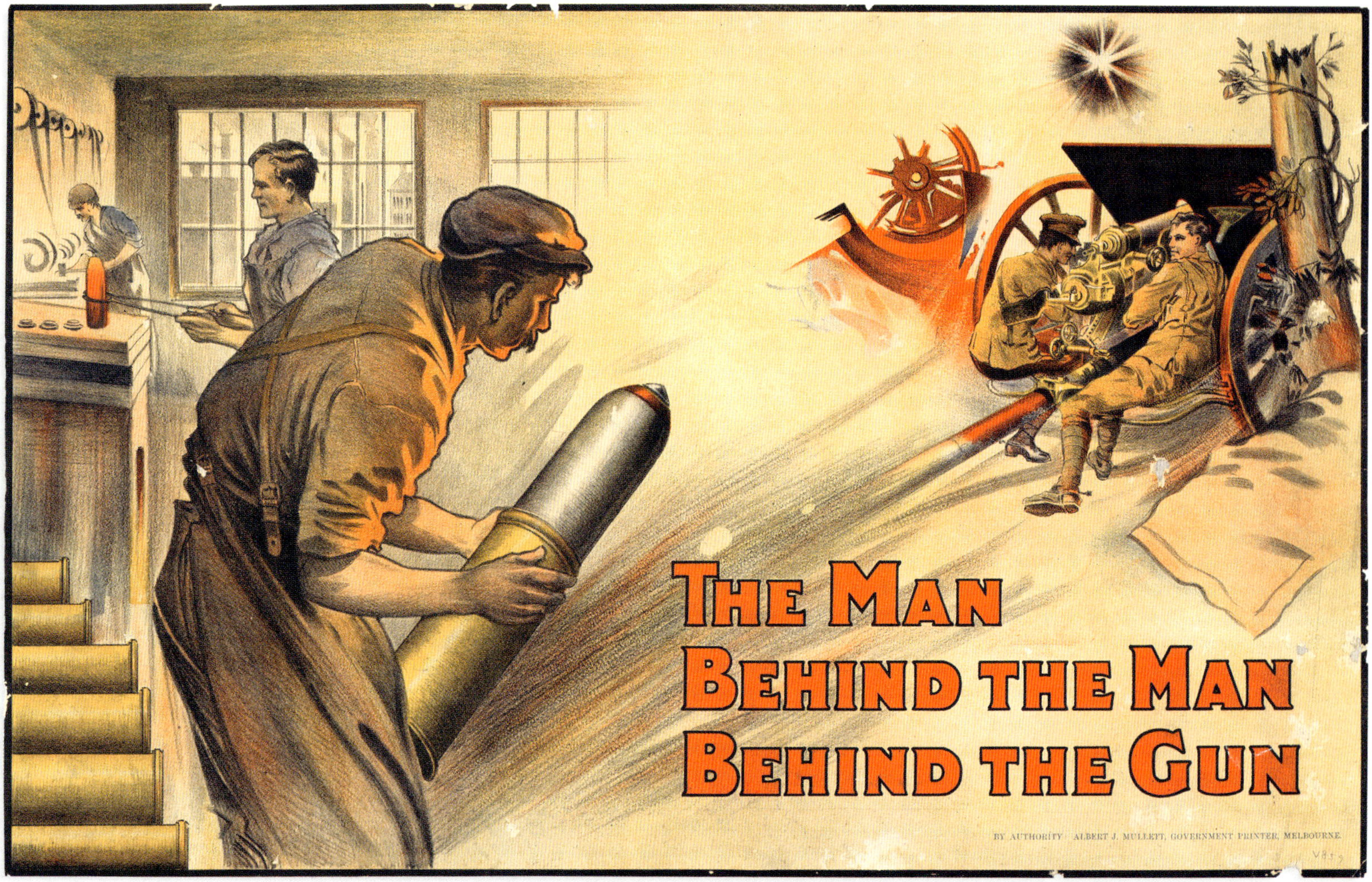

ABOVE **The Great War's insatiable desire for armaments:** A recruitment poster celebrating the 'man behind the man behind the gun'. In fact, many of these workers were women. *ARTV00859 courtesy Australian War Memorial.*

industry was left desperately short of manpower. Men were needed to meet the Great War's insatiable demand for armaments – guns and explosives, battleships and rifles, tanks that lumbered across no-man's-land, fragile aircraft that took war to the air.

Able men were so few that the British authorities soon recruited women to work in munitions factories, and an appeal went out to the dominions. Australia sent none of its women (though many offered their services), but did send 6000 men. Thomas Manns was amongst them; he sailed on a troopship for civilian service overseas.

The conditions in the factories were appalling. It was not just the hazards of the industry – the poisonous chemicals that turned skin yellow, faulty and dangerous machinery, and the ever present possibility that volatile ordinance would explode. The pay and conditions were abysmal by Australian standards. Men worked a fifty-four hour week for half the wages they received back home. The cost of living, the quality of accommodation, the food and the climate in Britain also left much to be desired.

Manns may well have been a patriot but he was also a man who knew the value of skilled labour, and he had a wife to provide for as well. He began work at the Royal Gun Factory in Woolwich, but lung trouble and an abdominal injury forced him to take on lighter duties. The problem was that light work didn't pay well at all. In December 1917, as the factories geared up to meet the German Spring Offensive, Manns wrote a letter of complaint. According to the officer in charge, Manns:

> *. . . did not consider the rate high enough to support himself and wife . . . stated that he had served three years in the army and he expected better treatment . . . [Demanded] they give him something more suitable.*

In January 1918, Manns used the language of a living breadwinner's wage pioneered by unionists in Australia and New Zealand: 'He should continue endeavours to get justice done, as he had sacrificed his health for his country.' Eventually the authorities conceded. A medical officer certified him unfit for work and Australia agreed to fund the cost of repatriation.[2]

Manns would not sail home without his wife. She was pregnant at the time and he refused to leave her. With little other income, he took on work sawing timber in Bedford. Just two days before the Armistice was declared, Manns fell forty feet from a ladder. A man who had survived wounds from Gallipoli, and the risky business of one of Britain's largest munitions factories, was fatally injured felling the branch of an oak tree.

So far as Mrs Manns was concerned, her husband had died for the war effort. She wrote to the Minister of Defence asking that Thomas be buried as a soldier would be, in the military cemetery at Harefield adjoining the hospital where he had stayed. His body lies there to this day, not far from the bodies of other Australian soldiers. The fortunes of war had treated them differently, but had led them to a common graveyard.

Of the 6000 Australians who served as munitions and war workers, more than sixty died overseas. Many who survived complained that their health had been broken by war service – danger and hardship was clearly not confined to the front line. In recognition of their services, munitions workers achieved some, though not all, the repatriation benefits extended to returned servicemen. But the title of 'war worker' never acquired the same kudos as 'digger'. Ironically, many of those men, Thomas Henley Manns included, had served in the AIF before taking up that second tour of duty overseas.

Today Harefield is the site of Anzac Day services. An official party from Australia House travels up from London and local schoolchildren lay flowers on Anzac graves. One of the tombstones reads simply 'munitions worker', but this too was the grave of a man present at the Landing, an Anzac by any other name.

Mrs Manns gave birth to their son a few months after the death of her husband. She called him Henley in honour of his father and she chose the middle name 'Anzac'. Hadley Anzac Henley Manns served in the Second AIF, just as his father served in the First. And he too lost his life in war.

BELOW **Harefield today:** The AIF burial ground adjoining St Mary's Church in Uxbridge outside London. Harefield Estate was owned by Charles Billyard-Leake, an Australian expatriate who married a British heiress and secured his own private fortune. Free use of his estate as an AIF hospital was his contribution to the war effort. The tombstones were first put in place in 1917, the patients at the hospital and Billyard-Leake himself contributing to a subscription fund to remember fellow countrymen and mates. They were not replaced with official IWGC tombstones after the war. *Courtesy Bruce Scates.*

SOURCES AND FURTHER READING: This account is based on Henley Manns' service dossier NAA: B2455, MANNS THOMAS HENLEY; his Red Cross Wounded and Missing file AWM 1DRL/0428; and his official record as a munitions worker NAA: MT1139/1, MANNS THOMAS HENLEY. There are substantial holdings in the National Archives of Australia relevant to the munitions workers scheme. Some of the most useful of these are NAA:536/1/929; NAA:536/1/1998; NAA: 536/1/3605. A good introduction to the topic is provided by Tony Griffiths, *An Industrial Invasion: Australian Civilian Volunteers in British Factories 1916 to 1920* (Sydney: Topech Engineering, 2010). We thank Mr Griffiths for suggesting some of these lines of enquiry. The authors also acknowledge the assistance of Roger Gage, a parishioner of St Mary's Church and the organiser of Anzac Day services in Harefield.

A most particular friend

JOHN HUTCHINSON

In the soft light of early evening, John Hutchinson was shot by a sniper at Gallipoli. The bullet sped through his back and shattered his spine. It would take Private Hutchinson over two hours to die.

It is said that in the last moments of life, as the darkness closes in, a dying man's thoughts turn to the ones he loves. John Hutchinson thought only of his sergeant.

'Casualty lingered in pain,' Sergeant Matthews reported to the Red Cross. 'He was quite conscious to the end and gave a message to his very particular friend, Sgt Carson of the 8th Battalion.' By the time that interview was recorded, Carson and the 8th had been transferred to France, and the battalion had suffered hundreds of casualties. But that final message from a dying man made an indelible impression on Sergeant Matthews' memory.

Hutchinson did not use the words soldiers usually chose to describe their friendships, 'cobber' or 'mate'. Perhaps because this relationship seemed something other than that, something more intense and more familiar. There was intimacy there that Sergeant Matthews did not quite understand, and certainly didn't approve of:

> *Casualty was very much attached to Sgt Carson and the boys referred to them as Lord and Lady Carson . . . Sgt Carson stuck to him so closely.*[1]

ABOVE **Gay people also gave their lives in war:** A delegation of gay ex-servicemen attempt to lay a wreath at the Shrine on Anzac Day. 'I don't mind poofters,' Bruce Ruxton told a party of journalists, but he said that if his son was queer he would probably 'have to shoot him'. *Courtesy Jay Watchorn and the Australian Lesbian and Gay Archives.*

'It was supposed that casualty had plenty of money', Matthews continued; why else would a man in Sergeant Carson's position curry such favour? But John Hutchinson was a labourer from Kyneton, Victoria, and left all his worldly possessions to his mother. If Carson took him on as a 'particular friend' there must have been some other reason. That mocking phrase, 'Lord and Lady Carson' may not have been a reference to class at all, it perhaps served to identify two men whose private companionship set them apart from their mates, and whose very behaviour was deemed suspiciously effeminate.

Here we should sound a word of caution. You can read too much into a single paragraph from a single file, and we can't assume that our emotional sensibilities today are the same as those in the past, even if that past was barely a hundred years ago. In truth, we know virtually nothing about Hutchinson's and Carson's relationship and we can never know what these two men's sexual preferences may have been.

What we do know is that homosexuality was illegal in early twentieth-century Australia. And we know homosexuals faced imprisonment and dishonourable discharge from the Army. As Oscar Wilde famously remarked, gay love was a love that dared not speak its name, especially in the close confines of Gallipoli. Its expression and its extent are hidden from history.

We can also state with confidence that homosexuals served then, just as they serve now, and that patriotism, loyalty and a sense of duty are not defined by sexual preference. Today, the rights of homosexuals are (technically) respected in the services. But men and women suspected of being gay still experience the kind of satire and contempt John Hutchinson and his sergeant encountered. And many still believe that queer men and lesbian women are simply unworthy of the title 'Anzac.' Nowhere is that more apparent than in the history of Anzac Day.

In 1982, a group of gay servicemen representing the Australian Army, Navy and Air Force, sought to place a wreath at the Shrine of Remembrance on Anzac Day. A tribute of red and white roses, it honoured 'All our Brothers and Sisters' who lost their lives in war. The five-man delegation 'made a solemn and dignified approach to the shrine'. They didn't get far. In what the gay press dubbed 'Ruxton's ruckus', Bruce Ruxton, the President of Victoria's RSL, 'bellowed "stop those men" and waving his umbrella like a sword [formed] a human barrier across [the] . . . entrance to the shrine'.

Gay men were not permitted to lay their wreath in a memorial that purported to honour all Victorian servicemen. Nor were they permitted to march in what Bruce Ruxton called a separate 'poofter' delegation in the Anzac Day march. The leader, Mike Jarmyn, insisted he was not 'playing politics', let alone seeking any 'degradation of the Anzac Day tradition': 'We simply wish to publicly recognise the fact that gay people also gave their lives in war.'[2]

John Hutchinson lost his life at Anzac within forty-eight hours of the Landing, just as the sun faded over Samothrace. His family was no doubt told he died fighting for freedom, but was he really free to choose the one he loved?

SOURCES AND FURTHER READINGS: This story is based on the service dossiers of John Hutchinson NAA: B2455 HUTCHINSON J and William Carson NAA: B2455 CARSON WILLIAM EDWIN; and John Hutchinson's Red Cross Wounded and Missing file AWM 1DRL/0428. Attempts by gay people to commemorate their war dead are examined in Bruce Scates, *A Place to Remember: A History of the Shrine of Remembrance* (Cambridge: Cambridge University Press, 2009). For an introduction to the history of homosexuality in Australia see Garry Wotherspoon, *City of the Plain: History of a Gay Sub-Culture* (Sydney: Hale & Iremonger, 1991). The authors would also like to thank Olivia Killeen for directing us to the story of John Hutchinson.

A vacant look in his eyes

ALFRED ATKINS

We will never know why Alfred Atkins went to war, but we do know he was far too old to serve. Just after Christmas in 1915, the plumber from Geelong turned up at a recruiting office in Adelaide. A military clerk noted his thin greying hair and may well have spotted the spectacles the old man carried. Atkins gave his age as 45. In truth, he was closer to 60. The recruiting officer turned a blind eye – Atkins claimed three years of service in Ballarat's voluntary militia and, after the debacle of Gallipoli, trained men were desperately needed.

Just as we don't know why Alfred Atkins went to war, we don't know why he took his own life. An inquest into his death offers only the barest details: Atkin's body was discovered at a military camp in England where his unit had previously been stationed. He was fully dressed, 'with a razor in his hand, and his throat cut'. The court heard that Private Atkins had been missing for months. He had been granted twelve hours leave in May 1917 – not long after the battalion had returned from active service – and he had not been seen again until November. No one knew what he had done in that time, or indeed how he'd managed to survive in England 'illegally absent' from his unit. Atkins had not drawn pay since April.[1]

Captain Lucas was one of the last men to see Atkins alive. He interrogated the soldier on 17 November, while he waited for a warrant to return him to camp. Lucas confessed he gave Private Atkins something of a 'shakedown'. 'He seemed to be miserable,' Lucas told the court, 'and there was a vacant look in his eyes.' Lucas 'had heard Atkins had been sandbagged in London' – soldier slang for treating a man cruelly and unfairly. And in the course of the interrogation Atkins had told him his age was 64, three times the age of most other soldiers in his unit. With not much else to go on, the court returned a verdict of suicide 'whilst of unsound mind'. In a case like this, it did not do well to ask too many questions.[2]

BELOW **Alongside eighteen other Australian soldiers:** Atkins' grave lies alongside men who died at half his age. *Courtesy Bruce Scates.*

But we can ask why Atkins took his own life. No doubt his age had something to do with it. This was a young man's war, and a man in his sixties was hardly fit to fight it. Nor was it just the stamina required on the battlefield. Could a man like Alfred Atkins really 'fit in', especially amongst virile men determined to enjoy what may have been their last leave in London? Atkins had recorded his religion as Presbyterian; perhaps he was something of what was then called a 'wowser'. However one looks at it, there was a vast demographic divide between Alfred Atkins and the young men he served with.

Perhaps Private Atkins was ashamed. Captain Lucas would have made it clear how serious the charges were that faced him. Atkins had been illegally absent from his unit in wartime, neglected his responsibilities, and failed the men around him. For a man who had served before, who presumably had a strong sense of duty, the feeling of failure would have been overwhelming.

Suicide is often presented as a failing of character. And perhaps there was something missing in the life of Private Atkins. Despite his age, he had never married. He had no living relations and recorded his next of kin as '(Friend) Mr G Wilson' back in Adelaide. After Private Atkin's death, no one applied for his war gratuity. His medals, personal effects and a photograph of his grave were routinely dispatched to the next-of-kin. There is no record of a Mr Wilson requesting them. Perhaps this is just the story of a lonely old man who hoped the comradeship of war might be a substitute for some more intimate companionship.

The war, though, did not deal Private Atkins a good hand. He belonged to what was called 'the fighting 10th'. Whilst he was still in training, the battalion had been mauled at Pozières. In just six weeks there the AIF suffered 22 000 casualties. The 10th had gone on to fight in the bungled Battle of Bullecourt, a head-on assault on the heavily fortified Hindenburg Line. It is surely no coincidence that the old man left his unit within weeks of it returning to England. Perhaps the thought of the front line was simply too much for him. Whatever Private Atkins had seen – or heard or done – must have been horrific. With a terrible resolution, this old man slit his throat from ear to ear.

Alfred Atkins' body was cold and stiff when they found him. It was bundled up in a blanket, taken to Fargo Hospital and left in the mortuary until the inquest was concluded. In death, at least, the man who'd been 'sandbagged' by his mates was treated with respect and dignity. Atkins' body was sent 'by request of unit', to the 2nd Training Battalion AIF for burial at Sutton Veny. His oak coffin was lowered into consecrated ground in the shadow of St John's Church, and placed alongside 'eighteen other Australian soldiers'. Captain Bradby read the service and a sturdy wooden cross was driven into the earth. In 1923, that cross was replaced with the standard war graves commission tombstone, but no one composed an epitaph for Alfred Atkins.[3]

ABOVE **Standard tombstone:** The grave of Alfred Atkins in the military plot at St John's Church, Sutton Veny. Suicides were not always buried in consecrated ground. Military authorities made an exception for Private Atkins. *Courtesy Sally James.*

SOURCES AND FURTHER READING: This story draws on the service dossier of Alfred Atkins NAA: B2455, ATKINS ALFRED; and contemporary newspaper reports both in Australia and Britain. The authors would like to thank Greg and Sally James for their assistance in obtaining the details of Atkins' grave in Sutton Veny.

I baptise thee 'Anzac'

TASMAN MILLINGTON

On 25 April 1922, Tasman Millington walked down to the water's edge at Anzac Cove, an infant child cradled in his arms. The baby boy was wrapped in a thick, warm shawl. And just as well – like the morning of the Landing, seven years before, a bracing wind whipped across the Aegean. Millington steadied himself on the shingle, as slippery now as the day he first came ashore. With a tenderness uncommon in a soldier, he handed his son to the clergyman standing beside him. The old man splashed the ancient sea across the newborn's head and a strong, solemn voice rang out across the water: 'I baptise thee in the name of the Father, and the Son and the Holy Ghost.' And so Tasman Millington's only child was named.

Millington had every reason to bring his newborn to the shores of Gallipoli. When he had fought there in 1915, the beach had been a place of death and suffering. Now, with his young wife, Ruth, beside him, this became a place of life, renewal and joy. And although the christening name may have been Bernard, the name 'Anzac' stuck. Nor was that surprising. What better name was there for the son of this Gallipoli veteran charged with the care of Gallipoli's graves?

Millington and his wife would live in Turkey for over fifty years. At first they set up home in Kelia, literally bordering the battlefields. Millington would walk that lonely landscape almost every day. The bones of the dead were brought in from the gullies, reverently buried in purpose-made graveyards, marked with tombstones shipped all the way from England. Millington took care to bury men as close as possible to where they fell. In that way, the landscape became their memorial. Quinn's and Courtney's, Baby 700 and the Nek battlefields were remade as graveyards. Men had died to hold that ground, Millington said, and in a sense they held it still.

Unlike the sprawling cemeteries in Flanders or on the Somme, most of the graveyards he marked out were tiny. Plugge's, on the first ridge the Anzac forces had taken,

held the bodies of fewer than twenty men. But Gallipoli was not the same as the mechanised murder of the Western Front. Here, death seemed somehow less anonymous.

Creating the cemeteries was hard enough. An army of Greek stonemasons, exiled White Russians and Turkish peasants worked under Millington's careful direction. They terraced the hillsides, shifted tons of earth and hauled into place great blocks of freshly chiselled stone. The last memorial, Lone Pine, was not completed until 1929, and decades later Millington would still find bodies in the scrub around it.

The labour of establishing the gardens proved equally exacting. Gallipoli, then as now, was a place of extremes. The cold was so intense it cracked stone in winter. In August, hot, dry winds baked the clay ridges bare. It was hardly the place for an English country garden but Millington planted roses, primrose and lavender over the bodies of his countrymen. He sowed lawns in what was once a barren wilderness, and tended the graves as a mother would that of her own. And on the ridges he struggled to plant

ABOVE **Carrying the scent of wild thyme:** George Lambert's *Gallipoli Wild Flowers*. Lambert began the painting in 1919, when he embarked on his own pilgrimage to Gallipoli. Ruth Millington also sketched the flora of the Dardanelles and, like Lambert, collected hundreds of specimens. Some of these she took to Hobart when she visited Tasman's elderly parents in 1934. There was great interest in her work – strong enough to warrant a public exhibition in Hobart. *ART02838 courtesy Australian War Memorial.*

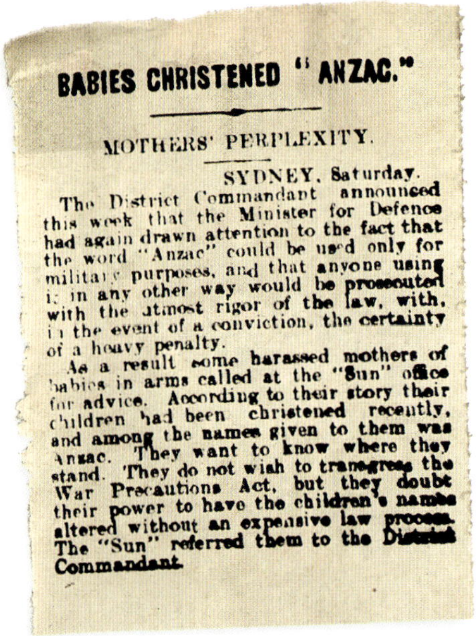
BABIES CHRISTENED "ANZAC."

MOTHERS' PERPLEXITY.

SYDNEY, Saturday.

The District Commandant announced this week that the Minister for Defence had again drawn attention to the fact that the word "Anzac" could be used only for military purposes, and that anyone using it in any other way would be prosecuted with the utmost rigor of the law, with, in the event of a conviction, the certainty of a heavy penalty.

As a result some harassed mothers of babies in arms called at the "Sun" office for advice. According to their story their children had been christened recently, and among the names given to them was Anzac. They want to know where they stand. They do not wish to transgress the War Precautions Act, but they doubt their power to have the children's names altered without an expensive law process. The "Sun" referred them to the District Commandant.

ABOVE **What better name?:** Reports of a spree of Anzac babies named in Sydney. Despite strict legal prohibitions on any commercial exploitation, families chose this name for sons and daughters alike. One family at Maclean on the Clarence River even named their baby boy 'Anzac Dardanelles'. The government could do little to curb popular enthusiasm and turned a blind eye to most non-commercial use. Ballarat Courier, *28 August 1916 courtesy National Library of Australia.*

something of Australia and Aotearoa/New Zealand: rimu and blue gum were raised in Kew Gardens and taken as seedlings all the way to Anzac. This corner of a foreign field would be made, Millington hoped, a little more like home.

It was not until the early 1920s that this was a place fit for visitors. Even so, as soon as the war had ended the first pilgrims came. Millington remembered one old man who travelled all the way from Gippsland, desperate to find a son lost in the bungled campaigns of the August Offensive.

It fell to Millington and his wife to comfort these determined travellers. By 1925, they had a small cottage in Chanak and often received visitors from Australia, Britain and New Zealand. Millington would take them across the straits in a War Commission motor launch and drive them over the gullies and the ridges in the Commission's (and the peninsula's) only car. 'A rather dilapidated Ford', as one Australian pilgrim recalled, spluttering asthmatically across the landscape. The Ford's engine seemed to strain and almost falter on every punishing slope – just as men had in 1915.[1]

Pilgrimage in Millington's day was very much the prerogative of the privileged. The first organised tours did not take place until the late 1920s and cost more than a year's wages for a white, skilled, male worker. But if Australians could not make their way to Gallipoli, Tasman Millington would send Gallipoli to them. On Anzac Day 1935, he and his wife trod that same careful path again along the shoreline of Anzac Cove, close to the place where their boy had been christened. The old soldier dug his hands deep into the earth and Ruth picked wildflowers gleaming in the spring sunshine. A week before Armistice Day, 'a parcel of soil from Gallipoli, and a bundle of foliage picked from the environs of Anzac Cove' arrived in Sydney on the Orient liner the *Orien*. What the newspapers called 'historic earth' was taken to the Anzac Memorial in Hyde Park and stored in a bronze urn like some sacred relic. The flowers Ruth had picked were 'placed on the graves of returned soldiers' and they still carried the scent of the wild thyme scattered across the cliffs of Anzac.[2]

What then of young 'Anzac' himself? Like his father, Flight Sergeant Bernard 'Anzac' Millington also went to war, serving in the Royal Air Force. He survived both his father and his mother.

Tasman Millington died in England in 1962. He is buried beside his wife in Sidcup Cemetery, Kent, hundreds of miles from the graveyards he helped establish and 8000 miles from home.

SOURCES AND FURTHER READING: This account draws on the service dossier of Tasman Millington NAA: B2455, MILLINGTON TASMAN; Foreign Office records in the National Archives, UK, PRO FO 141/520; the Bean Papers in Canberra AWM, Series 5, 3 DRL 8042; and contemporary newspaper reports. Further details on the creation of Gallipoli's cemeteries can be found in Bruce Scates, *Return to Gallipoli: Walking the Battlefields of the Great War* (Cambridge: Cambridge University Press, 2006); Bill Gammage, 'The Anzac Cemetery', *Australian Historical Studies*, vol. 38, no. 129, 2007, pp. 124–140; and Bart Ziino, *A Distant Grief: Australians, War Graves and the Great War* (Crawley: University of Western Australia Press, 2007). Millington's life is captured in a semi-fictional account in John Samuels, *Millington's Mission* (Pymble: HarperCollins, 2002).

A vast tide of grief
FRANK ROBERTS

On Friday, 13 September 1918, Garry Roberts boarded an electric cable car at Princes Bridge and set off for his offices in the city. The tram clattered to a halt at the very end of Bourke Street, almost opposite the grand Italianate building where he worked. It was a bright morning in Melbourne and the first flush of spring sunshine seemed to have brought the city to life again. Roberts quickened his pace, entered the building through its ornate wooden doors and walked down a columned corridor leading to a stairwell.

A senior accountant in the Melbourne Municipal Tramways Board, Roberts knew how to act like a man in authority. He removed his hat, proceeded to his office and noticed a cablegram waiting on his desk. It sat there in its buff envelope, *OHMS* printed starkly in the corner. Roberts may have assumed it was an urgent communication from the Tramways. A man in his position dealt with many such cablegrams each year. But Friday the 13th was an unlucky day for the Roberts family.

'I opened it and read to my dismay and grief that my dear brave soldier son had been killed in action.' Thus began, as Roberts put it, 'the most awful day in our lives'.[1]

Garry Roberts' son Frank had been killed at Mont St Quentin twelve days earlier. It had taken that long to relay the message from the battlefields of France to the distant metropolis of Melbourne. Roberts' first response was one of confusion, disbelief and denial. Frank had survived over two years of war, and that war was now fast approaching its end. Could the authorities be mistaken? Perhaps some other 'brave soldier son' had been 'taken'. Like many faced with the death of a loved one, Roberts harboured the guilty hope that this might just be someone else's grief. The entries in his diary that week began the process of staring loss in the face:

> *I went immediately to the Red Cross enquiry office, but they knew nothing.*

I then went to base records office and had my fears confirmed. I returned to the Red Cross enquiry office and gave them a donation and thanked them.

For a time, Roberts returned home to the family's townhouse in Hawthorn. There is no record of what he did there that day (although in the months to follow he would often sleep in his son's room, hoping to feel his boy's presence again). Roberts spent over five hours in that empty building crowded with memories. It was almost seven in the evening when he caught the train to Ferntree Gully.

It was a long and jolting journey from the city to the bush. Roberts got off at the end of the line at Belgrave Station and set off on foot for the family property 'Sunnyside'. There his wife, Berta, was waiting. 'A wearisome and depressing walk,' he recorded:

a hot wind blowing. Berta met me at the [bottom of the] hill . . . with a faint hope that I would not confirm the sad news. But I had to tell my brave son's brave mother that our first born had died a hero's death in France to help to save mankind.

There was no saving Garry and Berta from their grief. Within hours, their immediate family had assembled around them and Garry retold the story of that 'awful' day again. The next morning, the couple made their way to Warwick farm, a neighbouring property where their daughter-in-law, and once their son, had lived. Forewarned by Garry, Ruby's father had broken the news to his daughter. It had been a long night:

We tried to comfort the poor girl the best we could but it was a distressing time. . . . Ruby greeted me with, 'It isn't true father, is it?' and I had to reply, 'yes, girlie, it is,' and she cried, 'Oh! my Frank, my little Nancy will never see her father.'

Frank Roberts had sailed off for war within a few weeks of Ruby falling pregnant. He would never hold his baby daughter, Nancy. Nor would one of Nancy's tiny booties reach her proud father. That parcel, sent by his loving Ruby, was returned to the Roberts family months after Frank had been killed, that cold word 'Deceased' scrawled across it. It was not uncommon for families like the Roberts to receive correspondence from dead sons months after war had claimed them. It was like hearing a voice from a grave.

Garry Roberts' life didn't end with the death of his son. Instead, he turned to the business of remembering. Every other week in his diary he noted some kind of anniversary, marking time when it seemed to have ended, landmarks in what historians have called the 'nothingness of grief':[2]

23 July: This would have been Frank's birthday

8 August: Frank in big battle

4 January 1920: My dear son Frank (Pte FW Roberts No 6874 C Company

OPPOSITE **One man rather than many:** Charles Web Gilbert's memorial to the Second Division raised on the slopes of Mont St Quentin. It bore a striking likeness to Frank and was destroyed when the German Army returned to the town in World War Two. *P02205.011 courtesy Australian War Memorial.*

21 Battn AIF) was killed in the capture of Mt St Quentin in France this day 16 months ago. His body lies in a cemetery near Péronne.

Garry commenced what he called 'Frank's Memorial book'. From his 58th birthday to the day of his death, there was not a single day he did not attend to it. It swelled with careful transcriptions of Frank's letters, cuttings from obituaries, detailed accounts drawn from reluctant comrades of the battle that claimed his son.

Making memory was an elaborate and time-consuming process but it kept despair at bay. By the time it was completed, Frank's book numbered several hefty volumes, as impressive a monument as an obelisk carved in stone.

The memorial books may have been a private undertaking but they reminded Garry Roberts he was never alone in his loss. Hundreds of sympathy letters are pressed securely in the volumes, each writer clutching at words that might bring comfort: pride in a 'duty nobly done'; hope for 'strength in God'; reassurance that 'in time the burden of sorrow will be easier to bear'. In a way, the most eloquent letters are also the sparsest.

'I feel I don't know what to say to you,' Edith Jones wrote, '[after] seeing the news about Frank in last night's *Herald* . . . Oh why did he go, I am so sorry for you.'

Amidst the 'deep heartfelt regret' there is also bewilderment and anger: 'This horrible war!' Annie Duncan declared. 'When will it end? It is draining this country of the very best.' Annie understood 'the terrible blank' left in Garry Roberts' life. The great tide of grief we call the Great War had swept away so many.[3]

Garry Roberts' grieving took on a very public dimension and it was expressed with an intimacy seldom easy for men. He distributed memorial cards to friends and family, raised a tablet to Frank in the Stock Exchange, and played a role in the Sailors and Soldiers Fathers Association of Victoria, a kind of fraternity of the bereaved ('Carry on Dad', their brave motto).

At the end of the war, Garry began a long correspondence with Charles Web Gilbert, determined to raise a memorial to the Second Division. It would take the shape of an Australian soldier bayoneting a German eagle on the summit of Mont St Quentin, the fortress where Frank and over four hundred other Australian soldiers had been killed. Thanks to Garry's friendship with Gilbert, the statue bore a striking resemblance to his boy. Garry provided photographs of Frank to ensure a 'good likeness', inspected 'beautifully modelled' casts of the memorial, and persuaded Frank's younger brother Bert to pose at a sitting. To most, the memorial would be a symbol of Australian sacrifice on the Western Front, where the Second Division alone suffered over a thousand casualties. But for Garry Roberts the statue at Mont St Quentin was one man rather than many – his 'darling boy', his Frank.[4]

Garry Roberts died in 1933, still grieving the loss of a boy on the other side of the world. In 1940, the German Army marched again on Mont St Quentin. Web Gilbert's bellicose digger was one of the few war memorials they destroyed, the sight of their butchered national symbol simply 'too much' for them.[5] Frank's books survived though, page after page of clippings and cuttings, letters and photographs; one man's 'exhaustive search for solace'[6]. Frank's descendants still keep that pair of baby booties, a very private, very fragile memorial, but one that proved more lasting than a monument cast in bronze.

ABOVE LEFT **His body lies in a cemetery near Pèronne:** John and Bertha Monash on their pilgrimage to Frank's grave in France. This was the only time Monash returned to the site of an old battle or visited the cemeteries where his men were buried. Frank originally shared a grave with several others of his platoon. The bodies were exhumed and reburied individually some time after the war. *H82.288/15 courtesy State Library of Victoria.*

ABOVE **A very private, very fragile memorial:** The baby booties Frank would never see. They remain a memorial to the loss of a father, and a family. *Courtesy Mark Warren.*

SOURCES AND FURTHER READINGS: This account is based on an exhaustive scan of the Roberts Papers held in the State Library of Victoria MS8183; as well as Frank Roberts' service dossier NAA: B2455, ROBERTS FRANCIS WILLIAM; and Red Cross Wounded and Missing file AWM 1DRL/0428; and contemporary newspaper reports. Several historians have explored this rich collection, Joy Damousi, *Labour of Loss: Mourning, Memory and Wartime Bereavement* (Cambridge: Cambridge University Press, 1999); Pat Jalland, *Changing Ways of Death in Twentieth Century Australia* (Melbourne: Oxford University Press, 2002); Tanja Luckins, *The Gates of Memory: Australian People's Experience and Memories of Loss and the Great War* (Perth: Curtin University Press, 2004); Bruce Scates, *Return to Gallipoli: Walking the Battlefields of the Great War* (Cambridge: Cambridge University Press, 2006). The most detailed and eloquent account and one which succeeds in bridging military, cultural and social history is provided by Peter Stanley, *Men of Mont St Quentin: Between Victory and Death* (Melbourne: Scribe, 2009). The authors thank Deb Tout-Smith and the descendants of Frank Roberts for access to family memorabilia.

The hands of our own men

DAISY SCHOEFFEL

Daisy Pearse was a fourth-generation Australian. She belonged to one of the oldest white families in Fremantle and achieved some acclaim in Australia as an author. But Daisy married Alfred Schoeffel – a German.

When war broke out, she was living in Fiji with her husband and his cousin. Both these businessmen were long-term residents of Fiji and both had been naturalised as British citizens. But that did not protect them from being summarily deported to Australia for internment with their wives and children. Some seventy women were dealt with in this way, all escorted by Australian soldiers, bayonets fixed to their rifles. Daisy was sent to the so-called family camp at Bourke in New South Wales:

> *We arrived . . . just before dark [and were taken to an old] brick building, formerly the 'Empire Hotel'. Here the Sergt Major told each family what room to go to. We had just time to have a glimpse at my room and then darkness set in; there was no light of any kind. When at last I was able to get some candles from a store nearby and [we] were able to see the state of the rooms we had to live in, we women after that hot and long journey just broke down. I wished to God I could die and my babies with me! In my room were two broken bedsteads and nothing else but filth and dirt. This building had been empty for over 2 years.*
>
> *Later on in the evening we were told that there were straw sacks below and if we wanted them to come and get them; there was no other bedding or pillow of any kind. At 10 o'clock that night, we were told that if we wanted anything to eat to come to the kitchen. We were shown a pile of filthy dirty rusty tin plates, a tin mug (dirty). There was some sort of stew rice in a bucket, dirty and greasy, which had previously been used to wash the floor*

with. Needless to say I had not a taste of food for 24 hours after arriving in Bourke. I politely asked the Sergeant Major could I have a plate to make my baby some food, and he answered 'There's the plates (pointing to the filthy rusty tin ones) that the Australian Government give to the German prisoners'. I looked him fair in the face and said 'I am neither a German nor a prisoner, but an Australian woman!' He said 'If you were not a German prisoner you would not be here!'[1]

Daisy Schoeffel was indeed a German prisoner. Well into the twentieth century, a woman took on her husband's nationality the moment she married. At the outbreak of war, some 35 000 Australian residents had been born in Germany, Austria and Hungary, and in the eyes of the authorities their dependents were as suspect as they were. Daisy Schoeffel had, after all, 'chosen' to be a 'Hun'.

In addition, there were entire communities who were descended from early German settlers and who retained, in the view of the official war historian, 'a sentimental attachment to the land of their origin'.[2] In the hysteria of wartime, some 6000 suspected 'enemy sympathisers' were interned; several had sons serving in the First AIF.

Very few of these 'enemy aliens' presented any threat to the nation they had adopted as their home. To speak German, to have a German name or, absurd as it may seem, German 'appearance' was enough to warrant suspicion, investigation and sometimes imprisonment. In short, these individuals were different, not dangerous. Imprisonment served personal as well as political motives: what better way of removing a successful business rival than by alerting authorities to an enemy in our midst?

Hunting 'the Hun' became a way civilians could involve themselves in a conflict taking place far away. It brought the war home to Australia. Readers of the Sydney paper *The Mirror* thrilled to stories of Germans still 'at large' in the city. Among these 'enemy aliens' was Edmund Resch, the brewer, and the shipping agent Oscar Plate, whose home at Elizabeth Bay (suspiciously!) overlooked the naval dockyards of Garden Island.

BELOW **All too much:** Emma Rohrmann's body is buried in Queanbeyan Riverside Cemetery. She was 35 years old at the time of her death. In 1961, her remains were reinterred at the Tatura German War Cemetery in Victoria. By that time another generation had suffered internment during wartime. *POO121.001 courtesy Australian War Memorial.*

Patriotic women, many of whom had menfolk serving abroad, believed the anti-German campaign was a practical way of helping them, and avenging the lives of loved ones lost in Europe. An Anti-German Women's League advocated compulsory military service and pledged their support 'for the destruction of the enemy'. In 1917, its officers wrote to the Prime Minister informing him there were 'at least 148 employees with foreign names' in key positions in the public service.[3]

The harassment of German families was yet another gauge of how the Great War divided Australian society. The war bred fear and suspicion, and narrowed the definition of what it meant to be Australian. There was much the same experience in Aotearoa/New Zealand – where immigrants from

Germany had made an equally vital cultural and economic contribution.

At the end of the war, Daisy Shoeffel received no redress, no apology, and certainly no compensation. But at least she survived the experience. After enduring forty degree heat in the tin huts at Bourke, she (and many fellow internees) were transferred to Molonglo Internment Camp near Canberra. 'I felt this sudden change of climate . . . and the barracks were very badly built and kept out *neither rain nor wind* and this told on my health more every day.'

It was all too much for Mrs Emma Rohrmnn, who contracted pneumonia and died of heart failure the same month the war ended. In 1919, all the internees of the camp were deported – including some seventy-seven children. Australia was intent on purging a German presence from our shores, though Daisy Shoeffel insisted on her right to return to her family in Fremantle.

'What hurt us more than all the insults and hardships,' she wrote to her Member of Parliament in Western Australia, 'was the fact we should have to suffer all this at the hands of our men and in our own country!' It would not be the last time Australia would condemn a woman by virtue of her marriage, or that children would be held in custody and 'treated as criminals'.[4]

SOURCES AND FURTHER READING: This story draws on Daisy Schoeffel's entreaties to the Honourable H. Gregory, Member for Fremantle NAA: CRS 457, item 406/1. It also draws on several government reports relevant to internment in NAA: MP 367/1, 567/10/189. The best study of the experience of German-Australians remains Gerhard Fischer, *Enemy Aliens: Internment and the Homefront Experience in Australia, 1914–1920* (St Lucia: University of Queensland Press, 1989); and Klaus Neumann and Ilma O'Brien's contribution to Martin Crotty and David Roberts (eds), *Great Mistakes in Australian History* (Sydney: New South Books, 2006).

ABOVE **Intent on purging the German presence:** The memorial at Trial Bay in New South Wales. The German prisoners commemorated here died during their internment. This memorial – erected by their comrades – was blown to pieces by returned diggers in 1919. Sydney Mail, *16 July 1919 courtesy National Library of Australia.*

My broken heart

FRANCES EDGEWORTH SOMERS

Today, it is impossible to imagine Melbourne's skyline without the Shrine of Remembrance. A great granite sentinel, it sits on the summit of the Domain, seen from every corner of the city and, when it was first built, seen from Port Phillip Bay as well. The Shrine was the first thing visitors saw on their arrival by sea to Melbourne and was the last sight to farewell them as they left. And it was built to stand forever. The granite from which the Shrine was fashioned is one of the hardest stones known to humankind. In the 1920s, the symbolism of that was simply compelling. The names of men whose bodies were rotting in the mud of Flanders, bleached to the bone by desert winds, blown apart by high explosives, were carved on the face of the memorial. Reborn, reconfigured, the classical lines of the Shrine had rendered them whole again. But Melbourne's war memorial might well have been very different.

To the generation that built the city's memorial, the form it took was by no means inevitable. All great monuments are controversial, but this memorial, arguably, was one of the most controversial in the world. Controversial partly because of its appearance – a curious cross between a pyramid and the Parthenon – but mostly because of its cost. With a price tag of over £200 000, Melbourne would raise one of the most expensive war memorials in the world.

Many believed that the money could be better spent elsewhere. Other designs were cheaper and many were more practical. Melburnians debated bridges over the Yarra, memorial hospitals, bell towers that would sing out remembrance, and giant illuminated statues of diggers that could serve as lighthouses on the bay. But by far the most likely contender was a cenotaph. And in fact a cenotaph served as Victoria's first memorial long before the massive structure of the Shrine was complete.

A cenotaph was first raised on the steps of Parliament in 1926, the symbolic centrepiece of that year's Anzac Day procession. It was a scaled down replica of Edwin

ABOVE **Melbourne's memorial might well have been very different:** An artist's impression of a cenotaph raised at the top of Spring Street. Note the dome added to the Parliamentary Buildings, another monumental vision that never eventuated. Herald, *6 July 1926 courtesy State Library of Victoria.*

Lutyens' Cenotaph in Whitehall and, like its London counterpart, it was originally intended as a temporary memorial.

But in both London and Melbourne, the moment the cenotaphs were built – flimsy structures of plaster and timber – one letter after another, one public meeting after another, demanded they be made permanent, set in the heart of those great cities forever in stone. Melbourne's Cenotaph stood in the heart of the city, not relegated to the outskirts of the Domain. Once mourners had placed their flowers there, it became a place of pilgrimage, the site to which they would go to grieve. And for many, the form that memorial took was uplifting, the strong vertical lines of the Cenotaph gave it a kind of weightlessness, unlike the heavy, horizontal structure of the Shrine. Many were pleased that Melbourne's (temporary) memorial was modelled on the one that stood in the heart of Empire. And all were delighted with its cost.

A faithful replica of the Cenotaph could be built for less than £10 000 and the remaining money could be used to help the victims of the war. Finally, remembering had an urgency all of its own, and it would take ten years to build the Shrine. 'A Bereaved Mother' wrote to the Argus that:

> *by that time many mothers and fathers will have passed away . . . In the meantime could we not have a cenotaph . . . on which we could lay our wreaths and flowers?*[1]

The literal translation of cenotaph is an empty tomb. This was a surrogate grave for those with loved ones buried far across the seas.

Frances Edgeworth Somers was one of many who favoured a simple cenotaph over what some unkindly called 'a useless stone pile' on the Domain. She wrote to General Sir John Monash, Chairman of the state's Memorial Committee, and put forward her ardent view on the type of monument Melburnians should raise. Her letter underscores the intimate nature of remembrance, its human face:

> *I am the mother of three sons who served in the war, two of whom have fallen . . . I am convinced that only a cenotaph similar in design to the one in London will appeal to the hearts of those who have suffered grief in the war, and that it will prove a living force and a comfort to thousands. Many wonder why the English Cenotaph makes such an appeal especially to the mothers of the fallen but I have never wondered . . . Also we can get close to it, touch it with our hands, and place our flowers there so easily. . . [Should not our] disabled soldiers . . . be assisted in every way possible instead.*[2]

Mrs Edgeworth Somers' eldest boy, Noel, went missing at Gallipoli in 1915. Despite vague hopes he may have been taken prisoner, nothing more was heard of him. All her life she imagined that unmarked grave by the Aegean, a body left in the scrub of the gullies and covered by wild thyme.

Noel's brother, Gervase, enlisted within days of his 18th birthday, determined to follow the example his two older brothers had set. A 'dear little boy', he was killed in France just a few weeks before the war ended. News of Gervase's death only reached the family after the Armistice, when a friend in England finally initiated inquiries. Mrs Edgeworth Somers 'took the loss of her two sons so [very] badly'; 'a terrible blow' made all the worse by false hopes, inconclusive news and the long trial of waiting. She had a claim to speak for the bereaved.[3]

In the end, the Shrine was built against the wishes of a great many of Melbourne's mourners. A voluntary poll was conducted by the *Herald* and of the 23 000 people who participated, 20 000 voted against the Shrine. Once complete, the Shrine was seen by many as a soldiers' rather than a mothers' memorial – the first dawn services were exclusively the preserve of men.

Disenfranchised from the formal structures of remembrance, women like Mrs Edgeworth Somers sought other places to grieve. She helped fund a cross of sacrifice in her hometown of Mornington. It bears the image of a woman laying to rest the slain body of a soldier, just as she wished she could have done. She also funded an honour roll in the town hall, a handsome wooden panel on which the names of the dead were inscribed in gold. And she wrote poetry to remember Noel and Gervase, tributes in words far more heartfelt than a monolith of stone.

> *Little son with deep blue eyes*
> *Like shadows on the azure skies*
> *Sun kissed curls that seemed to dance*
> *Do you really lie in France*

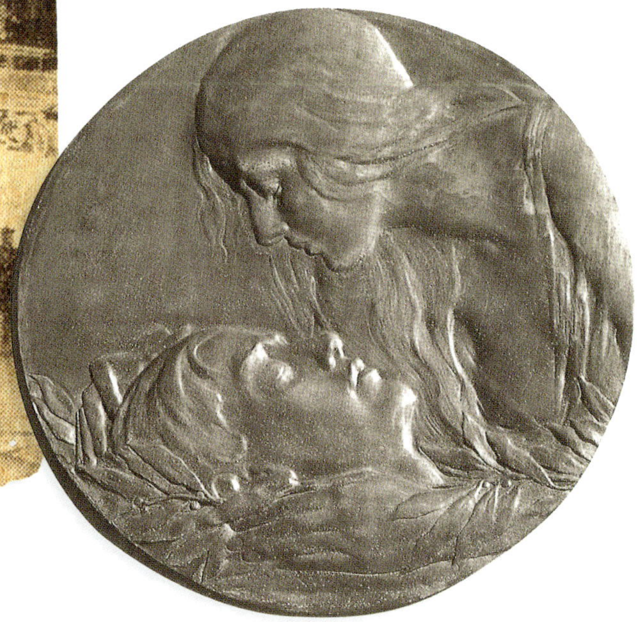

ABOVE RIGHT **Laying to rest the slain:** Dora Ohlfsen's sculpture on the face of Mornington's Memorial. Ohlfsen was one of several female artists whose work was declined by the Trustees of the Shrine. All the sculptures there were completed by men, and the work of veterans was preferred. The sculpture reminds us how memorials perform the function of the Cenotaph, a place where the absent body of the dead becomes present again. Herald, *25 April 1930 courtesy State Library of Victoria.*

ABOVE **The intimate nature of remembrance:** A group of women inspect the wreaths placed on Melbourne's original and alternative shrine. One senses the accessibility of the memorial unlike the distant edifice raised on the Domain. *Courtesy Greg James.*

Son whose eye ever grew darker blue
Hair that lost its golden hue
Eyes that looked with open glance
Do you really lie in France

Soldier son that left that day
Kissed me softly, seems so gay
I wonder do you know, perchance
My broken heart lies too in France.[4]

SOURCES AND FURTHER READING: This story draws on the service dossiers of Noel, Geravse and Neville Edgeworth Somers, NAA: B2455 SOMERS NOEL TRAVERS EDGEWORTH; NAA: B2455 SOMERS GERVASE LOUIS EDGEWORTH and NAA: B2455 SOMERS NEVILLE EDGEWORTH; and the Red Cross Wounded and Missing files for Noel and Geravse AWM 1DRL/0428; as well as a comprehensive scan of their school paper, *The Xaverian* and other contemporary newspaper reports. Mrs Edgeworth Somers' vision is expressed in her submission to Sir John Monash, which can be found in the Monash Papers, MS 1884, box 35, folder 324, at the National Library of Australia. The authors would like to thank Nick Hughes, Senior History Teacher at Xavier College, Melbourne, for his valuable assistance with this story, and the Mornington Historical Society whose website features Somers' poems. Debates surrounding the shape of Melbourne's memorial are considered at length in Bruce Scates, *A Place to Remember: A History of Victoria's Shrine of Remembrance* (Cambridge: Cambridge University Press, 2009)

The Great Fuck Up

CECIL TARRANT

Cecil Tarrant immigrated to Australia in 1910. His hometown was Treharris, in the Taff Bargoed Valley, South Wales. As with many young men, emigration promised something better. But five years after his arrival in Australia, Cecil was sailing back to Europe, a young recruit in the 15th Battalion.

Cecil's war was brief and it was bloody. At first he was sent to the nursery sector at Armentières, to be schooled in what the generals called the 'Art of Trench Warfare'. But there was very little art in what followed. Cecil Tarrant and his battalion were thrown into the carnage of Pozières. The 4th Division relieved the 2nd in the defence of the ruined township, and, like them, faced days of incessant bombardment. Then came the disastrous assault on Mouquet Farm, yet another costly attempt to take the high ground at Thiepval. July to November 1916 is known in the history books by the august title of the 'Battle of the Somme'. Soldiers like Cecil had a far better name for it – they called it the 'Great Fuck Up'.

It was at Mouquet Farm that Cecil received a gunshot wound to the face. His jaw, mouth and nose were shattered. Cecil spent a year and a half hospitalised in France, suffering an endless series of operations. Then he was moved to Sidcup Hospital in England for further treatment. From 1916 to 1919, Cecil Tarrant underwent forty-two separate surgeries, his jaw was rebuilt, dentures fitted and an 'appliance' placed in his left nostril. The wounds never seemed to heal and Cecil often bled profusely from the mouth. From the day he was wounded on the Somme, every breath he took, and every meal he ate, would be an effort for Cecil Tarrant.

Private Tarrant belonged to a generation determined to defy disability. Intent on earning a living for himself, he took on forty-five acres of farmland in the Tweed Valley, near Murwillumbah, just south of the Queensland border. But his injuries proved one of many handicaps. Cecil knew next to nothing about the local land, the seasons were

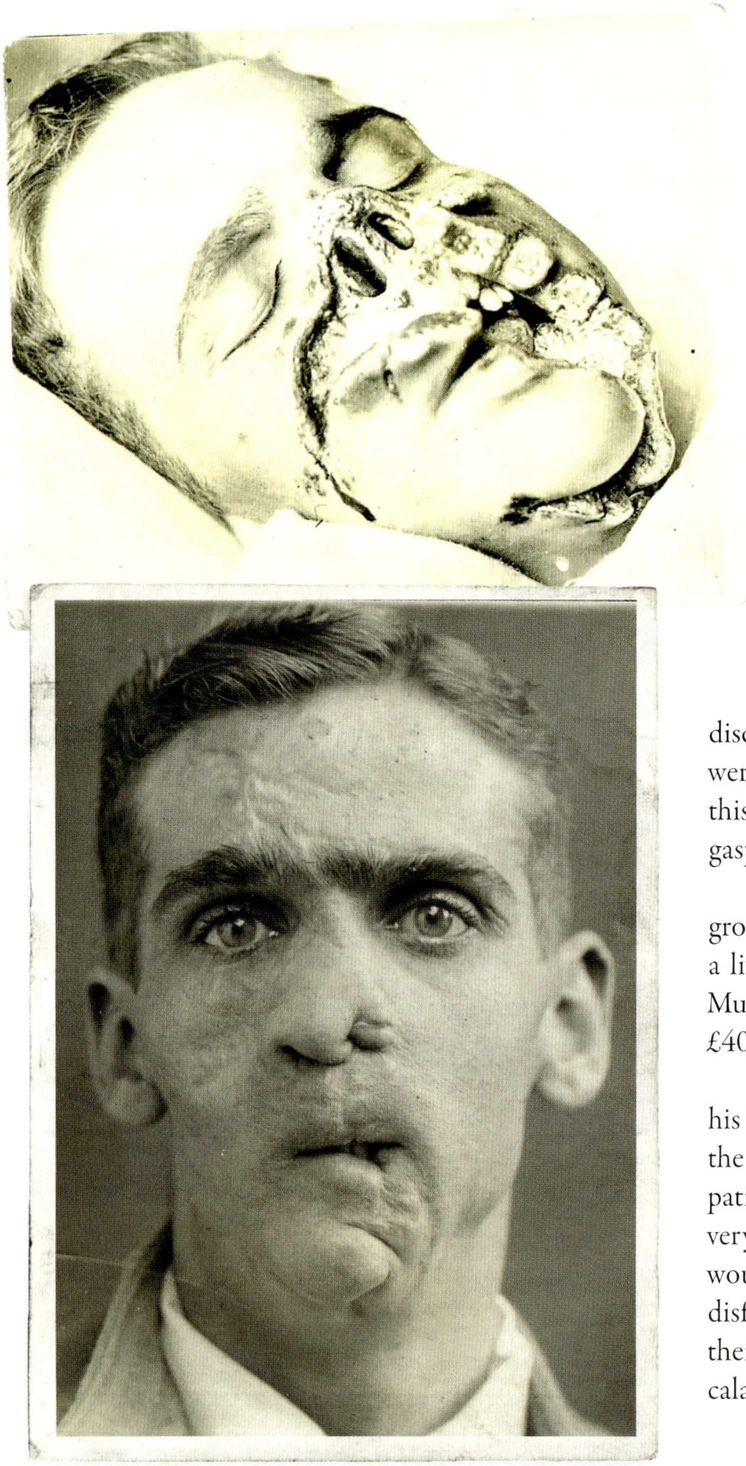

bad and the markets indifferent. In his first year at Eungella, the farm yielded barely three cases of bananas per week, and returns from the dairy were minimal. Soon Cecil Tarrant's debts were mounting.

On 25 April 1921, crowds gathered by war memorials all around Australia. They listened to speeches that honoured the bravery of soldiers and the debt the Empire owed the fallen. Honouring the debt to the living was quite another matter. At the very moment that these commemorations took place, the local bailiff charged into Tarrant's home, repossessed the family's furniture, confiscated a herd of dairy cows, and took whatever he fancied in farming equipment.

The Murwillumbah community was outraged. It was bad enough such a thing should happen at all, let alone on Anzac Day. A town meeting was called to discuss the treatment of Private Tarrant. Horrific photographs were shown to the audience, a graphic illustration of the way this faceless man had been pieced back together. The assembly gasped at the raw wounds, 'a mute tribute to colossal suffering'.[1]

The mayor declared that Tarrant's farm was 'hardly fit to grow an [onion]' and that 'it was impossible for him to make a living on it'.[2] Rural communities are often close-knit, and Murwillumbah came to the aid of Cecil Tarrant, raising over £400 to help him.

Cecil Tarrant returned to the UK. Little is known of his life there. What we do know is that many men failed on the land in Australia, so many it taxed the funds and the patience of even the most caring rural township. And it seems very probable that this was not the last time Cecil Tarrant's wounds became a perverse kind of 'asset'. It was only the most disfigured men, the men who wore the wounds of war on their bodies, who could move communities to charity in the calamity of the Great Depression.

SOURCES AND FURTHER READING: This story draws on Cecil Tarrant's service dossier NAA: B2455, TARRANT CECIL WILLIAM; his repatriation file NAA: C137, R90115; and contemporary newspaper reports. For studies of soldier settlement in this part of Australia, see Murray Johnson, 'Promises and Pineapples: Post-First World War Soldier Settlement at Beerburrum, Queensland, 1916–29', *Australian Journal of Politics and History*, vol. 51, no. 4, 2005, pp. 496–512; also Bruce Scates and Melanie Oppenheimer, *The Last Battle of the Great War: Soldier Settlement in Australia* (Cambridge: Cambridge University Press, forthcoming).

ABOVE **A mute tribute to colossal suffering**[3]: Cecil Tarrant suffered terrible facial injuries in battle. These images show his initial wounds and the progress made by 1918. *Se71-171 Cecil Tarrant Photographs courtesy Royal Australasian College of Surgeons.*

Friendship knows no boundaries

MARGARET THORP

In July 1917, the newly formed Women's Compulsory Service Petition League met in Brisbane's School of Arts Hall. It was a cool winter's night, with a sharp breeze rising up from the river. But in the hall itself the atmosphere could not have been more heated. Around three hundred women had crammed into the building. Many wore stern black dresses, evidence, one participant claimed, that 'the majority were mourning the loss of a loved one'– a son, husband or father 'who had either gone down in the conflict or will come back maimed or impaired'.[1]

It was a sombre crowd but also an angry one. The Women's Compulsory Service Petition League called for the conscription of all eligible men, demanding that those who had thus far 'shirked' their duty be sent immediately to the Front. The chair, Anna Paterson, told the gathering that 'her three sons were in the firing line' and that due to disloyal elements in their midst all their lives were now in peril.

Voluntary enlistment had been falling since the debacle on the Somme. By 1917, the Allies could barely replace the dead and the wounded, let alone meet the needs of a new and equally bloody offensive in Flanders. The Australian people had rejected conscription in a fiercely contested referendum the previous October (and they would vote again against conscription later in the year). But the meeting that night called on the government to introduce compulsory military service without the mandate of a plebiscite and 'without further delay'. Victory would come at a cost, a determined Anna Paterson declared. To defend what they called 'liberty and freedom' the loyal women of Brisbane were prepared to sacrifice democracy itself.[2]

Not all the women in the hall that night agreed. Margaret Thorp, feminist, pacifist and Quaker, rose to move an amendment. A cluster of about thirty supporters sat around her, a small island of dissent in a huge tide of patriotic fervour. With some difficulty, Thorp made her way towards the platform. She reminded the Chair that the

ABOVE **An army of 10,000 mothers, wives, sisters, and sweethearts:** A huge public demonstration of women on Empire Day, appealing to Australian men to enlist. Sydney *Mail, 29 May 1918 courtesy National Library of Australia.*

MRS. P. LAWRENCE
JANE ADDAMS
ANNA MOLLOY
PEACE
PEACE DELEGATES ON NOORDAM

conscription of human life was a grave and contentious matter, and that the Australian electorate had voted 'overwhelmingly' against it. 'The boys who had gone overseas went on a voluntary basis,' she continued. In Australia, no man had been forced to bear arms, a point that distinguished our young democracy from all the conscript armies compelled to fight in Europe.[3]

Thorp had spoken for less than a minute before the interjections began. As voices were raised, scuffles broke out and the meeting descended into pandemonium. Those who opposed conscription were called disloyal, pro-German, un-Australian. 'You haven't anyone at the Front,' one woman insisted, an unfounded claim in fact, as many of the 'Antis', including Thorp, had relatives serving overseas. As Miss Thorp continued to speak, she was 'pulled about, clawed and hustled'. One woman tried to drag her from the platform. Only by desperately clinging to a table did Margaret remain on the stage. But not for long:

> *[S]uddenly, a number of wild women in the front of the audience surged on the 'rostrum' and Miss Thorp was shamelessly assaulted. She was punched and scratched, thrown off the platform, rolled on the floor, kicked, punched, and scratched again, and at last was carried, pushed or thrown out of the doorway. All the time there was a hideous roar of voices.*[4]

It says much about the mettle of Margaret Thorp that she returned 'still calm and determined' to the meeting. She also had the good sense to bring a policeman. At that point, the most belligerent patriots suddenly became 'extremely quiet and retiring'.

The fair-minded constable appealed for fair play. Miss Thorp had every right to attend a public meeting, he explained, as did her fellow members of the Women's Peace Army. And the purpose of opening the floor for discussion was a frank and respectful exchange of views. But the pro-conscription lobby would have none of that. Rather than debating the issues, someone struck up a rousing chorus of the National Anthem. When Thorp began to speak again she was met with 'counting out', hoots, catcalls, and 'various other performances'. Then fighting broke out again. 'No one,' the papers reported:

> *was so seriously hurt as to require medical aid [but hats] and clothes were in many cases battered and torn, and several Labor women subsequently showed scratches and bruises that had resulted from the 'catty' tactics of the militarist females.*

Miss Thorp was the most badly shaken of all. Twice she had been ejected from the meeting and twice she'd marched boldly back into the building, her 'spirit undaunted'.[5]

Margaret Thorp became the cause célèbre of the peace movement overnight – the *Worker* dubbed her the 'angel of peace' – but her career in the anti-war movement had begun much earlier.

Women's
Peace Army
QUEENSLAND BRANCH.

Member's Name
Address
Date Issued

President: Miss Clio Jensen, M.A.
Vice-Presidents: Mrs. Miller and Mrs. Lane.
Secretary and Treasurer:
Miss Thorp,
Pied a Terre, Borva Street,
South Brisbane.

HEAD OFFICE:
LATROBE STREET, MELBOURNE.
Hon. Secretary: Miss CECELIA JOHN.

ABOVE **A feminist critique of nationalism and violence:** The Women's Peace Army described itself as an educational agency devoted to breaking down the barriers between nations and challenging the inequalities that fostered war. *Society of Friends Collection courtesy State Library of New South Wales.*

OPPOSITE **A just and lasting peace:** Delegates to the 1915 Women's International Congress aboard MS *Noordam*. Those who sought a negotiated settlement to the conflict were dismissed as 'peace cranks' or worse. In fact, these women (and others like them) sought peace with justice, and condemned the arms race, jingoism and rampant imperialism that plunged Europe into war. *Ggbain 18848 courtesy United States Library of Congress.*

ABOVE **Calm and determined:** A portrait of Margaret Thorp around the time of the Brisbane School of Arts riot. A male dominated press damned the 'emotionalism' of the meeting, accusing women of hysteria. By contrast, Margaret seems restrained and demure. *Courtesy the Religious Society of Friends.*

Born into a Quaker family in England, Margaret had been schooled in pacifist principles and taught to value free speech and independent thought since childhood. Margaret immigrated to Queensland on the eve of the Great War and threw herself into the work of the Australian Freedom League. The League sought the repeal of the 1912 Defence Act, requiring children to attend cadets, drill in military formation and learn the use of arms. By 1914, 5732 minors had been imprisoned for resisting military training and over 20 000 boys or their parents had been prosecuted. Lads of 16 had been confined in the cells of military prisons, subjected to verbal and physical abuse, and sentenced to solitary confinement and half rations.

Margaret deplored the militarisation of youth, and established a Children's Peace Army to promote Quaker and socialist ideals. She believed schools should educate children to build a better nation and a fairer world and teach the practical values of tolerance and cooperation.

When war broke out most of the country responded with enthusiasm. Recruiting offices were overwhelmed with volunteers, patriotic groups formed to assist with fundraising, and politicians and the press rallied around the cause of Empire. But Margaret called on Australians to remember the cost of human conflict. She believed war was 'immorality made legal', that it involved a sordid 'wholesale slaughter by machinery' and could only end in 'tragedy' and 'devastation'. Fighting on such an appalling scale would breed 'hatred and revenge' and one world war would lead inevitably to another. 'Justice and reason,' she concluded, 'cannot be served by mechanical brute force.'[6] Margaret called on Australia to negotiate a just and lasting peace. In 1914, very few listened.

As the war progressed and casualties in Europe mounted, Australian society became more and more divided. The fracas in Brisbane's School of Arts was symptomatic of the fear, resentment and anger that gripped the nation. Determined to win the war, punish Germany, and avenge the loss of loved ones, pro-conscription movements urged greater and greater sacrifice. The War Precautions Act imposed severe penalties for any activity deemed prejudicial to recruiting, and Margaret herself became the subject of military surveillance.

In a country that claimed to be fighting for freedom, her activities were monitored, her correspondence intercepted, and her home raided in search of anti-war literature. Intelligence officers described her as a 'fully qualified communist', sympathetic to banned organisations like the Industrial Workers of the World (a militant anti-war union), 'anti-British, pacifist and sometimes out-and-out revolutionary'.[7] In response, the Women's Peace Army fielded a feminist critique of nationalism and violence, its manifesto declared:

> *WE UNITE with the Women of All Nations . . . WE FIGHT AGAINST THE SYSTEM which compels Emperors, Czars and Kings to march their people to slaughter.*[8]

Pro-conscriptionists like Anna Paterson claimed those who opposed the war or themselves refused to fight were cowards. But Margaret's brother, also a Quaker, went to France. Unwilling to take up arms against his fellow man, Joseph served in the Quaker's Ambulance Unit. He nursed the wounded midst 'the continual booming of the guns', and risked his own life to save the lives of others.[9]

Nor could Margaret herself be called a coward. She showed the moral courage to stand up for her beliefs. And the physical courage to leave Australia for war-torn Europe in 1919 to aid an army of starving refugees. Margaret was amongst the first aid workers to visit Soviet Russia, a country stricken by drought, famine, disease and a bitter civil war. 'The land was a brown desert,' she wrote in her memoirs, in some districts 'over 90% of the children under three died of hunger.' Margaret remembered their bodies piled in the streets, naked and emaciated.[10]

All her life, Margaret Thorp would work to aid the disadvantaged. In the interwar years, she helped establish the New South Wales Society for Crippled Children and served as one of its first welfare officers. When the Second World War wreaked even more havoc across Europe than the First, Margaret returned to Germany and worked as a volunteer for the British Red Cross. In the 1950s, she became a Foundation Member of UNICEF, and later, in the 1970s, a supporter of the Moratorium Movement opposing the conscription of Australian youth to fight in Vietnam.

Margaret befriended the homeless, pleaded the cause of refugees and welcomed immigration from Asia. She championed the cause of war orphans and called for their resettlement in Australia. 'The children know nothing of politics,' she declared, 'and their agony cries out above national barriers.'[11]

'Who are the real national heroes?' she asked. 'Surely they are the men and women who do the little things of life in a big way, putting their best energies and interest into their work and whose friendship knows no boundaries.'[12]

Margaret Thorp was a woman whose friendship knew no boundaries – who worked to bring all war to an end.

SOURCES AND FURTHER READING: This story draws on intelligence records on Margaret Thorp in NAA: A402/W245; the Religious Society of Friends in Australia Papers concerning Margaret, including her unpublished journal on peace work and an unpublished autobiography in the Thorp Papers, Society of Friends collection, in the State Library of New South Wales, ML 1209/78, boxes 1 and 2; as well as contemporary newspaper reports. For earlier studies of the Women's Peace Army see Raymond Evans, '"All the passion of our womanhood": Margaret Thorp and the Battle of the Brisbane School of Arts' in Joy Damousi and Marilyn Lake (eds), *Gender and War: Australians at War in the Twentieth Century* (Cambridge: Cambridge University Press, 1995) pp. 239–253; Bruce Scates and Raelene Frances, *Women and the Great War* (Cambridge: Cambridge University Press, 1997); Hilary N. Summy, *'Peace Angel' of World War 1: Dissent of Margaret Thorp* (St Lucia: Australian Centre for Peace and Conflict Studies, 2006); Raelene Frances, 'Women's Mobilisations for War (Australia)' in Ute Daniel, Peter Gatrell, Oliver Janz, Heather Jones, Jennifer Keene, Alan Kramer and Bill Nassan(eds), *1914–18 Online International Encyclopedia of the First World War* (Berlin: Freie Universität Berlin, 2014). The authors gratefully acknowledge the assistance of the Religious Society of Friends (the Quakers) in compiling this account and in particular Jenny Madeline, co-convener of the Quaker exhibition, *World War One: Quaker Witness to Peace and Non-Violence*. Further details of Thorp's life can be found in the *Australian Dictionary of Biography* (under her married name of Margaret Sturge Watts).

A lost soul

WILLIAM RILEY

When some people die, a whole world mourns their passing – the loss is sorely felt by family, community and friends. But other deaths are more anonymous. In the Great War, thousands perished almost unnoticed, lives cut short almost before they had begun.

William Riley was an orphan. His parents died of tuberculosis when he was very young. William was separated from his two sisters and they would never meet again. He was sent to the Burwood Boys' Home, an institution pledged to rescue 'destitute or uncared for' boys from 'depraved immoral or other dangerous surroundings'.[1] William was taught the rudiments of reading and writing, schooled in scripture and gardening, then told he must make his own way in the world.[2]

Within weeks of his eighteenth birthday, William joined the Army. Perhaps it was patriotism, perhaps the chance of earning a living, perhaps there was nowhere else to go. William served fourteen months with the 60th Battalion, and we will never know what kind of a family they became to him. He fell ill within weeks of arriving in France, was shipped away to England and died.

William Riley's personal effects made a pathetic little bundle: a pen and a notebook, a French coin and pocketknife, some cigarettes and a Bible, the usual assortment of socks, comb, handkerchief and scarf. But Base Records had no next-of-kin to send them to. They were wrapped up in brown paper, bound with string and forwarded to the Boys' Home in Burwood. William had also kept two letters. There is no record of who they were from. Perhaps it was his guardian appointed at the orphanage, perhaps the nurse who cared for him through sickness, perhaps one or even both of his sisters had learned of his service overseas.

More than likely, these letters were written by a stranger. William's name was probably chosen at random by one of a dozen patriotic societies working to 'keep up morale'. Women, young and old, sent off parcels of comforts and wrote cheery correspondence to men they would most likely never meet.

In the 1920s, there was no one to choose William Riley's epitaph. His grave reads like a roll call, noting his rank, battalion and age. Nor was there anyone to receive his medals, medallions or memorial scroll issued by a 'grateful King'. Those trinkets of condolence were mass produced in England and issued to grieving families across the Empire, honouring around one million dead.

Even so, it would be wrong to claim that William had no one. A Miss Halligan from Ballarat wrote for details of his death. Perhaps she also wrote the letters William Riley had kept. William left what little money he had to her, and the nurse who showed some little kindness to a sick and vulnerable child. The pay still due to him from the Army was bequeathed to the orphanage, the only 'real' home William had known. In time the orphanage also received his medals, pledging to care for them in the absence of any relative the military authorities could find. Interestingly, William used the term 'Burboys' in addressing the Home. Perhaps that familiar abbreviation was even a term of endearment.[3]

Today, still, that orphaned soldier boy is remembered. Mrs Betty Horskins of Glen Waverley chanced on the lad's story in her research and it is William she remembers each Remembrance Day:

> *How sad, a young man who belonged to no one. To have not a soul that was family . . . There being no loved ones to accept his medals . . . the authorities asked if the Boys' Home would accept them. The Committee agreed – I wonder where the medals are now. Fancy fighting and dying then what little you owned and what you were entitled to ends up with a committee.*[4]

Mrs Horskins became a kind of fictive kin for a boy without a family, one of countless thousands who endured 'the awful events' of the Great War. But no one knows the answer to her question about the medals. Burwood Boys' Home was disestablished in 1972. The mementos it had pledged to 'preserve in a suitable manner' have vanished without trace.[5] So too, in a sense, has William Riley. A young man, of whom nothing is left bar the official record, 'a lost soul' Betty Horskins has adopted as her own.

ABOVE **Smart lads:** A few of the 'orphaned', 'destitute' or simply 'uncontrollable' boys sent to Burwood. The home 'for the rescue and training of boys' was situated in 'fine, healthy country' a few miles (then) from the metropolis of Melbourne. These boys were institutionalised at around the same time that William was, trained 'to be of use in garden or on farm' and taught to become a 'wage-earner'. Perhaps the Army promised William a more regular or remunerative occupation, or perhaps it was just the promise of adventure. The Spectator, *23 June 1899.*

OPPOSITE **Trinkets of condolence:** The memorial broach issued to mothers on the death of their sons. In William's case the memorialisation process is underscored by absence. His mother died over a decade before him. A memorial broach for her was never made. *Snape family memorial broach courtesy Walter Barber.*

SOURCES AND FURTHER READING: This account draws on William Riley's service dossier NAA: B2455 RILEY WILLIAM ERNEST; and contemporary newspaper reports. The authors thank Mrs Betty Horskins, Shirley Swain and Kim Wheatley for their help. For further reading on the experiences of soldiers from orphanages see Frank Golding, 'Making Men of Our Boys: Soldiers from the Ballaret Orphanage in World War 1' presented at Approaching War: Children's Culture and the War 1980–1919, UTS, December 2011.

What should never happen again

HUGO THROSSELL

In July 1919, Captain Hugo Throssell VC, a West Australian hero born and bred, led the victory parade through his hometown of Northam. It was a bright, sunny afternoon. A light breeze caught the flags lining the streets and played with the emu plume perched on Throssells' hat, the celebrated hallmark of every Light Horse man.

Throssell rode a big bay gelding, an officer's sword swung at his side, and the dull bronze of the Victoria Cross was pinned proudly on his chest. Hundreds cheered as he passed them. This was their lad, their 'Jim', the boy from Northam who had been awarded the Empire's highest award for gallantry.

BELOW **Badly mauled at Gallipoli:** A badge commemorating the assault on the Dardanelles. Although Throssell was not present for the Landing, he survived some of the bloodiest fighting at the Nek and Hill 60. He came to remember his time on the peninsula with bitterness and regret. *Courtesy Melbourne Museum.*

The procession wheeled to a halt at a large platform mounted outside Tattersalls Hotel. The Salvation Army Band struck up, a massed choir of the town's churches sang 'God Save the King' and the whole town seemed to join them. Hugo Throssell took his place amongst the eldest and wealthiest men of the district. Throssell was well connected – the Premier of Western Australia, who sat beside him, was a close family friend.

The crowd listened respectfully to the usual speeches by churchmen and politicians. But it was 'Jim' they had come to hear. A charming man, tall and handsome, his speech began with heartfelt thanks for his reception. 'It was good to be back in old Northam,' he bellowed joyfully, and to receive 'dozens of warm handshakes' as he strolled through the town. Throssell delighted the crowd with 'humorous references to his exploits', tales of the football field and the boxing ring. Soon he had his old school chums and the entire community eating out of his hand.

He paused a moment and the crowd waited for tales of that next great adventure, a thrilling account of how the hero of Gallipoli earned the VC. But here, Hugo Thossell's speech took a quite unexpected turn. During the past five years he had seen much of the world and now left childhood dreams of the glories of war behind him:

Nearly five years ago I rode through the streets of Northam in charge of eighteen men, who were amongst the first to enlist . . . Of that eighteen, seven are lying either in Gallipoli, Palestine, or France. . . . War had made me a Socialist . . . I have seen enough of the horrors of war, and want peace. After four years of war, after the loss of nearly eight million lives, with a total of eighteen million wounded, of whom six million are permanent wrecks . . . [how was it] still possible for individuals to make colossal fortunes by the manufacture of armaments . . . If the people do not want war, we must scrap this rotten old system of production for profit and organise . . . for the well being of the community as a whole.[1]

ABOVE **The highest award for gallantry:** A photograph of the handsome Hugo Throssell. This studio portrait was probably taken in London towards the end of the war. Throssell had been hospitalised on several occasions for illness and wounds. *A03688 courtesy Australia War Memorial.*

'You could have heard a pin drop,' Hugo's wife, Katharine Susannah Prichard wrote to a fellow communist, Nettie Palmer. 'Jim himself was ghastly, his face all torn with emotion. It was terrible – but it was magnificent.'[2] Those who believed in the cause of the Empire would never forget what was said that day and few would forgive.

Hugo Throssell spoke with conviction. One of the boys he rode out with from Northam five years previous was his younger brother, Ric. They'd shared a close bond and all through their childhood the two mischief-making lads had been inseparable. But Ric was killed in the Battle of Gaza, just one more casualty in that desperate desert war against the Turks:

On the night that Ric disappeared, Hugo crawled across the battlefield under enemy fire, searching in vain for his brother among the dead and dying, and whistling for him with the same signal as they had used when boys.[3]

Ric was buried beneath the shifting sands of the Sinai Peninsula. Hugo was never the same again. In fact, he was one of the damaged men to whom his speech had referred. Hugo Throssell had been badly mauled at Gallipoli. One of the few officers to survive that 'fool's charge' at the Nek, he was thrown into equally costly fighting at Hill 60 near Suvla. For several days, the Ottomans and Allies battled over a hill so tiny it resembled, in the official historian's words, a 'swelling on the plain'. In this place, 'murderous bomb, rifle and machine gun fire' left the trenches 'choked with dead.'[4]

In the action that earned him his VC, Throssell fought continuously for forty-eight hours, refusing to retire until ordered (twice) to do so. By then, wounds covered most of his body and a bomb blast had driven fragments of uniform, including the metal shoulder badge that read 'Australia', deep into his arm.

The wounds Throssell suffered at Gallipoli and then later in Gaza would plague him for the rest of his life. But earning a VC didn't win any particular favours with the repatriation authorities. Successive medical boards classified him 'partially incapacitated', noted he was 'depressed' and 'sleeping badly' and that his defective vision was progressively becoming worse. 'Metal splinters entered eye at Gallipoli,' Dr C.W. Courtney scribbled in his notebook, '[even so] I do not consider patient eligible to receive glasses at Departmental expense.'[5]

Perhaps Courtney had heard about the speech Throssell made at Northam, and the unorthodox, left-wing company the husband of Katharine Susannah Prichard had come to keep. Consorting with known communists was not considered behaviour becoming of an officer, let alone a VC winner. 'Manner somewhat nervy,' one doctor recorded, 'looks older than he is.'[6] Intelligence officers were detailed to monitor the war hero's 'leaning towards socialism'.[7]

Forced to resign from a government post by those who opposed his politics, Throssell's finances went from bad to worse. The Depression of the 1930s rendered much of his property worthless, his farm was failing and so too was his health. Along with the wounds inflicted on the battlefield, Throssell had contracted meningitis in hospital. He suffered what he called 'brain storms', searing pains that pounded in his head. And he was alone: Throssell had insisted his wife accept an invitation to visit the Soviet Union, believing only a brave new social order could avert the outbreak of yet another war. His 'all consuming love' had gone when he needed her most.[8]

Early one Sunday morning in 1933, Hugo Throssell walked from his bedroom to a latticed verandah looking out on the bush. He sat in his favourite wicker chair, rested his feet on the balcony, and shot himself in the head. The bullet that killed him was fired with a Webley service revolver. Remembrance Day, honouring the heroic dead, had passed just a week before.

RIGHT **A latticed verandah, looking out on the bush:** The site of Throssell's suicide. The Throssell family home now serves as a writer's retreat, honouring the career of Katharine Susannah Prichard and the memory of the man who loved her. *Courtesy Bruce Scates.*

Throssell wrote a brief message before raising the revolver to his temple. 'I can't sleep, and I feel my old war head.'[9] The authorities found a note with his will and personal papers:

> *I have never recovered from my 1914–18 experiences and with this in view, I appeal to the State that my wife and child get the usual war pension. No man could have a truer mate.*[10]

They buried Captain Hugo Throssell VC with full military honours. His medal and sword were placed on the coffin, as was a union flag. Politicians and returned soldiers, some of them the same men who had hounded him since that fiery speech in Northam, mourned 'a fallen hero'. 'He died for his country,' said the chaplain, 'just as surely as if he had perished in the trenches.'[11]

A few weeks later, his widow returned from abroad and reluctantly accepted a pension:

> *I consider that his 'grateful country' made it impossible for my husband to live. He thought he had to die to provide for his wife and child . . . I could not accept anything that cost him his life; but . . . I have no right to interfere with what he sought to do for his son.*[12]

Katharine never recovered from the loss of her husband. But she threw herself into her work, devoting the rest of her life to the same ideals Hugo spoke of in Northam. Ric Throssell, Hugo's son, sold his father's VC, donating the proceeds to the campaign for nuclear disarmament. In 2008, Karen Throssell became a peace ambassador to Turkey and walked the ground her grandfather fought on:

> *I think my grandfather would have been very proud of me for making this journey . . . My brief visit . . . has left me feeling that I should . . . acknowledge Anzac Day, acknowledge it as our Peace Day – a day to remember what happened not just to our own loved ones but to remind us of what should never happen again.*[13]

ABOVE **He died for his country:** Hugo Throssell's grave in Karrakatta Cemetery. The Light Horse Association, Throssell's old school and the Northam RSL restored the monument in 2014. 'Courageous in war' it reads, and 'steadfast in peace'. No mention is made of the circumstances of Throssell's death or of his pacifist beliefs. *Courtesy Bruce Scates.*

SOURCES AND FURTHER READING: This story draws on Hugo Throssell's service dossier NAA: B2455, THROSSELL HUGO VIVIAN HOPE; his repatriation records NAA: K60, C5723 and NAA: PP6441/1, M5273; and reports by postwar intelligence agencies on both Hugo and his wife NAA: A6119/42 and NAA: A6119 vols. 1–7. The authors have also drawn on a detailed survey of contemporary newspaper reports; C.E.W. Bean, *The Story of Anzac*, vol. 11 (Sydney: Angus and Robertson, 1924) and autobiographical accounts by Hugo Throssell's family, namely Katharine Susannah Prichard, *Child of the Hurricane* (Sydney: Angus and Robertson, 1963) and Ric Throssell, *My Father's Son* (Melbourne: William Heinemann Australia, 1989). For the most recent biography of Throssell's life see John Hamilton, *The Price of Valour* (Sydney: Pan Macmillan, 2012) and for the most nuanced reading of his death, Pat Jalland, 'A Private and Secular Grief', *History Australia*, vol. 2, no. 2, 2005, pp. 42–57. For work on Katharine Susannah Prichard see Pam Portman and Sally Clarke, *Katharine Susannah Prichard: Her Place* (Western Australia: Gooseberry Hill Press/Katharine Susannah Prichard Foundation, 2010). Note also Prichard's semi-autobiographical account, *Intimate Strangers* (Sydney: Angus and Robertson, 1937). The authors would also like to acknowledge the kind assistance of Peta Alderman, Manager of the Commonwealth War Graves Commission in Western Australia, and Julie Wells.

The second Count of Monte Christo

LEO GALLI

It has often been said that truth is the first casualty in war. We will never know the 'truth' about Leo Galli.

To some, Galli was a patriot, an idealist, even a hero. Italian born, but a naturalised British subject, Galli was amongst the first to volunteer. From the moment he put his pen to the Army's enlistment papers he projected an intriguing persona. Over a hundred clerks, labourers, artisans and businessmen called at the recruiting desk at Randwick that day, but Galli was the only man to describe his calling as 'Geologist'. The address of his next-of-kin, his mother, was recorded as the Vatican and, in Catholic company especially, Galli boasted his uncle was the Pope's trusted secretary. Though barely 33, Professor Galli claimed extensive military service. He'd served a year in the 4th Infantry Militia (terminated by what he called 'mutual consent') and held (so he said) a commission as Second Lieutenant in the 91st Infantry Regiment of the Italian Army. Eight thousand miles from Rome, most of these claims were taken at face value. Professor Galli secured the rank of Lance Corporal.

Galli sailed to war with the first contingent. Again, if we can believe his account, he was popular with the men and soon emerged as a natural leader. There was no Catholic priest on HMAT *Afric* and (at the suggestion of the padre, we're told), Galli took on the pastoral care of '300 Catholic boys'. 'All the boys faithfully said their prayers,' Galli told a company of grieving mothers back home in Australia, 'and before the landing at Gallipoli, [I] asked them to kneel down and [pray] before they took to the boats. They did so.'[1] Such an assurance may well have brought comfort, especially in the large Catholic audiences he addressed. But like so many of Galli's claims it has proved impossible to verify.

Landing on Gallipoli, Lance Corporal Galli was told to advance up the ridges. 'The Australians fought like lions,' he told applauding audiences across the country.

They did their duty to a man 'and he had seen them die with a smile on their lips'.[2] But Galli appears to have seen very little of the Australians in action. He was evacuated on the same day he landed, most likely with the first boatloads of wounded. The absence of any apparent injury on Galli himself soon roused the suspicion of authorities.

Lieutenant Paine told his commanding officer that he judged the man a 'deserter' and 'malingerer'. Galli could not say by whose authority he had left his platoon. When 'asked what was the matter with him', he 'could not give any clear account of his actions ashore'. In the space of twenty-four hours, Galli claimed to have been 'shot in the leg', 'dazed' by shellfire, affected by rheumatism, sciatica and an ingrown toenail. He was placed in the cells but released by the surgeon after twenty-four hours 'as he was continually crying and protesting'. 'It was,' the surgeon explained, 'very difficult when a patient said that he was suffering from some complaint to prove that he was not.'[3]

Proving anything about Lance Corporal Galli proved equally difficult back in Egypt. '[I]t was impossible to [ascertain] whether he really has the pains he says he has or not,' an examining doctor noted, '[though] he most certainly makes the most of his troubles.' Galli complained of aching arms and legs, but the doctors found no swelling, no abnormalities and their patient's temperature was normal.[4]

ABOVE **A thousand new recruits:** A recruiting poster appeals for reinforcements. Leo Galli would have brandished posters like these as he lectured audiences across the country. *Courtesy Melbourne Museum.*

The simplest explanation was the one Lieutenant Paine had seized on: that Galli was a malingerer, a deserter and quite probably a coward. But the wounds soldiers suffer in battle are not always entirely physical in character. At this early stage of the war, conditions like Galli's were often attributed to shell shock, a nervous condition thought to be linked to the 'commotional' impact of an explosion. However sceptical the doctors might be, shell shock was a possible diagnosis:

> *He told me [he] thought he must have been punched down by the concussion of the shell as he remembered nothing after the advance began until he found himself recovering consciousness on the ground not far from the beach.*

Galli may have made the most of his complaints and even perhaps exaggerated any injury, but military authorities were hardly neutral observers. Major J.C. Holdrich Leister had served as a surgeon in the British Army since the Boxer Rebellion, including a lengthy tour of Imperial outposts. An advocate of muscular Christianity and an enthusiast for the Boy Scout movement, he had scant regard for this visibly distressed Italian 'evidently of a very neurotic temperament'. '[A]nd I lay stress on this', Leister added, as if the two page report had not already made his position obvious.

Soldiers like Galli hardly measured up to the Anzac ideal, replete with those British characteristics of stoicism, bravery, and coolness under fire. They were a liability on the line, unreliable, undisciplined, even (in the racially charged and gendered language of the day) hysterical.[5]

Invalided back to Australia as medically unfit, the 'scholar soldier', as he liked to be called, was commissioned as a recruitment officer.[6] Officers in the field may have found Galli wanting, but at home he served the purposes of the authorities admirably. Few Gallipoli veterans had returned and those who had – often lacking a limb or their sight – were more than likely prejudicial to recruiting. Galli, on the other hand, was described as a clever speaker, informative and impassioned, and something of a hit with the ladies.

'He is a smart looking man above the average height of the Italians,' a paper in Mount Gambier told it readers:

> *His speech was strongly flavoured with the accent of his country, and it was thus sometimes difficult to follow him at times when he became excited with his subject. But the audience understood him fairly well and cheered him again and again.*[7]

It is hard to say what excited Galli most – the lurid descriptions of Hun atrocities or *Boys' Own* accounts of Australians storming the beaches.

As Galli's lecturing tour progressed, his limp became more pronounced and his war stories more fanciful. Initially, Galli was introduced as a wounded man lately returned from Gallipoli. By 1918 it seems he had been wounded several times, once 'severely', and even lost the sight in one eye. His Italian war service grew proportionately: Galli was promoted to First Lieutenant and he had somehow been transferred from the 93rd Infantry Regiment to a dashing post in the cavalry. He now claimed to have been a soldier since boyhood, fighting with the 'Garibaldian Legion . . . against the Turks' at the tender age of 16. At the same time, Leo Galli garnished his academic credentials. In what was called 'a strange combination of professions', he was introduced to one expectant audience as 'a Lieutenant in the Italian Army', a sergeant in the Australian forces and 'a Professor of Archeology to the Vatican in Rome'.[8]

So far as the authorities were concerned, the truth of any of these claims was immaterial. They understood Galli's recruiting tours were a performance first and foremost, and their advertisements wilfully colluded in an increasingly elaborate deception. Professor Galli of Gallipoli was always billed as the principal attraction, but support acts included 'animated pictures of the Australians in Egypt and other places', martial selections from camp brass bands and other 'popular items' likely to attract an audience.

The lectures themselves were promoted as 'an intellectual treat'. Galli's willingness to range across topics as diverse as the position of the Vatican on the war, the German psyche, and the intricacies of European politics was welcomed (it was said) by isolated communities across Australia. Sergeant Galli's address 'was one of the finest and most impressive orations ever delivered to a Murchison audience,' one Victorian paper declared, 'and his intricate knowledge of European diplomacy much appreciated.' 'Citizens,' a like-minded paper in Adelaide bellowed, 'the views of this eloquent Italian will set you thinking more deeply than ever.'[9]

However contrived some of his credentials may have been, Galli claimed his own legitimacy. That audience in Murchison, Victoria was no doubt perplexed by developments eight thousand miles distant. Galli placed them at the centre of world affairs, his explanations both plausible and empowering. Here was an eyewitness to the Landing at

OPPOSITE **A smart looking man:** The photograph of Leo Galli in the front of his book. *Scattered War Leaves* is a curious blend of history, fiction and autobiography – lines from Galli's recruitment speeches are woven throughout it. The author dedicated his book to 'The Chivalrous Defender of the World's Civilization and Progress'. *Professor Leo C Galli,* Scattered War Leaves *(Melbourne: Advocate, 1918) courtesy Rare Books Collection, Monash University.*

ABOVE **Told to advance up the ridges:** The cover of Phillip F.E. Schuler's Pictures of the Battlefields of Anzac (Melbourne: Osboldstone, 1916). Schuler's collection of photographs and anecdotes rivalled C.E.W Bean's accounts of the campaign. Galli learned more about the fighting on Anzac from these publications than from his own limited experience. *Courtesy Rare Book Collection, Monash University.*

Gallipoli, a man who spoke with authority about Teutonic aggression, and a valued Italian ally convinced of British righteousness.

Perhaps most significant of all, the cosmopolitan Galli broadened the appeal of the Allies at a time when war made Australia more and more insular. He wore both an AIF and an Italian uniform – 'as proud of that khaki as [he was] the more brilliant [colours] of his own army'. And just as the conscription campaigns divided Australia along sectarian lines, a Catholic advocated even greater sacrifice for Empire. Leo Galli, a man of 'Franco-Italian extraction', appealed to what he frequently called the 'brotherhood of nations'. 'I care not whether men be white or dark,' he told white communities bordering Coomeragunga Native Reserve:

> *... and I resent the attitude of some who speak of those plucky recruits as merely 'blacks'. Those men should be grateful to the Mission men offering to go and fight, who are not going to go themselves. I honour these recruits, and so I think will every true man possessed of a Christian and patriotic spirit.*[10]

This was a far more complex and inclusive formulation than the usual patriotic urgings to avenge Australia's fallen. Certainly Galli's ability to speak to what was called his 'co-religionists' was welcomed by the authorities. Few prominent Catholics were prepared to countenance conscription and, as a recruiting official noted, many were 'unsympathetic towards this war on account of being of Irish descent and having a hereditary grudge against ... Great Britain.'[11]

Did Leo Galli succeed? In the course of a tour that stretched from southernmost Victoria to tropical Cairns, Galli claimed credit for four thousand new recruits and almost without exception his talks were well attended. But the audience was not always the one authorities hoped for, as eligible men often stayed away. Patriotic workers, parents anxious to hear news of sons serving abroad, and the appropriate civic dignitaries listened appreciatively, but they were not the ones needed to fill each month's recruiting quota. In the last two years of the war, the First AIF suffered 35 000 dead and over twice that number wounded. As the country grew more and more war weary, even a man as charismatic as Galli failed to persuade the uncommitted.

What we should think of Galli himself is a far more open question. Patriot or charlatan? Shell-shock victim or outright coward? A fighter committed to a cause or a flagrant opportunist? Perhaps the enigmatic Signor Galli was a mixture of all those things. What is beyond dispute is that the Italian community in Australia paid a heavy price for the Great War, and not just in the number of volunteers who willingly went to fight it. We may not have introduced conscription, but Italy did. A few days before

Anzac Day 1918, 'Australian soldiers with bayonets' rounded up Italian citizens for deportation. For all Galli's talk of freedom's cause, coercion forced his countrymen back to the battlefields of Europe.[12]

And what became of Leo Galli? After the war, he continued – as many men did – to trade on his war service. Galli wrote an unsuccessful book and fielded an even less successful film. Then he migrated to New Zealand. A bemused official in Wellington's Returned and Services Association read a brief account of Galli's life and dubbed him the second 'Count of Monte Cristo'.[13] Despite his service in the First AIF and the fact that he was a naturalised British subject, Galli was interned as an enemy alien for most of the Second World War. He also came under investigation as an 'unorthodox medical healer'. It seems Signor Galli had changed his uniform yet again and now styled himself a 'former medical adjutant, Italian Army'. Leo Clement Galli died in 1964 in Auckland.[14]

SOURCES AND FURTHER READING: The authors gratefully acknowledge the assistance of Raelene Frances in researching and writing this story, which draws on Leo Galli's service dossier NAA: B2455 GALLI L; Intelligence case file NAA: MP 16/1; general correspondence on Galli during his time as a recruiting sergeant NAA: MP367/1; as well as a scan of contemporary newspaper reports and close reading of his novel *Scattered War Leaves* (Melbourne: Advocate, 1918). We have also referred to the Royal College of Surgeon's biographical register for John Leicester and Karen Agutter, 'Captive Allies: Italian Immigrants in World War One Australia', Close NLA, 2009, nla.gov.au/openpublish/index.php/australian studies/article/view/1558/1865.

BELOW **He had seen them die with a smile on their lips:** The graveyard at Ari Burnu, not far from where Galli landed in 1915. His evacuation on the first day meant that he survived this punishing campaign. *Courtesy Bruce Scates.*

Never the same as before he left

JIM SOORLEY

Horseshoe Bend, New South Wales, 20 September 1918. St Paul's Parish Hall in Church Street is decorated with all the flags a tiny Maitland town can muster. Streamers trim the room and an eager community, all dressed in their Sunday best, waits to welcome home the town's returning heroes. As soon as the young men arrive, the cheering begins, one patriotic toast follows another and a slightly tipsy crowd sings 'Home, sweet home'. 'There's no place like home,' the song called out. All the blokes who'd made it back from Europe agreed with that.

The mayor interrupts the celebrations and speaks solemnly to the crowd. He tells these soldiers how proud the community is of its gallant men: they had proved themselves worthy of Horseshoe Bend and Australia. The mayor wishes each returned soldier a long life, happiness and prosperity. Sadly none of that awaits Jim Soorley.

Officially, he was Private Reginald James Hackett, but that name never felt right to him. As a baby, Jim had been adopted by Annie Soorley and he was raised as part of her large and loving family. As far as most folks in the district were concerned, he was another Soorley.

When Jim was just shy of 21, he enlisted. He was sent to Belgium with the 34th Battalion, fought at the Battle of Messines and was struck in his elbow by a shell. At the casualty clearing station, the doctors amputated part of his arm. It was a hurried, desperate procedure – most operations were on the battlefields of the Salient. Weeks later in an English hospital, the doctors had to operate again. This time they cut further up, the young man's arm was no more than a stump now.

After a year at war, Jim had got himself an 'Aussie', a wound serious enough to spare him from Passchendaele and send him back to Australia. Jim returned to Horseshoe Bend in February 1918, but he was a very different man to the one who'd left.

It was hard to explain to anyone who hadn't gone overseas. 'At night time, I live again through the whole horrors of war,' he told his family. Every time he closed his eyes it all came back to him.[1] Unable to sleep, Jim would take long, lonely walks. The only rest he seemed to get was when his body collapsed from exhaustion. And even then sleep was fitful. Jim would wake suddenly in a terrible fright, screaming in the night, wrestling with unseen demons.

Jim Soorley didn't turn to drink, as many of the men in his condition did, but he became more and more self-conscious, painfully aware of the empty sleeve that hung at his side, the stump that stuck out at an angle. He barely ate, and smoked an unbroken chain of cigarettes. Every day he looked thinner, sicker and more weary. The Soorley family were terribly worried – though Jim was still a good lad, he was 'never the same as before he left'.[2]

One night must have been worse than most. On the morning of 18 September 1918, Jim was found lying in his bed, his left hand clasped around his revolver. He'd been at war for nearly two years, tried for eight months to find his place again back home, and now he had put an end to all the horrors.

In early twentieth-century Australia, suicide carried a deep social stigma – even more so than today. The position of the Catholic Church was doctrinaire and unyielding. To take one's own life insulted the love of God and defied the Church's teaching. The Bishop of Maitland announced that the young soldier, one of his flock, could not be buried in consecrated ground. The members of the West Maitland Returned Soldiers' Association were outraged.

Jim Soorley, they declared, was 'a splendid type of Australian'.[3] They knew the kind of man he'd been before the war had damaged him. They called a branch meeting in the same hall where returned men had been welcomed home, and demanded the Bishop reverse his decision:

> *[We], members of the West Maitland sub-branch of the Returned Sailors and Soldiers Imperial League, emphatically and unanimously protest against the disgraceful treatment shown to our late comrade.*[4]

Where Jim Soorley was to be buried became a matter of great controversy. The debate divided the community, and challenged the authority of the Church. Letters to the press document the outrage. 'Horror' denounced the Bishop's 'unChrist-like attitude':

> *[How could a man of God refuse] Christian burial . . . [to one] who had left his health and reason and one of his limbs on the blood-stained fields . . . Would gentle Jesus refuse this duty to the dead soldier? Believers in his teaching answer, no.*[5]

Another, whose author signed off with the apt 'RIP', pleaded the case of the Catholic community:

BELOW **We do not wish future generations to point the finger of scorn at the burial place of our late comrade[11]:** The West Maitland RSL led the public outrage that Jim was 'denied the services of his church'.[12] Jim now lies in consecrated ground, buried under the name of Private Hackett, with the Soorley family. *Courtesy Tania and Garry Hackett.*

What a pang to this young soldier's relatives and friends when they hear the Congregation being requested to pray for the souls (named) departed and his name not mentioned? Not on the honour roll of the church! Cruel, beyond thought![6]

But most interesting of all were letters to the press that dismissed religious scruples altogether. 'Ex-Sgt' clearly believed his status as a returned soldier mattered far more than any knowledge of scripture. 'God alone knows how he suffered', he wrote, 'fighting for you and for me'[7].

In a similar vein, 'Mr Nicholson' reminded the community that 'this lad fought for us that we might live and his death was directly attributable to his loyalty.'[8] The debt to those who fought was far more compelling to these correspondents than the pious pronouncements of the clergy.

In the interwar years, Anzac became something of a 'secular religion', with its own high priests, its own distinctive rituals, and a clearly defined congregation. Nowhere is that more apparent than in the way returned men reclaimed the body of Jim Soorley.

Setting out from the Soorley home, a cortege made its way through the streets of West Maitland. At the head of the procession were twelve soldiers holding reverse arms, followed by the local cadet band playing the solemn and stately 'Dead March from Saul'.

Then came the returned diggers in uniform, 'the more severely injured in a drag'.[9] Jim's coffin, draped proudly in a Union Jack and decorated with elaborate wreathes, was escorted by six comrades. Marching at the end of the procession was the West Maitland Water Brigade, the mayor and the president of the district's patriotic fund. Crowds gathered by the roadside to honour a fallen soldier at home, and as the procession passed by the town's orphanage, children stood by to pay their respects.

An impressive crowd assembled by the grave site and appealed, 'May God have mercy on his soul.' The party fired a salute and the Last Post echoed throughout the cemetery as Jim's body was lowered into the ground. The town's Catholic priest was in attendance of course, but that day it was the way soldiers honoured their own that mattered.

Eventually the Church relented. Reassured by the Coroner's finding that this 'nerve shattered and crippled' man had ended his life in a fit of temporary insanity, the Bishop found room for compromise – and forgiveness.[10] Jim Soorley's remains were removed at night several months after they'd been buried. The body was placed at last in consecrated ground, the same earth where Jim's adoptive mother would eventually be buried. His epitaph reads, 'Sweet Jesus have mercy on his soul'.

SOURCES AND FURTHER READING: This account draws on Private Reginald Hackett's (aka Jim Soorley) service dossier NAA: B2455 HACKETT RJ; and contemporary newspaper reports. For the most convincing exposition of Anzac as a secular religion see Ken Inglis, *Sacred Places: War Memorials in the Australian Landscape* (Carlton: Melbourne University Press, 1998).

A garden of memory

DOROTHY GILBERT

In March 1919, just a few months after the fighting had ended, the mayoress of Adelaide convened a meeting in the Town Hall. Its purpose was to raise a women's war memorial, and all the principal charities and patriotic associations were involved. The League of Loyal Women, as they called themselves, faced the usual debates and choices. Should their memorial be utilitarian or monumental, a hospital or some 'symbolical figure'; where should it be sited; how was the money to be raised?[1] It was decided:

> *The memorial was to be in the nature of a shrine and the site a hallowed spot where the mothers wives sisters and friends . . . [could] place their tributes of love . . .* [2]

For that reason the women rejected a site on North Terrace where South Australia's official war memorial was eventually to be raised. They chose instead a piece of parkland, bordered by the river and the cathedral. Here, they decided, 'a garden of memory' might be made. And not just any garden, either. Having lost two brothers in the war, one in Gallipoli and one in France, Dorothy Gilbert had a very clear idea in mind.

> *It is the wish of my Executive Committee [to borrow the designs of the Imperial War Graves Commission] making for the women who will never see the graves of their men, a place of quiet and repose, a 'Garden of the Unforgotten.'*[3]

Hedged with yew and cyprus, fragrant with rose and rosemary, it would '[c]reate for us in miniature, in the heart of our city, a garden which should instantly call to mind those other gardens covering many an area of Northern France and on the slopes of Gallipoli'.[4]

ABOVE **Opening a memorial with a funeral:** Soldiers and mourners gather for the dedication of the Cross of Sacrifice in Adelaide. The number of floral tributes remind us of the role memorials played as a focal point for grief: they were surrogate tombs for bodies lost in battle. The Australasian, *6 May 1922 courtesy National Library of Australia.*

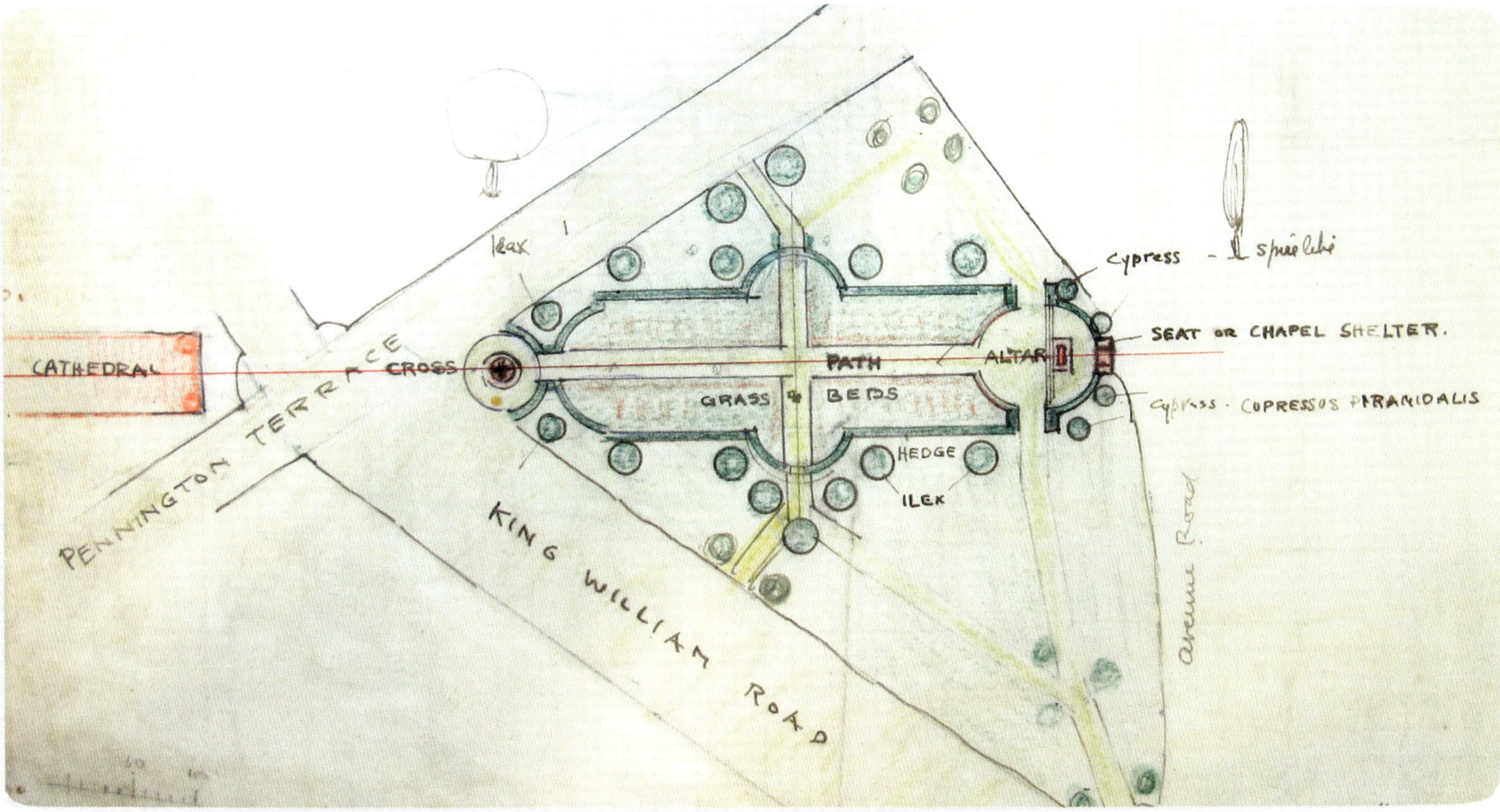

What Dorothy Gilbert called a 'garden' looked like a graveyard. Internal paths were set down in the figure of a cross, and flowerbeds of rosemary made to resemble plots. Both were aligned with the two great motifs of Europe's war cemeteries, Sir Reginald Blomfield's Cross of Sacrifice and Sir Edward Lutyens' Stone of Remembrance: they 'appeal to us tremendously', Gilbert wrote to the Commission, 'because most of us will never see the graves of our men [our] design [will] shadow [your own]'.[5]

Recreating the cemeteries of Europe in a stretch of Adelaide parkland was not to be thought 'morbid', the The League of Loyal Women insisted. On the one hand, it reflected a sense of belonging to an Empire so many had died for:

> *. . . wherever our men lie and wherever that cross is seen throughout the world, and throughout the centuries, it shall be known as the British Cross of the Great War. If that is to be so we should like our Memorial one link in the chain . . .* [6]

On the other, it made possible an imaginary pilgrimage; not an actual voyage, but a journey of the heart and the mind. Standing in her Garden of Remembrance, Dorothy Gilbert imagined similar garden cemeteries on the other side of the world.

> *The families of the men who have fallen can perhaps appreciate better than others the form of the Memorial Cross and Stone. They have seen both pictured in the book sent to them by the War Graves Commission. The Women's Memorial is in the form of a garden [featuring] an exact*

ABOVE **The two great motifs of Europe's war cemeteries:** Sir Reginald Blomfield's Cross of Sacrifice and Sir Edward Lutyens' Stone of Remembrance sketched on the plan for Pennington Gardens. In fact, the cross was a collaboration of several Great War architects, and all found its ambiguity appealing. The religious (such as Dorothy Gilbert) saw this as the paramount symbol of Christianity; others could relate to its martial quality, a sword set squarely at the cross's centre. This made the cross acceptable to many religious faiths within the British Empire. It also spoke to a growing number of agnostics. Dorothy Gilbert was the first of many to borrow this design from the Imperial War Graves Commission. *Sketch from the minutes of the Women's War Memorial Committee, SRG89 courtesy State Library of South Australia.*

OPPOSITE **A journey of the heart:** The figure of a mother reaches out towards the spirit of her son. Raynor Hoff's arresting sculpture is a key feature of South Australia's National War Memorial on North Terrace, Adelaide. *Courtesy Bruce Scates.*

reproduction of those two monuments, so that anyone entering . . . will feel at once that somewhere, on some battlefront, the man they personally know is lying under the shadow of the [same] War Cross facing the [same] War Stone . . . [7]

The Loyal Women of Adelaide opened their memorial with a funeral. In April of 1922, in the week preceding Anzac Day, the names of the fallen were placed in an urn, taken to the cross, and buried beneath its foundation stone. Amongst the thousands of slips of paper were the names of Dorothy Gilbert's two brothers, one buried near a similar cross in France, the other, whose body was never recovered, swallowed up by the carnage of Gallipoli. 'The graves of the front', Dorothy Gilbert declared, had been linked forever 'with the homeland'. And the Garden of Remembrance had laid their memory to rest. [8]

SOURCES AND FURTHER READING: This account is based on a detailed scan of the League of Loyal Women's Papers SRG684 and the Minutes of the Women's War Memorial Committee SRG89, both held in the State Library of South Australia. For further discussion of women's place in the culture of commemoration and their representation in memorials themselves see Ken Inglis, 'Men, Women and War Memorials: Anzac Australia', *Daedalus*, vol. 116, no. 4, Fall 1987, pp. 35–59; Catherine Speck, 'Women's War Memorials and Citizenship, *Australian Feminist Studies*, vol. 11, no. 23, 1996, pp. 129–145; for the use of the cross in memorials see Bruce Scates and Rebecca Wheatley, 'War Memorials' in Jay Winter (ed), *The Cambridge History of the First World War*, vol. III (Cambridge: Cambridge University Press, 2014) pp. 528–558.

BELOW **A Garden of the Unforgotten:** Blomfield's Cross of Sacrifice stands guard over the imagined graves of a memorial garden. Great care was taken to replicate the designs of the Imperial War Graves Commission cemeteries in Belgium and France, enabling an imaginary journey to those real graves a world away. *Courtesy Bruce Scates.*

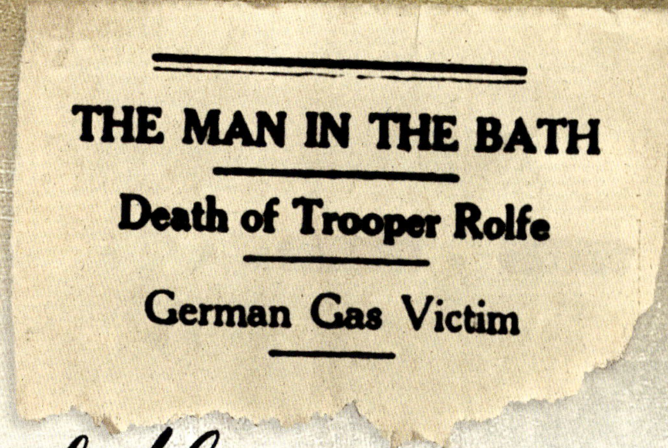
THE MAN IN THE BATH

Death of Trooper Rolfe

German Gas Victim

The man in the bath
SAMUEL ROLFE

The first successful large-scale gas attack occured outside Ypres. The Ypres Salient had long been known for suffering, and in the early afternoon of 22 April 1915 it provided the setting for one of the Great War's greatest horrors. A special detachment of troops, the first to be trained in the science of chemical warfare, opened the valves on nearly 6000 steel cylinders set out along the German defensive perimeter. Within ten minutes, more than 160 tons of asphyxiating chlorine gas lifted into the air and floated towards the opposing French trenches.

The use of gas took the Allies by surprise. The line folded across a six-kilometre front as French and Algerian troops retreated in terror. The slow-moving wall of gas killed more than 1000 Allied soldiers, and seriously wounded 4000 more. A British soldier serving nearby captured the pandemonium:

> *[I watched] figures running wildly in confusion over the fields. Greenish-gray clouds swept down upon them, turning yellow as they traveled over the country blasting everything they touched and shriveling up the vegetation . . . Then there staggered into our midst French soldiers, blinded, coughing, chests heaving, faces an ugly purple colour, lips speechless with agony, and behind them in the gas soaked trenches, we learned that they had left hundreds of dead and dying comrades.*[1]

That attack was the first of many. There were dozens of types of gas developed during the Great War. The Allies and the Germans competed for new ways to blind, choke, cripple and kill the enemy. Historians have dubbed this 'the race to toxicity'.[2]

Mustard gas was first used in July 1917. It drifted in a heavy cloud across no-man's-land, poisoning everything in its path and settling in the trenches. Mustard gas blinded

ABOVE **The Man in the Bath:** A headline on the death of Samuel Rolfe. Virtual confinement to a bath mirrored the claustrophobic imprisonment of the trenches. Although it checked the searing pain of mustard gas burns, boric acid caused its own cruel discomfort. The Man in the Bath became a metaphor for Australia's postwar trauma and reminds us of the way the horrors of war spill into peace time. As late as 2013, an elderly woman remembered visiting the men in the baths in a Repatriation Hospital in Melbourne. A child at the time, she was horrified by the suffering concealed behind the screen and wondered what comfort, if any, these long-suffering men took from her visit. The North Western Courier, *15 December 1924 courtesy National Library of Australia.*

men while they fumbled with their masks. It blistered any exposed skin on contact, scarred bronchial tubes and damaged the lining of the lungs. In the worst cases of exposure, mustard gas could burn skin and flesh down to the bone.

Men severely affected by gas seldom recovered – that, of course, was the intention. Taking a gassed man out of the line weakened the enemy's defence, but keeping him alive posed a cost to the state long after his evacuation. The 'whispering men', as they were called, haunted the streets of postwar Australia, a pathetic burden on the community and their families.

Repatriation files suggest something of their misery: 'Patient is unable to keep any food down. Is weak and breathless. Suffers from giddiness, constant nausea, severe abdominal pain.' 'Has no confidence in himself,' one doctor added; a reminder that a physical injury often shaped a mental outlook.[3]

Gas cases often lingered for years in hospitals and sanatoriums. While they were able, they gulped down tonics for their stomachs, breathed through medicated atomisers and swallowed bottlefuls of painkillers. Wheezy, dizzy, weak and listless, coughing blood and spitting mucous, gassed men died years after they were injured. Samuel Rolfe was one of them.

Private Rolfe was badly gassed near Albert in France, discharged 'medically unfit' and sent home. They called him 'the Man in the Bath'.[4] Mustard gas had blistered much of his skin and there was 'a scaly feeling all over his body and face'.[5] Any treatment in such a case was likely to be palliative. Immersion in a tub of special fluid numbed his pain just a little.

BELOW **Lungs dissolving:** Thousands of atomisers like these were distributed to gas victims in the aftermath of the Great War. At best they offered temporary relief. At worst they were virtually useless. *British Red Cross Collection, London courtesy Bruce Scates.*

For almost four years Samuel Rolfe virtually lived in a bath of boric acid. A screen was drawn around his tub in the Prince of Wales Hospital. Visitors – and there were never many – spoke to Samuel though a screen, never seeing his eyes, never touching his body. The Man in the Bath lived in a kind of liquid prison. Rolfe's family lived in Inverell and could seldom come to Sydney.

In December 1924, Samuel Rolfe's condition suddenly altered for the worse. 'Skin condition unchanged,' a doctor jotted down in his casebook a few days later. 'Had a convulsion two days ago, struggled violently, since then patient has lapsed into a coma. His breathing is laboured and his chest full of mucous.'[6]

As with many a gas victim, Rolfe's lungs were dissolving. The Man in the Bath would drown in his own fluids.

Samuel Rolfe died of war-related

causes just a week shy of Christmas 1924. Gas would go on killing men decades after the fighting had ended. Over 1.3 million men were casualties of gas attacks during the Great War.

ABOVE **One of the Great War's greatest horrors:** Masked men drill for a gas attack. Donning this protective clothing hampered soldiers in the line, adversely affecting their vision and agility. And often the masks proved ineffective. Gas was one of the war's most inhumane weapons – in this image, the masks dehumanise the wearers, conferring a cruel anonymity on their suffering. *Courtesy State Library of Queensland.*

SOURCES AND FURTHER READING: This story draws on the service dossier of Samuel Rolfe NAA: B2455, ROLFE SAMUEL EARL; his repatriation file NAA: C138, NC043642-01; and contemporary newspaper accounts. For a brief history of chemical warfare prior to the Great War see Arthur Butler, *Official History of Australia Army Medical Service in the War of 1914–1918,* vol. III Special Problems and Services (Canberra: Australian War Memorial, 1943). For general histories of gas warfare see L.F Haber, *The Poisonous Cloud: Chemical Warfare in the First World War* (Oxford: Oxford University Press, 1986); William Moore, *Gas Attack! Chemical Warfare 1915–1918 and Afterwards* (New York: Hippocrene Books, 1987); Robert Joy, 'Historical Aspects of Medical Defense Against Chemical Warfare,' in Frederick R Sidle, Ernest T Takafuji and David R Franz (eds), *Medical Aspects of Chemical and Biological Warfare* (Washington, DC: The Borden Institute, 1997); Stéphane Audoin-Rouzeau, '1915: Stalemate' in Jay Winter (ed), *The Cambridge History of the First World War,* vol. I (Cambridge: Cambridge University Press, 2014) pp. 65–88; G. Fitzgerald, 'Chemical warfare and medical response during World War I', *American Journal of Public Health*, vol. 98, no. 4, 2008, pp. 611–625; Amos Fries and C. J. West, *Chemical Warfare* (New York: McGraw Hill, 1921); Albert Palazzo, *Seeking Victory on the Western Front: The British Army and Chemical Warfare in World War I* (Lincoln: University of Nebraska Press, 2000).

Written out of history

WILLIAM IRWIN

Beneath the cloisters of the Australian War Memorial in Canberra, not far from where the names of the nation's dead are etched forever in bronze, two rows of stone gargoyles gaze out on the reflection pool. They were placed there in the 1940s, carved in situ just as the memorial was nearing completion. According to memorial guidebooks, the gargoyles represent 'the original inhabitants of the continent' prior to European arrival, and link white Australians to a 'land of great antiquity'. To the east are set the heads of an emu, koala, platypus, possum, goanna, swan and cassowary. The menagerie continues on the western side of the building, where a kangaroo, wombat, bearded dragon, Tasmanian devil, cockatoo and dingo look down blankly at dignitaries and visitors.

The gargoyles might well be an attempt to Australianise a building decidedly Byzantian in inspiration. No doubt they are also a reference to medieval carvings guarding the most sacred cathedrals in Christendom. But in one respect at least, this odd assortment of animals is deeply offensive. Alongside the creatures of the bush are the crude and caricatured images of an Aboriginal woman and man.

Aboriginal people were present at the founding of the Anzac legend, and today they have claimed their rightful place there. But acknowledgement of their contribution to the First World War and subsequent conflicts has been a slow and awkward process. At first there was the problem of denial and invisibility. Aboriginal people were not permitted to enlist – though clearly many did so – and service records seldom acknowledge Indigenous descent. This was quite literally a case of being written out of history. C.E.W. Bean, the Australian War Memorial's first director and principal author of the official history of the First AIF, made one passing reference to a single Aboriginal soldier in several thousand pages of narrative. It was as if the Aboriginal person was there purely as some kind of adornment, rather like those gargoyles chiselled into the fabric of the memorial itself.

William Irwin was the man Bean deigned to mention. In many ways, Private Irwin was an exemplary soldier and the embodiment of the very legend Bean helped to create. Born at Coonabarabran, Irwin acquired all the skills and resources of the archetypal bushman Anzac, travelling extensively across the north-west of New South Wales, shearing, droving and taking on what jobs he could. But unlike white workers, William Irwin lived in a world of seemingly arbitrary restrictions, and the authorities could have him sent back to the mission station at Quirindi at any time they chose. Perhaps it was that quest for manly independence so admired by Bean that led Irwin to volunteer for overseas service. He joined the AIF in January 1916, at a time when the desperate need for men relaxed the restrictions on Indigenous recruitment.

Private Irwin fought with the 33rd Battalion. He was wounded in action during the Battle of Messines, and again at Villers-Bretonneux a year later. Right towards the end of the war, Irwin took part in a costly assault on Mont St Quentin. In desperate fighting on this strong point of the Hindenburg Line, Irwin earned the Distinguished Conduct Medal, and became the first Aboriginal soldier to be so decorated for bravery. His citation records 'conspicuous gallantry and devotion to duty':

> *Single-handed, and in the face of heavy fire, he rushed three separate machine-gun nests, capturing the guns and crews. While rushing a fourth, he was severely wounded. His irresistible dash inspired the whole of his company.*[1]

ABOVE **Not much to remember him by:** A photograph of William Irwin rests beside his grave at Daours Communal Cemetery on the Somme. This is one of the few images that survive of this Indigenous soldier decorated for distinguished conduct in the field. It was placed there by pilgrims honouring Aboriginal service in 2014. The Connecting Spirits program undertakes regular pilgrimages to the graves of black diggers. *Courtesy Bruce Scates.*

'Magnificent gallentry', to be sure – but it claimed William Irwin's life. He died of shrapnel wounds the following day and was buried, thousands of miles from his ancestral lands, in a cemetery on the Somme.

The family of William Irwin – six siblings in all – did not have much to remember him by. Indeed they only learned of his death when a letter marked 'Not delivered: deceased' was returned to Quirindi station.[2] When the shipping finally became available, a parcel of belongings was sent back from Europe. It contained virtually nothing of material value: a box of needles, two rings, a damaged metal wristwatch. But a few photographs and letters to his family reassured them he hadn't forgotten them; two religious books buried deep in his kit suggest William never lost his Christian faith.

When William Irwin's medals were issued to his next-of-kin in the early 1920s,

ABOVE **Gazing out on the reflection pool:** The sandstone sculpture of the 'Male Aborigine'. Set beneath cloisters recording the names of the nation's dead, the sculpture symbolises the marginalisation (and denigration) of Aboriginal people in the Anzac narrative sanctioned by the War Memorial. The Memorial has consistently refused to acknowledge in its galleries the war fought against Aboriginal people. *Courtesy Romain Fathi.*

that longing for something more was rekindled. 'I am very much concerned as to my brother's fate,' William's oldest brother, Harry, wrote to the authorities. 'Can you please advise at once if there is any of his property in the care of your department? How am I to proceed to recover it.'[3] It wasn't just that there was so little that added to the grief of Aboriginal families. Few white families could afford to travel to war graves overseas; but without a passport or citizenship, and numbering amongst the poorest Australians, no Aboriginal person could.

Twenty years after William Irwin's death, the manager of the mission approached Harry and asked to borrow his brother's service medals and DCM. The posthumous award for gallantry would feature in an Anzac Day ceremony planned for Caroona Aboriginal School. After the service, none of William's medals were returned to the family. They had, the manager insisted, been 'mislaid'. In 1996, the descendants of William Irwin appealed yet again for the return of William's medals to their 'rightful owners'.[4] They're still waiting for their return today. And a hundred years after the Landing at Gallipoli, the Australian War Memorial – a memorial raised to record the nation's loss in all military conflicts, and flanked by those quaint Aboriginal gargoyles – still refuses to recognise decades of frontier war that robbed Aboriginal people of their land.

SOURCES AND FURTHER READING: The authors respectfully acknowledge the Gomeroi people of New South Wales and their elders, past and present. This account is based on sources in the public domain, most importantly the service dossier of William Irwin NAA: B2455, IRWIN, WILLIAM ALLEN. The authors acknowledge Brad Manera, Executive Manager of the Anzac Memorial in Sydney, who alerted them to this story and who has facilitated the community's attempt to recover Irwin's decoration. The medals in question will be stamped with his name and service number: William Irwin, No. 792. For general studies of Aboriginal people in the First AIF see Philippa Scarlett, *Aboriginal and Torres Strait Islander Volunteers for the AIF: The Indigenous Response to World War One* (Canberra: Indigenous Histories, 2013); Alick Jackomos and Derek Fowell, *Forgotten Heroes: Aborigines at War from the Somme to Vietnam* (Melbourne: Victoria Press, 1993). The authors await the important work of Mick Dodson, John Maynard and Jack Pearson into Indigenous service.

Like a broken doll

MARGARET BROADHURST

In the years before the war took hold of the world, Margaret and Tom were just sweethearts falling in love. The young dressmaker and carpenter lived in Prahran and the two had been courting since 1912. Although they'd discussed marriage it seemed far in the distance; they were both so young, after all. But as the clouds of war gathered and Tom signed up for service, it seemed only proper that things were made official. Tom proposed to Margaret with a diamond ring, and their engagement was announced.

Throughout the war they exchanged hundreds and hundreds of letters. After a while, though, Margaret noticed that Tom's correspondence had slowed. She worried when she learned that he had been admitted to hospital with illness, but nothing prepared her for his letter in 1917.

> *My dear Dolly . . . Well, I am sorry to say that there is a nurse here in England whom I like very much; in fact I love her. So it rests with you what we do. You said in your letter that should I love another girl in another country that is the end. So I am letting you know that I love another, and whom I should like to make my wife. This girl – I have met her in England – is the only one I could make happy in marriage.*

Margaret couldn't remember making any such concession to her fiancé. Tom continued his letter, trying to explain how he'd ended up so ill:

> *You remember I told you I was in hospital with diphtheria. Well, after seven weeks, they*

BELOW **Sweethearts:** The young couple became engaged before Tom set out for the war. The Prahran Telegraph, *13 February 1915 courtesy National Library of Australia.*

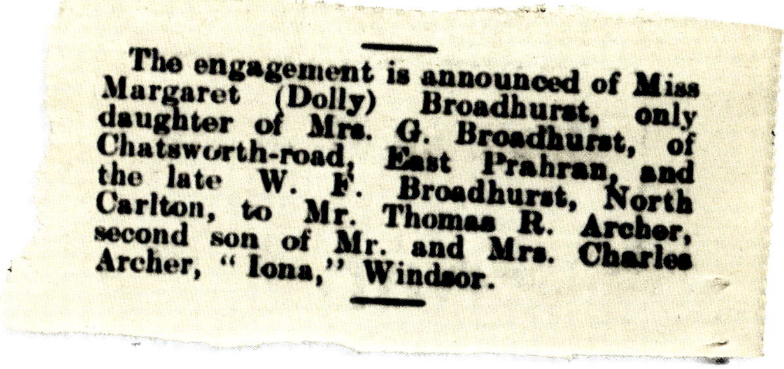

The engagement is announced of Miss Margaret (Dolly) Broadhurst, only daughter of Mrs. G. Broadhurst, of Chatsworth-road, East Prahran, and the late W. F. Broadhurst, North Carlton, to Mr. Thomas R. Archer, second son of Mr. and Mrs. Charles Archer, "Iona," Windsor.

found out I had not diphtheria, but a syphilitic throat. God knows where I contracted that disease, for I know it was not caused through any fault of my own. I have looked after myself in every way. The only place I can think of is in the dirt of Egypt as where I got it . . .

This letter was a great shock to Margaret. She was devastated that the future she'd planned had evaporated and she was furious that she'd spent some fifty pounds stocking her glory box with cutlery, linen and other things to make a home for her and Tom. She wrote back to him:

My dear Tom, your letter has come as a great shock to me, and I want more reasons. Remember, I will not say I will let you free. You have known me five years, and, at all accounts, this woman three months, yet you say you love her . . . This is a great upset, and I do not care what becomes of me; and remember you are responsible for what I do, for I am a miserable girl . . . I have received a note from England, telling me you had V.D: but I cannot believe it. If you say you have got what you have got you can't marry for years, so what do you think I am? . . . The folly of it all was that I had too much love and affection in you . . . I would like the address of this nurse you have. I will tell her all about this, for she ought to know. Can it be you, dear, who has written to a girl you really love? . . . I want to say a lot; but my head is swimming, so I must close, hoping you are well; but you have left me a broken doll.[1]

Perhaps it had been the 'soothing touch' and the 'gentle eyes of a ministering angel';[2] perhaps it was the time and distance away from Margaret, or the cold reminders of life and death, that made falling in love with another woman possible for Tom.

Tom claimed he never received Margaret's last letter. In March 1917, he married his young English nurse, Belinda. The couple moved to Australia after the war.

Margaret was hopelessly sad but she was also affronted by the dishonesty of her fiancé. She thought he ought to pay. Margaret took Tom to the Supreme Court, suing her former beloved for £750 in damages for breach of promise. On the day of the trial, she stood in the witness box and told the judge how her heart and Tom's promises had been broken. It all became too much and the fragile young woman fainted. The judge allowed her to compose herself in the fresh air before she continued her testimony. 'You left me like a broken doll,'[3] she cried to Tom and the courtroom.

The judge found in Margaret's favour and ordered the young soldier to pay his former fiancée £150. Tom had just eight pounds to his name, no property, no savings in the bank, just a paltry pension and an insufficient and unsteady wage. With nowhere near the sum found against him, Tom was declared insolvent.

Margaret was heartbroken at losing Tom, but part of this young woman's distress was likely her worry that she now might never find a husband. After the war, Britain had two million 'surplus' women, an already unequal sex balance worsened by a lost generation of men. Australia experienced a similar demographic change, albeit on a smaller scale. Whatever the reason, many young women would never marry after the war. A cohort of spinsters is an abiding memory in postwar Australia. The majority of men who enlisted in the AIF were single, and so the war also affected the pool of eligible bachelors in Australia. Quite apart from the terrible loss of life during the war, there were tens of thousands of men who died slowly in the years beyond 1918. And of the returned men, countless came home so deeply damaged by their physical and psychological injuries, so changed by their experience, that they felt unable to marry.

The women of that generation who, because of the war, never married, have been described as 'imaginary widows'.[4] In the early twentieth century, most women were expected to become wives and mothers. Female fulfilment was thought impossible in any other role.

However, not all women found their single status a burden. Some women discovered that as spinsters they had the opportunity to pursue satisfying and remunerative careers. Some also developed relationships that had once seemed off limits – many women established close and compassionate friendships with those of their sex. In some cases, these were lesbian relationships.[5]

Margaret Broadhurst did find a husband, though; she married Harold Bower in 1923. Tom Archer died in 1940 at the Caulfield Repatriation Hospital; he was 47 years old, hardly an old man. He left behind his beloved Belinda and their four children.

ABOVE **Imaginary widows:** After the war, many women worried that there were not enough men to go around. Truth, *3 February 1917 courtesy National Library of Australia.*

Sources and further reading: This story is based on contemporary newspaper reports of the court case; the Supreme Court record, Broadhurst v Archer, PROV VPRS267, unit 1652, no. 308, 1917; and Thomas Archer's service dossier NAA: B2455, ARCHER T R. For an examination of Britain's 'surplus women' see Virginia Nicholson, *Singled Out: How Two Million Women Survived Without Men after the First World War* (London: Viking, 2007); and for work on 'imaginary widows' see Kate Holden, 'Imaginary Widows: Spinsters, Marriage, and the "Lost Generation" in Britain after the Great War', *Journal of Family History*, vol. 30 no. 4, October 2005, pp. 388–409.

A meddlesome priest

THE REVEREND BERNARD LINDEN WEBB

BELOW **The Religious Significance of the War:** Three of Reverend Webb's pacifist sermons of 1915 were published as a pamphlet by Quaker William Cooper. Webb's views on the immoral and injurious nature of the war caused heated debate in Australia's Methodist circles. *Courtesy National Library of Australia.*

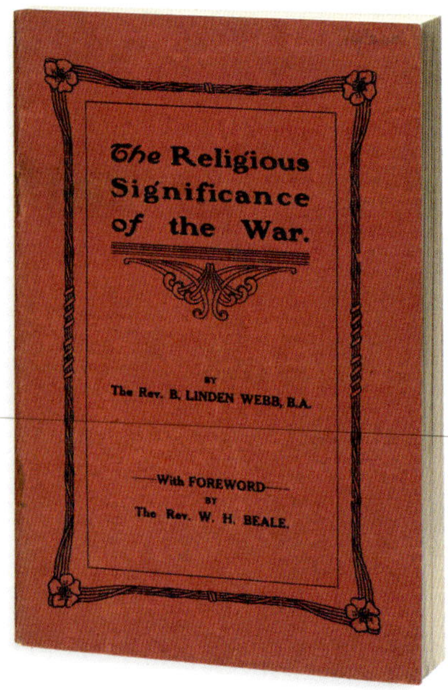

By January 1915, the world had been at war for almost four months. Schooled in the doctrines of Nelson and Wellington, generals had dreamed of swift breakthroughs, rapid advancement and vast encircling movements that would capture the capitals of Europe. Instead, massive opposing armies dug in along a thin corridor of ground that divided one side of the Continent from another. By 1915, the Great War had become a static war, characterised by trenches, barbed wire and seemingly incessant artillery bombardment. It was the first industrialised war of the twentieth century and it was fought on a scale, and with an intensity, past generations would not have thought possible.

As the new year dawned, the churches of the Allied nations summoned their congregations to prayer. Australian and New Zealand troops had barely begun their garrison duties in Egypt, and Gallipoli had not yet been thought of. Even so, everyone at home knew it was only a matter of time before their loved ones joined the fray. By 1915, the war had claimed the lives of tens of thousands of soldiers from across the British Empire. Our turn was coming.

The first Sunday that year saw fiery sermons right across the nation. Catholics and Baptists, Anglicans and Presbyterians pleaded the righteousness of the Empire's cause and called young men to service. But the small Methodist congregation of Hay, in the New South Wales Riverina, found themselves listening to a different kind of address. At the outbreak of war, Hay's Methodist minister, the Reverend Bernard Linden Webb declared himself a pacifist. Three months into the slaughter, his belief that war was wrong remained unshaken. 'This war is not in keeping with our profession of

Christianity,' he thundered from the pulpit. 'It is the outcome of materialism, worldliness, godlessness.'[1]

Reverend Webb called on his congregation to remember that Christ's message was one of peace. And he reminded them of the terrible price they would pay for racing unthinkingly into conflict:

> *Science is being prostituted to the terrible business of making instruments of destruction; and thousands upon thousands of lives are being ruthlessly sacrificed . . . the days are coming when tales of blood and iron will no longer thrill us but sadden and disgust.*[2]

ABOVE **We're Off. Join Us. It's Up To You:** Of the sixteen men in this photo who left Hay for war in 1915, two were killed in action, and another three died of wounds or illness. Eight were wounded at the front, and ten hospitalised for illness. Two men were shell shocked, two contracted venereal disease, and another two returned to Australia permanently incapacitated. Two of those men won Military Medals, while four were punished for misdemeanours. All were under thirty when they enlisted, with the average age being 21. *Courtesy Laura James.*

Hay's Methodist congregation found itself divided. Many thought their preacher's views were 'idealistic and impractical', but not a few were swayed by his passionate advocacy of peace. Twice more Webb took to the pulpit to denounce the war Australia and the Empire were fighting. Hay was one of the first communities in Australia to openly debate the justice of a conflict that would eventually divide the nation. But the beginning of 1915 was still a long way from the bungled battle of the Somme or even the bloodletting of Gallipoli. Enthusiasm for the war was such that conservatives had not yet sought to impose conscription.

Fifteen young men from Webb's parish joined up, almost 20 per cent of the congregation. Each new recruit left a father, mother or sibling behind to take the pews every Sunday morning. It says much about the man that so few of these families chose to stay away. Perhaps because this pacifist priest, resolutely opposed to war, attended the farewells for each and every one of those boys, waved them off at the railway station, and presented every one of them with a 'lucky' keepsake. Webb never placed his own principles above the welfare of the young men who now, more than ever, needed his strength, support and spiritual guidance. Nor did he avoid donating what he could to help the sick or wounded in their hour of need.

In time, the Great War claimed the lives of four lads from the congregation, and another nine were to become seriously sick or wounded, some returning home with missing limbs and horrific facial injuries. Faced with such grievous loss, the people of Hay found their difficult priest harder and harder to tolerate. A junior circuit steward of the church quit his position when his son was maimed in France. Others still turned to their minister for comfort, religion a stronger force than politics. Some quite probably came to accept Webb's position – and no doubt wished they'd opposed their sons joining up in the first place.[3]

The Reverend Webb's views made him something of a celebrity – and not just in one quiet town in the Riverina. Supported by William Cooper, a well-known Quaker and pacifist, Webb published his three sermons as a pamphlet. It was read by many

ABOVE **The question that divided Australia:** Australians were sent to the ballot box twice during the Great War to decide the question of conscription. It was a debate that split Australians into two camps with ramifications that continued for years to come. *Courtesy State Library of Victoria.*

within and beyond the church and attracted savage criticism.

A bitter debate broke out in *The Methodist* newspaper. Webb was accused of 'turn[ing] the blind eye' to the realities the Empire would face if it were not to meet German aggression with force.[4] Church officials publically censured him for his 'extreme narrowness of vision'; some reviled him as a traitor.[5] Only two like-minded souls defended Webb's pacifist convictions. They did so anonymously. A church founded by the prince of peace was now a staunch ally of the Empire.

The debate came to a head in 1916. That year the Methodist Church – like most other churches in Australia – declared their support for compulsory military service. It may have been a real possibility that the Empire faced defeat, or perhaps the belief that compulsion would somehow share the sacrifice more evenly. Whatever the reason, compulsion is always at odds with tolerance, diversity and freedom. Many thought this meddlesome priest would have to go.

Reverend Webb was always a man of principle. He could not remain in a church that had departed so fundamentally from Christ's teaching. A week before the first plebiscite was held, he handed his resignation to the president of the Methodist convention, regretting that his views on the war 'did not coincide with the attitudes of the church upon that question'. One of the ten commandments Webb had been taught as a novice was 'Thou Shalt Not Kill'; to force others to kill was simply unconscionable.[6]

Not long after leaving the church, Linden Webb left Hay for Sydney. It was easier for a discredited parson to make a living there, and no doubt his position in so small a country community was now untenable. But many were sorry to see him go. Even those with family serving overseas had come to value their preacher's care and friendship. With the defeat of the first conscription referendum and then a second, the views of Linden Webb seemed vindicated.

The Great War in general – and the conscription referenda in particular – divided Australian society. The smaller the community, the deeper the fault lines, particularly in country communities. Debate over the justice of the war and the means to fight it would divide homes, neighbourhoods and congregations for many years to come. And those debates claimed their own kind of casualties, the Reverend Webb, a good man hounded from his church, amongst them.

SOURCES AND FURTHER READING: This story is based on Webb's 1915 publication *The Religious Significance of the War* (Sydney: s.n., 1915) and accounts from contemporary newspapers, most particularly *The Riverine Grazier* and *The Methodist*. The authors also gratefully acknowledge the work of Ian Beissel on the life of Reverend Webb. For further sources see Robert Linder, '"Galilee Shall at Last Vanquish Corsica": The Rev. B. Linden Webb Challenges the War-Makers, 1915–1917', *Church Heritage*, vol. 11, no. 3, March 2000, pp. 171–83; Don Wright and Eric G. Clancy, *The Methodists: A History of Methodism in New South Wales* (Sydney: Allen & Unwin, 1993); Michael McKernan, *Australian Churches at War: Attitudes and Activities of the Major Churches* (Canberra: Australian War Memorial, 1980).

Her war never really ended

RACHAEL PRATT

Many have told the story of Sister Rachael Pratt. All have admired her courage, her commitment, her endurance. Like many of the young men who went to war, Sister Pratt lied about her age. She was already in her forties when she volunteered for service overseas, and certainly far too old for the hardships that lay before her. Pratt sailed for the Dardanelles in May 1915. She first served on hospital ships, every cabin and even the decks crammed tight with the wounded. In August, the military authorities sent Sister Pratt to Lemnos. She found what passed for a hospital there in a state of chaos:

> *the wounded began to arrive . . . Dysentery was a scourge on the island . . . many of the wounded fell prey to the disease . . . cold weather brought frostbitten patients . . . It was pitiable to see gangrene feet.*[1]

After Gallipoli, Rachael Pratt continued nursing in Egypt, then England, then France. At every post she worked tirelessly for the welfare of the men in her care, tending to the needs of the sick and wounded. She wrote hundreds of letters home to Britain, New Zealand and Australia, assuring grieving mothers that the sons they loved had not died alone, had not died in pain, had died bravely. It must have been hard to always sound convincing.

Rachael Pratt's own bravery was never in question. In 1917, German aircraft bombed the casualty clearing station where she worked. It may have been a mistake – for obvious reasons, hospital facilities were located near transport lines, which were legitimate military targets. Or it may have been part of a deliberate military strategy. By 1917, this was a total war, mass mechanised slaughter with little pretence of compassion or chivalry.

Sister Pratt was severely wounded in the attack but continued to nurse her patients until she collapsed. Evacuated to England, she was presented to the King and awarded the Military Medal 'for bravery under fire'. That made her something of a celebrity, both in London and also back home in Australia. But Rachael Pratt enjoyed little of the limelight. 'The war is awful', she wrote to her family in 1917, 'and I simply cannot discuss it . . . There is no prospect of it ending.'

The first Australian woman to receive the Military Medal, and one of the few nurses to be decorated, Pratt's war service has long been celebrated. But what came after the war is seldom mentioned.

Rachael Pratt never recovered from her injuries. A shard of shrapnel would remain lodged in her lungs for the rest of her life. She returned to Australia suffering chronic bronchitis and developed what the medical authorities called 'war neurosis'. Had she been a man they might have called it shell shock, but women were not supposed to come under fire. For a male-dominated medical establishment, apt to regard any nervous disorder as a female malady, 'neurosis' seemed the right word for a woman.

Rachael was admitted to Berklea Private Hospital for the mentally ill in 1938. Initial assessments of her condition were dire: 'depressed and melancholic', one doctor wrote, 'worried the whole of her waking hours'. Another noted their patient was 'unable to face anything'. Having retired from private nursing, Rachael Pratt 'had lost all self-confidence . . . has no companionship . . . and no practical purpose in life'.[2]

She was transferred to Merton Private Hospital in Melbourne, where her 'mental outlook' worsened. An element of desperation crept into the case notes. A Dr Godfrey noted:

> *[No] improvement whatever . . . [she] requires careful vigilance as she is suicidal . . . Last week she secured a pair of nail-scissors, and hid them in her clothes. They were missed . . . on her being searched, she transferred them to her vagina. She then admitted her intention was to open a vein in her wrist.*[3]

At Merton, Rachael was treated by 'modern methods'. In August 1939, doctors began a course of Cardizol injections, a circulatory and respiratory stimulant. Doses were high enough to create convulsions and send the body into seizures. When this therapy failed, the doctors administered Somnifaine 'at such a frequency as to maintain a condition of narcosis for three to four weeks'.[4] That treatment also failed.

Worried by the cost, efficacy and perhaps the humanity of such treatment, medical staff drew the inevitable conclusion. In October 1940, Dr Godfrey made one of his final entries in the casebook: 'prospects of ultimate recovery must now be regarded as improbable'.[5]

Sister Rachael Pratt died in the Heidelberg Repatriation Hospital in March 1954. After her time in mental hospitals she never successfully returned to civilian life. Her war had never really ended.

ABOVE **A state of chaos:** This photograph was taken not far from where Australian nurses established their primitive hospital on Lemnos. It does not convey the crowded conditions of the island or the appalling circumstances in which the nursing staff found themselves. *Courtesy Bruce Scates.*

LEFT **Wearing the medal she clearly deserved:** The studio portrait often reproduced of Rachael Pratt. This appearance of composure is at odds with the story of her later life. *P05664.001 courtesy Australian War Memorial.*

In many regards, Rachael Pratt's story is an important one. And here we face the choice of what we choose to remember and what we decide to forget in our narratives of war. No one denies Sister Pratt's bravery, or her humanity, or her selflessness. Her photograph, wearing the medal she clearly deserved, is reproduced in newspapers every Anzac Day. But no one prints a picture of a frail and frightened woman driven mad by her nightmares. Telling the whole truth about war, and not just some of the story, requires its own kind of courage.

SOURCES AND FURTHER READING: This story draws on Rachael Pratt's service dossier NAA: B2455 PRATT R; her repatriation file NAA: B73, H5789; and Rachael's reflections on nursing on Lemnos in *Reveille*, vol. 6, no. 12, Aug. 1933. For further reading on Australian nurses see Jan Bassett, *Guns and Brooches: Australian Army nursing from the Boer War to the Gulf War* (Melbourne: Oxford University Press, 1992); Kirsty Harris, *More than Bombs and Bandages: Australian Army Nurses at Work in World War I* (Newport: Big Sky Publishing, 2011); and Alice McConnell, *Women in War: Lemnos–Gallipoli 1915* (Melbourne: Artek Productions, 2015).

That Other War

REGINALD BIGGS

Reginald Biggs sat down to write his memoirs in 1942. At the very moment the old journalist turned to his typewriter, Australian militia at Kokoda were struggling to turn back the Japanese advance. The Second AIF faced a battle at least as difficult as the First – and Australia seemed threatened by defeat and invasion. Biggs – or Ashmead, as he liked to call himself – gazed out on the little garden next to his study in Launceston. Then his fingers sped with practised ease across the keyboard, thumping out each letter: T-H-A-T O-T-H-E-R W-A-R.

At the time, the title seemed obvious enough. But then (as today), 'that other war' had other unintended meanings. Biggs' reminiscences were different to the genre of 'war books' that preceded it. Most of these had a tendency towards 'big noting': one old soldier after another recounted his martial exploits and explained (often with embarrassing bluster) the part he played in winning the war. In comparison, the claims made in *The Other War* were modest – and often Reginald Biggs was not the centre of the story.

Little more than a boy when he went to war, Private Biggs served as a signaller.[1] He was often near the front line, often shelled, often gassed and often afraid. At Messines his best mate had been killed beside him, cut down by machine-gun fire as they approached the German lines. But Biggs never went 'over the top' brandishing rifle and bayonet in pursuit of an unseen enemy. '[All] honour to those grand infantry privates who often got the rotten end of the stick,' he wrote, 'rather than to the generals who sit back in comfort out of danger and hear about the victories which the humble soldiers have won for them.'[2]

Nor was this a simple story of righteous Allies versus the evil Hun. It didn't dwell on the difference between Australian troops and their British contemporaries. The callous incompetence of high command is a much laboured theme in most Australian war writing. Biggs was equally critical of his own side. There was 'another war' being

fought alongside the battles – a class war that didn't cease when men put on uniform. In the early days of the war, Australia's officers were largely drawn from the ranks of the powerful and privileged. Those 'lazy well fed officers' thought they were 'Gods', Biggs complained. 'Would be aristocrats,' they treated enlisted men 'no better than cattle'.[3] And the most passionate passages of the book dealt not with German atrocities but our own. Without recourse to the death penalty to enforce discipline in the line, Australian authorities resorted to more use of Field Punishment No. 1 than many other Allied armies. It reduced 'brave and good soldiers' to 'trembling nervous wrecks':

> *Professional bashers . . . working in teams of half a dozen overwhelm a prisoner and belt the life out of him. Their brutality reigns the moment a prisoner is [subjected to Field Punishment No 1]. The flogging was not with whips but a repeated bashing with fists, and with kicks when he fell and lay on the ground.*

And that was in addition to hours of being strung up to posts, usually in the open, with ropes bound so tight that they cut off the circulation. Many soldiers suffered gangrene after this treatment, sometimes resulting in the amputation of hands or feet. Biggs believed Field Punishment No. 1 was the invention of sadists, carried out by monsters. He was appalled Australia's proudly volunteer army could be subjected to this.[4]

And there was one other important way that *That Other War* was different to most World War I memoirs. The interwar period saw the rise of what some called 'stench literature'. In often quite sensationalised detail, veterans dwelt on the horrors of battle – the mud, the rats, the mechanistic murder of Flanders and the Somme. Biggs had seen too much of the slaughter to sanitise it. In sparse and disciplined prose, the boy

ABOVE LEFT **Old Pop:** A souvenir from Poperinge. The town was several kilometres behind the lines and offered welcome relief from the horrors of the Ypres Salient. 'Pop's' diversions catered for every taste and every budget; the YMCA dispensed free refreshments, Talbot House offered spiritual guidance, and a range of bars and brothels plied their trade amongst the troops. Biggs partook of several of these pastimes and, like many of his comrades, was fined for being absent without leave in the town. *Courtesy Bruce Scates.*

ABOVE **The makeshift chapel of Talbot House:** One of the shrines inside the informal church where Reginald Biggs came to pray. Talbot House was established by Captain 'Tubby' Clayton, the 'jovial padre' – and fellow Australian – Biggs took a shine to. The entrance to the club was adorned with a sign reading 'Abandon Rank All Ye Who Enter Here'. It was a sentiment the democratic private strongly approved of. Biggs later established a chapter of Toc H (the Christian society that ran Talbot House) in Tasmania. *Courtesy Bruce Scates.*

ABOVE **Simply having a bit of fun:** A studio portrait of the Anzac Coves, an Australian Pierrot troupe who entertained at the Front, behind the lines, and even at Buckingham Palace. Of the ten men pictured here, eight are dressed in Pierrot clown costumes and two are dressed as women. The proceeds from their shows were donated to the Australian Comforts Fund. *Courtesy State Library of Queensland.*

cadet from the *Examiner* captured the 'continuous din' of the front line, 'the constant anxiety and danger'; the ghastly sight of men butchered on the parapet, 'the perennial misery of trench mud'.[5]

The Other War also told of times outside the actual fighting. 'Life was blissful in our leisure hours,' Biggs remembered, hearty meals at village *estaminets* washed down by bowls of coffee and plentiful *vin blanc* or *vin rouge*, served 'by a lovely blonde'. Biggs walked through beautiful woods beyond the 'broken countryside', gazed on the wonders of ancient cathedrals, and 'felt closer to God than I have ever been' in the makeshift chapel of Talbot House, a soldiers' club in Poperinge. He performed in plays alongside the 'Anzac Coves', flirted with pretty nurses, mastered jokes of 'a war time flavour' and discovered Paris – a city 'full of kind-hearted ladies who wanted to make the soldiers happy on their leave'.[6] This life behind the lines introduced him to a world a God-fearing teetotaller from Launceston was never likely to see otherwise.

When Biggs returned to Belgium and France half a century later, a solemn pilgrimage across the battlefields was not the only thing on his mind. What he liked to call 'fraternisation' – and simply having a bit of fun – was at least as important as commemoration and mourning. In 1967, he wrote a series of letters to the organisers of

Operation Amiens, a plan to return some thirty diggers to the Western Front for the fiftieth anniversary of the Battle of Villers-Bretonneux the following year. Worried that things were starting to look a bit too serious, he reminded the organisers of what might well be called 'that other war':

> *I fully recognise that this tour is partly dedicated to a purpose, namely, a pilgrimage to the battlefields and certain war memorials with the aim of a tribute to the memory of our Fallen Comrades; also that, as the Dept. of External Affairs is identified with it, courtesy receptions at some embassies and consulates are unavoidable.*[7]

But Biggs' recognition and approval were two quite different matters:

> *. . . those who are planning the arrangements must equally bear in mind . . . that the veterans are spending their life savings to see as much as possible of the battlefields and their old rest areas to which they became strongly and sentimentally attached. With this in mind, I have just been studying a large area map of France . . . and drafted out an itinerary.*[8]

Of course there were the obvious landmarks, the 'many marvels to see and enjoy' all throughout Paris. On the battlefields, Biggs longed to travel the line again, and visit Lille, the German-held town 'we looked longingly at . . . from our trenches'. Other longings would surely be understood by every old soldier:

> *. . . the bus could take us to Armentières via the rest and training area we used to go back to. (I'd love to call at the billet . . . near Becourt . . . to see whether that fine girl and my company's friend Marie is still there.)*[9]

'Doubtless several in your party would like to revisit old "Pop",' Biggs continued, 'lots of diggers frequented Talbot House in Poperinghe', its warm fires, spacious lounge and cheery atmosphere had been a welcome escape from the cold cramped horror of the trenches.

A number of the '68 pilgrims threatened to 'wag it' if the trips to the cemeteries weren't balanced by time in bars, cafes and other places 'diggers frequented'.[10] And most were appalled that an Anzac Day service planned in England might prove a very formal occasion. Fred Cahill (an old friend of Biggs and the tour's official organiser) struggled to explain their 'requirements' to (somewhat bewildered) British veterans. The wreath-laying and ceremony at Whitehall was all very well, but '[h]ere in Australia Anzac Day is dedicated to . . . fraternisation'. Would it be possible to host some drinks, the letter politely inquired; 'tea and cakes' would not quite be the go, perhaps something a little stronger. Above all: 'Speeches are not our favourite pastime; [no more than] a word of welcome and a reply from our leader'. Music, on the other hand, was entirely acceptable, 'We always have [a] . . . community song from our World War I repertoire.'[11] Writing yet another letter, Reginald Biggs expanded on his own ideal itinerary:

ABOVE **That fine girl and my company's friend:** F T Whitcroft depicts a first encounter between an Australian soldier and a mademoiselle behind the lines. The relationships troops established with civilians ranged a huge emotional spectrum, from respectable and platonic to casual and commercial sex. A happily married man when he wrote his memoirs, Biggs emphasised the innocent nature of these liaisons – but like most troops he was issued with prophylactic kits and could also purchase condoms (which the diggers dubbed 'dreadnaughts'). Whatever precautions he might have taken, Biggs was admitted to hospital with VD in 1917. *'The Prodigal Sun: Homeward Ho! On H.M.A.T. "Mahia"' in Chronicle and Caricature courtesy National Library of Australia.*

In England, why not a sentimental trip to Salisbury Plain . . . ? In France, [let's do] a round trip . . . through our old rest areas . . . Then have a couple of days doing Paris (wonder whether the Hotel All Nations brothel is still functioning?)[12]

Though well into his seventies, Reginald Biggs, it seems, was still fully functional. For a good time in Paris, he would happily forgo all but a day's rest on the homeward journey. In the twilight of his life, battlefield feats seemed far less memorable than youthful exuberance and sexual adventure – this was 'that other war' Reginald Biggs chose to remember.

Scholarship on the Great War now stands at a crossroads. Some argue that historians have placed too much emphasis on the horrors of battle, forgetting that most of a soldier's time (on the Western Front, at least) was spent out of the line and that there life assumed a kind of normalcy. Why focus on the casualties when many men escaped unwounded? Why exaggerate the hardships when men in rest camps were sometimes better housed, fed and cared for than they had been as civilians?

This revisionist line is fraught with danger. While it is true that not every man was wounded or killed, every survivor feared death or maiming. Nor could life behind the lines – an interlude in constant carnage – ever really escape the totality of wartime. Drink and sex only ever offered fleeting oblivion. Men like Biggs missed the friends, the family, the simple comforts and reassuring certainties left behind them.

Even so, his testimony reminds us that there was 'that other war': moments of compassion, friendship, even joy amid the madness. Towards the end of his life Reginald Biggs told a historian that though he marked every Anzac Day with what he called 'a kind of reverence', it symbolised a sacrifice unimaginable to those who had not seen it.[13] But he also never forgot the other side of war.

SOURCES AND FURTHER READING: This story is based on Reginald Biggs' autobiography *That Other War* (Launceston: privately published, 1983); his correspondence with the RSL in regards to the 1968 pilgrimage to the Western Front AWM 3DRL6037; his service dossier NAA: B2455, BIGGS R A; and his repatriation file NAA: P107, H12148 PART 1 and 2. We have also benefitted from the 1987 documentary *The Unknown Soldier* directed by Gus Howard and written by Russell Fewster, with an interview with Biggs before his death filmed by David Foreman. For further reading on relationships behind the lines, see Susan R. Grayzel, 'Mothers, Marraines, and Prostitutes: Morale and Morality in First World War France', *The International History Review*, vol. 19, no. 1, Febuary 1997, pp. 66–82; and James Curran, 'Bonjoor Mardemwazell! Diggers Discover Gay Paree', *Wartime*, no. 3, 1998, pp. 37–41; and Craig Gibson, 'Sex and Soldiering in France and Flanders: The British Expeditionary Force along the Western Front', *The International History Review*, no. 3, September 2001, pp. 535–79. For a comparable account to *That Other War* see Joseph Maxwell, *Hells Bells and Mademoiselles* (Sydney: Angus and Robertson, 1932).

Their name liveth for evermore?

ABAS BHAWOODEEN GHANSAR

Abas Bhawoodeen Ghansar's life was far from an easy one. He was born in Bombay (now Mumbai) at the height of the British Raj. Like thousands of subject Indians, Ghansar was raised a Christian and almost certainly educated in one of the many mission schools established in India. That rudimentary education, and the opportunities offered by a great port city, enabled Ghansar to travel from one outpost of the Empire to another. The young man worked his passage to Australia via London and landed in Sydney in 1907.

Compared to the slums of Bombay, Australia must have seemed a land of opportunity. A prosperous nation with seemingly limitless possibilities, it offered the chance to build a new life and escape the teeming millions of India. But as for many immigrants the promise fell short of reality. The early Commonwealth was intent on creating a white Australia. Suspicious of 'coloured labour', Indian workers like Ghansar were relegated to the fringes of the economy. He became a hawker on the streets of Sydney, living off what he could sell and what he could carry.

When trade was doing well, Ghansar took a room in lodgings, but often he slept rough, catching what rest he could in laneways and parklands. Hawking was a life of constant movement – vagrancy laws meant he drifted from town to town, trying to stay one step ahead of the authorities.

Abas Bhawoodeen Ghansar lived with the possibility of deportation every day of the eighteen years

BELOW **In and out of hospital:** Sutton Veny in southern England. Abas Bhawoodeen Ghansar spent time here in 1917. An Australian hospital, this image captures the character of the white Australian troops who were treated there. We do not know if Ghansar would have mixed well with any of these men; if anyone took a photograph of him, it has not survived in the historical record. *H01343 courtesy Australian War Memorial.*

he spent in Australia. And come the war, there was yet another chance to remove coloured labour from a fervently British and largely monocultural Australia. India was part of the Empire, and by 1917 the loss of white troops was making Britain increasingly reliant on the vast reserves of coloured manpower across its colonies. That October, Ghansar offered himself for service at Victoria Barracks, Sydney. A recruitment officer looked askance at this malnourished black man, his body pitted with smallpox scars and his feet blistered from walking.

Almost 40, barely five feet, four inches in height and weighing less than 130 pounds, Ghansar would not have been accepted some months earlier. But that very week the Allied advance on Passchendaele had stalled in the mud of Flanders. Now the Army would take almost anyone. A man born in Bombay donned an Australian uniform and was sent off to fight in Europe; such was the transnational reach of the first global war of the twentieth century.

By any measure, his was not a distinguished record of war service. Worn out by a life on the road, Private Ghansar spent more time in British hospitals than he did in the field in France. His constitution, used to the hot climate of Australia and the subcontinent, broke down in the freezing conditions of Europe. He suffered bouts of influenza and severe tonsillitis, and was also treated for VD.

In July 1918, barely nine months after leaving Sydney, Private Ghansar was deemed medically unfit to serve by the military authorities. A doctor at Horseferry Road, London, listened to Ghansar's complaint of pains all over his body. Though only in his forties, Ghansar showed signs of 'premature senility'. The doctor raised the age of his patient to 45 in his notes, perhaps to discourage any second thoughts by an army hungry for men. In his opinion, Abas Bhawoodeen Ghansar 'was of no use to us as a soldier' and was ordered back to Australia.

For a time, it seemed Ghansar had been offered a second chance. His war gratuity and deferred pay made it possible to purchase a grocer's store in Pyrmont. And in 1922 he married. Annie Buckley was 50 years of age, and we know nothing of the circumstances – personal or financial – that brought them together. But repatriation was seldom easy for white diggers, and certainly not for a black man. The business failed to thrive, and Annie died in the first year of the marriage.

In 1926, Ghansar returned to the subcontinent. We have found no record of what became of him there. There is no acknowledgement of his service on any monument raised in Australia, let alone the few memorials that survive in India. Abas Bhawoodeen

ABOVE **The transnational reach of the world's first global war:** Charles Burleigh's painting of wounded Indian troops in the music room of the Royal Pavilion, Brighton. The Pavilion was used as a military hospital for Indian troops in 1915. The authorities assumed the exotic surroundings would be to the liking of troops from the subcontinent. *The Music Room of The Royal Pavilion as a Hospital for Indian Soldiers courtesy Royal Pavilion and Museums, Brighton and Hove.*

OPPOSITE **For the British Empire:** A souvenir booklet issued for the first Anzac Day in Queensland. This is a rare depiction of Australian soldiers serving alongside the so called 'coloured' troops of the Empire. *Anzac Day Booklet 1916 courtesy National Museum of Australia.*

Anzac.-The Dawn.
25th April, 1915.

A. J. Cumming, Government Printer, Brisbane, Queensland

Anzac Day.

25th April, 1916.

For Classes V & VI.

Ghansar is not a name that 'liveth for evermore'.

Over a million Indian troops fought for the British Empire in the Great War, and 62 000 of them died. Another 87 000 Indian troops died in the Second World War. Britain did not grant independence to India until 1947, and then only after a long and bitter struggle. It's debatable if the war Abas Bhawoodeen Ghansar fought in was waged to defend freedom and democracy, but he would see neither in his lifetime.[1]

SOURCES AND FURTHER READINGS: This story draws on Private Ghansar's service dossier NAA: B2455, GHANSAR A B; his other military records NAA: B741, V/3124 and NAA:MT1486/1. The authors look forward to reading Peter Stanley's revealing study of the relationship between Indian and Australian troops on Anzac, *Die in Battle, Do Not Despair: The Indians on Gallipoli, 1915* (Solihull: Helion & Company, 2015). The history of Indian hawkers in Australia is an area yet to be fully explored. For a captivating introduction see Hanifa Deen, *Muslim Journeys* exhibition uncommonlives.naa.gov.au/muslim-journey/stories/camelees-andhawkers.aspx

ABOVE **Few memorials survive:** A war memorial in the grounds of St George's Church in Kochi, India. Over a million troops were raised in India and some 60 000 died. Even so, few memorials were erected and – seen as vestiges of colonialism – many were destroyed in postwar independence struggles. This memorial commemorates a British regiment that served in India and then on the Western Front. Lutyens' India Gate was raised in New Delhi to honour (but not to name) Indian servicemen, and a memorial to Indian seamen still exists in Mumbai. *Courtesy Bruce Scates.*

The ugliness of Anzac

MARY BOOTH

From the moment of the Landing – and even before that – that single word 'Anzac' acquired any number of meanings. Originally it was just an acronym. Devised by impatient clerks at Army Headquarters in Egypt, ANZAC was simple shorthand for the Australian and New Zealand Army Corps. But it also came to represent a place – the site where Australasian troops first landed in Turkey – a particular group of servicemen and women (initially veterans of the Dardanelles campaign), and a set of values, attributes and beliefs. Anzac may well have been born on the slopes of Gallipoli, but like any legend, the Anzac mythology gained a life all of its own. And it was never just the property of men.

Back home in Australia, Anzac meant everything to Mary Booth. She had volunteered for service overseas, but was rejected (as was every other female doctor) by a male-dominated military hierarchy. A patriot and imperialist at one and the same time, she helped to create the legend we live with today. Committed to her war work, Mary Booth often invoked the stoic determination of the diggers. She called on the community for greater and greater sacrifice, campaigned vigorously for conscription, appealed to that Anzac spirit as she urged everyone to do their bit. Dr Booth founded the Soldiers' Club in Sydney, a vibrant social centre offering nourishing meals, non-intoxicating drinks, and healthy entertainments for men on leave. And well before the war was won, Mary Booth channeled the rhetoric of Anzac into the work of remembrance. It was Dr Booth who organised the first pilgrimages to soldiers' graves. Under her leadership, groups of women (most with loved ones still serving overseas) decorated the graves of returned servicemen who had died of illness or wounds. They did this on Anzac Day, their floral tributes brightening 'the graves of the brave'.[1]

At war's end, Booth led what she called an 'Anzac pilgrimage' to the wharves at Woolloomooloo. Every April the gates there were 'hung all over with flowers', sprigs of rosemary, handwritten messages and other 'tokens of remembrance'. [2] 'It was through these gates that nearly all of the boys passed', Booth explained to her compatriots. Here young men 'made their final farewells' and sailed off to war and eternity, and here women came, clad in black, to remember them. She arranged for an Anzac memorial fountain to be built at Woolloomooloo, one of the first such monuments completed in the wake of the war and, she proudly added, 'the only memorial erected by women, from all parts of New South Wales, in honour of all the[ir] men.' [3]

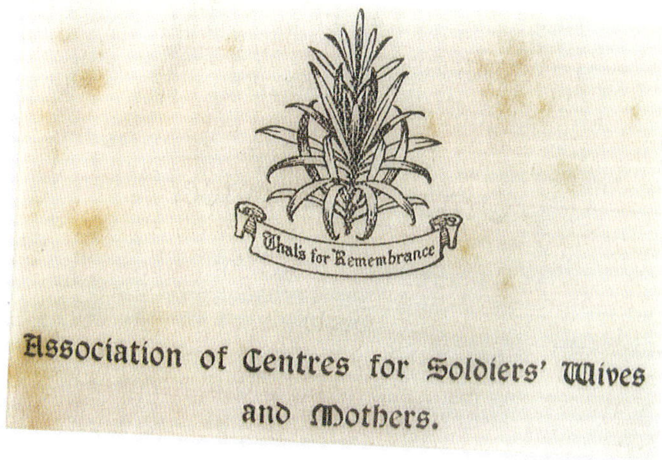

ABOVE **The work of remembrance:** Masthead of the Centre for Soldiers' Wives and Mothers. The Anzac Fellowship of Women first popularised rosemary as a symbol of remembrance during Anzac Day. *Anzac Fellowship of Women papers NLA: MS 2864 courtesy National Library of Australia.*

OPPOSITE **An architect of Anzac:** Arguably Mary Booth did more than any other woman to secure Anzac Day in the postwar period. *Portrait of Dr Mary Booth by J.S. Watkins courtesy National Library of Australia.*

Honouring those men became the mission of the Anzac Fellowship of Women, yet another group Dr Booth founded in 1921. It continued its work – with Booth as president – until 1956, and was the only civilian organisation granted the right by Prime Minister Billy Hughes to use the name Anzac. That work was as indefatigable as Mary Booth herself. Along with Anzac Day and Armistice Day services, pilgrimages to soldiers' graves, and community singing in honour of the diggers, the Anzac Fellowship of Women organised essay-writing competitions in schools 'to pass the message on to the next generation', and established an Anzac Festival Committee pledged to safeguard 25 April as a 'sacred day' of remembrance. With Governor-General Lord Gowrie and Lady Gowrie as patrons, the Anzac Festival Committee lobbied for the day's gazetting as a public holiday; they sponsored artistic endeavour – rather than football or racing – to mark what they called 'the Anzac Season' and made April the month where the achievements and 'inseparable union' of Empire and nation were celebrated. By a happy coincidence, Shakespeare's birthday, the Landing at Gallipoli, and the festival for England's patron saint, St George, fell within days of each other in April.

Few idealised the Anzacs as much as Mary Booth; few were as intimately involved in the making of that Anzac mythology. But Mary Booth was also acutely aware of what might well be called the ugliness of Anzac – the appalling human consequences of war and the failings of the Anzac himself.

In 1916, Dr Booth set up the Centre for Soldiers' Wives and Mothers to care for the women the Anzacs left behind. Throughout the war – and well beyond it – she organised charitable assistance for women beaten, abandoned, abused or neglected by their men. Her case notes offer a frank insight into a deeply traumatised society. Many soldiers, she noted, seemed to bring the war home with them, addicted to acts of violence, hardened to human hardship, changed forever by what they had seen and done.

There were times Dr Booth was sympathetic, and times she made excuses for them – those shell-shocked men who couldn't control their shaking let alone their actions, cripples unable or unwilling to provide for their families, men eaten up by their anger and frustration. Many veterans, Booth admitted, had 'suffered greatly'; war had

ABOVE **Never just the property of men:** A woman pins her tribute to the wharves at Woolloomooloo. A rough working place every other day of the year, the gates were transformed by tributes every 25 April, briefly feminising a world of masculine labour. *DG ON4/2026 courtesy State Library of New South Wales.*

left them human 'wrecks' and killed much of the good in them.[4] Some sad boys just 'couldn't settle down', or went 'off drinking' with old comrades who understood their pain. There were 'badly wounded soldiers' who couldn't hold down a job, men old employers wouldn't take back, those who took to crime in sheer desperation.[5]

The Anzacs Booth knew were often anything but angels. Sidney Galloway was one of the first to enlist; he boasted the service number 28 and served at Gallipoli. Maria Galloway married him when she was barely 16 – Sidney was just the sort, Booth thought, to take advantage of a woman. On his return from war, Galloway was 'very brutal to his wife', locked her and their baby out of the house, drank heavily and gambled away almost everything. He was in prison when Maria, living with her parents, 'barely able to keep her and child and . . . expecting another baby', sought help from the Centre.[6]

Frank Thomas, service number 190, may have been 'mildly gassed' during the war, but he too was a man 'of very bad character'. His wife overlooked much 'for the sake of the children' but 'in September last she took them to the Children's Court owing to his attempted interference with his little girl'. Acquitted for want of evidence, he promptly deserted his family.[7]

Private Herbert Bulmer, yet another patriot of 1914, was also a bigamist, with one wife in Australia and another in England.[8] Private John Whealy enlisted right towards the end of the war and saw just a few months of service overseas, but expected his 'wife to keep him on his return'. Whealy sported a tattoo reading 'Love Emily' on his left arm. He had need of reminding. By 1920, Emily Whealy, a 'nice little woman', had 'pawned nearly everything', was 'in very ill health' and lived in fear of beatings from her husband. Like Whealy, Joseph Bryson 'would not work', a wounded knee his excuse to 'lie in nearly all the morning'. Bryson ill-treated his wife, refused to provide for her or his two children, and complained when the government cut back his pension for varicose veins.

These men weren't the simple victims of war – they were (in Booth's opinion) 'bad men' to begin with. William Cordiner 'did not support [his wife] before going to war' and was hardly going to do so on returning to Australia. A veteran of the Somme, he took all the money his wife had saved while he was away, and then deserted her and their five-year-old daughter.[9] Most proved as great a failure in war as they were in marriage – the aforementioned Whealy was punished for gambling and drunkenness on the voyage out, and kept under close arrest during his return to Australia. His war service suggests a deeply dysfunctional man, one charge following another.

In cases like these, Booth chose to champion the women rather than the Anzacs. And here we see a paradox. Though intensively conservative (and a candidate for the National Party), Mary Booth was also a feminist. She told these women to stand up for their rights and demand their share of a returned man's entitlement; she offered women shelter from their violent husbands and even encouraged some to leave them. On one hand, Booth believed 'good wives made good husbands' but some returned men, she admitted, were simply 'too bad' to reform. Marriage was a contract that conferred mutual obligations.[10]

BELOW TOP **Bad men to begin with:** In this familiar larrikin image of the first AIF, the men lounging about are presented as likable figures. Booth saw through that façade as she dealt with families abandoned and abused by 'idle wasters'. Gazette *(London), 28 February 1919.*

BOTTOM **A deeply traumatised society:** One of the 'faceless men' Booth could not help but pity. Bertram Byrnes had his face shot away in France. Unable to chew, he lived much of his life on slop food and struggled to provide for his family. *NAA: C138/2, M55451 courtesy National Archives of Australia.*

An architect of Anzac in the postwar period, Mary Booth attended countless commemorative functions and the dedications of countless memorials. Each time she spoke of the righteousness and valour of the men those monuments honoured. But she also knew that many men fell well short of the clichéd Anzac ideal. The legend, she was the first to admit, had its limitations.

SOURCES AND FURTHER READING: This account is based on a detailed study of the records of the Anzac Fellowship of Women, particularly the case studies compiled by Dr Booth for the Centre for Soldiers' Wives and Mothers NLA: MS2864. These case studies have been cross-referenced with service dossiers. For studies of the work of the Anzac Fellowship of Women see Bruce Scates, *Return to Gallipoli: Walking the Battlefields of the Great War* (Cambridge: Cambridge University Press, 2006); also Bruce Scates, 'The Unknown Sock Knitter: Voluntary Work, Emotional Labour, Bereavement and the Great War', *Labour History*, no. 81, 2001, pp. 29–49. The sexual politics of Booth's generation are discussed by Jill Roe, *Stella Miles Franklin* (Pymble: Fourth Estate, 2008). The lives of Australian doctors who served in the Great War are the subject of Susan Neuhaus and Sharon Mascall-Dare, *Not for Glory: A Century of Service by Medical Women to the Australian Army and its Allies* (Brisbane: Boolarong Press, 2014). For disreputable Anzacs see Peter Stanley, *Bad Characters: Sex, Crime, Mutiny, Murder and the Australian Imperial Force* (Millers Point: Pier 9, 2010).

War Horse
THOMAS GOODWIN

ABOVE **The men who look after their animals the best:** Indian troops tending their mules at No. 2 Outpost. These troops, along with the Zion Mule Corps, played a critical role at both Helles and Anzac and showed great concern for the animals placed in their care. Goodwin was also critical of the way the Greeks on Lemnos treated their animals. He saw them 'struggling along' with impossible loads, and often these 'poor miserable looking' creatures were 'flogged and abused'. *Edward G. Williams Collection PH-ALB-212p18-1 courtesy Auckland War Memorial Museum.*

Thomas Goodwin's transport arrived off the coast of Gallipoli on 25 April 1915. He remembered being roused by the gunfire around five o'clock in the morning as British warships bombarded the coast for miles around. For a time the ships steamed dangerously close to the stream of shrapnel coming from the shore, 'so close in fact that the wash [from exploding shells] splashed over our stern':

> *As we stood off [Anzac] we saw the First Division Australian Infantry land, heavens it was awful. How men managed to gain a footing there is a mistery [sic] . . . In the meantime, the Navy blazing away like fury. The old* Majestic, Triumph, . . . The Queen Elizabeth *with her 15 inch guns beautiful weapons too I can assure you, and a lot more battleships that I don't remember the names of. An incident that has impressed on my memory was a man with a Helio signalling he was on a hill signalling to someone on the beach, he was there a number of hours signalling away shrapnel bursting around him. Presently the Helio stops flickering. No need to say what happened.*[1]

Unable to unload their cargo of men, guns and horses, the transports sailed on to the Gulf of Saros. A few landing parties were sent ashore, feints to confuse Gallipoli's defenders. And the escorts continued to bombard the coast. 'We opened fire on a wireless station and blew it to pieces. We also smashed up a village.' For over a week, Thomas Goodwin observed war from a distance, marvelling at the might of naval power. Then the 2nd Battery of the Field Artillery Brigade (guns, men and horse-drawn carriages) landed at Helles on the toe of the peninsula.

Some sixty-seven horses were packed onto a pontoon and towed ashore by paddleboat. It was a difficult operation. Each animal had to be lifted up in a harness and lowered over the side of the vessel. Twisting in the air, some almost plunged to their deaths. The pontoon came ashore at V Beach, quite close to where the *River Clyde* and her cargo of British Tommies had run aground. 'It was a terrible place to unload horses,' Goodwin noted in his diary; shells were still 'screeching over' and the beach itself was pitted with the hurried graves of the dead.[2] From the ruined Ottoman fortress of Sedd-el-Bahr, Goodwin's party marched less than a mile inland. They took up a position near wells captured by the Allies and within an hour's march of their front line. For six months, Goodwin's battery would serve at Helles, the only place then on Gallipoli where so large a contingent of horses, guns and wagon trains could be stationed:

> *A few remarks about our daily routine may be interesting. Revallie [sic] 6:30 AM. Water feed, and muck out, groom etc. Breakfast 7.30. After breakfast, fatigue [and] draw rations, in the meantime some three horses are sent up to the Battery . . . The water cart horses are then sent . . . At 11.30 with water feed and etc again. Dinner is then served, the men are at liberty to go for a swim.*[3]

The semblance of order here is deceptive. At any time in that 'routine' a shell could land and send terrified horses stampeding down the line. 'No place here is safe,' he scribbled in his diary, 'you are [always] under fire.' Every day, he recorded a careful tally of wounded and dead. By June, as the hot weather made the stench of unburied corpses 'unbearable', Goodwin described conditions as 'dreadful': 'a lot

BELOW **A terrible place to unload horses:** A horse in a sling lifted over the ship. This dangerous procedure was used to load and unload horses during the campaign. *A01237 courtesy Australian War Memorial.*

of our drivers breaking down, nerves [simply] gone'.[4] Most of the Brigade's work had to be done in darkness; water, ammunition and all the necessities of war were carted laboriously up to the firing line. 'Many a night we have been out to after midnight', Goodwin wrote, man and beast alike exhausted by their toil.[5] On just a few occasions he approached the front in daylight. He was appalled by what he saw there:

> *[T]he dead and the wounded of both sides lying out [in open ground] as thick as flies . . . Three New Zealanders, killed in action about three months ago, their bodies were only got and buried yesterday. A prayer book found on one had a note in it, saying, if anything should happen to him to return it to an address in New Zealand. It seems a horrible thing for bodies to be left out all the time, but I can assure you it cannot be avoided. If a man only had to show his head above the parapet, it is certain death.*[6]

Thomas Goodwin's diary is one of the few extended accounts Australian soldiers kept at Helles. Some ten miles south of Anzac, the flat ground of the peninsula was held by the British and the French – aided by an army of colonial troops from Africa. As such, Australians and New Zealanders often forget the war at Helles – although this part of the peninsula actually bore the brunt of the fighting. It also saw the bungled Australian assault on Krithia, a bloodbath as bad and as pointless as the Nek and one that claimed the lives of just as many Anzacs.

Goodwin's account is also one of very few to focus on the role of horses at Gallipoli. The men of the Light Horse were dismounted when they came ashore at Anzac, though a few daring despatch riders raced between the beaches. But at Helles, horses (particularly the horses of the Field Artillery) helped to hold the line. And Thomas Goodwin was well aware of that.

The farrier from Sydney was often critical of the soldiers who served beside him at Helles. Goodwin claimed reinforcements were so poorly trained that they had to be

BELOW **The Light Horse:** George Lambert's iconic sculpture, originally a tribute to the men and their mounts who served in Palestine. Horses were used as transports as well, and over a million died in the course of the war. The Light Horse was not permitted to repatriate their chargers. Many were shot by the men themselves to prevent them falling into Arab hands. *Courtesy Bruce Scates.*

sent back to Egypt; he described the men of D Battery as 'the biggest lot of wasters I ever saw'. He poured scorn on any officer he thought callous or incompetent. And the greatest abuse of all was reserved for the French, who were lazy and 'unsanitary' and, worst of all, ill-treated their horses:

> *Talk about cruelty to animals. I have seen horses taken to water, with hardly a leg to stand on. Bullet wounds (septic) on legs and bodies with pus running out. Another favourite habit is jagging the mouth of the horse. I have seen their mouths bleeding, horses on wagon lines packed close together, nicking and biting one another, legs swollen, heels galled and horses . . . [sick with] colic . . . They also eat any horse that is killed by the enemy.*

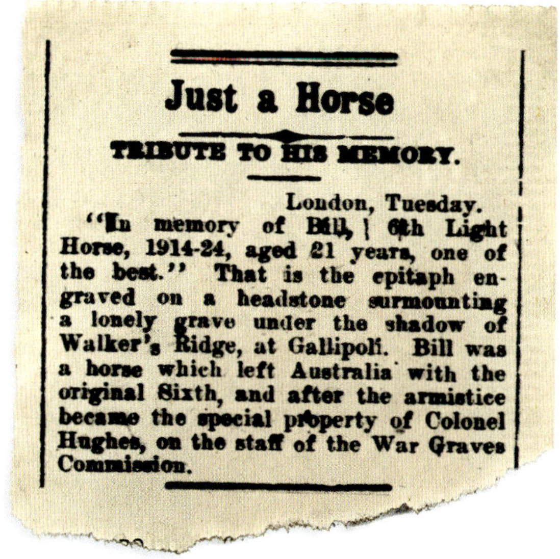

Just a Horse

TRIBUTE TO HIS MEMORY.

London, Tuesday.

"In memory of Bill, | 6th Light Horse, 1914-24, aged 21 years, one of the best." That is the epitaph engraved on a headstone surmounting a lonely grave under the shadow of Walker's Ridge, at Gallipoli. Bill was a horse which left Australia with the original Sixth, and after the armistice became the special property of Colonel Hughes, on the staff of the War Graves Commission.

ABOVE **Beautiful creatures:** Bill was a Waler who served at Gallipoli. In 1924, the Imperial War Graves Commission unit stationed at Anzac took the unprecedented step of marking his grave with an official memorial. The epitaph – 'one of the best' – signals the great respect the men of the Light Horse felt for their mounts. Albany Advertiser, *3 December 1924 courtesy National Library of Australia.*

Not that this can be attributed to any contempt for foreigners. 'The men who look after their animals the best are the Indians,' Goodwin continued. He had often seen them lead a thousand mules to water, beautiful creatures clearly loved and cared for.[7]

While the men may have been found wanting, Goodwin's horses never failed him. It was not just their feats of endurance, as sick, hungry and tick-ridden animals laboured to bring supplies to the front line. The most graphic accounts in the diary are of exploding shells wreaking havoc on the wagon train, mauling the bodies of men and beast.

> *19/5/1915. 2236. Brown Geld[ing], 3240, Bay Geld[ing]. These horses were the first to be killed by a 5-inch shell. It went through the neck and chest of one, and the hips of another. The first one mentioned was killed outright. The other had to be destroyed. A third horse was knocked insensible . . . When this happened . . . I was going over towards the horses, and heard the shell coming . . . The concussion knocked me off my feet . . .*

The following day Goodwin described the wounding of the major's charger:

> *This was a shocking case. When I discovered it the horse had his nosebag on feeding. I saw the blood running out through the ventilation holes of the bag. At first I thought it was hopeless. When we dressed and we found two teeth out and the jawbone shattered.*

Through Goodwin's patient nursing, the major's gelding was saved. But he couldn't help others:

> *23/8/1915 . . . this time shrapnel got in amongst us, every horse turned about and bolted back to wagon line . . . I was tending to the wounded horse . . . I never in all my experiences heard a horse cry so piteously. She was staggering about when I shot her.*

ABOVE **Poor dumb animals paid the price:** The war horse features in a monument dedicated to all animals who suffered in the war. The memorial near Hyde Park, London, was an initiative of Princess Anne. Its plaque reads: 'They had no choice'. Neither did the conscripts some armies forced to serve. *Courtesy Bruce Scates.*

Goodwin and his horses would go on to serve on the Western Front, in conditions (as Stephen Spielberg's *War Horse* has shown) as bad as Gallipoli, if not worse. But the cruelty of the peninsula, and the suffering of the men and animals that served there, was etched forever in his memory. 'This is a game of waste', Goodwin wrote after yet another day of 'awful slaughter' – and it was poor dumb animals that paid the price of it.[8]

SOURCES AND FURTHER READING: This account is largely based on the service record of Thomas Goodwin NAA: B2455, GOODWIN T; and the diary of Thomas Goodwin ML MSS 1598, State Library of New South Wales. We thank Nathan Wise for kindly drawing our attention to the diary and providing photocopies of the same. His work has also explored Goodwin's identity as a skilled worker, an identity that helped to construct his experience of war; see 'The Lost Labour Force: Working-Class Approaches to Military Service during the Great War', *Labour History*, no. 93, November 2007, pp. 161–76; also *Anzac Labour: Workplace Cultures in the Australian Imperial Force during the First World War* (Basingstoke: Palgrave Macmillan, 2014). For a useful account of the role horses played at Gallipoli see Michael Tyquin, *Gallipoli: The Medical War* (Sydney: UNSW Press, 1993) and more generally Jillian Oppenheimer, *Horses and Guns: Poss Nivison's War with the Australian Field Artillery Brigades on the Western Front 1915–1919* (Walcha: Ohio Productions, 2005).

The land held a secret
BERROL MENDELSOHN

There's a place in Flanders where a small blue flower grows; in one particular field – so the locals say – and that place only. A farmer first noted the flowers in 1919, not long after the Germans had retreated. Try as he may, the farmer could grow no crops in that field. Not sunflowers, nor canola, beet nor barley. Only that small blue flower took purchase in the soil, shaded by the woods around it. The field adjoined Pheasant Wood, in the tiny French hamlet of Fromelles. And the land there held a secret.

A few years before the people of Fromelles returned to their homes, Abigail ('Abbie') Mendelsohn wrote the first of many letters to the authorities. Her son Berrol had been killed in a 'terrible battle' not far from those same woods. The official telegram, she protested, was simply not enough; 'my heart is aching to know how he lost his dear life.'[1]

> *Up to the present I have not received one word from [the commanding officer] of my son's Bttn or any member of [his] company. Just one letter from the Jewish chaplain conveying his sympathy . . . I am just heartbroken at this great loss, and my distress has been considerably intensified at not getting any details. Can you help me? I do hope you will be able to find out where my darling hero lies buried. I know nothing at all, and I have not had one night's sleep since I received this dreadful news . . . It is nearly 6 months since my son was killed and so far none of my letters have been returned, neither have parcels . . . I value every article he possessed and would like to have them to keep forever.*[2]

In time the details drifted in – though they offered little solace to a mother who had lost 'an ideal son'.[3] Berrol's life had been full of promise – a handsome lad with a bright career ahead of him, he was accomplished at sport and one of Bondi's best swimmers.

BELOW **An ideal son:** Lieutenant Berrol Lazar Mendelsohn. Growing up in Sydney, Berrol loved the sea and was a keen member of the Bondi Swimming Club. He was 25 years old at the time of his death. Sydney Morning Herald, *11 August 1916 courtesy National Library of Australia.*

ABOVE **One particular field:** The French historian Annette Becker directs an Australian pilgrim to one of the blue flowers growing beside Pheasant Wood. Fromelles was a German base for much of the war and here, as in other occupied towns and cities, the civilian population had either fled or been forcibly evacuated. *Courtesy Bruce Scates.*

OPPOSITE **Invited to compose an epitaph:** The inscription chosen for Berrol Mendelsohn 's grave. It was a sentiment his grieving mother would have approved of and suggests the task of mourning the dead can be passed from one generation to another. *Courtesy Patrick Daly.*

And at the age of 25 that life had been tragically cut short. The men who fought beside Lieutenant Mendelsohn confirmed his death was instantaneous – and that he had died bravely. 'I was with him . . . when he was hit by a shell,' Private Johnson told a Red Cross worker. 'I saw him just before he died and again after he was dead. He did not seem to suffer.' Mendelsohn had led the charge, urging men on to the German parapet. 'He was a game man alright', Private Johnson added.[4]

Many of Mendelsohn's belongings were eventually returned to his mother. The personal kit left behind in the trenches at Fromelles, a trunk transported from Marseille, even an identity disc taken from his body by the Germans. A hessian parcel containing an assortment of books, clothing and photographs finally reached the family home in Mosman in 1921, a full five years after Berrol's death. 'Such poor little sad articles,' Mrs Mendelsohn wrote to Major McLean, 'and my boy had so much which I would love to treasure.'[5] Was there a chance, she asked, that another parcel might still come? Abbie Mendelsohn longed for the watch she'd pressed in Berrol's hand as he sailed off to war. The authorities would recognise it readily enough, it was inscribed with a message she herself had chosen, 'God be with you'.[6]

And then there was what Mrs Mendelsohn called the 'saddest trial' of all, not knowing what became of that 'dear boy's' body. On the eve of Anzac Day 1919 she wrote yet again to Major McLean. How he must have dreaded her letters:

> *I have waited and waited, in the hope that you might have been able to get some information for me . . . I have so far received no tidings of his burial place, the only news I have had from the front was that his body was never recovered from the trenches. He was killed in action in France on 20 July 1916, and that is all I know . . . Each time I have written to you . . . [I've felt] sure you will do all you can to help me . . . and I often think that if I knew where my dear son was buried it would be some . . . consolation.*[7]

Two years later Mrs Mendelsohn was still waiting. Towards the end of 1921, the authorities dispatched a memorial scroll bearing the grateful message of the King. That only triggered a new spate of enquiries:

> *Enclosed please find the receipt for the memorial scroll. I am still waiting, and hoping to hear that the grave of my darling son has been found, but so far have not had that consolation. Could you possibly give me any address I could write to for information and anyone I could enquire from re the above? I would even write to Germany to enquire if they could find out for me if I knew whom to write about it . . . The heartbreaking thought of not knowing where my darling son lies buried is always with me and it would give me much to know where.*[8]

It was the last such letter that Mrs Mendelsohn would write. She died in 1945, 80 years of age, 'tormented by not knowing where [Berrol's body] lay'.[9] And that mystery would remain unsolved until 2010, when the first bodies from that field in Fromelles were recovered and identified.

AUSTRALIAN IMPERIAL
FORCE
LIEUTENANT
B. L. MENDELSOHN
55TH BN. AUSTRALIAN INF.
20TH JULY 1916 AGE 25
תנצבה
GREATLY LOVED SON OF
SALI AND ABIGAIL
BELOVED BROTHER OF ZILLAH
ARTHUR ESTELLE FELIX OSCAR

The exhumations from a mass gravesite at Fromelles were deeply controversial. An expert panel was appointed in 2005 to investigate the claim that German Forces had buried Australian and British dead in three deep pits dug not long after the battle. The government's default position was that the men were buried elsewhere. Those men unaccounted for may have been recovered after the war and buried as unknowns. Those pits may have been dug for some other purpose. Despite aerial photographs taken in 1917, despite evidence that bodies were carted to that very field, despite page after page of verbatim testimony, Canberra refused to initiate a physical search. Then one of the historians appointed to the panel produced compelling new evidence: a letter had come to light confirming that War Graves units in the 1920s had acknowledged the existence of these mass graves, and had searched for them but never found them. Faced with the growing weight of archival evidence, besieged by lobby groups and embarrassed by the media, the government capitulated. In 2007, it returned to a task the authorities had effectively abandoned in 1921 – Australia would resume the search for the missing.

In many ways the government's reluctance is understandable. Opening the graves at Pheasant Wood has also opened something of a hornet's nest. It set an alarming precedent. There are any number of unidentified graves littered across Flanders and the Somme, and no shortage of documentation suggesting where they might be. If this search began, others would be sure to follow. And to what lengths should we go now to identify these men? In the 1920s, enquiries were exhaustive; specially trained units sifted through belongings and remains hoping to put a name to the missing. Today, forensic techniques and DNA testing have made that search an exacting – and expensive – science. From 2007 to 2010, Australia would spend more money identifying war dead from nearly a century ago than it gave in foreign aid to many third-world countries.

Then there is what you might call the inequality of commemoration. Mrs Mendelsohn longed for news of the burial place of her son; she would die never knowing. Almost a century on, science now offers the certainty denied the generation that most needed it. Can the great-great nephew of a soldier grieve in the same way for a man he never knew? Can he claim any kind of closure? Finally, in commemoration – as in war – there are winners and losers. Australian and British dead recovered from the mass pits of Fromelles were reverently reburied barely a kilometre away in a purpose-built cemetery. No one has recovered the bodies of Algerian troops also slaughtered on the fields of Flanders: who cares to put a name to them? The moral, ethical and political questions raised by the exhumation at Fromelles may never be answered – least of all by historians.

Those blue flowers still grow in the field at Pheasant Wood – and fresh plantings of roses, daisies and dahlias line new graves in which the dead are buried. As the cemetery was laid out, the soldiers' next-of-kin were invited to compose an epitaph. And as in the 1920s, the War Graves Commission vetoed

BELOW **A wreath shaped in the Star of David:** A tribute by the Jewish Ex-Servicemen's Association. Over a thousand Jewish Anzacs served in the AIF during the Great War. Thousands of Jews also fought for Germany, their sacrifice a tragic prelude to the rise of fascism in Europe. *Courtesy Bruce Scates.*

any sentiment deemed 'inappropriate'. The dedication of the graveyard took place in July 2010, ninety-eight years since the day of the battle. A large party of descendants attended, as did several thousand other pilgrims. On that bright summer's day, the Cross of Sacrifice, the last to be raised on French soil, was piled high with tributes: wreaths of red poppies, crosses bearing the names of the dead, a posy of flowers a schoolgirl picked from her garden, photographs carried all the way from Australia.

On a corner of the white stone, the Jewish Ex-Servicemen's Association laid a wreath shaped in the Star of David. It was placed there in honour of Berrol Mendelsohn and the mother who never stopped searching for him.

SOURCE AND FURTHER READING: This story draws on Berrol Mendelsohn's service dossier NAA: B255, MENDELSOHN BERROL LAYAN; his Red Cross Wounded and Missing file AWM 1DRL/0428. For extended discussion of the Expert Panel's deliberations see Bruce Scates, 'Finding the Missing of Fromelles: When Soldiers Return' in Martin Crotty and Marina Larsson (eds), *Anzac Legacies: Australians and the Aftermath of War* (Melbourne: Australian Scholarly Publishing, 2010) and also an opinion piece on the ethics of recovering the war dead, 'Unknown then and even more so now', *Sydney Morning Herald*, 17 July 2007. The course of the excavations is considered in Julie Summers (ed), *Remembering Fromelles: A New Cemetery for a New Century* (Maidenhead: CWGC Publishing, 2010). Fromelles is the subject of ongoing research by French, British and Australian historians. The authors thank Annette Becker, Lucy Noakes and Sally Carlton for their comments; Lambis Englezos (who ably led the principal lobby group); pilgrims interviewed in the course of this research during funeral services in 2010 and 2014; Oliver Mendelsohn; and Marika Vicziany. For a recent French perspective see Annette Becker, 'Ceux de Fromelles', *L'Histoire*, no. 66, January 2015.

ABOVE **Buried as unknowns:** A cluster of unidentified graves in Trois Abois Cemetery. These Australian soldiers were also killed in the Battle of Fromelles. The government's position was that most of the missing of Fromelles were buried in isolated graveyards like this one surrounding the township. The arithmetic never added up. *Courtesy Bruce Scates.*

ABOVE RIGHT **Still missing from the battle:** The names of the unrecovered dead line the walls of V C Corner Australian Cemetery and Memorial. The remains of 410 unidentifiable dead were also buried here. Mindful that a mass of graves 'known only to God' might distress grieving families, the authorities buried the men en masse – and marked two great plots with a cross of roses. Mendelsohn's name was once inscribed on the panel here, alongside over a thousand others. It was removed after his burial. *Courtesy Bruce Scates.*

Her hands are never still

MADAME CHARLOTTE CRIVELLI

Most Australians touring the Somme visit Villers-Bretonneux – and with good reason. It is here that Australia raised a national memorial, a tall white tower looking out across the killing fields of France. The names of over 10 000 men are inscribed here: those whose bodies vanished in the carnage, who 'have no known grave'. And stretching down from the Memorial to the Missing are row after row of tombstones, each as white and upright as the tower set behind them. Over 400 Australians are buried at Villers-Bretonneux. They rest alongside the graves of soldiers from Britain and the dominions, and 266 men who could never be identified. Their homeland will never be known.

Most of these men were killed in the German spring offensive of 1918. While historians debate the role the First AIF played in turning back that onslaught, none would dispute that this was a turning point of the war. In a way, Villers-Bretonneux marked the beginning of the end of the fighting – a tiny hamlet on the outskirts of Amiens carved its name in history and secured a place on the itinerary of every battlefield tour.

No visit to Villers-Bretonneux is complete without a tour of its museum and school. Thousands of visitors pass through the building annually; some study the contents of glass cases and bookshelves, others gaze in wonder at intricate carvings of Australian wildlife (a postwar gift to the school) lining the Assembly Hall's walls. Every Australian visitor also reads the message shouting in green and gold across the school ground: '*N'oublions jamais l'Australie*' – Never forget Australia.

Australia did not forget Villers-Bretonneux. In the aftermath of the Great War, communities large and small contributed to the rebuilding of the town, and money raised mostly in Victoria helped establish the school. What we have forgotten is who was behind that mammoth labour: Madame Charlotte Crivelli, a French expatriate who settled in Albert Park.

In 1915, Madame Crivelli established the French Red Cross Society of Victoria.

ABOVE **A French wife and mother:** Madame Crivelli managed fundraising efforts, and personally contributed to the charity projects for her home country, France. The photographer noted that the image didn't do her justice; that it couldn't show 'the way her smile goes sparkling all over one as she talks'. The Argus, *10 May 1947 courtesy National Library of Australia.*

It was the beginning of an unpaid career in war work that would long outlast the war itself. 'A bundle of energy', Crivelli organised appeals, officiated over fundraising events, and personally packed a veritable mountain of goods for France.[1]

Throughout the war her society held soirees, fetes and dinner parties; organised parades, flower stalls and performances; and embarked on one collecting drive after another. Victorians responded generously – and not just with money. Rolls of flannel, reams of paper, cartons of books, razors, scissors, pillowslips and buttons were bundled together and sent overseas. Most of these donations went to a military hospital outside Paris where Madame Crivelli's son Dr Louis Crivelli, and her sister, the wife of the former French Consul in Melbourne, worked. By 1916, Crivelli had raised enough money in Victoria to equip a ward of forty beds named after generous Melbourne suburbs or donors.[2] And by the end of the war, the Society had raised a staggering £207 233 in funds – the equivalent of several million dollars today.[3]

But Madame Crivelli's war work did not stop there. 'As a French wife and mother', the cause closest to her heart was the *Societe d'Assistance Maternelle et Infantile*.[4] This particular charity helped the wives and widows of French soldiers and their babies, offering them legal, social and medical protection. Pregnant women were housed, fed and cared for, and once their child was born both mother and baby were sent to a maternity home to convalesce. In a city stricken by wartime deprivations, the organisation provided food and housing for the hungry and the homeless. Between August 1914 and August 1915, 37 085 children were born in Paris, and the *Societe d'Assistance Maternelle et Infantile* assisted over 34 000 of them.[5]

Madame Crivelli appealed to patriotism and motherhood at once, urging an alliance between the mothers of Australia and France. The former were asked to empathise with the plight of children orphaned, maimed and disadvantaged by war. '[G]ive a pillow for their heads', Madame Crivelli pleaded:

> *Give food and clothing, so that, when your own little ones go to bed at night, your heart will not be sad at the thought of other babies who have suffered so much when their young lives should be full of peace and smiles.*[6]

This call raised £20 832 over the course of the war, providing French children and their mothers with the necessities of life.[7]

Yet still Madame Crivelli felt she could do more. Appealing again to a sense of shared identity, she implored the schoolchildren of Victoria to come to the aid of war orphans in France. They responded by collecting over £1000 in a single year.[8] Madame Crivelli then launched the French Ambulance appeal, securing the purchase and equipping of fourteen vehicles in 1917.[9] She asked for clothing and blankets for refugees, welcomed French colonial troops on leave to Australia, and urged childless couples to adopt French children orphaned by the war.

BELOW **N'oublions jamais l'Australie:** A kiss from France sent across the ocean. Embroidered cards like this one were often posted home by nurses and soldiers serving abroad. They laid a foundation of goodwill that Madam Crivelli's fundraising efforts would build on. *Courtesy Laura James.*

Even after the fighting had ceased and the French Red Cross Society had closed, Madame Crivelli's war work continued. Not long after the signing of the Armistice she established the After-War Relief Society for France. At a time when most war workers were putting aside their collection tins and knitting needles, she rallied again to the cause. 'Help is needed in France for the crippled, the blind, the consumptive soldiers; for returned prisoners, for the women, babies and war orphans.'[10] Her beloved homeland may have no longer been a battlefield, but she saw there was still a war to be won.

The pact between France and Australia was mutually binding. Australian mothers had sent their sons to war; Charlotte Crivelli now helped them bear their loss. Through her sister in France, she organised some of the first wreath-laying ceremonies on the Somme. Photographs were taken of the carefully tended graves of Australian soldiers, and forwarded to those who most mourned their absence.[11] In this, Madame Crivelli acted as a kind of fictive kin to grieving families; through her, those disenfranchised by distance from the battlefields found a way of connecting with the graves of loved ones far away.

BELOW **Madame Crivelli's war work continued:** Madame Crivelli is presented with a bouquet of flowers at the award ceremony for her Legion of Honour, in recognition of her lifetime of service. She was the first woman to receive the honour in Australia. Sunday Times, *23 July 1916 courtesy National Library of Australia.*

Madame Crivelli was well aware of the devastation of Villers-Bretonneux, and knowing of its connection with Victoria, began to seek assistance for the town. Plans were put in place for French Week, a fundraising festival to be held in Melbourne in aid of that tiny town on the Somme. It took place in the last week of August 1921, coinciding with the anniversary of the Battle of Amiens. Under the refrain of 'By Diggers Defended, Victoria Mended', the festival received an overwhelming response from the community. Throughout the city of Melbourne, its suburbs and even in regional Victorian towns fundraising efforts were organised. Stalls selling flowers, buttons and postcards crowded the streets; a charity football match at the Melbourne Cricket Ground raised £200 alone; night concerts, picture shows and performances were held in venues large and small; and, at the top end of Collins Street, a reconstruction of the ruined town in miniature was displayed.

Victorians soon became familiar with the distress and suffering facing the citizens of Villers-Bretonneux, and at the conclusion of French Week, £24 275 had been raised.[12] It says much for the generosity of Victorians that communities financially and emotionally exhausted by giving could be asked to give yet again. And this money was raised while Victorians grappled with the needs of their own veterans returning home to Australia, a legion of blind, crippled, wounded and insane.

Some of Victoria's most prominent citizens pledged their support to rebuilding Villers-Bretonneux; Sir John Gellibrand and Sir John Monash argued for the adoption of the town by Melbourne. But again it was Charlotte Crivelli's genius for fundraising that secured the project's success. In 1921, she appealed again to the schoolchildren of Victoria to aid their counterparts on

the other side of the world. And she succeeded in convincing the Director of Education, Frank Tate, to divert most of the funds leftover from the war effort to the aid of the town. A gift of £12 000 was presented from the children of Victoria to the children of Villers-Bretonneux. It laid the foundations of a new school and began a lasting relationship between Australia and France.[13]

In postwar Australia, many hoped for a new epoch of peace and prosperity. The gesture of rebuilding that corner of war-torn France symbolised a faith in a new and better world. But the same orphaned children rescued by Madame Crivelli from the slums and streets of Paris would march to war in much the same uniform as their fathers, and the town of Villers-Bretonneux would soon be occupied again.

SOURCES AND FURTHER READING: This story draws on a detailed survey of contemporary newspapers. An extended study of the relationship between Victoria and Villers-Bretonneux, featuring the work of Charlotte Crivelli, appears in Laura James, 'A Little Piece of Australia in France: Memory, Loyalty, Nationalism in Historicising the Relationship between Victoria and Villers-Bretonneux' (BA honours thesis, University of Melbourne, 2010). For further reading on Villers-Bretonneux and Australia see Allan Blankfield and Robin Corfield, *Never Forget Australia-N'Oublions Jamais L'Australie: Australia and Viller-Bretonneux, 1918–1993* (Hawthorn: Villers-Bretonneux 75th Anniversary Pilgrimage Project Committee for the Royal Victoria Regiment, 1994); and Linda Wade, 'The Reconstruction of Villers-Bretonneux 1918–1922' in Martin Crotty and Marina Larsson (eds), *Anzac Legacies: Australians and the Aftermath of War* (Melbourne: Australian Scholarly Publishing, 2010).

ABOVE **The foundations of a new school:** The community of Villers-Bretonneux gathers to lay the first stone of a new building. Note the coupling of Victoria and Villers-Bretonneux; their coats of arms are linked and circled by the flag of St George. *School Paper, September 11, 1923 courtesy State Library of Victoria.*

ABOVE RIGHT **Appealing to the schoolchildren of Victoria:** Fundraising badges and medals issued to young Australians. Events like Children's Flower Day mobilised vast reserves of unpaid child labour in support of the war effort. After the war, much of the money raised was pledged to the rebuilding of Villers-Bretonneux. *Courtesy Laura James.*

I am against all wars

ARCHIBALD BAXTER

In April 1918, Archibald Baxter woke to find himself in a hospital bed in Boulogne. He had been unconscious for several days. The medical officer working in the 'mental ward' was troubled by his patient's condition. Baxter's body was 'emaciated, fleshless, with the skin drawn over the bones'. Though barely 27, he looked much older – his nerves had gone to pieces, his muscles had wasted away, and he had clearly lost several stone. Every serving doctor in France had seen badly damaged men, but this particular case puzzled him. There wasn't an inch of Baxter's body that wasn't battered and bruised. 'How have you come by those marks on your body?' the doctor asked. 'Had you been blown up by a shell?'

'No,' Baxter replied in a 'hollow whisper', 'I am against this war, I am against all wars.'[1]

The enemy did not exact the wounds the doctor examined that day. Nor were they self-inflicted. Several of the men admitted to the mental ward had shot themselves to escape the fighting. The doctor's job was to nurse them back to health, so they could be tried for 'cowardice' and shot again. But Archibald Baxter wasn't a soldier – even if the New Zealand Army insisted on treating him as one. Baxter was a conscientious objector. He had been starved, beaten and tortured at the behest of senior army officers. His own countrymen – not the Germans – had done all this to him.

'I told him what had happened to me,' Baxter remembered some years later. 'I watched his face. It altered. . . ' At several stages in his story, the doctor stopped him, wondering if Baxter might be suffering from delusions, hoping none of this could actually be true. But it was. Archibald Baxter had refused to fight, disobeyed his orders, and cast aside his uniform. The authorities were determined to maintain army discipline, discourage dissenters and 'make an example of him'. A principled man's unwilling service became an almost unrelenting regime of physical and psychological abuse.[2]

It began back home in Otago. By 1916, voluntary recruitment was failing. The New Zealand Army had suffered 7473 casualties of the 8556 who served on Gallipoli; losses on the Somme the following year were even worse. With men increasingly reluctant to enlist, the government claimed it was unable to meet its quota for reinforcements. Despite considerable opposition, a conscription bill was pushed through the parliament. Unlike Australia, there was no chance to vote 'No' in a referendum. Even more severe than British legislation, New Zealand's Conscription Act allowed for few exemptions.

A Christian socialist who attributed war to greed and empires, Baxter's opposition was deemed 'political' and he was sent to prison. So too were 272 others. In late 1916 Baxter was transferred to an army camp near Wellington. Trentham was his first taste of military discipline. Refusing to work, or to wear army denims, he was sentenced to solitary confinement and allowed only bread and water. He then faced a court martial and a further eighty-four days' hard labour. Baxter remained defiant, despite yet another sentence of forced detention in the barracks. That principled intransigence – and the overcrowding problem posed by so many dissenting men – convinced the camp commandant to send some of the 'conscies' overseas. There the British Army would no doubt know how to deal with them.

ABOVE **Courage is not monopolised by those who carry a gun:** A portrait of Archibald Baxter after the war. All his life he worked for the cause of peace. *1/2-037732-F courtesy Te Puna Matauranga O Aotearoa/National Library of New Zealand.*

Fourteen dissenters were spirited onto the troopship *Waitemata*, the authorities hoping their forced deportation might be kept a secret. Baxter and his compatriots were confined to the ship's clink. A tiny cabin, 'stuffy and ill ventilated', it soon stank with the vomit of seasick men. They were issued with uniforms – and again refused to wear them. They were marched on deck, stripped naked 'in front of men assembled to watch' and forcibly dressed in uniform. Baxter later wrote in his memoirs:

> *The feeling of the crowd appeared to be mixed. There was some laughter, some jeering and a gramophone somewhere played 'Onward, Christian Soldier' but there were also shouts of, 'Stick it out! Stick to your principles!' The hands of the man who put the uniform on were trembling . . . 'Don't blame us,' he murmured. 'We don't want to do it, we have to.'*[3]

It says much about the character of Archibald Baxter that he remembered these compassionate voices amongst the violence and ridicule, the 'gentleness and humanity' that challenged the 'military machine'.[4] He believed most soldiers were decent men, compelled to do indecent things.

The *Waitemata* arrived in Plymouth on Boxing Day, 1916. For a time Baxter and the ship's other detainees were confined to freezing prison cells in Britain. Their refusal to wear a uniform left them virtually naked, while a poor diet (and little of it), forced

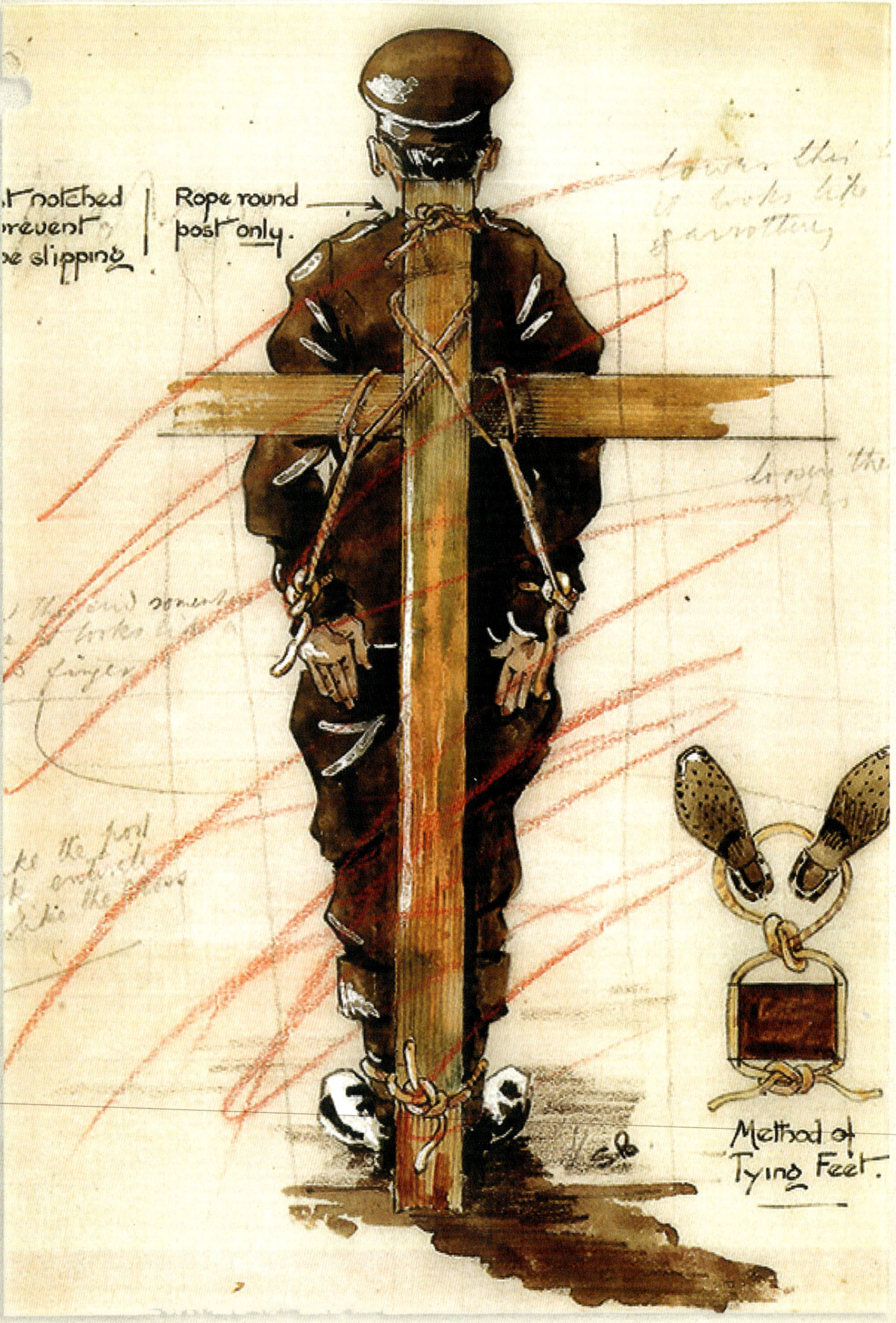
Rope round post only.
Method of Tying Feet.

labour and abuse took a steady toll. Then Baxter was shipped across the Channel to France. And the closer he came to the fighting, the more brutal his treatment became.

In October 1917, Baxter found himself in Étaples, a training camp where men were made accustomed to conditions up the line. The commander, Lieutenant Colonel George 'Hoppy' Mitchell, was a 'war hero' twice wounded in battle. He was determined to break Baxter's spirit, and sentenced him and three others to suffer Field Punishment No. 1. The soldiers called it 'the Crucifixion'. Baxter explained why:

> *[The sergeant] tied me to [a post] by the ankles, knees and wrists. He was an expert at the job and he knew how to pull and strain at the ropes till they cut into the flesh and completely stopped the circulation. When I was taken off [many hours later] my hands were always black with congested blood . . . I could get no proper grip with my feet on the ground . . . was strained so tightly up against the post that I was unable to move body or limbs.*[5]

The punishment continued over several weeks, regardless of Baxter's deteriorating health and a sharp turn for the worst in the weather. One day, Baxter and another particularly 'difficult' prisoner were tied up in a blizzard:

> *In a short time we were white with snow from head to foot... The cold was intense... A deadly numbness crept up till it reached my heart and I felt that every breath I drew would be my last.*[6]

Baxter survived this, only to face violent beatings by men brutalised by war. He was also exposed to heavy shelling near the front line.

Alongside this physical punishment was psychological abuse. Every day began with orders and reprimands barked in his face. Every day food was withheld, promises broken and arbitrary punishments exacted on a whim. One particular sergeant repeatedly raised his revolver to Baxter's head and threatened to pull the trigger. And all the time the threat of execution hung over Archibald Baxter. Five New Zealanders were executed during the war, for 'cowardice', desertion and simply being unwilling or unable to fight. Baxter never signed the enlistment papers thrust before him; he never admitted that the New Zealand Army had any legitimate authority over him. Had he done so he may well have been tied to another post and shot.

The authorities never broke Baxter's spirit. In the end it was simpler to declare him insane. In mid-1918, Baxter was transferred from Boulogne and admitted to a mental hospital in Middlesex, England. Another doctor diagnosed extreme 'melancholia'; that would lead eventually to a discharge on medical grounds. 'His ideas about war amount to an insane obsession,' the doctor recorded in his case notes, '[patient is] dull, depressed and apathetic. [His] memory [is] poor [and he] is indifferent to everything.'[7] But Archibald Baxter had not forgotten his principles, refusing to obey orders or shoulder a rifle to the end. Nor was he ever indifferent to the human cost of war.

OPPOSITE **The crucifixion:** War Office instructions on inflicting Field Punishment No. 1. When it was first introduced, soldiers' arms and legs were spread across the wheels of a gun carriage – outstretched limbs formed a cross. Field Punishment No. 1 was common in all the Allied armies. As Baxter explained, crucifixion cut off the flow of blood through the body – many men suffered gangrene and had feet or hands amputated after a spell on that cross. *Courtesy War Office, London, 1917.*

ABOVE **Tied to a post: The** memorial flanking the old execution post at Poperinge. Britain issued a posthumous pardon to men executed for 'cowardice'. Five New Zealanders were shot by their own side during the war. These men were posthumously pardoned in 2000. *Courtesy Rohan Gerrard.*

Archibald Baxter was sent home towards the end of the war. In the 1920s, he resumed his political work and was active in the New Zealand Labour Party. He remained a pacifist all his life and represented Aotearoa/New Zealand at the War Resisters' International Conference in Copenhagen in 1937. His eldest son, Terence, followed in his father's footsteps and was imprisoned for opposing compulsory military service in World War Two.

In 2014, the New Zealand government digitised Baxter's service records, along with those of several other conscientious objectors deported during the war. Ironically they can be accessed today on a website called 'Discovering Anzacs'. Archibald Baxter was never an Anzac – and courage is not monopolised by those who carry a gun. His testimony reminds us that it was not just soldiers who suffered for their convictions. And that in order to 'defend freedom' governments were prepared to sacrifice freedom itself.

SOURCE AND FURTHER READING: This account is largely based on Archibald Baxter's service record and autobiography, *We Will Not Cease: The Autobiography of a Conscientious Objector* (Whatamongo Bay: Cape Catley, 1980). Another useful primary source is Harry Holland's impassioned defence of civil liberties, *Armageddon or Calvary: The Conscientious Objectors of New Zealand and 'The Process of their Conversion'* (Wellington: Maoriland Worker, 1919). There are a number of useful studies of conscription in Aotearoa/New Zealand including Paul Baker, *King and Country Call: New Zealanders, Conscription and the Great War* (Auckland: Auckland University Press, 1988); PS O'Conner, 'The Awkward Ones – Dealing with Conscience 1916–18', *New Zealand Journal of History*, vol. 8, no. 2, 1974, pp. 118–133. For comparable studies in Australia, see Bobbie Oliver, *Peacemongers: Conscientious Objectors to Military Service in Australia, 1911–1945* (Fremantle: Fremantle Arts Centre Press, 1997). The authors have also drawn on Chris Pugsley's study of discipline in the NZEF, *On the Fringe of Hell: New Zealanders and Military Discipline in the First World War* (Auckland: Penguin, 1991). Above all we thank David Grant whose brilliant study of Baxter and Mark Briggs inspired this story, *Field Punishment No 1: Archibald Baxter, Mark Briggs & New Zealand's Anti-militarist Tradition* (Wellington: Steele Roberts Publishers, 2008).

The stone carver
DAPHNE MAYO

The Great War is a story Australia and Canada share. In 1914, the two young dominions rallied to the Empire's cause. Both rushed to send contingents of soldiers, nurses and airmen to Europe; both placed their infant navies at the service of Great Britain; both raised hundreds of thousands of pounds to help the war effort. In the course of the conflict Canada mobilised 620 000 of its eight million, Australia 420 000 out of five million. The losses the two countries bore are remarkably similar. Some 60 000 Australian dead are scattered across the battlefields of Gallipoli and Palestine, France and Belgium. Canada fought mostly on the Western Front, where 67 000 died.

Nor do the parallels end there. For both Australia and Canada, the Great War helped define a new sense of national identity. It was not just that this was the first major military conflict in which either country had fought, or the scale of loss, or that both countries produced their own exemplary leaders with strategies quite distinct from British command – General Sir John Monash on one hand, General Sir Arthur

BELOW **Overwhelmingly masculine:** The men of Queensland march to war. Despite being a women's memorial, the figure of a nurse is obscured at the end of the procession; perhaps that was deliberate. A voluntary worker herself during the conflict, Daphne Mayo was acutely conscious of women's marginalisation in war. *Courtesy Tina Donaghy.*

ABOVE **Cutting grief into stone:** Daphne Mayo completing the finishing touches to the Women's Memorial in Anzac Square, Brisbane. Shaping this memorial was a physical ordeal, it was difficult, dirty and dangerous work. The Australasian *6 May 1922 courtesy National Library of Australia.*

OPPOSITE **An elfin like creature:** Known as 'Queensland's girl sculptress', Daphne Mayo's work won a number of prizes and scholarships but (being a woman) it was difficult to compete in what was considered a largely male sphere. Mayo was one of the few women to be admitted to the Royal Academy Sculpture School in London, its director stating that she would bring credit to the Academy 'even if she was but a woman'. Here she holds *Winged Victory*, a sculpture completed in 1912 and eerily anticipating the outbreak of war. *Courtesy State Library of Queensland.*

Currie on the other. Serving overseas, Australians and Canadians saw what distinguished them as a people; they longed for the landscapes and the accents left far behind them. 'Home' ceased to be Great Britain and many became critical of the class-bound inequalities and oppressive traditions of Empire.

Of course, there were differences as well: Canada introduced conscription, Australia did not; Vimy Ridge marked a great Canadian triumph, Gallipoli a terrible defeat; the Western Front looms large in Canadian remembrance; few remember a small contingent from Newfoundland slaughtered beside the Anzacs on the plains of Suvla. Even so, the stories that bind us seem stronger – back when the war was fought and first commemorated, and arguably still today. And nowhere are those stories more compelling than in the great memorials raised at Villers-Bretonneux and Vimy.

Australia's National Memorial looks out over the fields of the Somme; Canada's commands the flat ground of Flanders. Both were completed just a few months before the Second World War began and both were built on ground heavy with Australian or Canadian sacrifice. Canada's memorial takes the form of two shafts stretching high into the sky; Australia's a soaring white tower flanked by semi-cloistered walls. In each case, the stone carries the names of the missing – boys from Vancouver and Quebec, Hobart and Darwin swallowed up by the battlefields around them.

In 2001, the Canadian writer Jane Urquhart brought the story of her country's memorial to life. *The Stone Carvers* is a tale of love, loss and redemption set in the 1930s. Its central character is a young woman, Klara, whose lover, Eamon, is killed in France. Nothing is left of Eamon's body, there is only that name set in stone to remember him by. In Urquhart's story, Klara somehow makes her way to Vimy and, disguised as a stonemason, undertakes work only thought fit for men and helps to build the memorial. It's her calloused hands that carve the features of the monument's central sculpture, fashioning Eamon's likeness into stone, carving out her grief for eternity.

On the other side of the world, at around the same time as Klara's imaginary journey was set, the Australian artist Daphne Mayo set to work on Queensland's state memorial. Unlike the strong vertical lines of Vimy and Villers-Bretonneux, the monument took the shape of a circular colonnade, a ring of Doric columns modelled on an ancient temple in Greece. Mayo's memorial was set beneath it – a tribute by the women of Queensland to their men who marched to war. In Mayo's memorial they are marching still. The bas-relief shows a procession of warriors, their heads bent slightly down in stoic resolution, a horse-drawn gun carriage central to their train. The image is sombre, almost funereal; they are 'marching as to war but also to a burial'.[1] And, ironically perhaps for the women's memorial, it is overwhelmingly masculine. Daphne Mayo

had suggested a design highlighting women's war efforts at home and overseas. The committee opted instead for a tribute to branches of the armed services, and the single figure of a nurse can barely be seen.

Carving the memorial was a physical and emotional labour for Daphne. Physically she was never very strong. Her fiancé, Lloyd Rees, described her as 'a short elfin like creature, with a mass of golden locks and voluminous blue eyes, and often with a sickly pallor due to her chronic asthma'.[2] Frail and exhausted, Daphne would rise early in the morning hoping to escape the heat of Brisbane's sun.

> *I used to get up at the first crack of dawn, toast a crust of bread and a slice of bacon, and get into my little car and off to the job. Sometimes it was still so dark when I got there that I had to wait until it was light enough to see – this would probably be about 5 o'clock. At 9 am it was so hot working against the stone wall that I nearly fried. Then I packed up and went home and was back again at four in the afternoon, working until dark.*[3]

But it was not just the heat that was taxing. Daphne carved her figures with devotion, mindful that in the faces of those soldiers, sailors and airmen, mothers, wives and sweethearts would see the men they'd lost. And leading the procession is her own brother Richard, a lad who went to war at 22, served in Egypt and died of war-related causes seven years after the fighting had ended. Like Klara in Urquhart's story, Daphne had cut her own grief into stone.

BELOW **A lad who went to war at 22:** Captain Richard Mayo leads a procession of fallen warriors. Mayo served in the Australian and New Zealand Mounted Divisional Train. That fact, and the inspiration of a similar memorial in Edinburgh, almost certainly influenced Daphne's design. *Courtesy Tina Donaghy.*

SOURCES AND FURTHER READING: This account is based on a study of both Canada and Australia's National Memorials. For the Australian memorial see Laura James, 'A Little Piece of Australia in France: Memory, Loyalty, Nationalism in Historicising the Relationship between Victoria and Villers-Bretonneux' (BA honours thesis, University of Melbourne, 2010) and Linda Wade, 'The Reconstruction of Villers-Bretonneux 1918–1922', in Martin Crotty and Marina Larsson (eds), *Anzac Legacies: Australians and the Aftermath of War* (Melbourne: Australian Scholarly Publishing, 2010). Daphne Mayo's life and work is captured by Judith McKay and Michael Hawker, *Daphne Mayo: Let There be Sculpture* (Brisbane: Queensland Art Gallery, 2011); for consideration of her work in the civic sphere see Judith McKay, 'Daphne Mayo and a Decade of Public Monuments for Brisbane', *Art in Australia*, Autumn 1982, p. 360. For a study of Vimy, and memorials in general, see Bruce Scates and Rebecca Wheatley, 'War Memorials' in Jay Winter (ed), *The Cambridge History of the First World War*, vol. III (Cambridge: Cambridge University Press, 2014) pp. 528–558. The authors would like to thank Geoff Bird and Raynald Lemelin for their advice on the Vimy memorial. We have drawn further biographical information from Mayo's private papers held by the University of Queensland and a typescript of her interview with Hazel de Berg held by the National Library of Australia. Mayo's own reflections on the role of sculpture are surveyed in *Art in Australia*, no. 72, August 1938, p. 12. The authors thank Tina Donaghy for her valuable assistance.

I seem to dream of blood

WALTER DEXTER

The Reverend Walter Dexter marked his second wedding anniversary somewhere off the coast of Egypt. He had left Australia five months earlier, one of twelve army chaplains charged with the spiritual care of the First AIF. Dexter remembered to jot a loving line to his wife, Dora, that day, mindful that he would tear the duplicate pages from the binding and send them back by the next mail to Australia. But when that mail might be delivered was an open question. Two days before, news of the *Novian*'s destination had swept through the ship's company – Dexter, and the men who sailed with him, were destined for the Dardanelles. He scribbled excitedly in his diary:

> *As soon as we get outside the harbour we learn our orders. We are bound for Lemnos . . . and are to be ready to disembark 24 hours after we leave Alexandria. We are to take 48 hours provisions, and our water bottles filled for we may not be up to get food or water for three days and our landing [at Gallipoli] will probably be opposed. Anyhow we are in for the most historical event of the war and can but pray that our boys will not be found wanting.*[1]

Dexter slept on the deck that night – or at least tried to. The *Novian* was crammed with men and equipment, including four pontoons purpose-built for the Landing. There were 1200 men on a cargo ship never intended to carry passengers. They competed for space in the dark, crowded hull with over three hundred horses. A brisk wind and rough sea left Dexter drenched with spray, but it was better than the suffocating heat below deck.

When the ship reached Mudros, it shared thc harbour with a hundred other vessels. Dexter gazed in amazement at one of the largest armadas ever assembled in modern times; a flotilla of craft large and small would land French, British, Indian and Anzac

ABOVE **One of the most eloquent testimonies of the campaign:** A description of the pyramids before sunrise. Dexter's eye for beauty in the landscape made the horrific conditions at Gallipoli more bearable. He had travelled extensively through the Near East prior to his arrival in Egypt. A Master Mariner before the war, Dexter had even ferried pilgrims to Mecca and professed a deep respect for Islam. *Diary of Chaplain W.E. Dexter, 15 December 1914, PR00248 courtesy Australian War Memorial.*

ABOVE INSET **I wanted to bubble and cry:** Barges of the wounded towed to transports off Gallipoli. The sight of these men moved Dexter to tears. Confident of a swift victory, the Allies were woefully unprepared for such casualties and made provision for only two hospital ships within easy reach of Anzac. *A02740 courtesy Australian War Memorial.*

troops on the Gallipoli peninsula.

The Landing would not take place until two weeks later, and it would be opposed. In the hazy light of the early morning, Dexter could just make out the strings of boats rushing towards the shore under tow by destroyers. Each boat was packed full of men, and the water around them 'simply churned up by rifle fire'. Landing furthest to the north, the 7th Battalion was caught in enfilade fire; that part of the beach seemed 'almost impregnable' and men were cut down well before reaching the shore. By early afternoon, the boats of the 7th had made their way back, several still laden, but now with a silent cargo of dead. It was, Dexter noted, 'our first real touch of war' and again, mindful of history, he took a moment to record it:

> *They had probably been there from about 7am and no one had time, or place, to remove them. Just as they were killed so they sat in the bottom of the boat and had grown stiff in a sitting attitude. The wounds were mostly head wounds and death must have been instantaneous. One sat in the bottom with his arm over [an oar] and as the boat bumped and rocked so his head just nodded in a peculiarly inane way. One almost felt like asking him not to be so silly. Each boat had about 6 inches of water stained with blood and in one boat . . . lay another man face down. On top of these bodies were placed the stretchers that were to go ashore, [while on the destroyers] the dead and dying would be laying about their decks. [Some of the men, especially those about to land] got very sick . . . . The boys will not forget 25 April in a hurry.*

Nor would Walter Dexter. Forbidden to land with the men, he passed that day and the ones to follow it tending to the wounded:

> *I formed a dressing station in the tween decks . . . and also dressed one part of the deck just as they lay. I wanted to bubble and cry and take them in my arms and soothe them for their nerves were all wracked as well as their actual wounds. Instead I joked with them . . . and gave them cigarettes to smoke while I pulled the hard bandages from the wounds . . . No water is used . . . for fear of septic poisoning . . . Men with part of the hand, or an arm, blown away go clean out and faint as the iodine begins to sting. In the tween decks the air is terribly fetid just like a butchers shop that has not been cleaned for a month. The smell of stale blood with perspiration is particularly trying and . . . cutting away the old bandages the nose is very often only a few inches away . . . At 11:30 pm we knocked off for the night . . . [but the] horrible smell of the blood seemed to hang to me and would not go away. I seemed to dream of blood all the time.*[2]

The casualties were such that Dexter's ship was sent back to Egypt, crammed this time with the dying and wounded. A fresh breeze blew across the decks but still the smell of blood seemed to linger:

OPPOSITE **The cruelty of war:** A glimpse of the burial of the dead during the armistice in May 1915. Dexter took this photograph through one of the steel loopholes protecting the trenches. The chaos of no-man's-land with its broken terrain and twisted barbed wire is all too apparent. *J04970 courtesy Australian War Memorial.*

[It] never seems to pass away from us . . . one thinks it will remain with us till [my] dying day. You go to sleep with it in your nostrils, and you wake up with it. Your food seems to take on the taint and your hands, though disinfected a hundred times in the day, seem to be the same.

And yet amid the brutality of war a man of God could still find tenderness and compassion:

[The men] do not seem to feel for themselves, only for their chums. When the shrapnel was flying around the boats amongst those hit was a young fellow who was shot somewhere in the body. Alongside him was one of those hard-case bushman that one would never suspect . . . . of feeling for anything or anybody. He was also in awful pain but as the young fellow alongside him was groaning and writhing in his agony the hard-case, as he could not speak, just stroked the other one's arms as a sign of his sympathy . . . and tried to soothe him as a father with his boy. Oh God the cruelty of war.[3]

In his time at Gallipoli, Dexter acted as the father of his men. He was the first chaplain to land and the last to leave, tending his boys as best he could amid the squalor and carnage of the peninsula. His diary remains one of the most eloquent testimonies of the campaign; graphic descriptions of the fighting interspersed with almost lyrical passages describing wildflowers and sunsets, 'picturesque' valleys ablaze with shrapnel, the song of the skylark heard alongside exploding shells. Dexter comforted the living and buried hundreds of the dead, especially during the armistice called in May:

Amongst this awful mass of dead Turks were some of our boys who had been killed on the first and second days fight and had lain there since. Many of the missing could now be classed as dead, the bodies were horrible to look at being black and swelled up stretching out the clothing and in many cases when they were touched falling to pieces.[4]

By June, the peninsula was one long graveyard, the trenches of the living often carved through the bodies of the dead. Dexter's own dugout looked out on 'two little crosses made of twigs and not as thick as a pencil'. 'I see them as I write,' he jotted in his diary, 'not 30 feet away' and swept by gunfire. Men marked the final resting places of the fallen as best they could – a line of stones laid on the heaped earth, a name scratched on a beaten jam tin. Dexter seemed to see the 'pathetic little crosses' everywhere; 'there is no gully or hilltop free from graves'.[5] Then came the August Offensive and a new spree of killing. As the trenches of Lone Pine filled with bodies and maggots, Dexter and the chaplains who worked beside him buried 'miles of dead'.[6]

When the time came to evacuate in December, leaving behind the dead was one of the hardest tasks the Anzacs faced. 'I hope *they* don't hear us marching down the deres,' one man grumbled to his mates.[7] Dexter spent his last days on the peninsula 'searching the hills and gullies seeking isolated graves', carefully marking their location on the

sketches and maps that line the pages of his diary.[8] He began the task of turning the landscape itself into a memorial:

> *I went up to the gullies and through the cemetery scattering silver wattle seed. If we are to leave here I intend that a bit of Australia shall be here . . . I suggested to the general that a letter should be left for the commander of the Turks asking that our graves should be respected.*[9]

In time, Dexter knew Anzac would become a place of pilgrimage. But the freezing winters of Gallipoli killed all the wattle he planted, and far from respecting our graves those 'pathetic little crosses' were burnt for firewood.

Dexter himself went on to serve in France and Belgium. He was awarded the Military Cross for 'zeal and devotion to duty', visiting front-line troops and tending to the stricken and wounded 'regardless of personal risk'.[10] Right to the end, the fighting parson shared the hardships of his flock. Walter Dexter, like many of the men he served with, failed as a soldier settler. His death in 1950 was hastened by the gas he was exposed to during the war.

SOURCES AND FURTHER READING: This account is based on Dexter's service dossier NAA: B2455, DEXTER W E and extensive diaries AWM PR00248. For a compelling introduction to the war service of AIF chaplains see Michael McKernan, *Padre: Australian Chaplains in Gallipoli and France* (Sydney: Allen & Unwin, 1986). The authors also acknowledge the Dexter family. The Dexter Papers form the basis of a special exhibition in the National Anzac Centre in Albany. For an exemplary reading of narratives of war (and one that informs all this book) see Bill Gammage, *The Broken Years* (Canberra: Australian National University Press, 1974).

ABOVE LEFT **This awful mass of dead:** Dexter's photograph of the burials in May 1915. A carpet of dead stretched all the way from the Chessboard in the north to Bolton's Ridge in the south. Dexter took this photograph surreptitiously – photography breached the conditions of the armistice. *H03947 courtesy Australian War Memorial.*

ABOVE RIGHT **I intend that a bit of Australia shall be left here:** Walter Dexter at Gallipoli. The crest in the background marks the second ridge, the edge of the Anzac firing line. The proximity of the trenches was a dramatic contrast to Dexter's later service in France, though even he contrived to get as close as he could to the men charged to his care. Dexter had served as a soldier himself in South Africa, and was awarded the Distinguished Conduct Medal. He knew better than most 'the cruelty of war'. *J05400 courtesy Australian War Memorial.*

But for the grace of God

JOSEPH BOLTON

Jack and Joseph Bolton both went to war. There was not much more than a year between the two brothers, both engine cleaners from Sydney. Joseph embarked for active service overseas in March 1916. Always just a step behind, Jack followed him eight months later. From that moment on, their parents, Lydia and George, began the long ordeal of waiting.

Private Joseph Bolton fought in the Second Battle of Bullecourt, the AIF's second attempt to break the heavily fortified Hindenburg Line. On the first day he was struck by a shell, and on the second he died. In the first three weeks of May 1917, the AIF suffered over 7000 casualties.

Consumed with grief and fearing for Jack's life, Lydia and George both wrote to the authorities: '[Is there] any possible chance of [Jack] being transferred ... out of the firing zone,' a fretful father pleaded, 'he has been twice wounded and the loss of his younger brother at Bullecourt makes me anxious.' Lydia's letter appealed, 'I only hope my other son will be spared to me.'[1]

He was, but more by luck than intervention from the authorities. Jack was discharged medically unfit at the end of the war. By that time the scars of battle covered most of his body.

The family faced the maiming of one son and the loss of another. 'Just away, not forgotten,'[2] Joseph's memorial notice reads. Joseph's body *was* far away, buried in a grave on the other side of the ocean. A sense of distance made the grieving almost unbearable.

ABOVE **On the first day struck by a shell, on the second he died:** Joseph Claude Bolton. This studio portrait was taken shortly before he sailed from Sydney. Joseph was 21 years of age. *H06292, courtesy Australian War Memorial.*

Back in Sydney, Lydia laboured to build some connection to her dead son. She gathered together what mementos she could. At her request, the authorities sent the standard parcels – a photograph of the grave, the King's commemorative scroll, a few of her son's belongings bundled up in plain, brown paper. In 1922, Lydia received a copy of *Where the Australians Rest*, a sketchbook of cemeteries distributed to mourning families. C.E.W. Bean, who edited the booklet, hoped Australians would 'read the book, and gather from it at any rate the sort of surrounding in which their boys lie'.[3] Lydia and George imagined the journey to their son's grave. A hasty sketch in Indian ink was all they had to go on.

In 1924, Lydia saw a newspaper article about the Young Australia League Tour to Europe. Founded in 1905, the League's philosophy was 'education by travel'. Its purpose was to send young men overseas, introduce them to the world and widen their horizons. They were convinced that taking such a journey 'adds to the storehouse of individual knowledge, broadens the outlook and brings first-hand information in a way never reached by book study'.

The 1924 European Tour included excursions to France and Belgium, and some forty Australian boys made up the contingent. It was one of the earliest youth pilgrimages, organised well before British schoolchildren travelled to Menin Gate or the battlefield excursions run by the Ypres League in the 1930s. The tour cost around £250, more than twice the yearly earnings of a skilled, white, male worker. In the interwar years, pilgrimage was a privilege enjoyed by very few Australians.

Lydia Bolton would never be able to afford to visit her son's grave. But perhaps others could make the journey for her, embarking on a pilgrimage by proxy. Lydia wrote to the League in July 1924. She sent the location of her son's grave and begged the boys to visit it.

BELOW LEFT **The scars of battle:** The Young Australia League boys investigate a crater near Fleurs, not too far from Baupame where Private Joseph Bolton was killed. One of the Young Australia League boys, Thomas Donnan, noted on the back of this photograph that 850 Germans were killed here. *Thomas Donnan Papers courtesy Rare Book Collection, Monash University.*

BELOW **Cemeteries still being completed:** The Young Australia League boys inspect the graves in Adelaide Cemetery. These temporary crosses were not replaced with permanent headstones until the mid-1920s. *Thomas Donnan Papers, courtesy Rare Book Collection, Monash University.*

When the Young Australia League arrived in France, they were warmly welcomed. At French Army Headquarters, Marshall Foch marched along their ranks, inspected their uniforms and applauded their discipline. They 'represented a great nation's sons', he told them, mindful of the number of Australian dead buried in his soil. The League were the 'sons and brothers of those who fought with France': 'You boys are met here with great and deep sympathy. France will never forget the Anzacs.'[4]

At Amiens, the boys were met by Major Phillips, Superintendent of the Somme War Graves. His familiar Australian accent was something of a relief to them. Together they travelled across a landscape marked with the scars of battle:

> *They penetrated into uncleared areas hitherto not visited by tourists, where they found live shells and wrecked aeroplanes and guns. The lads inspected trenches and 'pill boxes' and the German division headquarters dug-out, all as in wartime . . . [At Albert] the boys climbed to the top of the ruined cathedral. At Delville Wood rain fell unceasingly, and the lads saw the typical muddy conditions in which the soldiers lived during the wet season in war time.*[5]

Many of the vast cemeteries and great memorials were still being completed, and the landscape was littered with the debris of war. Death and destruction lay all around them. The boys found bodies that could never be buried, 'all churned up in the mud' of the Somme. '[W]e saw several skulls,' one boy scribbled in his diary, '[and the] bones of a man's foot [encased] in [a] boot.'[6] Once thriving townships were now nothing more than ruins.

North of Amiens, the League began their pilgrimage by proxy. They made their way to Vaulx Australian Field Ambulance Cemetery, a tiny graveyard on the edge of the Somme. It wasn't difficult to find Private Bolton's grave buried alongside thirty other Australians. On a dull spring day, they carried out a makeshift service and laid a wreath for a family half a world away. The boys took photographs of the grave, careful to include French caretakers tending the cemetery. Before they left, they picked a posy of forget-me-nots to carry all the way home to Australia. Most of the boys who made that journey were not much younger than Joseph Bolton. But for the grace of God, his grave could have held any one of them. We know from the correspondence that Lydia gained much comfort from that pilgrimage to that corner of a foreign field forever her own.[7] Joseph's grave reads 'Peace, Perfect Peace'.

SOURCES AND FURTHER READING: This story draws on the service dossiers of Joseph and Jack Bolton NAA: B2455 BOLTON J C and NAA: B2455 BOLTON J G; Joseph's Red Cross Wounded and Missing file AWM 1DRL/0428; Thomas Donnan's diary, 1924 Young Australia League Tour, Rare Book Collection, Monash University; Young Australia League Papers, 7292A, State Library of Western Australia; and contemporary newspaper reports.

For justice and freedom

CYRIL AND RUFUS RIGNEY

Rufus Gordon Rigney and Cyril Spurgeon Rigney were two brothers who went to war. Ngarrindjeri men, they were born where the Murray stretches down to the sea, on Port Macleay Aboriginal Mission, a hundred miles south of Adelaide.

Port Macleay is the name Europeans used – a name imposed by the first white missionary. Raukkan, meaning 'meeting place', has been the Aboriginal name for this place since time immemorial. The traditional lands of the Ngarrindjeri people extend from Lake Alexandrina, where Raukkan is situated, twenty miles up the Murray; they include the length of the Coorong and encompass coastlands as far as Encounter Bay. By the turn of the twentieth century the best of that vast estate had been taken by white farmers; the mission was established on a narrow strip of the Narrung Peninsula, on what most saw as marginal country. Over-clearing by the whites destroyed the habitats where Aboriginal people had hunted for generations, increased salinity levels in the lake and generally damaged a fragile ecology. It was a pattern of environmental degradation mirrored throughout much of Australia.

Port Macleay functioned as a Christian mission until 1916, after which the Aborigines Protection Board established by the government administered it. 'Protection' was a misnomer. At the time Rufus and Cyril enlisted, Ngarrindjeri people were not permitted to speak their language, the community was isolated and institutionalised, and traditional practices were vigorously discouraged. Instead, the mission trained Aboriginal people to work on the fringes of the white economy. Both boys recorded their occupation as 'labourer' on their attestation form when they signed up for war.

ABOVE **Swallowed up by the Salient:** Cyril Rigney's name appears alongside thousands of others on Menin Gate's Memorial to the Missing. The attack on Messines Ridge launched the Third Battle of Ypres – in the next few months it would cost the AIF 38 000 casualties. *Courtesy Bruce Scates.*

Perhaps it was the hope of something better than toiling on a farm that persuaded Rufus and Cyril to enlist; perhaps – as for many white recruits – it was the lure of travel and adventure. In Rufus's case at least, it may have been the strong sense of family obligation at the core of Aboriginal culture. Cyril signed up in April 1916; Rufus would follow his elder brother to war four months later. Both lads wrote on their enlistment papers that they were 19, but Rufus was actually 16. Had they been white, they would have required their father's consent, but the Protector of Aborigines – not the boys' parents – was deemed to be the legal guardian of all Indigenous people. William Garnet South, a man Rufus had probably never met, duly signed his papers.

It turned out to be his death warrant. Cyril was killed at Messines in 1917. Rufus died at Passchendaele three months later.

We know little of the circumstances of Cyril's death, or whether his remains were recovered from the battlefield. Like thousands of other troops from all over the world, the body of this Ngarrindjeri man was swallowed up by the Ypres Salient. Rufus was initially reported missing rather than killed in action, and the uncertainty regarding his fate prompted a series of Red Cross enquiries by his family.

'He was wounded in the hop over at Passchendale [sic],' George Fox told the authorities, 'shot through the lungs, . . . [he] was left in a shell hole'. Another of his comrades hurried to wrap a bandage around the wound but the lad was 'very bad'.[1] Private Rigney died not long after in the hands of the Germans.

Almost ninety years after the brothers left Australia, Victor and Verna Koolmatrie journeyed to Belgium. They carried part of their country with them – sand from the dunes of Ninety Miles Beach, earth from the banks of the Coorong, soil gathered from the shores of Lake Alexandrina and the edges of the Murray. All these places were shaped by the ancestral hero Ngrunderri during the Dreaming; these sites were sacred to Cyril and Rufus and will always be a part of them.

BELOW **Heroes of the Great War:** A studio portrait of Rufus Gordon Rigney (fifth from the left, top row). The service dossier notes his 'dark complexion' and includes a letter consenting to his enlistment from the Chief Protector of Aborigines. The Chronicle, *9 February 1918 courtesy National Library of Australia.*

ABOVE **A loss dearly felt:** The memorial window to the Rigney brothers raised by the community. Note the appeal to 'Justice and Freedom'. Aboriginal service in World War One and subsequent conflicts helped to secure citizenship – but not until the 1960s. *Courtesy Bruce Scates.*

The parcel of soil was scattered on the moist turf of Harlebeke New British Cemetery where one of the two boys was buried; the distinctive notes of a didgeridoo cried out across Flanders to the other. Clad in red paint and loincloth, Victor performed the dance of the Kangaroo and the Emu. It was a freezing winter's morning but the great-great nephew of Rufus Gordon Rigney leapt high into the frosty air and landed close by his grave. And as Verna Koolmatrie spoke, reading a tribute to her ancestor, that cold place seemed a little warmer.

Ngarrindjeri people will always remember Rufus and Cyril Rigney, just as they will always care for the country that they came from. The grieving began in the church where the two boys were taught the Bible, and where today a memorial window shines in their honour. Nine from that mission went away to war, fighting, the stained glass tells us, not for 'King and Empire' but for 'Justice and Freedom'. The loss of those two boys was dearly felt by the community.

'I think about all that crying . . . when I was a little girl,' Doreen Kartinyeri, niece of Cyril and Rufus, remembered. 'My mum, my dad, and the other old ladies used to come to sit with my grandmother and they'd howl for days, a couple of days before and a couple of days after every Anzac Day.'[2] And every other day of the year, Cyril and Rufus's names gleam in gold from Raukkan's war memorial.

We do not know the exact number of Aboriginal people who lost their lives in the Great War, nor the number who fought for the country that long denied them citizenship. We do know that 'Justice and Freedom' has been a long time coming for Indigenous Australians – and that the service of Rufus and Cyril Rigney was one of many sacrifices.

ABOVE **Ngarrindjeri people will always remember:** The war memorial at Raukkan. Here, vivid Indigenous imagery is put to a commemorative purpose. In 1924, a returned man from the community marched at the end of the Anzac Day procession in Adelaide – but Aboriginal people have also devised their own ways of remembering. Note the church in the background where the memorial windows to the Rigney brothers (and two other men who died in the Great War) is set. *Courtesy Bruce Scates.*

SOURCES AND FURTHER READING: The authors respectfully acknowledge the Ngarrindjeri people of South Australia and their elders, past and present. This story draws on the service dossiers for Rufus and Cyril NAA: B2455, RIGNEY RUFUS GORDON and NAA: B2455, RIGNEY CYRIL SPURGEON; and Rufus's Red Cross Missing and Wounded file AWM IDRL/0428. See also Mike Sexton, 'One service charged with extra emotion', *The 7:30 Report*, ABC, 25 April 2005, transcript available: abc.net.au/7.30/content/2005/s1353096.htm. Further details of the transfer of Raukkan land can be found in *Australian Quarantine and Inspection Service Bulletin*, February 2005, number 1/2005.

We gratefully acknowledge our debt to Clyde Rigney, who facilitated our visit to Raukkan, and Verna Koolmatrie, who welcomed us to the community and generously shared her memories. Thanks are also due to the Indigenous playwright Wesley Enoch who alerted us to the existence of the memorial window and who wove their story into his remarkable play, *Black Diggers*. Finally, we acknowledge the work of Julie Reece, whose 'Connecting Spirits' commemorative tour honours Indigenous service. Studies of Ngarrindjeri Anzacs were pioneered by Doreen Kartinyeri, see *Ngarrindjeri Anzacs* (Adelaide: Aboriginal Family History Project, South Australian Museum and Raukkan Council, 1996) and more generally Doreen Kartinyeri and Sue Anderson, *My Ngarrindjeri Calling* (Canberra: Aboriginal Studies Press, 2008). This account also benefits from the scholarship of Diane Bell, *Listen to Ngarrindjeri Women Speaking = Kungun Ngarrindjeri Miminar Yunnan* (Melbourne: Spinifex Press, 2008); *Ngarrindjeri Wurruwarrin: A World that Is, Was and Will Be* (Melbourne: Spinifex Press, 1998). For general studies of Aboriginal people in the First AIF see Philippa Scarlett, *Aboriginal and Torres Strait Islander Volunteers for the AIF: The Indigenous Response to World War One* (Canberra: Indigenous Histories, 2013); David Huggonson, *Too Dark for the Light Horse: An Exhibition of Photographs & Documents Depicting Aboriginal Involvement in the Australian Army at the Albury Regional Museum, August 11th–September 27th* (Albury, 1988); Alick Jackomos and Derek Fowell, *Forgotten Heroes: Aborigines at War from the Somme to Vietnam* (Melbourne: Victoria Press, 1993). The authors eagerly await the important work of Mick Dodson, John Maynard and Jack Pearson into Indigenous service.

A motherly chat at the Cheer Up Society

ALEXANDRINA SEAGER

All three of Alexandrina Seager's sons enlisted in the first week of the war, and her youngest boy, George, was barely 17 when he was killed at Gallipoli. It was partly the absence of her own boys that persuaded her to turn to patriotic work. From the outbreak of the war, right to its very end, Annie Seager (as she preferred to be called) devoted herself to the care of South Australia's soldiers. She may have lost her own son but she became, in time, 'the little mother' of many an Anzac.[1]

Annie's most ambitious task was the establishment of a Cheer Up Society in Adelaide. Its purpose was to boost morale amongst the troops: concerts and singsongs, picnics, luncheons and many a farewell dinner were organised by Annie and her army of voluntary helpers. A mother of country boys herself, Annie knew all too well how young men could feel adrift in the city. For some, even a place as small as Adelaide could be lonely. The Cheer Up's journal, predictably dubbed *Cheer Up*, recorded one of Mrs Seager's 'motherly chats' with her soldiers:

> *'What's wrong old chap?' she asked. 'You look down in the dumps.' He glanced at her suspiciously, but the winning smile was too much for him. 'Oh, I dunno,' he replied. 'I feel rotten. Got no friends . . . I ain't used to crowds, you see.'*
>
> *'No friends!' she exclaimed. 'There are 150 friends here at least, all proud and anxious to be your friend, and of any other man in the King's Uniform. Here, girls, come and cheer up this boy.'*
>
> *In a twinkling he was surrounded by a coterie of the white-clad Cheer-Ups (they always dressed in white), and it was soon hard to recognise the morose individual in the merry-faced lad, with his hands full of peaches, cracking jokes with the girls.*
>
> *That soldier shortly became a prime favourite in the camp. It was the*

BELOW **Mother to the Anzacs:** 'Annie' Seager in her Cheer Up attire. In her early forties when this photo was taken, she was described by contemporaries as 'pretty, blue eyed, petite [and] charming', just the sort some diggers might take a shine to. *SRG 6/34/1 courtesy the State Library of South Australia.*

Cheer-Ups' way. Show them a soldier who was lonely, and they simply stormed him and jollied him into a brighter existence. [2]

A good time, to be sure. But Annie Seager and her Cheer Up girls also served a more serious moral purpose. Many mothers wrote to the Society to thank them for watching over their children. 'He is our baby,' one declared, 'just 18 years of age, and the temptations of the city are quite unknown to him.' For such young men from the bush, the girls provided 'clean, healthy amusement', an alternative to pubs and brothels keen on the custom of lonely, displaced men.[3] And the memory of those 'dear Australian girls' was thought to make them better soldiers.

On the eve of his departure for Egypt, Lieutenant Colonel Frederick Miell praised the example of this 'highest type of womanhood':

> *I know that many men in the 9th are better fellows today because of the interest taken in them by the girls of the 'Cheer-Up' Society . . . All of the boys will fight better because they know they have such treasure to fight for . . . and I earnestly pray that the mothers of the good fellows will have reason to be proud of [them]. Cairo is the wickedest city on earth, but we are trying to keep them straight . . . God bless the dear girls of C.U.S. . . . their influence is greater than they think.*[4]

OPPOSITE **The highest type of womanhood:** Cheer Up girls, dressed in Cheer Up uniforms outside the Cheer Up Hut in Adelaide. Note the boy scouts, another source of voluntary labour crucial to the war effort. *PRG 280/1/42/94 courtesy State Library of South Australia.*

BELOW **Violets for Remembrance:** Annie Seager was the first to adopt the violet as a commemoraitve symbol, and Violet Days were observed throughout Australia long before the Flanders poppy came into currency. The women's memorial garden at Victoria's Shrine profiles the violet as a female form of remembrance. *Courtesy The Shrine of Remembrance.*

Farewelling the boys was an easy matter. The return of crippled and wounded men was infinitely harder. As one Cheer Up girl recalled, those 'grand fellows', whom the Society 'sent away in the full glory of their manly vigour, return[ed] shattered and nerve-stricken wrecks'. Dancing with the lads had been fun, but how did one entertain the maimed, the blind or those who had been driven out of their senses?[5]

By the end of 1916, a steady stream of wounded were making their way back to Adelaide. The grand outdoor parties of the Cheer Up Society were replaced by basic meals in a hastily assembled hut on the banks of the Torrens. Though it was well furnished and set in beautiful parkland, the Cheer Up Hut could not have been very cheerful. New recruits, treated to a last lunch before departing for the war, were surrounded by hundreds of portraits of the fallen and tablets recording the names of those who had died since their return to Australia. And wounded men often outnumbered the able. In 1916 a special chair was installed to hoist the crippled up onto the balcony. Intended as a place of lighthearted amusement, the hut became a haunting blend of hospital, memorial, recreation room and madhouse.

It was also an institution staffed and managed almost entirely by women. A self-published poet, Annie wrote often of the 'Empire's stainless honour' and the 'bravest and the best' of Anzac.[6] Her verse was 'composed . . . on the spot', 'set to music' and 'committed to memory'.[7] But the girls working at the hut had little time for poetry; they faced dirty and demanding work, tending to the needs of men made more helpless than children. And there was certainly little 'glory' in that never-ending stream of dishes:

CHEER-UP S^CTY
ONLY SOLDIERS & SAILORS ADMITTED

About 10 000 meals monthly were being served in the Hut, apart from the farewells and similar functions; but we shall later quote even better figures! Readers, you can picture the amount of hard toil which surrounded the operations at the Hut, and the organisation required to keep matters going in apple-pie order.

Think of the wash ups, for instance. Mountains of dishes and cutlery were tackled daily by those voluntary workers, after waiting on hungry soldiers who 'took a power of keeping up with'.

It was the day by day regularity of the things that made it so exhausting, and the frequently interspersed farewells and other large functions rendered the task at times simply Herculean. Often a large gathering would terminate at 8 o'clock, but the Cheer-Ups could not finish the task of washing and drying the dishes until after 11 o'clock.

A farewell to 1000 men would involve the use of at least 3000 pieces of crockery, and 4000 pieces of cutlery and spoons! It was a common experience for girls to be on duty for 13 hours continuously, and they 'stuck it' for years, smilingly and uncomplaining . . . [8]

ABOVE TOP **A steady stream of wounded:** One of the first of the injured men to return, overwhelmed by a sea of patriotic well-wishers. Sir William Snowden, editor of the conservative daily *The Register* and one of the Cheer Up supporters, fronts the picture. *PRG 280/1/15/637 courtesy State Library of South Australia.*

ABOVE BOTTOM **Determined to offer what comfort they could:** A badge issued by the Cheer Up Society to raise funds for soldiers. The cheerful salute, 'Hats off to the Infantry', made light of the trials of war. *Courtesy Melbourne Museum.*

Just how many volunteer workers 'stuck at it' right through the war is open to speculation. What's beyond doubt is that voluntary work generated its own kinds of inequalities. While Annie Seager liked to pose as the selfless mother of the Anzacs, she was also paid (quite well) by donations raised by the Cheer Up Society. And with all the important work of fundraising and social networking to consider, the senior members of the society seldom had to deal with the dishes.

Annie Seager's Cheer Up Hut shut down at the end of the war. Ironically it reopened in the depression of the 1930s, a temporary shelter for unemployed soldiers sleeping in rags on the banks of the Torrens. The hut was demolished in 1972 and the site is now occupied by Adelaide's Festival Hall. But a plaque on the northern wall still pays homage to the Cheer Up Society's work and the women of Adelaide who were determined to offer what comfort they could to their soldiers.

SOURCES AND FURTHER READING: This story draws on a survey of contemporary newspaper reports; occasional publications by the Cheer Up Society; reminiscences by contemporaries; and the published work of Alexandrina Seager. For an earlier study of Seager and the Cheer Ups see Bruce Scates and Raelene Frances, *Women and the Great War* (Cambridge: Cambridge University Press, 1997) and for voluntary work more generally, Bruce Scates, 'The Forgotten Sock Knitter: Voluntary Work, Emotional Labour, Bereavement and the Great War', *Labour History*, no. 81, November 2001, pp. 29–51.

In Australasian hearts
KARANEMAR POHATU

From the first day of the Landing to the very last day of the campaign, Quinn's Post was the most perilous section of the Anzac line. Here one army collided against another, the trenches of Allied and Ottoman forces barely metres apart. You could see Quinn's from almost everywhere at Anzac. Perched on the second ridge of the Sari Bair range, it guarded the gullies beneath it. And you could hear Quinn's as well. 'The haunted house', men called it.[1] Every day and every night, the blasts of exploding bombs, the rattle of guns and the piteous cries of the wounded echoed ominously down the valley.

Quinn's was also the most critical part of the line. If the embattled garrison fell, Turkish troops would rush down Monash Gully, overwhelm the fragile defences of Anzac and sweep the invaders into the sea. That is why men died to hold Quinn's. And they hold it still. Just to the north of subsided gun pits, on one of the few slopes that could be terraced against erosion, 473 men are buried or commemorated. Remains were gathered in from hurried graves, collapsed trench lines and the open heights of the ridges within a year of the war's end. Fewer than 300 could be identified, but every bag of bleaching bones was reverently reassembled, lowered into the earth and honoured with its own memorial.

Eric Cotterill was one of the men buried at Quinn's – reburied, actually. His body was not placed there until the 1920s when his earlier grave on nearby Pope's Hill was almost obliterated by flooding.[2] At around the same time, Lieutenant Cotterill's family was asked to choose an epitaph. It remains one of the most eloquent inscriptions chiseled into stone at Gallipoli.

BELOW **Proving themselves warriors:** The Maori Pah at the northernmost end of Anzac. Maori troops performed the Haka before setting off for Chunuk Bair in the August Offensive. Technically serving as Pioneers they suffered casualties disproportionate to their numbers. *P05859.006 courtesy Australian War Memorial.*

BELOW LEFT **Proving themselves warriors:** Maori art carved in the hills of Gallipoli. The Australasian, *16 October 1915 courtesy National Library of Australia.*

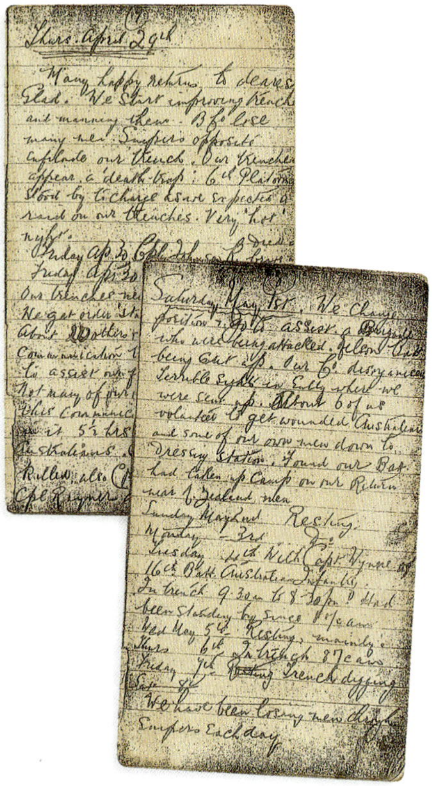

ABOVE **Quelling the terror erupting around them:** A soldier remembers his sweetheart in the 'death trap' of the trenches. Private Charles Thomas Scates' diary captures the frenzied nature of the fighting at Quinn's and records the bravery of the men who died beside him. This young man served with the Royal Marines Light Infantry; servicemen from across the British Empire fought and died at Quinn's. *Diary of Private Thomas Charles Scates, RMLI, 29 April 1915 courtesy Bruce Scates.*

His Grave Lies
Southward of the Line
In Australasian hearts

Though soldiers from across the British Empire are buried at Quinn's – as are the remains of many of their enemy – the Post belongs first and foremost to Australia and New Zealand. New Zealand troops were amongst the first to occupy Quinn's. One 'fern leaf' (as New Zealanders were usually called then) likened their foothold on the cliff face to the steep sides of Tasman Bluff on the coast near Nelson. Another reckoned the distance across no-man's-land was not much more than the width of the average street in Wellington.

Australians too likened Quinn's to the places they'd left behind them. The 17th Battalion, raised mostly from Sydney, called sections of the line 'Five Ways' and 'Martin Place', and christened the main sap running into the 'Post Broadway'. This was a way in which men sought to normalise the unreal world of battle erupting around them; familiar, even endearing terms quelled the terror.

Quinn's was a place Australia and New Zealand quite literally shared. It was not just that responsibility for the garrison rotated during the course of the campaign – Quinn's was held successively by Queensland's 15th Battalion, the Wellingtons under Malone, and brigade after brigade of Australian Light Horsemen. In the first desperate hours of the Landing, with all the battalions hopelessly intermingled, composite units of Australian and New Zealand troops found themselves fighting together, driving back one murderous Turkish attack on the Post after another. It was at Quinn's that the old animosity between these colonial cousins finally broke down and that quaint term 'Australasian' (as Cotterill's grave attests) came back into currency. Under fire, mates depended on one another regardless of which side of the Tasman they were born. The quarrels that had broken out in the bars and brothels of Cairo were promptly put behind them.

According to the cemetery register, barely a dozen New Zealanders were buried at Quinn's, but that means very little. The remains of men from Otago and Auckland, Canterbury and Wellington are littered across the hilltops and gullies nearby, a reminder that New Zealand units bore the brunt of the fighting over much of summer. And of course not all New Zealanders wore their country's uniform. Then, as throughout much of the twentieth century, the workforces of Australia and New Zealand were virtually interchangeable – shearers, miners and seamen regularly crisscrossed the Tasman. Many Australians were in New Zealand when war broke out and many New Zealanders in Australia. Robert Stone was one of these.

Robert Stone was not his real name. Karanemar Pohatu was a Maori man from Te Hanke near Hastings. He migrated to Australia four years before the outbreak of war and worked as a labourer and shearer. His brother, Tohana Pohatu, was unsure of Karanemar's age, but the attestation papers claim he was 21 when he enlisted. Just six months later Karanemar Pohatu was killed defending Quinn's and buried hastily near the ridgeline. 'He was fair for a Maori', Tohana Pohatu wrote, and perhaps changing his name to Stone – the English translation of Pohatu – was a way of cloaking his cultural identity. We do not know if Karanemar shared Tohana's loyalty to the Crown – Tohana ended his letter with a rallying call for Empire: 'God Bless you all. God Save the King.'[3]

Like Indigenous communities in Australia, Maori had suffered much in the course of British colonisation. Their land had been taken, their culture disrupted, and their population decimated. For Maori, military service asserted the rights and entitlements of citizenship, as it did for Aboriginal people. But there was one important difference between the experience of Aboriginal and Maori servicemen.

In Australia, the refusal to recognise Aboriginal soldiers as Indigenous, and insistence that all recruits be of 'predominantly European descent' meant that Indigenous servicemen were integrated throughout the First AIF. Their duties, their pay, their responsibilities and in some cases their opportunities were the same as white servicemen. In New Zealand, by contrast, Maori were marshalled into quite separate units under the strict command of white officers. Men who once had been warriors were relegated to noncombatant duties and formed into Pioneer battalions – they were intended to carry shovels rather than rifles at Gallipoli. Of course, Maori would prove themselves warriors again and again in the course of the campaign, and petitioned military authorities to play an active role in the fighting. Even so, the fact remains that had Karanemar Pohatu enlisted at home in Hawke's Bay he too would have been forced into that subordinate position; perhaps that is one of the reasons he chose to enlist – cloaked in that fair skin – in Australia.

Karanemar Pohatu died on the second day of the campaign, as the battle for Quinn's Post raged all around him. What serves as his grave is marked by a special memorial, the epitaph chosen not by his family but by military authorities. 'Their glory shall not be blotted out' was the standard inscription employed for any memorial where the exact location of a body buried nearby could not be determined. But perhaps it is a fitting tribute. Whatever the case, Cotterill and Pohatu were remembered 'southward of the line' and 'Australasian hearts' were wounded by their passing.

ABOVE **A place Australia and New Zealand shared:** An early tribute to the fighting on Anzac. Note the fusion of national and imperial loyalties - on Gallipoli men from both sides of the Tasman were keen to prove themselves 'worthy sons of Empire'. *Courtesy State Library of Queensland.*

BELOW **Guarding the gullies beneath it:** Quinn's Post, the most perilous section of the Anzac line. To the far left, the entrance to Shrapnel Valley is visible. Losing this position would mean the narrow beachhead would soon be overwhelmed. Thosands of Ottoman soldiers were killed attacking Quinn's; many Anzacs died defending it. *Courtesy Bruce Scates.*

SOURCES AND FURTHER READING: This story draws on the service records of Eric Cotterill and Robert Stone NAA: B2455, COTTERILL E R and NAA: B4255, STONE ROBERT. The most accomplished history of New Zealanders at Anzac remains Chris Pugsley's *Gallipoli: the New Zealand Story* (Auckland: Raupo, 2008). See also *Te Hokowhitu a tu: the Maori Pioneer Battalion in the First World War* (Auckland: Reed, 1995). Maori service is also considered by James Cowan, *The Maoris and the Great War: A History of the New Zealand Native Contingent and Pioneer Battalion, Gallipoli, 1915, France and Flanders, 1916–18* (Auckland: Whitecombe and Tombs, 1926); also see Peter Stanley, *Quinn's Post: Anzac, Gallipoli* (Sydney: Allen & Unwin, 2005). C.E.W Bean's return to Quinn's is considered in *Gallipoli Mission* [1948 edition] (Sydney: ABC Books, 1990) where he ponders its strategic significance. For a fictional recreation of the same see Bruce Scates, *On Dangerous Ground: A Gallipoli Story* (Perth: UWA Publishing, 2013). The authors thank Meleah Hampton for alerting us to Pohatu's story.

SIGNALLER ELLIS SILAS, 1916.

ANZAC. DAWN MAY 3. 1915. I SHALL NEVER FORGET THE INDESCRABLE SCENE IN THE GULLY IT WAS CHOCKED WITH DEAD AND WOUNDED, THESE POOR LUMPS OF CLAY HAD ONCE BEEN MY COMRADES, MEN I HAD SMOKED AND WORKED, AND LAUGHED & JOKED WITH, OH GOD! THE PITY OF IT! IT RAINED LEAD IN THIS GULLY, ALL ROUND COULD BE SEEN THE SPARKS, WHERE THE BULLETS WERE STRIKING; IT WAS AMID THIS HAIL OF BULLETS THAT GEN' GODLY CALMLY DID MY PUTTEE FOR ME, I IMPLORED HIM TO TAKE COVER, KNOWING WE COULD ILL SPARE THE LOSS OF A GENERAL; BUT HE WOULDN'T HEAR OF IT, EVERY SECOND I WAS EXPECTING TO SEE HIM HIT, BUT NOT UNTIL HE HAD DONE UP MY PUTTEE, WOULD HE MOVE; THEN WITH AN AMUSED CHUCKLE, HE PASSED HIS HAN ACROSS THE TOP OF HIS CAP, AT THE SAME TIME REMARKING, "THAT WAS A PRETTY NEAR THING", A BULLET HAD SINGED THE TOP OF HIS

The joke of the battalion

ELLIS SILAS

Ellis Silas wasn't cut out to be a soldier. His first attempt to enlist, in Perth, Western Australia, in the first week of war, failed miserably. Already in his thirties, of slight build and frail constitution, the artist originally from London was deemed unsuitable for service. He tried to join up as a medic in September; this time, the authorities relented and took him on as a signaller.

Silas soon regretted this decision. His first days in Blackboy Hill training camp east of Perth were simply 'terrible'. It wasn't just the 'filthy' conditions, or the pointless drill, or the boredom of all that 'flag waving'. Sensitive and self-conscious, Silas found 'the rough society of Bushmen' uncomfortable, their manners coarse and their language 'frightful'. He longed for the 'quiet', reflective world of his studio, found it difficult to sleep, and told his captain he could not bear to shoot a man. Nor did the artist adjust to military discipline. Distracted by 'a rather fine sunset', he found himself 'standing alone [on Parade], the remainder of the squad having marched off'. The drill sergeant 'exploded'. Silas took to wearing his slouch hat in a rather jaunty fashion. 'I thought it looked nice,' he confided in his diary, 'but individuality does not find favour in the army; doing everything like everybody else does. It is a nuisance.'[1]

Signaller Ellis Silas embarked from Albany in December 1914. Most soldier diarists were reflective on leaving Australia's shores – but the artist even more so as he jotted in his notebook:

> *A greyish day . . . Nature is sad, she weeps for us as we steam away close to the great bluffs of the coast of Western Australia. Far away astern of us there are a few specks getting ever smaller – the last sight of . . . the land which has been so much to me . . . which now I am leaving perhaps forever.*[2]

ABOVE **Not about to sanitise his experience:** Silas prepares to paint his trauma onto the canvas. He was commissioned by C.E.W. Bean to paint images of his time at Gallipoli. Bean was keen to capture the testimony of the men who had actually fought there. *Source P02801.002 courtesy Australian War Memorial.*

OPPOSITE **The dead piling up:** Silas's sketch of the gully (aptly named Shrapnel Valley) choked with dead and wounded. White faces turned up towards the sun became his abiding memory of Gallipoli. *ART90803 courtesy Australian War Memorial.*

On ship, he found refuge in reading and the voyage itself had its attractions, 'a brilliant sky above, glorious blue below'. Even so, Silas confessed to a 'kind of wish-I-were-dead sort of feeling . . . cooped up with 3000 men', many of whom found him odd and eccentric: 'I cannot get used to the rough conditions with which I am surrounded . . . How I hate this terrible life.' Silas was seen as something of a 'snob', his sketchbook often his only company.[3]

Aloof and intellectual, Ellis Silas was hardly a paragon of Anzac mateship. But even to the roughest of bushmen he would prove himself on Gallipoli. In the first dangerous weeks ashore, he scribbled and sketched in the tense spaces between battles. His diary and his artwork remain one of the most compelling accounts of the campaign.

Ellis Silas was there from the first day of the Landing. He recorded an 'awful feeling of utter helplessness' as they drifted in under fire; 'we were packed so tightly in the boats and so heavily laden with our kit that, had a shot hit the boat, we should have had no chance of saving ourselves'. The beach was a 'scene of utter carnage', and the ridges that awaited him even worse, 'groans and screams everywhere, calls for ammunition and stretcher bearers,' the dead piling up in shallow and shell-swept trenches.

The first night Silas thought 'the dammed noise of the guns' would send him 'to pieces': he felt weak and tired and wondered how long he could stand it. But Ellis Silas acted the soldier he never was – braved enemy fire in the most perilous sections of the line and kept furiously waving his flags when every other signaller in his section was dead. He remained at his post 'four days and four nights without a rest', narrowly escaped death on at least a dozen occasions and saved – by his devotion to duty – the lives of hundreds of men, including a large party of New Zealanders wandering into a 'nest' of Turkish soldiers.

On 29 April 1915, Signaller Silas learned he'd been mentioned in despatches. He responded to that honour with characteristic ambivalence. On the one hand, Silas insisted he'd done nothing exceptional:

> *It is curious on the battlefield how unconscious one is of having accomplished anything . . . I do not feel that I have done anything more than my duty – where so many men are doing fine things I do not see what utter use it is giving medals.*

On the other, a man whose 'one great fear' was that he would 'fail lamentably' brimmed with a sense of relief and satisfaction:

> *[I've] shown the lads that Signaller Silas, the joke of the Battalion, was able to do his bit with them, and also to show a somewhat sneering world that artists are not quite failures on the battlefield.* [4]

BELOW **Crusading at Anzac:** Portrait of a wounded Turkish prisoner. The title of Silas's sketchbook reminds us of the way that age-old fear and prejudices were mobilised to fight the Gallipoli campaign. But this sketch of a wounded prisoner suggests a far more sympathetic view of the enemy. Silas's diary also recorded the suffering of an Ottoman soldier shot through the lungs, facing his God alone far from friends and family. *ART92679.004 courtesy Australian War Memorial*

Ellis Silas showed that there was a place for artists in war and that a sensitive, somewhat eccentric man need not fail his comrades. His personal courage, that ability to rise above the fear every soldier felt, earned the admiration of the very men who once shunned him.

Equally importantly, Silas's own view of those same men was transformed. 'In Cairo I was ashamed of them,' he jotted down on his first day at Gallipoli, 'now I am proud to be one among them.' The bonds men felt in battle bridged an immense cultural difference, as bohemian and bushman, foul-mouthed soldier and well-read artist endured a common ordeal. Eventually, however, that ordeal broke Ellis Silas. He was evacuated from the peninsula suffering shell shock, enteric fever and exhaustion. Silas was unconscious or delirious for several days and then spent several weeks in hospital. Like many men far more stoic than himself, he never truly recovered from his war service.[5]

ABOVE **Drifting in under fire:** Silas captures the Landing at Gallipoli. The 16th Battalion came ashore later in the day, the first wave (at dawn) faced no such opposition. But this image of gunfire lashing the water dominates popular memory of the first day at Anzac. *ART90807 courtesy Australian War Memorial.*

FOLLOWING PAGES **The dead were part of our life at Gallipoli:** Roll Call at Quinn's Post after the disastrous charge of 9 May. What Silas called 'a thin line of weary, ashen-faced man' testifies to the fury of the fighting. Silas added that the dead to the right could not be buried for several days 'as we were so hard pressed by the Turks'. *ART02436 courtesy Australian War Memorial.*

Ellis Silas was one of only three artists to record Australian participation firsthand on Gallipoli – and he was the only one to paint battle scenes after his time there. Silas had always believed the purpose of art was to be truthful. Here too the softly spoken man from London showed a rare kind of courage. A public eager for stories of heroism, and used to grand canvasses romanticising battle, were confronted with hasty, brittle sketches done in the field, and brutal images of the carnage at Gallipoli.

Some found this far too challenging, accusing Ellis of 'morbid sensationalism'. But the artist who had served as a soldier was not about to sanitise his experience. 'The dead were a part of our life at Gallipoli,' he told the comfortable salon circles. Silas and his sketches were summoned by Royal Command to a viewing at Buckingham Palace. Queen Mary graciously 'consented to accept a copy of Silas's forthcoming book', but otherwise said very little.[6]

Ellis Silas never really left Gallipoli behind him, even though his later work might be viewed as therapeutic. In 1922, he travelled the Pacific, lived in native villages and sketched soft and sensitive portraits of life in the islands. Eventually the Australian War Memorial purchased three of his Gallipoli sketches; many of the remainder were published in a slim volume entitled *Crusading at Anzac*. General Sir Ian Hamilton, Allied commander of the bungled campaign, wrote a brief appreciation in the foreword. It was far more prescient than any of his commands at Gallipoli: 'Though treating so largely of death, [these images] are so lifelike; though grim, they do justice also to the gaiety and good humour which never deserted any of our troops in the trenches; though slight, they seem solid and serious enough to such of us as were there.'[7]

SOURCES AND FURTHER READING: This story draws on contemporary newspaper reports; Silas's diary (held by the State Library of New South Wales); relevant war diaries; Silas' Gallipoli sketches in *Crusading at Anzac, AD 1915* (London: British-Australasian, 1916); and his service dosier NAA: B2455, SILAS ELLIS. His repatriation files are still not available. The authors thank Janda Gooding (former curator of the art collection at the Australian War Memorial) for the opportunity to view Silas's work in the original. Previous appreciation of Silas's life appear in Betty Churcher, *The Art of War* (Carlton: Miegunyah Press, 2004) and Peter Stanley, *Quinn's Post: Anzac, Gallipoli* (Sydney: Allen & Unwin, 2005).

The mystery of the Water Diviner

THOMAS MURRAY

Thomas Murray Sr's firstborn son was taken by the war. Perhaps there is nothing so exceptional in that. Nor was his love for his son any greater, or any less, than a million other fathers all over the world. Grief knows no nationality. Stripped of their uniforms, the sons of Turkey and Serbia, Britain and Belgium all look the same.

Tom bore his father's name, worked alongside him on the family's property in Gippsland, broke in the stock and opened up the land. The Murray family was the first white family to settle in Buffalo; 'Fairy Nook', their quaint and rambling colonial homestead, still stands. Father and son were close, but perhaps no closer than fathers and sons in any other rural community. And young Tom's achievements were shared by the sons of many a farmer. He was one of the darlings of the district, captain of the footy team, champion batsman, the boy the girls wanted most to dance with, the man with a plan.

In 1914, Tom mounted his horse and rode to the recruiting station at Meeniyan. Like his father, he was a patriot. That, and the infectious lure of travel and adventure, made him determined to serve overseas. He joined the 8th Light Horse, alongside other lads from the district. By March he was in a training camp in Egypt, by May, in the Dardanelles. By August he was dead.

Like many fathers, Thomas Murray found the death of his boy impossible to deal with. A family friend remembered that strong, sensitive man breaking down, his face struggling for 'control', his heart 'convulsed' with grief.[1] And like many who lost their sons in war, Thomas clung to the hope that the authorities might be mistaken. No body had been brought in from the battlefield, so perhaps there was a chance that Tom had been taken prisoner. There is a quiet desperation in Thomas's correspondence with Base Records, a piteous struggle with the inevitable:

ABOVE **One of the darlings of the district:** T.R. Murray prior to his departure overseas. Murray enlisted in the Infantry and served later in the Light Horse; note the distinctive emu plume. *Courtesy Lyn Skillern.*

His number was altered in the firing line . . . and he had been lately raised in the ranks to Lance Corporal. No 766 would be the number stamped on his identification disc. Kindly assure me whether there was any possibility of a mistake having arisen in consequence of the change in numbers . . . and greatly oblige.[2]

No such assurance was forthcoming. 'I regret I am unable to hold out any hope of there being an inaccuracy,' Major McLean wrote in reply. He would write much the same letter to a thousand other families.[3]

In many ways, the loss of Trooper Murray on Gallipoli and the grief of the father left behind in Gippsland is the experience of a generation. Though every death was unique and every loss intensely personal, the doubts, the pain, the anguish was much the same. But in one regard at least the story of Thomas Murray and his son is quite exceptional. In 1920, this old man from Gippsland became the first Australian father to make his way to Gallipoli; he would travel halfway across the world to search for his son.

Until now, it has been a journey steeped in mystery. There is only one fleeting reference to it in the standard histories of the period. In 1948, C.E.W. Bean wrote his account of his own return to the peninsula; *Gallipoli Mission* details his quest to retrace the old trench line, walk the 'sacred shore' of Anzac and 'solve the riddles' of that ill-fated campaign. Almost as an aside, Bean quotes a letter, correspondence from Cyril Hughes who returned to Anzac with the war graves units in 1919.

'One old chap managed to get here from Australia,' Hughes told Bean; he spent a few days 'looking for his son's grave' although the sight of the battlefield, still strewn

BELOW **Suicidal:** George Lambert's iconic depiction of the charge at the Nek. The 8th Light Horse was amongst the first to go into battle. Within minutes hundreds of dead were piled in a space the size of a tennis court, Trooper Murray amongst them. *ART07965 courtesy Australian War Memorial.*

ABOVE **To touch the shingle at Anzac:** The remains of a landing boat rusting away in the Aegean. At the time of Murray's journey, the battlefields were littered with debris and the skeletons of the dead. *Courtesy Bruce Scates.*

OPPOSITE **A powerfully deliberate act of remembrance:** Cover of a scrapbook compiled by a local in the district in the early days of the war. The special treatment of Murray's portrait therin suggests some connection to the family. *Courtesy Leongatha Historical Society.*

with the bones of the dead, was 'unspeakably distressing'. 'We looked after him [as best we could]', Hughes hastened to add, both men knowing the search was hopeless; 'he's pushed off to Italy now'.[4] Hughes did not name this sad but determined visitor, and there was no clue – other than age – to reveal his identity. But this single line of text inspired a feature-length movie, *The Water Diviner*, a film that claims to be based on true events, although the filmmakers had 'no information' about who this man might be.[5]

How do we know that old man who struggled up Walker's Ridge was Thomas Murray? In truth, there were very few other contenders to choose from. It was not just the horrendous cost. Even a steerage fare to Europe ran to sixty pounds – a good part of the yearly wage for a skilled, white, male worker. There was also the question of getting to Gallipoli. A pilgrim to Anzac in the early 1920s travelled by sea to Istanbul, then retraced his steps on a smaller vessel back down the Sea of Marmara to Chanak. From there, he hired a launch, if one could be found, to ferry him across the Dardanelles to Anzac.

Such a journey was long, difficult, dangerous and – in 1920 at least – illegal. The Straits of the Dardanelles remained as strategically important as they had been in 1915; Allied authorities struggled to keep them open through the long war of independence that followed the defeat of the Ottoman Empire. Issues of safety, and of course the 'unspeakable' sights of the battlefields, meant visitors were prohibited 'with the utmost rigour'.[6]

Murray was one of the few Australians with the capital and the resolution to make such a journey. Something of an adventurer, he had made his fortune on the goldfields of Western Australia before returning as a grazier to Buffalo. Like the rugged, self-reliant farmer played by Russell Crowe in *The Water Diviner*, Murray was a man used to 'roughing it'. He was old – almost 60 – just as Hughes had reported. But he was still one 'of the strongest men in the district', and better prepared than most for the rigours of the journey.[7]

That journey took Murray first to London. We know this from shipping records of the time and a telling column in the pages of the *British Australasian*. The latter was a journal kept by Australian and New Zealand expatriates living in London. It carried political commentary, sporting news from home, reviews of the latest books, plays and scandals and surprisingly exact itineraries of Australians passing through the Imperial capital. In 1920, the same year Hughes wrote to Bean in Australia, its regular feature, 'Australasians in Europe', reported Murray's visit:

> *Mr Thomas Murray has arrived from Victoria with the object of visiting the grave of his son, who fell at the charge of the 8th Light Horse at Walker's Ridge, Gallipoli, and the graves of other relatives in France. Mr Murray is at present in London. He will return home via America.*[8]

Solving the mystery of *The Water Diviner* is one challenge that confronts the historian. Another is to grapple with the many liberties this film – 'based on true events' – takes with history. In the film, the son survives – he had been taken prisoner by the Turks, chose to stay on after the war, and lived the life of a mystic in a Sufi monastery. That may seem an unlikely scenario, yet there is also a kind of emotional truth to it. Many parents (including, for a time, Murray himself) steadfastly refused to accept the death of their sons. They bickered over details with the authorities, wrestled with conflicting testimony, demanded the conclusive truth of a body. And enquiries initiated by the Red Cross often raised the very doubts they intended to solve.

'Missing' men were sometimes sighted long after a battle was over, seen on hospital ships making their way to Egypt, or reported only slightly wounded and likely to have been taken prisoner. The chaos of war made space for just such possibilities. And the most persistent and damaging hope of all was the thought that a man may have lost his memory. Somewhere, their son may still be alive, wandering nameless through the French countryside, confined to a hospital bed with amnesia, admitted with no proven identity to an asylum.

BELOW **Few of the bleaching bones could be identified:** Trooper T.R. Murray's name on the Memorial to the Missing at Lone Pine. Thomas Murray had hoped to find his son's grave, but when he trudged up to Walker's Ridge none of Gallipoli's cemeteries were completed. There was only a wasteland of bones scattered across the landscape. *Courtesy Rebecca Wheatley.*

In that light, a soldier whirling with the Sufis somewhere in central Turkey is not entirely fanciful. Perhaps it is no more desperate a hope than the thousands who embraced spiritualism in the aftermath of the war, determined to reach those they had literally lost in the war. Murray may have been the first Australian father to touch the shingle at Anzac, but his search expressed the longing – and unresolved pain – of an entire generation.

The Water Diviner holds out that hope. And like many a movie it clutches at a happy ending. Father is reunited with son, the dead are laid decently to rest, reconciliation – even romance – is found with a former enemy. And that is where Hollywood departs from history. The battle in which Trooper Murray lost his life was the charge at the Nek. A suicidal assault on one of the strongest Turkish positions at Anzac, there was little chance of survival. Men were cut down by machine-gun fire within yards of the trenches. In the space of a few minutes many were killed, many wounded, and not a single man taken prisoner.

Thomas Murray knew this when he walked the ground at Gallipoli. As the report in the *British Australasian* noted, he went with 'the object' of finding the grave of his son – that was the only solace Anzac could possibly offer him. And even that was denied. The remains of hundreds butchered at the Nek were not recovered until 1919, and few of the bleaching bones could be identified. Tom was interred in a mass grave not far from where he fell; as were hundreds of other boys, other fathers' sons.

We don't know if so inconclusive a pilgrimage offered Thomas Murray any kind of comfort. We know he returned to Gippsland to work the family farm. We know he would have seen his son's name etched in gold in the war memorial in Meeniyan. A few hundred men from the district volunteered, like Tom, for service overseas – fifty-five of them never came home.

The memorial takes the form of a broken column, signifying a life cut short – like young Tom's. Other families raised more fragile but equally poignant monuments to their dead. A tattered scrapbook survives to this day in the archives of Leongatha's historical society. An unknown hand has cut a photograph of Tom out of a local paper, bordered it with gold and set a laurel wreath above the head – a private but powerfully deliberate act of remembrance. We also know that the old man who made his way to Turkey outlived his son by twenty-four years, a long time to carry the burden of that grief.

Thomas Murray, the first Australian father to visit Gallipoli, is buried beneath a marble slab in Leongatha Cemetery. The epitaph is short and simple: 'In Loving Memory of our Dear Father'. That same love between a father and a child had sent Murray halfway across the world in search of the grave of his son. And the date of his death is particularly significant. Murray sacrificed his son in the Great War, promised as the war to end all wars. But in September 1939, the same month and year Thomas Murray died, the world went to war again.

ABOVE TOP **In loving memory of our dear father:** Thomas Murray's grave at Leongatha. The father was laid to rest in the way the son never was. *Courtesy Bruce Scates.*

ABOVE BOTTOM **The old man who made his way to Turkey:** A portrait of Thomas Murray, the real inspiration for the story of *The Water Diviner*. *Courtesy Leongatha Historical Society.*

SOURCES AND FURTHER READING: The mystery of the first father to visit Gallipoli was solved by a painstaking survey of extant copies of the *British Australasian* held in Melbourne, Canberra and London. T.R. Murray's details were accessed through his service dossier NAA: B4255, MURRAY THOMAS RICHARD, and details of his father's life were gathered through his contribution to the first history of the district, H.J. Malone, *A Short History of Central South Gippsland* (Melbourne, np, 1932). The authors thank local historians Joan Newman and Lyn Skillern for their assistance in compiling this account. Particular thanks are due to Kath and Ken Vagg for providing histories of the district, Dawn and Ashton Farrell (who remembered the Murray family) and the Leongatha Historical Society for access to their archives. The most extended account of early pilgrimages to Gallipoli remains Bruce Scates, *Return to Gallipoli: Walking the Battlefields of the Great War* (Cambridge: Cambridge University Press, 2006) and for a fictionalised account of such journeys see Bruce Scates, *On Dangerous Ground: A Gallipoli Story* (Perth: UWA publishing, 2013). Both books were provided to the producers of *The Water Diviner*, and the assistance of the National Centre for Australian Studies at Monash University is acknowledged in the credits of the film.

Out of the silence
THE UNKNOWN PATIENT

In 1916, the Unknown Patient was admitted to Broughton Hall, a 'mental facility' for returned soldiers in Sydney. Some said he'd been found behind the lines in France, wandering aimlessly and wearing a slouch hat. Others said that he'd been taken in by a group of soldiers roaming the streets of London. Everything about this man was a mystery.

Doctors noted their patient was 'shaky', 'nervous' and 'disoriented':

> *He states that people's voices, who are unseen, worry him by calling him a coward. His memory is so dull that he cannot enter any question except by answering 'I don't know, I don't know.'*[1]

They attributed his condition to 'the stress of the campaign', and, in the rambling conversations recorded in the asylum casebooks, sketched what might have happened to him. 'Patient had shock', 'was buried by sandbags as a result of a shell', suffers 'from Hallucinations of hearing' and frequent 'distressing dreams'. A doctor looked with clinical interest at the 'vacuous', 'semi-stuporous' expression on his charge's face and printed 'Recommended for discharge as permanently unfit' on the medical record.[2]

The Unknown Patient would remain in Sydney's Callan Park Mental Hospital for over a decade. They called him George Brown, a name so nondescript it might have belonged to anyone. Personal details were circulated to the press in the hope that someone might come forward – aged somewhere in his thirties, straight brown hair, blue eyes, 'two vaccination scars, one above the other'.[3] That – and vague and contradictory reports of a tattoo – wasn't much to go on.

In the late 1920s, returned soldiers' associations adopted the case, determined that an unknown comrade be reunited with his loved ones. Hundreds of 'anxious enquiries' flooded in, 'from fathers, mothers, brothers or sisters all over Australia, who fancy he might be the long-lost member of their family'[4]. Lost quite literally. In the wake of the Great War, tens of thousands of bodies vanished altogether – around a million dead were buried as 'Unknowns', never to be identified. Even a decade after the war, families hoped against hope that their missing menfolk might come home to them:

> *They cannot believe their father or husband or brother is dead – though officially reported killed or missing – because they received none of his personal belongings, not even the identification discs, from the Defence Department.*

First came the letters: 'piteous appeals are being received from all parts for a photograph,' one press report noted. Hundreds stared for hours at an expressionless face, imagining a son or brother aged by war, searching for some feature they might recognise. And then came the visits. 'A sad procession made their way to Callan Park Asylum,' an eyewitness reported, 'mostly parents who had cherished the fading hope that perhaps their boy had been wrongly reported missing.' They watched a man 'baulking furiously at the cameras brought in to photograph him' or standing 'lamblike', indifferent to his surroundings. After a while they turned away, thankful – perhaps – that their boy had been spared that, anyway.[5]

Almost a decade after the end of the war, the Unknown Patient was identified as George Thomas McQuay, a carpenter from Taranaki. McQuay signed up with the New Zealand Expeditionary Force in 1914, fought in Gallipoli and France and was posted as a deserter after the battle of Armentières. Perhaps that helped to explain the voice that shouted in his head, 'calling him a coward'.

In May 1928, George was reunited with his mother. Emma McQuay had crossed the Tasman with a fare raised by returned soldiers, as both the Australian and the New Zealand governments would do nothing to assist her. As Mrs McQuay explained to an eager reporter:

> *Think of it! Never a word since 1915; never a sign of George since the landing at Gallipoli! Not to know even that he had been killed, no report of him as 'missing' – just silence. . . when I have him home again, among the places and people he loved, he'll 'come back'. So many years here, with nobody to prompt him, nobody to care. He was only a number.*[6]

BELOW **He'll come back:** Mrs Emma McQuay and her son, reunited after years of absence. A cameraman captured a mother's anxious joy in the grounds of Callan Park Mental Hospital. Her hand is resting on George's shoulder as if reluctant to lose him. Sydney Morning Herald, *2 May 1928 courtesy National Library of Australia.*

UNKNOWN SOLDIER RECOGNISED BY HIS MOTHER.

MRS. E. L. McQUAY AND HER SON GEORGE REUNITED AT CALLAN PARK YESTERDAY.
For eleven years Mrs. McQuay had believed that her son was dead.

For all the spin of the press reports, the case of the Unknown Patient did not end happily. On the one hand, there were the hundreds who were turned away disappointed – a mother who wrote to the medical superintendent demanding some 'assurance they have no record of any other unknown patient'; a man had a vivid dream about his brother, a soldier killed at Pozières who 'suddenly returned from nowhere'. Another family from Hampton, Melbourne, wrote for a photograph, explaining 'strange to say, only a few nights ago one member of our family had a dream of her son having reappeared after 10 years. He was killed in the war'. In each case (and there were many), news of a man who had 'stepped out of the silence' rekindled hope and prolonged the process of mourning.

Nor was it quite true, as Mrs McQuay had assumed, that her son had 'come back' to her. Within weeks of returning to Aotearoa/New Zealand, the now known patient was admitted once again to an asylum where one doctor noted:

BELOW **Thousands of bodies vanished altogether:** The grave of an Australian soldier 'Known unto God'.Over a third of the bodies of Australia's dead could not be found or identified. For the families of these lost men, the case of George McQuay offered a last fragile hope that the missing might return to them. *Courtesy Bruce Scates.*

> *Lounges about in a hopelessly untidy condition. Is very childish . . . and cannot converse rationally . . . his table manners are repulsive. . . habits are filthy [he] drinks urine, licks spittoons, spits in cups, eats porridge with his hands.*[7]

Recent work by Jen Hawksley has retraced what remained of George McQuay's life: two more decades in and out of institutions, sometimes in the care of his family, sometimes locked away, always a burden to others. The Unknown Patient died in 1951, aged 64. He was buried in the soldiers' cemetery at Kopuatama. Veterans from both world wars attended the funeral and the Last Post was sounded over his grave.

SOURCES AND FURTHER READING: This story draws on contemporary newspaper reports; George McQuay's service dossier R10927130, Archives New Zealand; and the records of Callan Park Mental Hospital. The latter were accessed (with the kind assistance of Belinda Saunders) in 2004. The authors thank NSW Health for permission to view the same and the Australian Research Council for funding. The most detailed treatment of the McQuay case is given by Jen Hawksley, 'Long Time Coming Home: The Unknown Patient of Callan Park', in Martin Crotty and Marina Larsson (eds), *Anzac Legacies: Australians and the Aftermath of War* (Melbourne: Australian Scholarly Publishing, 2010) and her assistance is gratefully acknowledged. For similar cases based on asylum records see Tanya Luckins, *Gates of Memory: Australian Peoples Experience and Memories of Loss and the Great War* (Perth: Curtin University Press, 2004); Bruce Scates, *Return to Gallipoli: walking the battlefields of the Great War* (Cambridge: Cambridge University Press, 2006); Marina Larsson, *Shattered Anzacs: Living with the Scars of War* (Sydney: UNSW Press, 2009) and Alistair Thomson, *Anzac Memories: Living with the Legend* (Melbourne: Monash University Publishing, new edition, 2013). The authors thank the Friends of Callan Park (in particular Hall Greenland and Roslyn Burge) for their introduction to the important historic site.

Aftermaths

KATHLEEN SKINNER

After World War Two some 12 000 war brides left Australia. Hitched to glamorous GIs – far better paid and certainly better dressed than most Australian servicemen – they made new lives for themselves in the USA. But after World War One, the traffic was in quite the opposite direction. Around 15 000 European women, the vast majority from Britain, married Australian and New Zealand soldiers, boarded the troopships that had carried these men to war, and sailed for Australia.[1]

Australians found their young brides in all the places diggers frequented: the parks and pubs of London, cinemas and teashops, churches, museums, theatres – even the occasional brothel. Some of these women married for love, some for the hope of adventure or advancement, and many – thanks to the harsh moral standards of the day – because they had very little option. A large number of war brides carried babies with them. Australian and New Zealand nurses, most already exhausted by their war service, were expected to care for young mothers and their infants on the long journey back home. Some nurses resented yet another chore, and one AIF sister unkindly dubbed their charges 'the Aftermaths'.[2]

Back home in Australia, many disapproved – sometimes vocally – of these liaisons. As early as 1917, public criticism was directed at the fifty or so soldiers a week marrying in the 'old country'. *Soldier*, a journal aimed at servicemen and their families, was little short of indignant:

> *Of course, there is nothing to prevent Bill or Jim from marrying a Chinese if he wants to but he will scarcely be given a glad eye by the local lassies on his return. English roses are said to be good, if you pick a goodun, but why the rose when the wattle blossoms bloom in the golden light of this sun-kissed country.*[3]

There were no glad eyes for the servicemen's brides, either. Englishwomen were considered 'loose' by many Australians; how else could they have lured the men away from the fiancées and sweethearts they had left behind? And while an English rose was one thing, a woman from the Continent was quite another. French brides were deemed foreigners in ways British women were not; they spoke differently, dressed differently, expected far too much of Australian cuisine and had an insatiable thirst for coffee.

Kathleen Skinner was one of a few Belgian brides who made her way to Australia. Her wartime life reflected the ordeal of her country's occupation. She fled to a convent in Ghent when the Germans seized the city, escaped to Holland and then joined a flood of refugees crossing the Channel for England. For a time Kathleen was placed in another convent, but she never joined an order. By 1918 she was boarding in Fulbourne Road in Walthamstow, London, and earning an independent living as a typist.

We don't know when exactly she met Jim Agnew, from Kellyville, near Sydney, serving in the First AIF. It was almost certainly at the end of the war, when Private Agnew and his unit were stationed in the south of England. Nor do we know what persuaded her to marry him. But Jim did cut a handsome figure, especially dressed in the togs of the 2nd Division Athletic Team. That may have caught Kathleen's eye, or perhaps it was those soft brown eyes, or the prospect of owning land of one's own, albeit in Australia. Presumably, though, there were some things the convent girl of 18 and the virile athlete of 30 chose not to discuss: Jim had contracted gonorrhea in France and spent ninety-seven days in hospital.

ABOVE **A handsome figure:** Jim Agnew (left) and fellow members of the 2nd Division Athletic Team. The boys trained in England and were granted special leave to compete in Paris. Healthy recreations like sports were favoured by the AIF, and (it was hoped) kept men away from the bars and brothels. *P04284.001 courtesy Australian War Memorial.*

The couple were wed in the parish church at Sutton Veny six months after the Armistice was signed. En route to the service Jim may well have passed the giant impression of the Rising Sun, the symbol of the AIF, that idle diggers had carved into a chalky hillside. Before walking down the aisle, he would have passed the graves of dozens of his countrymen, at rest beneath the steeple of St John's. But for the grace of God, he too might have remained in England.

Kathleen Skinner travelled to Australia in 1920. Jim had come home several months before her on the troopship *Mahana*. Her initial impressions of her new home could not have been very favourable. Heavily pregnant, she suffered in the heat of the Sydney summer, and was obliged to turn to charity for assistance. But Kathleen's story is ultimately one of success and resilience. The young couple successfully farmed the land, and established new orchards near Maroota. Despite Jim being discharged as medically unfit (the family – though not the service record – speaks of Jim being gassed), they survived drought and depression in the interwar period. Jim and Kathleen raised five sons and three daughters. Most extraordinarily, Kathleen was reunited with a member of her family, her sister Lily, yet another escapee from war-torn Europe.

The union of a convent girl from Belgium and a sportsman from Sydney was one of the unexpected consequences of the Great War. But as innumerable 'aftermaths' suggest, there were a great many others.

SOURCES AND FURTHER READING: This story is based on Jim Agnew's service dossier NAA: B2455, AGNEW J J; repatriation file NAA: C138, M89334; a scan of contemporary newspapers; and family reminiscences accessed through Ancestry.com. We were first alerted to Kathleen's existence by her application for a place in the Women's Hospital during her confinement, see Centre for Soldiers' Wives and Mothers casebook, 3 March 1920, Anzac Fellowship of Women papers, 3 March 1920, NLA: MS2864. For further reading on war brides see Rebecca Britt, *Stories of Love and War: From the Collection of the Australian War Memorial* (Chatswood: New Holland, 2010).

BELOW **Carved into the chalky hillside:** The symbol of the AIF etched on the landscape of Sutton Veny. This is one of the ways idle men – impatient for repatriation – passed the time. *Courtesy Bruce Scates.*

ABDUL.
Ted Colles 3rd LHFA.

A lost opportunity

ALFRED MORRIS

Gallipoli has long been remembered as a campaign of lost opportunities. From the failed forcing of the Dardanelles to the bungling of the Landing, the push on the ridges in August and the stalled advance on Suvla, historians and generals alike have wondered if the outcome could ever have been different. Perhaps with more troops, firmer resolution, better timing or better luck, the allies might have succeeded. Whether the Anzacs could have won and what might have happened if they had remains a matter of pointless speculation. What is beyond dispute is that the Centenary of the Landing represents a lost opportunity for Australia.

As far as the official records are concerned, the story of Alfred Morris is rather unremarkable. The young journalist from Geelong enlisted in the first weeks of the war, and departed Australia with the first contingent. Trooper Morris served with the Light Horse Field Ambulance. He saw action at Gallipoli, was evacuated sick to Lemnos, and spent another two years in the deserts of Sinai. Morris was discharged medically unfit in 1917 and returned, nursing on a hospital ship, to Sydney. His service dossier – a bare record of postings and promotions – runs to less than fifty pages.

But as one might have expected of a journalist, Morris kept a diary, and here one finds a rather different story. A series of hastily scribbled notebooks, the diary contains the hallmarks of many soldier narratives. It begins with a lyrical description of the voyage, offers a compelling account of fighting 'and living like rabbits in a hole' at Gallipoli, takes a moment amid the 'awful din' of the guns to sketch a sunset over Samothrace, and records the incessant rumours that ran through that 'small city' of Anzac. Much of it is written with a frankness, intimacy and even an innocence that takes the reader by surprise. There is not much Morris failed to record in his 'beloved little diary', his one 'constant companion' through every day of his war service.[1]

Morris had hoped that the August Offensive would yield a swift and conclusive victory for the Allies; it was – as historians have noted – the last opportunity to 'break

OPPOSITE **Abdul:** Frederick Collis's caricature of the Turk is not so dissimilar to the account in Morris's diary. Collis admires the stoicism and dogged courage of a man he was encouraged to see only as the enemy; so too did Alfred Morris. *ART00046 courtesy Australian War Memorial.*

ABOVE **A sunset over Samothrace:** Morris' diary evokes many scenes such as this. He was acutely aware of the juxtaposition between Gallipoli as a place of horror and suffering but also a site of immense beauty. *Leslie Fraser Standish Hore, 'The Bacchant tolls the knell of parting day', World War I Sketches courtesy State Library of New South Wales.*

out' from the narrow beachhead at Anzac. As ships' guns boomed from the sea, shells whistled overhead and the men prepared to charge, Morris confidently predicted the greatest day in history. But that 'brave effort' ended only in slaughter.

> *Sunday 8th August*
> *It's a hard thing to write these lines as I would like to blot from my memory the thought of this awful day. . . . the casualties on both sides were enormous. We were evacuating the sap and along this all the mules, ammunition and reinforcements had to come up and the Turks knew this and poured shrapnel into it all day. It was Hell. They shelled the beach with the wounded lying [there] helpless as they could not be taken to the ships. We had to go backwards and forwards all day and night with our stretchers stepping over the dead, and being bumped by the mules. How we escaped was miraculous. Bullets went through our clothing, but it got four of our best men two killed and two wounded. Our patients in some cases killed on [their] stretchers. Dead were falling all around us . . .* [2]

Morris snatched only a couple of hours' sleep that night. As dawn broke he found himself in a 'congested trench' surrounded by the dead and dying:

> *we could not get them away, and it was awful to see them suffering. They were lying out in [the open] with the sun beating . . . down on them. We did every thing we could for them, made them tea, Bovril etc but the suffering cannot be described here in words. On the beach it was worse. The hospital ships are full they cannot get them . . . the smell from the dead near the beach is frightful.*[3]

One might have expected these scenes would have hardened Morris – and ruled out any possibility of sympathy for the enemy. But that is not the case. At several points throughout the diary, the young medic admires the 'great stand' made by Johnny Turk, and even the 'plucky' courage of their snipers. Turkish dead lying in the gullies are described as 'an awful sight', the 'effects of our guns' terrible. Morris recorded the case of wounded men, starving and flyblown, being offered water by Ottoman soldiers and shaking their hands. He took time to visit a party of Turkish prisoners on the beach. Amongst them was a woman, a camp follower, he noted, not a combatant – she was a reminder that these men, too, had wives and families they cared for.[4]

Trooper Morris continued to fight the Turk, and to believe in the cause of the British Empire. But there also remained a grudging respect for the man on the other side of the trenches, a recognition that both sides shared the terror of battle and the squalid conditions of war in the desert and at Anzac. In the gruelling advance through Palestine, Morris even risked his own life to save the life of the enemy:

> *On the other side of the redoubt . . . I could see a poor beggar of a Turk badly hit. So with my officer's permission I climbed down to him. [A] sniper fired five shots at me but they all went wide. I reached the poor beggar dressed his badly shattered leg and dragged him into the shade and gave him some morphia to allay his suffering. I left him then for a party of our men waving to me from the hill . . . I found four dead and three badly wounded, one had six wounds on him.*[5]

Compassion is a rare thing in war, and men – even medics – are often brutalised by battle. What makes Morris's diary so remarkable is its steadfast refusal to embrace the common caricature of the 'unspeakable Turk' or to casually dehumanise the enemy. That is not to say he did not feel fear, or hatred, or relief when their side rather than his was the one that suffered. Nor, like most Australian soldiers, was he averse to souvenirring from 'Abdul'. Morris voted for conscription in 1916. He would do whatever he thought necessary to secure an Allied victory.

Morris and his beloved diary came home to Australia. Mindful again that he was a witness to history, his accounts of the war on Gallipoli and in the Sinai were deposited in Sydney's Mitchell Library. And there was something else included in his papers. In August 1915, in one of those 'brutal days'[6] described so well in the diary, Morris found a tiny copy of the Koran clasped in the hands of a dead Turkish officer. A man – not much older than himself – had carried it into battle, just as men on Morris's side carried their Bibles.

And here we come to the lost possibilities of the Anzac Centenary. In 2012, an expert panel of historians advising the Anzac Centenary Board made a unanimous recommendation: Morris's Gallipoli Koran should be repatriated to Turkey. Every other panel advising the Board agreed; the sacred text would be placed again in Turkish hands on the hundredth anniversary of the Landing. This might have been a gesture of reconciliation in a bitterly divided world; it might have signalled tolerance, inclusiveness and diversity; and it might have recognised – as Alfred Morris surely did – that whatever uniform one wears, whatever language one speaks, and whatever religion one professes, we all share a common humanity. Nothing came of that proposal.

BELOW **A gesture of reconciliation in a bitterly divided world:** The Gallipoli Koran taken by Morris and now held in an Australian archive. The return of this sacred text would have signalled the enduring friendship between Australia and Turkey and built a bridge across cultural and religious differences. *Alfred Prichard Kington Morris Papers, ML MS 2886 courtesy State Library of News South Wales.*

SOURCES AND FURTHER READING: This story draws on the service dossier of Alfred Morris NAA: B2455, MORRIS ALFRED and his papers at the State Library of New South Wales ML MS2886. The authors thank Tracey Bradford for her assistance.

The loyalties of the Irish

JOSEPH O'GRADY

BELOW **Another 9th Battalion man:** Victor Colless, who served alongside O'Grady at Gallipoli. O'Grady's body was mutilated within months of joining the war. Although wounded more than once in his five years of service, Victor returned to Australia with limbs intact. *Courtesy Julie Wells.*

The 9th Battalion was the first ashore at Anzac. The rugged promontory where they landed goes by the name of Queensland Point to this day. In the early hours of the morning of 25 April 1915, Private Joseph O'Grady threw his pack down on the shingle, fixed the bayonet to his rifle and disappeared into the scrub.

We don't know how far Private O'Grady advanced that first day at Gallipoli. Nor, in all probability, did he. The maps were next to useless, the terrain unfamiliar and one ridge looked much the same as another in the thin morning light. Some of the men he landed with made it as far as Gun Ridge, the furthest point of the Australian advance. They stood on the crest of the peninsula and looked out across the Dardanelles into Asia and beyond. Then a massive Turkish counterattack turned them back.

At some stage in the advance, O'Grady was severely wounded. Two explosive bullets ploughed into his left arm, shattering the bone. Taken back to the beach, Private O'Grady awaited evacuation. Lying helpless on the shingle he was hit again and again. When medical assistance finally arrived, doctors amputated his arm below the elbow. There was no chance of saving it. Nor could they reach a shard of shrapnel lodged near his heart. O'Grady languished in squalid, overcrowded hospitals in Egypt for a few months before they sent him home.

Home at that stage of O'Grady's life was Brisbane – but it hadn't always been. Joseph O'Grady was born in Limerick, Ireland. He'd served with the 1st Battalion Royal Munster Fusiliers, fought the Boers in South Africa and taken part in the Indian Frontier War before moving to Australia. Then war broke out once more, and he enlisted to fight for Britain again the week the recruiting offices opened in Brisbane.

Economic need may have led O'Grady to enlist, or perhaps an Irish desire for travel and adventure. But whatever the motivation, it is clear that this particular Irishman was all too prepared to serve the British Empire and fight for its interests in distant outposts across the globe. O'Grady wrote with pride about his war service – twelve years in the British Army and three separate campaigns before, as he put it, 'I evidently met my Waterloo' at Anzac.[1]

ABOVE **An Irish love of travel and adventure:** Four men from the 9th Battalion mounted on camels near the Sphinx. A few weeks later, they would name a crumbling headland at Anzac after that remnant from antiquity. Statistically, at least one in every four men in the first AIF was of Irish descent. *Courtesy Julie Wells.*

A different kind of battle awaited O'Grady on his return to Australia. Prior to leaving Brisbane, he had worked splitting timber and was able to clear sixteen shillings a day – a very good wage for an unskilled labourer. But with only one arm, he could no longer swing an axe, and anything but 'light work' was beyond him. O'Grady suffered pains in his chest on any exertion, caused, he claimed, by the bullet 'the doctors have been unable to locate'.[2] A fracture to his skull had brought on a series of epileptic fits; they started with 'a sick hot feeling' followed by seizures and then unconsciousness.[3] O'Grady was granted a partial pension and expected to live on twenty-two shillings a week.

Like most returned men, O'Grady faced continuous medical reassessment and successive attempts to lower his pension. Some doctors were sympathetic – who could dispute the loss of a limb, after all? – but others proved suspicious. Dr Cameron noted his 'habitual' drinking, declaring him 'a fit subject for an inebriate home'. The fracture to his skull may not have been a war injury – no medical officer had noted that particular wound in the chaos on the beach the day O'Grady was struck.

It probably didn't help that O'Grady was Irish. The brutal suppression of the Easter 1916 rebellion in Dublin turned many Irish against the war effort, and much of the Catholic community in Australia was mobilised against conscription. After that, many questioned the loyalty of Irish soldiers, even those like O'Grady who served with the AIF.

Finally, the fact that O'Grady could still earn a little money encouraged some to think that with more effort he could earn a good deal more. '[On] his own admission he is going hawking,' one skeptical doctor noted. '[This] does not seem to me to be a case for medical sustenance.' In the tough postwar economy, even a one-armed man was expected to pay his way.[4]

But Joseph O'Grady's health steadily worsened; the artificial arm issued by the department blistered his skin, and even the weight of an overcoat was painful to bear. His attempts to supplement his pension proved spectacularly unsuccessful. 'Owing to my physical condition I am unable to do any work,' he told the pension board in 1922, '[and my] future prospects of earning are nil.'

By that time, O'Grady had a wife and child to support. He suffered pains in his back and chest, persistent headaches and giddiness, and was obliged to rest after the slightest exertion. In over a year, O'Grady had secured just two weeks' employment, first as a watchman at the exhibition grounds and then as an attendant at the Albert Square lavatory.[5]

We don't know if the indignity of a crippled soldier thrusting his one good arm down a lavatory pan lessened Joseph O'Grady's belief in the British Empire. He was certainly unimpressed by the inconsistent diagnosis from a series of skeptical doctors and angered that the military authorities persisted in calling him 'Lawrence' – a nickname he had acquired in India:

> *I have received no satisfaction whatever . . . [The] treatment that has been meted out to me on my return for the great sacrifices which I have made for the Empire has been very unsatisfactory indeed.* [6]

Nor can we say with any certainty that the 'shooting' pains and constant sense of uselessness helped push O'Grady to drink.

We do know that a man who had served as a soldier for a third of his life, and who'd been amongst the first ashore at Anzac, was struggling with both his physical and mental health by the time the Second World War broke out.

In June 1943, he fell backwards from a tram in Cavendish Street and slammed his head against the gutter. A neighbour helped him home and his wife, Ethel – assuming her husband was drunk – put him promptly to bed.

'[He] was very restless during the night,' she told the police later, 'and groaning a great deal.' The next day she was unable to rouse him; 'she noticed frothy blood coming from his nose' and his heavy irregular breathing 'alarmed her'. Joseph O'Grady was taken by ambulance to the Brisbane General Hospital and died a few hours later.[7]

Ethel claimed her husband suffered much from his wounds and that his death was due to his war service. Indeed the coroner's report tabled on O'Grady stated that the second fracture to his skull ran along the fault lines of the first – that fall from a tram car might not have killed him otherwise. A post-mortem examination extracted the last shards of Gallipoli from his body: a piece of shrapnel several centimetres in diameter.

The Limbless Soldiers' Association wrote to the repatriation authorities to plead the case of Ethel, now yet another war widow. But a drunken Irishman was not the stuff of heroes, especially not as a new generation of men gave their lives for the Empire. The cause of death was recorded as 'Injury to brain and skull, alcoholism', and NOT DUE TO WAR SERVICE was stamped firmly on Private Joseph O'Grady's papers.[8]

The O'Grady story, like many in this book, has only recently come to light. The release of repatriation papers locked away for decades in doctors' filing cabinets has made it possible to chart the postwar lives of those who volunteered in 1914. It reminds us of the aftermath of the Landing, extending our memory of Anzac well beyond that moment

O'Grady and his comrades stumbled ashore. And it complicates family narratives as well.

Joseph O'Grady was John Cronin's great uncle. John grew up – as did Joseph – in a republican part of Ireland. He recalls hearing the stories of Irishmen who fought against the British, rising up in doomed rebellions before finally wresting twenty-six counties of the South free from English rule in 1922. Another of his great uncles, Thomas O'Grady, fought with the Irish Republican Army; Thomas formed a flying squad in Limerick executing British informers and harassing British patrols.

John's grandfather, Stephen O'Grady – brother of both Joseph and Thomas – fought for the British Army in World War One. Upon his return, he joined the army of the Irish Free State. He fought on the side of Michael Collins in the Irish Civil War.

John remembered stories of men who nursed deep wounds and deeper resentments, traumatised by the battles fought on Irish soil. Joseph O'Grady's story adds yet another dimension to that narrative. It reminds us of how the Great War divided families as much as it did nations, and perhaps how an Empire betrayed its own.

In 2015, in honour of his great uncle and all who lost their lives in war, Johnny Cronin recorded a song. It's a song he's sung in the streets of Dublin, perhaps in the same pubs in which his great uncle Joseph O'Grady once sang. 'Tipperary to Fremantle Station' tells the story of a man whose life ended in Australia's first great battle on the Western Front, just as Joseph's life ended – in a way – on that day of the Landing. It is, Johnny tells us, an Irish way of remembering. The chorus of his song cries out against the anonymity of war, lending voice and identity to an unknown man recovered from that mass grave at Fromelles: 'But please don't call me soldier – that's not my name.'

BELOW **Sung in the streets of Dublin:** Songwriter Johnny Cronin strums a guitar in Ireland's capital. His song, 'Tipperary to Fremantle Station', explores the pain, loss and separation of war. *Courtesy Julie Wells.*

SOURCES AND FURTHER READING: This story draws on Joseph O'Grady's service dossier NAA: B2455 O'GRADY JOSEPH; his repatriation file NAA: BP709/1, M198 O'GRADY, JOSEPH (AKA LAWRENCE); and contemporary newspaper reports. For further reading on Irish men who served in the First AIF see Jeff Kildea's pioneering study, *Anzacs and Ireland* (Sydney: UNSW Press, 2007) and for a recent study of sectarian violence in Australia, Robert Bollard, *The Shadow of Gallipoli: The Hidden History of Australia in World War I* (Sydney: New South Publishing, 2013). The authors gratefully acknowledge the assistance of Omid Haidari and Tina Donaghy in accessing Brisbane sources and Dr Julie Wells (granddaughter of Private Victor Colless, another 9th Battalion man who landed with O'Grady on Gallipoli) who facilitated this story. Above all, we acknowledge the generous testimony of John Cronin, Joseph O'Grady's great nephew. You can hear Johnny's tribute to soldiers of the Great War at soundcloud.com/johnny-cronin/tipperary-to-fremantle-stationudio-track?utm_source=soundcloud&utm_campaign=share&utm_medium=email.

A love stronger than pain

BILL KEARSEY

Glencorse Wood is a small patch of forest in the south-west of Belgium. It is also the site of one of the most costly battles on the Ypres Salient, where several days of fierce fighting claimed many thousands of lives. In 1917, artillery shells shattered the woods beyond recognition, reducing ancient trees to skeletons, pitting the ground with craters, laying a landscape to waste. And those same shells battered the bodies of the men who fought there.

Private Bill Kearsey had been on the Belgian front line just sixteen days when he was caught in an artillery barrage near Glencorse Wood. A high explosive shell detonated beside him, killing many of the men around him. For a time, Bill lay bleeding on the battlefield, left for dead by wave after wave of advancing troops. Then Sergeant Jack Gaukroger, a mate from Inverell, chanced to recognise him and despite the speed and chaos of battle paused just a moment to feel for a pulse. They took the young soldier back behind the lines where doctors in the field hospital did all they could. Bill's life was saved, but not his body or his face.

Bill's enlistment portrait shows a remarkably handsome young man. There's a brightness of spirit in his piercing eyes. But on that day in the Third Battle of Ypres, shards of artillery shell drew a deep gash in Bill's forehead and, as the medical case notes tersely put it, 'obliterated' his sinuses. Bill was sent to England and admitted to Queen's Hospital in Sidcup, a specialist facility for those maimed by war. Over the next eighteen months surgeons would operate on Bill's face no fewer than twenty-nine times.

OPPOSITE **Remarkably handsome:** Bill Kearsey on the eve of his departure, a fit and handsome young man from Inverell. Bill thought his injury was not as bad as some of the other 'face cases' – he knew he wasn't as handsome as he'd once been but at least he was better off than some other men. *P10965.001, courtesy Australian War Memorial.*

When Bill got back to Australia in May 1919, he took up a lifelong battle with the scars of war. 'Live out of town, stay in the bush', Bill was told, because life would be easier away from uncomfortable stares and awkward questions. He followed that advice;

like so many other men with devastating facial wounds he hoped to find peace in the isolation of rural life.

After spending four years in hospitals, Bill set out to work the land. In his first year, he sunk most of his money into a block and planted several acres of wheat. Just before it came time to harvest, it rained for ten days solid. The land was flooded and his entire crop was lost. The following year, Bill tried again. This time the season was too dry and nothing grew in the hard brown earth. But the same resolute spirit that kept Bill Kearsey alive in Belgium led him to try again.

With what was left of his savings, Bill bought some scrubby land and a motley flock of sheep. Despite his wounds, he sheared one hundred of them single-handedly and sent a bale and bag of wool into town for sale. The bag never arrived; apparently it had been mislaid. Years of hard work had come to nothing. Like a lot of returned soldiers, almost all much fitter than himself, Bill Kearsey was staring failure in the face.

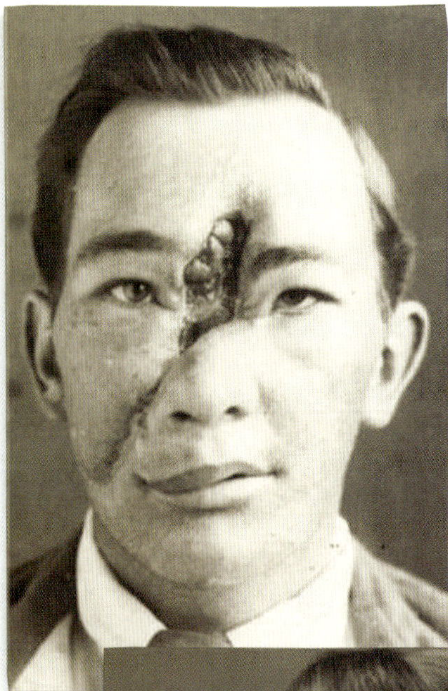

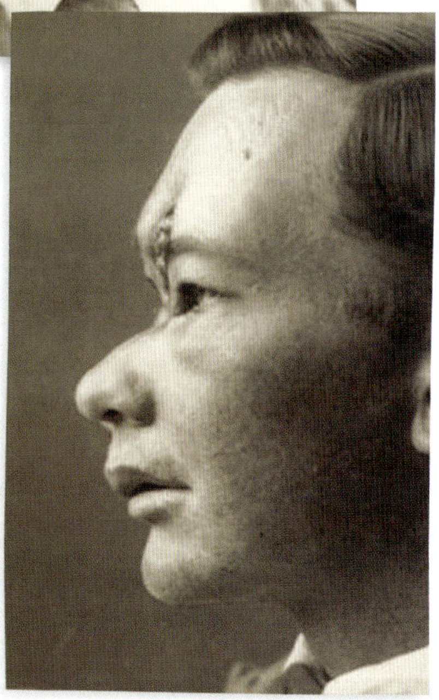

Bill Kearsey suffered severe sinusitis, chronic bronchitis, pain that split his shoulder blades and headaches that reached down into his neck. Often he was laid low for days, fluids leaked from his nose and his eyes, his wounds would sting and ache. These physical wounds were hard enough to deal with but 'nervy men' like Kearsey lived with their memories as well. Often his nights were restless; patchy sleep broken by terrifying dreams. When thunderstorms crashed in night skies Bill cowered, the loud rumbles and cracks of lightening reminded him of the explosion that changed his life. Despite all these setbacks, he persevered.

Farming is taxing in the best of seasons – physically exhausting and emotionally demanding – but Bill never shied away from it. Bill eventually built up an impressive holding, some 15 000 acres, stocked with cattle and sheep. Working the land became his solace, and his property was a source of immense pride.

Bill was a single man for much of his life. Despite his own disabilities he helped care for his elderly parents and his deaf brother, Stan. He certainly never thought of himself as a husband – a man with his face was hardly 'a catch' for anyone. Miss Verdun Frances Mary Forsyth, a young woman on the neighbouring property, disagreed. Though Bill was twenty-five years her senior, there was much she admired in this hard-working, self-sacrificing man. Verdun waited patiently as Bill built up the courage to propose. The couple were married in 1951.

ABOVE **Scars of War:** Bill Kearsey's facial wound. Dedicated surgeons constructed a new bridge for his nose from a bone graft. *William Kearsey Photographs courtesy Royal Australasian College of Surgeons.*

Verdun was named in honour of her French ancestry but her name was also a tribute to thousands of French soldiers who lost their lives in the war. The defence of Verdun, a small city in north-eastern France, claimed more casualties than any other single campaign: here the French Army was bled white by almost incessant fighting. To many of that generation, Verdun's name signified the Great War's sacrifice. She married a man whose face was an even more potent reminder of war's human cost.

In time the couple established a family. In 1960, 14-year-old Peter travelled out to Australia from an English orphanage as part of the Big Brother Movement and found employment on the Kearsey's farm. Bill and Verdun valued such a willing worker but they also enjoyed Peter's company, and the three developed a rare rapport. A few months later, Bill and Verdun formally adopted Peter as their son.

As Bill got older, his war injuries worsened. His aging body struggled to cope with its wounds. Life for Bill became what Verdun called 'an indurence [sic] test' and by the 1960s he was incapable of 'any useful work'. Bill's sight deteriorated dramatically until eventually he couldn't read or write and Verdun worried that it meant he was 'cut off from things'. As was the case in many homes of returned men, the matriarch took control of managing the household. Verdun drove her husband wherever he needed to be taken, corresponded on his behalf and guided Bill's hand into place when a signature was required. She also became his tireless advocate. Time and again, Verdun took issue with decisions of the repatriation authorities that she saw as cruel or arbitrary. Surely a man who had given his face and his health for his country was a 'deserving case'?[1]

Verdun died in 1969. Two years later Bill passed away and was buried alongside her in Inverell Cemetery. A soldier mauled by the artillery of the Great War died an '80-year-old diabetic whose kidneys packed in'.[2]

Peter Kearsey remembers his father as an incredibly generous man. That generosity of spirit took many different forms: in his will, Bill left substantial donations to the Red Cross, the church, Legacy and the Blind Society. And he was a man who, despite all he had suffered, was always there for his family. Bill provided for his wife and son for as long as his failing body would allow. It was a love far stronger and more enduring than the pain he suffered.

Bill Kearsey reminds us of a quiet type of courage; one not always noted in the heroic narratives of Anzac. Neither his war, nor his injury, came to define him; he became a farmer, a husband and a father despite all the odds. Today, life has returned to Glencorse Wood in Belgium. A green forest grows where once a terrible battle raged. Perhaps nature's resilience mirrors the resilience of this truly remarkable individual, a survivor of the Salient, and a man who built a new life for himself from the wasteland left by war.

BELOW **A loving marriage:** Bill and Verdun Kearsey on their wedding day. Their family was completed when they adopted Peter in 1960. *P10965.003 courtesy Australian War Memorial.*

SOURCES AND FURTHER READING: This story draws on William Kearsey's service dossier NAA: B2455, KEARSEY WILLIAM; and his repatriation files NAA: C138, R55422; NAA: C138, M55422; NAA: C138, H55422; NAA: C138, C55422. For further reading on facial injuries of the Great War, and a close study of Bill Kearsey, see Kerry Neale 'Without the Faces of Men: Disfigured Great War Veterans of Britain and the Dominions' (PhD thesis, University of New South Wales, 2015); and for a study of the surgeons of the Great War see Elizabeth Milford and David Watters (eds), *Anzac Surgeons of Gallipoli* (Melbourne: Royal Australasian College of Surgeons, 2015). The authors thank Deb Tout-Smith and Museum Victoria for their assistance. The authors also warmly thank Peter and Dessie Kearsey for sharing their memories of Bill.

A labour of love

WILLIAM KNOX

This is the final story in this book. And it might have been told in a dozen different ways.

William Johnstone Knox's story might have been about duty. Knox had served as a lieutenant in the Australian Field Artillery prior to the outbreak of war. He felt a deep obligation to serve and boarded a troopship a few months after his first – and only – child was born. Bill Knox left a young wife and his baby daughter behind him, a promising career in business, and political interests as well. Like hundreds of young men who put themselves forward, what he saw as his duty – to his country and his King – outweighed any thought of personal safety. Knox was a man destined to go to war.

By the same token, Knox's story might have been about privilege. The son of a successful businessman and the first Federal Member for Kooyong, he was raised at 'Ranfurlie', a stately home in East Malvern, one of Melbourne's wealthiest suburbs. He was educated at Scotch College, one of Melbourne's most expensive and elite 'public' schools. He gave his address on his attestation papers as the Melbourne Club, Melbourne's most exclusive private club. But Bill Knox was also a man who made his own way in the world. Expected to fend for himself the moment his education was completed, he struggled to keep his wife and child in a manner thought appropriate for middle-class society. Knox was not one of the idle well-to-do, but a man of enterprise, integrity and industry; a gentleman who went to fight an ungentle war.

Knox's story could have been about endurance. He would train in Egypt, fight on the slopes of Gallipoli, see action in France at Fromelles, Pozières, Messines, and along the Ypres Salient. An artillery officer, he went with his guns into the thick of the fighting. Teams of horses laboured to drag them into position, caked (he wrote) in frozen mud or trudging across desert sands. Bill Knox would witness some of the war's most savage fighting on the peninsula and in Flanders and the Somme. Gallipoli was

ABOVE **What he saw as his duty:** Bill Knox cuts a fine figure in his uniform. He would look very different after just a year's campaigning. *Courtesy Kate Baillieu.*

just one of several punishing campaigns: 'we only have 500 acres at Anzac and they can pump shells into any part of it'.[1]

And Knox's story might have been about courage. In August 1917, his battery came under heavy shellfire from enemy lines. 'At great personal risk from exploding ammunition' he extinguished a fire threatening to engulf his position. He was awarded the Military Medal for 'conspicuous gallantry' in the field.[2]

Like many of the stories in this book, Knox's might also have been about loss. He was killed in the push on Passchendaele in 1917. It might have been about pain and injury; his legs and chest were eviscerated by a high explosive shell and it would take the young man over twenty-four hours to die. Or it might have been about remembrance. William Johnstone Knox was commemorated in church, school and community; his name was carved in the polished blackwood of Melbourne Stock Exchange's Honour Roll; almost a hundred years after his death, he is still held up as an example to us all.

Bill Knox's story is all these things and more. But it is something far more intimate as well. All said and done, this story is about love.

Bill Knox loved the men who served beside him. It was not just the enduring friendship forged with fellow officers, decent chaps he shared a tent or a dugout with, 'a really good lot those fellows'.[3] Far from home, the young Knox acted as a surrogate father for the men who served beneath him. He cared for their welfare, wrote to their families, even brought them extra rations. And nothing was more hurtful to him than the loss of one of his boys. Knox wrote to his wife at the beginning of 1917:

> *I lost two of my best men yesterday Feltham and Robinson (the latter the little chap I asked you to send some foodstuffs to). They got blown up by a shell when returning from down near front line yesterday. Feltham was one of the best fellows in the world – cheery and popular with everyone. Young Robinson I told you about before – It just so chanced that it was a sticky job and I picked two of the best for it and lost them – I am very sad about it and a bit upset & nervy tonight – I sent out & got them brought in to bury near the Battery. I couldn't get a Padre so I had to read the burial service myself. The most trying thing I have ever done and more so as we were under heavy shellfire at the time – I was very fond of those two lads and wanted to do what I could for them properly – Fritz just commenced to hot us up with heavy stuff though I had tried to pick a quiet time . . . I had just commenced to read the service when we got it right and left . . . This is the way two fine brave lads went out and I am very sad and had to write their people tonight . . . It is desperately cold snowing for four days & now frozen hard and an icy wind blowing that almost cuts one in half . . .*[4]

BELOW **Putting himself forward:** Bill Knox leads his men through the streets of Port Melbourne en route to the transport ships. The streetscape of the town is still recognisable today. *Courtesy Kate Baillieu.*

ABOVE **A love that sustained them:** Diana, Mildred and Bill Knox in a stretch of woodlands in the south of England. At the time the photograph was taken Diana was barely two years old. Mother and daughter had crossed the world to be reunited with Bill. They shared just a few weeks together before being separated – forever – by war. *Courtesy Kate Baillieu.*

OPPOSITE **A child he never really came to know:** Bill watches his 'Bubby kins' test the water at Bognor. From the seaside resort you could just about hear the guns booming from across the channel. This was Bill's last leave. *Courtesy Kate Baillieu.*

Knox loved his baby daughter, Diana, a child he would never really come to know. He addressed her as his 'Bubby Kins' and always carried a photograph of her. In the close world of the trenches, he would stare at that image for hours on end, willing it somehow to life: 'I love that lovely little snap of her. The really nice one – with her mouth all pursed up in readiness for a smile and looking a picture of mischief.'[5]

And he loved his wife, a love that sustained him through the chaos and brutality erupting all around him. Throughout the war, Bill Knox wrote to Mildred on an almost daily basis. He described the horrors of the battlefield, the terror of the fighting, but also the love that kept him sane. Every letter to 'Mim' brims with intimacy and affection. She was his 'dearest girl', his 'dear old sweetheart', 'the most splendid perfect wife'.[6] Mim would read every letter time and again, put them carefully away, treasure their presence – that reminder of him – in her household. And in 1916, at great risk and expense, Mim and Diana travelled all the way to England. They spent a few precious weeks with Bill on 'Blighty leave' from France. The three of them walked the pebbled beach at Bognor; the only memory Diana had of her father was being lifted high up on his shoulders in the crisp sea air.

Within a matter of months of that visit, Bill was dead. A lifetime of grieving lay before Mim; like thousands bereaved by war she would not marry again. Diana would grow up without a father – as would thousands of other children, in countries all over the world.

When Diana died at the age of 93, her daughter and granddaughter carried her ashes to Belgium. Diana's ashes were tenderly placed in her father's grave, as was her wish. Kate, Diana's daughter, found Flanders a strangely peaceful place, a once battered landscape brimming with crops of barley and wheat. On a 'perfect summers day' she walked across green fields that had swallowed up a generation, and stood near the place where her grandfather had been killed. Kate plucked a few pieces of metal from the soil at her feet, shards of artillery shell dislodged by a farmer's plough. 'It seemed as though the war was still growling beneath my feet, rumbling on just below the surface.'[7]

Bill's letters to Mim survive, treasured and preserved by Kate to this day. They are a fragile record of a love that bound three people together and of the madness that tore them apart.

SOURCES AND FURTHER READING: This story is based on the service dossier of William Johnstone Knox NAA: B2455, KNOX WILLIAM JOHNSTONE and his family papers. The authors gratefully acknowledge the assistance of Kate Baillieu in accessing the latter. For an excellent account of Passchendaele and the campaign that claimed Knox's life see Robin Prior and Trevor Wilson, *Passchendaele: The Untold Story* (New Haven: Yale University Press, 2002). The diary of the 13th Field Artillery Brigade AWM4 13/40 informed this account. The authors look forward to Kate Baillieu's publication of her grandfather's letters and correspondence, and thank Kevin Fewster for alerting them to the importance of the same. Fewster's grandfather served alongside Bill Knox. We also thank Piet Chielens of In Flanders Fields Museum.

ACKNOWLEDGEMENTS

With every one of the 100 Stories, we feel we have one hundred people to thank. First and foremost we would like to thank the descendants and relatives of all the individuals examined in this book who entrusted us with their testimony and shared their family stories with courage and intimacy. In a way, this collection is an act of collaboration, told at the intersection of memory and history, and this book is all the richer for that. Individuals are warmly acknowledged alongside the stories of their families.

We have been especially privileged to hear Indigenous stories, spoken and recorded on both sides of the Tasman. Individuals and communities are, again, acknowledged in individual chapters but we also thank Monty Soutar (Manatū Taonga/ Ministry for Culture and Heritage, Aotearoa/New Zealand) and Wesley Enoch (Queensland Theatre Company and co-creator of the brilliant play 'Black Diggers').

As with any historical study, archives underpin this book. A number of libraries, archives, galleries and museums generously facilitated our research, most notably the National Archives of Australia, the National Library of Australia, Museum Victoria, all the state libraries and archives cited herein and a host of historical and heritage societies at a national, state and local level. Particular thanks are due to Anne-Marie Conde, Louise Doyle, Sean Debenham, Jean-Pierre Grenade, Kate Naughton and Shaun Rohrlach at the National Archives of Australia; Sue Roberts and her helpful staff at the State Library of Victoria; Martine Botha and her team at the State Library of Victoria Foundation; Chris Yeats of State Records New South Wales; Roger Lee and Andrew Richardson of the Army History Unit; Gina Pickering of the National Trust; Janda Gooding and Matt Trinca of the National Museum of Australia; Tracy Bradshaw and Elise Edmonds of the State Library of New South Wales; Linda Ferguson, Kerry Neale, Ricky Phillips, Susie Raymond, Meleah Hampton and Tim Sullivan of the Australian

War Memorial; Moira Drew at the Australian Red Cross; Cameron Hocking, Deb Tout-Smith and Linda Spoule of Melbourne Museum; Jillian Kohlhagen at Charles Sturt University Regional Archives; James Dexter of the National Anzac Centre in Albany; Ian Burke and Elizabeth Milford of the Royal Australasian College of Surgeons and Stephen Herrin of the Rare Books Collection at Monash University.

The 100 Stories is a trans-Tasman project and we are especially grateful to the archives and individuals who assisted our work in Aotearoa/New Zealand. We have consulted the rich holdings of the Alexander Turnbull Library, the Auckland War Memorial Museum and the Kippenberger Military Archive and Research Library; and we are especially indebted to Sally Carlton, Stephen Clark, David Grant, Denise Hill, Karen Hunter, Jock Philips, Chris Pugsley, Barry and Athena Reay and Kerry Taylor for their encouragement and support.

However central nation is to the Anzac narrative, Australian and New Zealand forces fought for the British Empire in the Great War. We are indebted to the British Library, the National Archives, Kew, the British Red Cross, the Imperial War Museum, London and the Liddell Hart Centre for Military Archives at King's College London. We also thank the Australian High Commission, Lucy Noakes of the University of Brighton, Martin Evans of the University of Sussex, Kevin Fewster of the National Maritime Museum and Carl Bridge, Ian Henderson and Simon Sleight at the Menzies Centre for Australian Studies at King's College London for hosting our research. A special thanks to Professor Ed Byrne, AC, Principal of KCL and our former Vice Chancellor at Monash who supported this project from its inception.

Key commemorative organisations have also aided our research. They include the Anzac Memorial (Sydney), the Commonwealth War Graves Commission, Legacy, the Returned & Services League (RSL), the Shrine of Remembrance (Melbourne), the War Widows' Guild, the War Widows' Association, the Australian War Memorial, the Soldier's Memorial Avenue, the Family and Friends of the First AIF, Friends of the Fifteenth Brigade, the students, veterans, politicians, teachers and support staff of the Victorian Premier's Spirit of Anzac Tour, and the Office of Australian War Graves and the Department of Veterans' Affairs. We thank those members of the Anzac Centenary Advisory Board who spoke out in support of this project; the Religious Society of Friends, Val and Mary Noone and all who promoted this project and helped to found the Peace Coalition in Melbourne. Special thanks are due to Serdar Baycan and Elizabeth Grigg who helped to raise the Seeds of Friendship Memorial in Melbourne acknowledging Turkey's and Australia's common loss in war.

In Aotearoa/New Zealand we thank the National Memorial in Wellington, the Auckland War Memorial Museum, and the New Zealand Returned and Services' Association. Further afield we owe a great debt to the Commonwealth War Graves Commission who care for the graves of servicemen and women killed overseas. The war dead are remembered in a different but no less important way by Jay Winter and Annette Becker of the Historial de la Grande Guerre, Péronne and Piet Chielens and Annick Vandenbilcke, of In Flanders Fields Museum, Ieper.

Monash University and the National Centre for Australian Studies hosted this

project. Alice McConnell worked tirelessly on this book and we owe her a great deal, Damien Williams and Catherine Tiernan provided valuable research assistance, Corrie McKee, Stuart Lees, Gerhard Zelenka, Tom Chandler, Rick Laird and Adrian Devey offered all manner of technical support. Mark Warren, Rob Pignolet, Lynne Butler and John Blyth produced excellent video material for the greater 100 Stories project. We also acknowledge the support of our Dean, Professor Rae Frances, and our President and Vice-Chancellor, Professor Margaret Gardner, AO. Monash University is a centre of World War I studies and all the participants in the History of Anzac Day project are warmly acknowledged. In addition to the individuals named above, we thank John Arnold, Frank Bongiorno, Martin Crotty, Robin Gerster, Keir and Andrew Reeves, Tim Soutphommasane, Peter Stanley, Graham Seal and Cora Trevarthen. Thanks are also due to Sharon Mascall-Dare, Russell Fewster, Brad West, Claire Woods and the cluster of scholars centred around the 'Narratives of War' research project in Adelaide.

Although this project was independently funded by Monash University, it inevitably drew on research materials generated by other projects. In particular we thank the Australian Research Council and our partner investigators State Records New South Wales, the Commonwealth Department of Veterans' Affairs and several of the cultural agencies cited above. The History of Anzac Day is an international project and we acknowledge our Turkish colleagues at Çanakkale Onsekiz Mart University, in particular Muhammet Erat, Azer Banu Kemaloğlu, Nurcan Şen and Mehmet Fatih Yavus.

We thank the formidable cast of historians whose scholarship informed and enriched this book. Most are named in individual chapters but we also signal our particular thanks to Melanie Oppenheimer, Ross McMullin, Jackie Huggins, John Maynard and Mick Dodson (all of whom served on the Anzac Centenary Advisory Board); Bill Gammage, Rosalie Triolo, Nathan Wise, and Ken Inglis, who first inspired our interest in Anzac. We could not have understood medical reports in several stories of repatriation without the specialist knowledge and insight of Dr Amshuman Rao, A.C. McFarlane AO, and Michael Sim; Mike Roper, Alistair Thomson and Marina Larsson also informed our reading of the same. The memory of the Great War has strayed far from the hands of professional historians. We thank Garry Snowden of the Conservation Volunteers, Lambis Englezos who did so much to recover the stories of Fromelles and Jim Claven and Tassos Ioannides who aided our research into Lemnos and Tom Keneally, whose literature has brought history to life. And we thank Nick Hughes and James Jacobs of Xavier College, Melbourne for their insights and advice. The usual caveat applies: the interpretation of these stories is our own.

ABOVE, OPPOSITE AND PREVIOUS PAGE **Rich holdings:** Items from the Military History collection of the Melbourne Museum and the State Library of Victoria. Material artifacts, oral histories and written archives inform this book. *Courtesy Melbourne Museum and State Library of Victoria.*

The book is enriched by the photography of Michael Coleman, Patrick Daly, Tina Donaghy, Romain Fathi, George Gemmill, Rohan Gerrard, Tania and Garry Hackett, Mike and Roz Goodwin, David Little, Phillip Marshall, John Savage and Nigel Starck. We thank Omid Haidari and Stephanie Woodbridge for accessing files interstate and Judy, Megan and Neil Travers for their encouragement and support.

The 100 Stories have a life beyond this book. They are a teaching resource for secondary school students; a digital history available online, a free university course delivered through Future Learn (UK), and are now being reconfigured (thanks to Paul Grabowsky, Lisa Mitchell and Ann Moir) as part of an orchestral performance. We acknowledge the work of all those who have extended and reinvented these stories and thank the many museums, galleries, archives, clubs and community groups who have exhibited these stories. It was our great privilege to present the stories at meetings of Rotary; the Lyceum, Athenaeum and Australian Clubs, the City of Sydney Historical Association, the History Teachers' Association, the History Council of New South Wales, the Gallipoli Memorial Club and the Family History Association. Particular thanks are due to Denis Baguley, Jean McAuslan and Neil Sharkey of Victoria's Shrine of Remembrance, the first institution to exhibit our stories.

The book itself was made possible by Penguin Random House. We thank our publisher Andrea McNamara who first recognised its potential, our ever patient editor, Andrea Davison, Laura Thomas our designer, and all the remarkable Penguin team.

Finally, we acknowledge the friends, family members and partners who stood by us in the making of the 100 Stories project. We extend our heartfelt thanks to Rae Frances, Alex Kiri Scates Frances, Will Scates Frances and Bob Scates; Tom Maher, Kim, Syd, Melissa Wheatley and Ben Torney; Greg Whiddon, Greg, Sally and Luke James. Laura's beautiful baby, Rose, was born just as this book began. For all of us, she represents the future so many men and women of the Great War generation were denied.

NOTES

HAROLD CANDY *(pp. 1–2)*

1 NAA: B2455, CANDY H J.
2 *Advertiser*, 4 August 1923.

LIZZIE ARMSTRONG *(pp. 3–5)*

1 *Register*, 5 February 1926.
2 *Daily News*, 17 March, 1920.
3 *British Australian and New Zealander*, 31 March 1927; *Sydney Mail*, 24 December 1927.
4 *Queenslander*, 6 November 1926.

BRIAN LYALL *(pp. 6–9)*

1 Lyall Papers, SLV, MS 10132.
2 Minutes of the Proceedings of the 41st Meeting of the Imperial War Graves Comission (IWGC), 17 January 1922, NAA: A2909 /2 A453/1/3.

DOUGLAS GRANT *(pp. 10–13)*

1 'The Story of Douglas Grant, the Black Scotsman' by John Thompson and Brian Hungerford [ABC radio feature script; box c21] NAA: SP1297/2.
2 ibid.
3 ibid.
4 ibid.
5 Letter from Douglas Grant to the Deputy Commissioner of Repatriation, October, 1927, and letter from Douglas Grant to the Deputy Commissioner of Repatriation, 4 March, 1928, NAA: C138, C70396 DOUGLAS GRANT.
6 Report from Medical Superintendent, Callan Park Mental Hospital 15 March, 1939, ibid.
7 Memorandum for O.I.C. Pensions Department, 22 October, 1948, ibid.
8 'The Story of Douglas Grant, the Black Scotsman' by John Thompson and Brian Hungerford [ABC radio feature script; box c21] NAA: SP1297/2.
9 ibid.

NOBLE BLACK *(pp. 14–15)*

1 Inspector's Reports, Soldier Settlement file, State Records NSW: 12/7421.
2 Medical file, 1 August 1931, NAA: C138/4, C29645 BLACK NA.
3 ibid.
4 Medical files, 25 August, 1 September 1931, ibid.
5 Personal History notes, Callan Park Mental Hospital, ibid.

NARELLE HOBBES *(pp. 16–17)*

1 Melanie Oppenheimer, *Narrelle: Nursing for Empire*, ABC Radio Hindsight Program, 28 March 2004.

PETER CHIRVIN *(pp. 18–21)*

1 *London Gazette,* 17 June 1919.
2 Witness statements at Court of Inquiry, 16 April 1919 NAA: B2455, CHIRVIN P.
3 *Port Pirie Recorder*, 28 April 1919.
4 Peter Chirvin to his mother Natalia Vassilievna, 23 June 1916, NAA: B2455, CHIRVIN P.

ALFRED SHARP *(pp. 22–25)*

1 *Box Hill Reporter,* 12 August 1916.
2 *Geelong Advertiser,* 12 September 1917.
3 A.T. Sharp to A. Fisher, 19 March 1917, NAA: A11489/1 2350/2.
4 *Williamstown Chronicle,* 16 December 1922.
5 *British Australasian,* 28 March 1918.
6 *British Australasian*, 17 April 1919; reports in the British Press that many pilgrims were Australasians 'on their way to visit the graves of soldier sons in France and Flanders', *Manchester Guardian*, 26 April 1921.
7 *Nottingham Journal*, 18 April 1921; *Cardiff Western Mail,* 25 April 1921; *British Australasian*, 17 April 1919, 14, 21 April 1921, 6 April 1922.
8 *British Australasian,* 1 May 1919; 21 April, 12 May 1921.
9 *Burnie Advocate,* 5 December 1922.

THE CARMAN BROTHERS *(pp. 26–27)*

1 NAA:B2455 CARMAN CC; NAA:B2455 CARMAN RC; NAA:B2455 CARMAN DW; Red Cross Wounded and Missing file AWM IDRL/0428 Clement Carman.

JAMES NEWMAN DANN *(pp. 28–29)*

1 Record of evidence, 17 September 1917, NAA: C138/4, C314427, DANN JN.
2 Soldier Settlement file, State Records NSW: 12/7293.
3 Doctor's notes, 16 May 1921, NAA: C138/4, C314427, DANN JN.
4 Soldier Settlement file, State Records NSW: 12/7293.

EMILY LUTTRELL *(pp. 30–31)*

1 Emily Luttrell to Minister of Defence, 23 June 1922, NAA: A1608, F27/1/7 Part 1.
2 Emily Luttrell to Minister of Home Affairs, 16 October 1922, ibid.
3 Emily Luttrell to the Minister of Home Affairs 6 March 1923, ibid.
4 Memo to Prime Minister, ibid.

ROWLAND LORDING *(pp. 32–33)*

1 *Fielding Star*, 19 May 1917.
2 ibid.
3 ibid
4 A. Tiveychoc (Rowland Lording), *There and Back: The Story of an Australian Soldier 1915–1935* (Sydney: Halstead Publishing, 1935), p. 240.

OLIVE PINK *(pp. 34–36)*

1 *Sydney Morning Herald*, 19 August 1932; B. Clark, *Our Formidable Olive*, Outback Voices website, www.outbackvoices.com/our-formidable-olive/our-formidle-olive accessed 1 May 2013.
2 *Sydney Morning Herald*, 16 May 1935.
3 Statement by Private William Hart, NAA: B2455 SOUTHERN HAROLD ALFRED.
4 Michael Jackson, *At Home in the World* (Durham: Duke University Press, 1995), p. 108.
5 Reg Harris, Olive Muriel Pink [Recollections of Miss Pink's personal life] *Bulletin* (Olive Pink Society), vol. 6, no. 2, 1994, p. 9.

WILLIAM BROWN *(pp. 37–39)*

1 Beatrice Brown to the Chief Officer of Pensions, 4 February 1920, NAA: C138/4, C29645.
2 Frances Brown to Pensions Department, 1 October 1922, ibid.
3 Frances Brown to Pension Office, 1923, ibid.
4 ibid.

ADAM WARDROP *(pp. 40–41)*

1 NAA: B2455, WARDROP ADAM GLADSTONE.
2 Letter from Lieutenant Colonel T.G. Wilson to Minnie Wardrop, 10 May 1919, ibid.

NORMAN GIBBINS *(pp. 42–45)*

1 Red Cross Wounded and Missing file AWM 1DRL/0428 Captain Norman Gibbins.
2 Violet Gibbins to Base Records Melbourne, 11 August 1916, NAA: B2455, GIBBINS N.
3 This was the philosophy she pursued before embarking on business ventures in New South Wales, advertisement for Cambridge Ladies' College, *Brisbane Courier*, 13 January 1904.
4 Violet Gibbins to Dr Mary Booth, undated letter (April 1921), Anzac Fellowship of Women Papers, NLA MS2864.
5 *Cairns Post*, 28 August 1935.

BERNARD HAINES *(pp. 46–49)*

1 NAA: B2455 HAINES C; NAA: B73, R14400.

HENRY HIGGINS *(pp. 50–54)*

1 Henry Higgins to Professor Frankfurter, 27 December 1918, Higgins Papers, NLA MS 2525, Folder 1; Nettie Palmer, *Henry Bournes Higgins: A Memoir* (London: Harrap, 1931), p. 233.
2 Correspondence Mervyn Higgins to his mother, Higgins Papers, NLA MS1057, Series 3, Box 7, see in particular letters dated 30 November 1914; 3, 9, 12 June 1916; 13 and 18 July 1915; 17 December 1916.
3 See correspondence between Henry Higgins and Major McClean 23, 28 and 30 January 1917, 28, 31 March 1917, 9, 12 April 1917 and Higgins to Senator Pearce, 31 March 1917, NAA: B2455, HIGGINS M B CAPTAIN.
4 See correspondence from Henry Higgins to the Imperial War Graves Commission, 25 February 1925, NAA: B2455, HIGGINS M B CAPTAIN; diary entry for 20 January 1924, Higgins Papers, NLA MS1057 Series 3.
5 Henry Higgins 'The grave at El Magdabha', Higgins Papers; see also diary entry for 20 January 1924, NLA MS1057 Series 3.

JOYCE MCGRATH *(pp. 55–57)*

1 NAA: B73, H12398.
2 ibid.
3 Jan Harper, *Plaster and Paint: John Colquhoun, Orthopaedic Surgeon and His Patient, Joyce McGrath, Portrait Painter* (North Melbourne: Arcadia, 2007).
4 ibid.

ALEXANDER MCKINNON *(pp. 58–60)*

1 NAA: B2455, MCKINNON A.
2 Major J.W. Pugh to Base Records, 19 April 1922, ibid.
3 Base Records to Mrs M McKinnon, 17 May 1922, ibid.

SAMUEL MELLOR *(pp. 61–64)*

1 NAA: B2455, MELLOR RICHARD.

HENRY TOVELL *(pp. 65–67)*

1 Norman Ellison, *Flying Matilda* (Sydney: Angus and Robertson, 1957).
2 ibid.
3 ibid.
4 Priest's sermon at service for Henri Tovell in his home town, AWM PR87/199.

FRANK WILKINSON *(pp. 68–69)*

1 Frank Wilkinson citation for Military Medal, 20 July 1917, Wilkinson Family Papers, courtesy Jill Fradd.
2 *Donald Mail*, 27 November 1917.
3 Soldier Settlement file, PROV VPRS5714, unit 1473, 4147/12.
4 Coroner's Inquest Frank, Elizabeth and Isabella Wilkinson, PROV VPRS24, 1927/1017.
5 ibid.

ETTIE ROUT *(pp. 70–73)*

1 Ettie Rout, *Two Years in Paris* (London: E Hornibrook, 1923), p. 49.
2 Letters from Women's Reform League, 2 February 1919 and YMCA Wellington, 24 December 1919, NAA: A1, 1920/3508 Ettie Rout – Question of admission to Australia.
3 Ettie Rout, *Two Years in Paris*, p. 11.

GEORGE IRWIN *(pp. 74–77)*

1 Sarah Irwin to Vera Deakin, 16 March 1917, Red Cross Wounded and Missing file AWM 1DRL/0428 George Roy Irwin.
2 *Sydney Mail*, 20 October 1926; 25 April 1931.

W.A. WINDEYER *(pp. 78–81)*

1 *Sydney Morning Herald*, 2 August 1922; *The Farmer and Settler*, 4 August 1922.
2 *Brisbane Courier*, 15 October 1921; *British Australasian*, 20 January, 29 September 1921; *Adelaide Register*, 15.October 1921; *Sydney Morning Herald*, 7 February 1920, 10, 26 October 1921.

ROYCE BAESEJOU *(pp. 82–84)*

1 *Albany Advertiser*, 27 April 1921.
2 *Albany Advertiser*, 12 August 1916.
3 *Official Report of the War Office Committee of Enquiry into Shell-shock* (London: His Majesties Stationary Office, 1922), p. 3.
4 *West Australian*, 24 May 1918.
5 *Albany Advertiser*, 20 September 1948.

ALLAN WHITTAKER *(pp. 85–88)*

1 *Argus,* 26 August 1915.
2 Coroner's Inquest Allan Whittaker, PROV VPRS24, 1929 428.
3 *Labor Call*, 8 November 1928.

ETHEL CAMPBELL *(pp. 89–93)*

1 Ethel Campbell, *The Life of Sam Campbell* (Durban, Natal: Singleton & Williams, 1938), p. 361.
2 ibid, p. 363.
3 ibid, p. 361.
4 ibid, p. 370.
5 *Kalgoolie Miner*, 27 March 1942.
6 Ethel Campbell, *The Life of Sam Campbell,* p.363
7 ibid, p. 387.

CORNELIUS DANSWAN *(pp. 94–96)*

1 Memo dated 23 July 1926, NAA: C138 R54054, C K DANSWAN.
2 *Murrurundi Times and Liverpool Plains Gazette*, 14 September, 1906.
3 Medical notes dated 21 May 1926; examinations by Dr Willock dated 1 June 1926, NAA: C138, R54054, C K DANSWAN.
4 Medical report dated 2 September 1926, ibid.
5 Medical report dated 21 May 1926, ibid.
6 Memorandum dated 13 December 1926; Flora Danswan to Director Lands Department, 24 March 1928; [undated] 22 March 1929, Soldier Settlement file, State Records NSW: 12/7052.

TOM ELLIOTT *(pp. 97–99)*

1 Ross McMullin, *Farewell Dear People* (Brunswick: Scribe Publishing, 2012), p. 113.
2 Red Cross Wounded and Missing file AWM 1DRL/0428 Major Thomas Patrick Elliott.
3 Letter from Pompey Elliott, cited in *Farewell Dear People*, p. 157.
4 Mary Elliott, Letter to Major Lean, 14 May 1918, NAA: B2455, ELLIOT TP.
5 Mary Elliott, cited in *Farewell Dear People*, p. 165.
6 Letter from Mary Elliott, cited in *Farewell Dear People*, p. 160.
7 Mary Elliott to Defence Minister, cited in *Farewell Dear People*, p. 167.

VERNON MULLIN *(pp. 100–103)*

1 *Argus*, 24 November 1950.
2 Sir Arthur Pearson to Mrs Mullin, letter printed in *West Australian*, 30 June 1917.
3 Sir Arthur Pearson, *Victory over Blindness: How it Was Won by the Men of St Dunstan's and How May Win It* (New York: George H Doran Company, 1919), p. 246.
4 ibid, p. 116.

JAMES FERGUSON *(pp. 104–105)*

1 Harry Gullett, 'Appendix – The Egyptian Rebellion in 1919, Volume VII - The Australian Imperial Force in Sinai and Palestine, 1914–1918' (10th edition), *Official History of Australia in the War of 1914–1918* (Sydney: Angus and Robertson, 1941), p. 793.
2 10th Australian Light Horse Regiment unit diary, March 1919 AWM4/10/15.

THE MAYNARDS *(pp. 106–108)*

1 'Ethnology: Tasmanian Tribes', *Queenslander*, 26 April 1924.
2 Lyndall Ryan, *The Aboriginal Tasmanians* (Sydney: Allen and Unwin, 1996), p. 243.
3 *Mercury*, 23 February 1931.

MAUD BUTLER *(pp. 109–112)*

1 *Weekly Times,* 1 January, 1916.
2 ibid.
3 ibid.
4 Intelligence Report, Melbourne, 25 December 1915, 'Miss Maud Butler, stowaway' NAA: MP/16/1 1915/3/1785.
5 ibid; *Singleton Argus,* 11 March 1916.
6 *Punch,* 11, May, 1916.
7 *Punch*, 1 May 1916; *Weekly Times*, 1 January 1916; *Farmer and Settler*, 31 December 1915.
8 *Soldier,* 5 January 1916.

CAROLINE GILBERT *(pp. 113–114)*

1 RC Devine to Caroline Gilbert, undated, in NAA: B2455, GILBERT RW.
2 We owe the phrase 'some gallant lie' to Siegfried Sassoon's poem 'The Hero', Collected Poems, (London: Faber & Faber, 1961).
3 Red Cross Wounded and Missing files, IDRL/0428 Private Albert Henry Gilbert.
4 Caroline Gilbert to Officer in Charge, Base Records, 10 February 1922 in NAA B2455, GILBERT ALBERT HENRY.
5 *Western Mail*, 7 August 1919; Caroline Gilbert to Officer in Charge, Base Records, 1 March 1918 in NAA: B2455, GILBERT ALBERT HENRY.

CHARLES KINGSTON *(pp. 115–118)*

1 John Oxenham, 'Discoverer of Missing Men: Major Allen of the A.W.G.S.' pp. 1-2, 4, NAA: A458/1 R337/7; *British Australasian*, 16 March 1922.
2 Statement and Evidence from Driver Bolan, Court of Inquiry, NAA: MP376/1, 446/10/1840.
3 Findings of Fact also statement by Driver Bollen, 26 March 1920, Court of Inquiry, NAA: MP376/1, 446/10/1840.
4 ibid; NAA: B2455 KINGSTON ALLEN CHARLES WATERS.
5 Testimonial dated 11 October 1920; Cablegram dated 27 October 1920, Court of Inquiry, NAA: MP376/1, 446/10/1840.

GORDON WALLACE *(pp. 119–122)*

1 OIC Report, 29 June 1921, NAA B73, M61609.
2 ibid.
3 Letter from Mrs Wallace, ibid.
4 Letter from H.B. Gullett, 31 May 1955, ibid.

THOMAS DOWELL *(pp. 123–125)*

1 Appellant's statement 16 September 1935, NAA: B73, M41646.
2 Letter 12 March 1935, Mr Dowell to the Repatriation Department, ibid.
3 Letter 12 March 1935, Mr Dowell to the Repatriation Department, ibid.
4 Letter 26 November 1934 from Dr Godfrey to Repatriation Department, ibid.
5 Letter 21 November 1935, Mrs Dowell to Repatriation Department, ibid.
6 ibid.
7 ibid.
8 Letter 26 November 1934 from Dr Godfrey to Repatriation Department, ibid.
9 Letter 21 November 1935, Mrs Dowell to Repatriation Department, ibid.

HILDA WILLIAMS *(pp. 126–128)*

1 *Sunday Times*, 15 December 1918.
2 *West Australian*, 25 April 1933.

BERNHARDT WALTHER *(pp. 129–132)*

1 *Greville Tregarthen, Sea Transport of the A.I.F.* (Melbourne: Naval Transport Board, no date).
2 The War Diaries of Captain Bernhardt Hermann Walther AWM PR00937, 25 April, 1915.
3 ibid, 26 April, 1915.
4 ibid, 27 April, 1915.
5 ibid, 28 April, 1915.
6 ibid, August, 1915.
7 Red Cross Wounded and Missing file AWM 1DRL/0428 Captain Bernhardt Hermann Walther.

CHARLIE BYRNE *(pp. 133–135)*

1 Charles Byrne to Undersecretary, 23 July 1923, Soldier Settlement file, State Records NSW: 12/7305.
2 Charles Byrne to Minister, 26 May 1923, ibid.
3 Memorandum, 1 November 1922, ibid.
4 Memorandum, 8 June 1923, ibid.
5 NAA: C138/4 M3444.
6 ibid.
7 ibid.
8 Memorandum, 17 August 1928; Charles Byrne to Undersecretary, 6 October, State Records NSW: 12/7305.
9 Memorandum 13 May 1929, District Surveyor's Report, 9 May 1932, ibid.

WALTER BAGENAL *(pp. 136–138)*

1 NAA: D63, H029717-01.

BERT CROWLE *(pp. 139–142)*

1 *The Mail,* 20 September 1916.
2 Herbert Crowle Papers AWM 1DRL/0227.

ROBERT PENNINGTON *(pp. 143–144)*

1 Alice Pennington to Federal Attorney General, 28 June 1916, in various papers re applications for permission to use the word 'Anzac', NAA: A432, 1929/3484 PART 25.
2 Secretary to the Federal Attorney General, 20 July 1916, ibid.

EVELYN (TEV) DAVIES *(pp. 145–148)*

1 Undated letter from Lemnos, Papers of Sister Evelyn Davies, AANS, AIF, AWM 3 DRL 3398B.
2 Grace Wilson, letter to her sister Minnie from Lemnos, 6 August 1915, AWM 3DRL 7819.
3 Louise Young, cited in Jan Bassett, *Guns and Brooches: Australian Army nursing from the Boer War to the Gulf War* (Melbourne: Oxford University Press, 1992) p. 48.
4 Letter dated 9 September 1915, AWM 3 DRL 3398B.
5 Letter dated 15 January 1916, ibid.
6 Letters dated 6 August 1916; undated letter from Netley, England, ibid.
7 Letter dated 17 October 1916, ibid.
8 Letter dated 11 October 1916, ibid.
9 Letter dated 30 November 1916, ibid.
10 Undated letter, England; letter dated 22 April 1917, ibid.
11 Letter dated 17 May 1916, ibid.
12 Letter dated 12 November 1916; undated letter, England, ibid.
13 Letters dated 15 January 1915; 15 July 1915, ibid.
14 Letter dated 11 October 1916, ibid.

ARTHUR RAE *(pp. 149–150)*

1 *Argus,* 1 August, 1914.
2 D.J. Murphy, 'Fisher, Andrew', Australian Dictionary of Biography, National Centre of Biography, Australian National University, http://adb.anu.edu.aubiography/fisher-andrew-378/text10613, published in hardcopy,1981; *Tamworth Daily Observer,* 30 September 1916; *Sydney Morning Herald,* 30 April 1917.

CHARLES CAMPBELL *(pp. 151–153)*

1 Charles Campbell to Walter Campbell, 10, March, 1917, Walter Campbell Memorial Trust, Charles Sturt University Regional Archives and University Art Collection, Wagga Wagga.
2 Charles Campbell to Christie Campbell, 11, April, 1917, ibid.
3 Charles Campbell to Walter Campbell, date unknown, ibid; I. Philpott, *The Birth of the Royal Air Force* (Barnsley: Pen & Sword Books Ltd., 2013) p. 210.
4 ibid, p. 291.
5 Charles Campbell to Christie Campbell, 8 October 1917, Walter Campbell Memorial Trust, Charles Sturt University Regional Archives and University Art Collection, Wagga Wagga.
6 Christie Campbell to Charles Campbell, 27, January, 1918, ibid.
7 Christie Campbell to Charles Campbell, 5, January, 1918, ibid.
8 Christie Campbell to Charles Campbell, 13, January, 1918, ibid.
9 Flora Samways to Christie Campbell, 1919, ibid.
10 Flora Samways to Christie Campbell, 1919, ibid.

EDITH MOORHOUSE *(pp. 154–156)*

1 *News,* 14 October 1925.
2 ibid.
3 *Sydney Morning Herald*, 25 June 1925.
4 Sister Leila Brown, AWM41, 946.
5 ibid.

PETER RADOS *(pp. 157–159)*

1 No copy of the letter survives, though it is referred to in NAA: B2455, RADOS PETER.
2 N. Rados to Red Cross, 28 September 1918, ibid.
3 N. Rados to Australian Imperial Force, 29 January 1919, ibid.
4 N. Rados to Australian Imperial Force, 30 May 1919, ibid.
5 Base Records to N. Rados, 8 March 1921, ibid.
6 N. Rados to Australian Imperial Force, 30 May 1919, ibid.

JOHN AND EDWARD SADLER *(pp. 160–163)*

1 Rodney Smith to Bruce Scates, 24 January 2014 (letter altered slightly with Mr Smith's consent for the purpose of publication).

JAMES ARDEN *(pp. 164–168)*

1 NAA: B2455, ARDEN, J.
2 Memo from Chief Secretary's Office, 4 May 1916, M. Austin to the Manager, Mr Galbraith, 5 July 1917 PROV Aborigines Protection Board, Accounts and Requisitions, 1 January 1916–1 January 1919, V/AF/092/03/01, VPRS 1694/P/0000, Unit 000002.
3 Letter from James Arden to Mr Callaway, Lake Condah, June 1912; Edith Bagnall to Chief Protector of Aborigines, 27 January 1917, Victorian Public Records Office, Correspondence and Reports, 1 January 1917, V/AF/091/01/05, VPRS 1694/P/0000, Unit 000003, Dscl 1917.
4 Letter from James Arden to Mrs Bon, Dunmore West, 12 June 1917; Letter James Arden to WL Galbraith, 7 July 1916; ibid.
5 Letter from W.L. Galbraith to The Secretary, Board for the Protection of the Aborigines, 23 February 1917, ibid.
6 Report from (Sgd) W.L. Galbraith, Manager to Acting Secretary, Department of Defence, Melbourne, 13 June 1917, ibid.
7 Letter from Mrs Galbraith, Lake Condah, 24 February 1917, ibid.
8 Memorandum from the Secretary, 20 February 1917, ibid.
9 Letter from James Arden to W.J. Ditchburn, Lake Condah, ibid.
10 Letter from James Arden to Mrs Bon, Dunmore West, 12 June 1917; ibid.
11 *Portland Guardian*, 17 June 1935; NAA: B2455, ARDEN, J.

ROSE VENN BROWN *(pp. 169–172)*

1 *Queenslander*, 26 January 1933.
2 *Daily Observer*, 30 October 1920; *Sydney Morning Herald*, 21 January 1933; *Times*, 30 May 1920.
3 *The Globe and Sunday Times War Pictorial*, 30 April 1917.
4 *British Australasian*, 11 March 1920; Rose Venn Brown, Letters dated 12 June, 3 September 1919; Catherine Boss to Miss Venn Brown, 24 June 1919, AWM 2DRL/0598.
5 Correspondence to Miss Venn Brown from C. Chasting, Ada McGregor, Ada Jurd, Elizabeth Macrea, June – September 1919, ibid.
6 Hannah Fenwick to Miss Venn Brown, 19 June 1919; ibid.

DAVID BISSET *(pp. 173–175)*

1 Form D. 16, in NAA: B2455 BISSET DAVID.
2 Mary Bisset to Secretary, 13 November 1918, ibid.
3 Agnes Gordon to Base Records, 20 December 1918, ibid.
4 Statement by Pte CC Bottomley, 8 February 1919, Red Cross Wounded and Missing file AWM 1DRL/0428 David Bisset.
5 Secretary to Mary Bisset, 25 March 1919, ibid.
6 Secretary to Mary Bisset, 1 July 1919, ibid.
7 *Brisbane Courier,* 18 September 1920.

FREDERICK WEIR *(pp. 176–177)*

1 NAA: B2455, WEIR, FREDERICK ROBERT.
2 Inspector's report, RSS Branch Office Memorandum, 31 December 1921; Soldier Settlement file, State Records NSW:12/7286.
3 Inspector's report, 1 September 1924, ibid
4 ibid.
5 Inspector's report, 3 November 1924, ibid.
6 NAA: B2455 WEIR, FREDERICK ROBERT.

MARY CHOMLEY *(pp. 178–183)*

1 Pte George Anderson, 48th Batt. A.I.F., Friedrichsfeld, 15 April, 15 July1917; Papers of Miss M E Chomley Australian Red Cross Society, POW Section, AWM 1DRL615 [749/19/20] Folder 2.
2 Tommy Taylor, Heilsberg POW camp, ibid.
3 Pte George Anderson, 48th Batt. A.I.F., Friedrichsfeld, 15 April, 15 July1917, ibid.
4 Statement by Capt John A Mott, 48th batt, Statements by Repatriated POWs, AWM 30.
5 Papers of Miss M E Chomley Australian Red Cross Society, POW Section, AWM 1DRL615 [749/19/20].
6 Caroline Moorehead cited in Nola Anderson, 'Dear Miss Chomley', *Wartime*, no. 21, p. 45.
7 Pte. Hubert Berning, 21st Australian M.C.G., Gustrow, 21 April 1918; Papers of Miss M E Chomley Australian Red Cross Society, POW Section, AWM 1DRL615 [749/19/20] Folder 2.
8 Gnr. Roy B. MxNeill, 102nd Howitzer Battery Australian Field Artillery, Gustrow, 17 February 1918; Papers of Miss M E Chomley Australian Red Cross Society, POW Section, AWM: 1DRL615 [749/19/20] Folder 4.

9 Gnr. Roy B. MxNeill, 102nd Howitzer Battery Australian Field Artillery, Gustrow, 17 February 1918; ibid.
10 Tommy Taylor, Captured Bullecourt 1917, Heilsberg POW camp.
11 Spr. W.L. Lawry, 6th Field Eng. A.I.F. Munster, 26 January 1917; Papers of Miss M E Chomley Australian Red Cross Society, POW Section, AWM 1DRL615 [749/19/20] Folder 4.
12 B M Lennan, 16 May 1919, Corowa; Papers of Miss M E Chomley Australian Red Cross Society, POW Section, AWM 1DRL615 [749/19/20] Folder 6.
13 ibid.
14 Frank Dean, 14th Batt. A.I.F., 1 January 1918, Frieburg; Papers of Miss M E Chomley Australian Red Cross Society, POW Section, AWM 1DRL615 [749/19/20] Folder 3.
15 Pte. Wat Finlay, 13th Batt. A.I.F., Soltau, 15 July 1918; ibid.
16 Letter from a mother to Miss Chomley, 2 April 1919, Mary Chomley papers AWM 1DRL/0615.

GORDON CORBOULD *(pp. 184–185)*

1 L. Parr, Rector St Thomas Balmain, to Captain in charge, Garden Island, 10 December 1914, Loss of the *AE1* AWM 50, 18/2.
2 WP Bainbudge, Rector, St Peters Church Eaglehawk, to Captain in charge, Garden Island, 11 December 1914, ibid.
3 Charles Thomas to Captain in charge, Garden Island, 15 December 1914, ibid.
4 *Sydney Morning Herald*, 13 September 1916.

GIOVANNI FERRANDO *(pp. 186–188)*

1 Royal Consulate of Italy for Australasia, 'Call to Arms and Repatriation', Italian Reservists Mobilization, NAA: MP367/1, 592/4/295.
2 President of the Italian Club 'Savoia' to Baron Sonnino, Rome, 10 September 1920, 'Italians- Enlistment in AIF and Calling up of Italian reservists, NAA: MP367/1 592/4/1116.
3 Giovanni Ferrando Writ, 25 July 1918, Giovanni Ferrando, NAA MP367/1 592/4/1086.
4 Affidavit by Cavalier Giovanni Ferrando lodged in the High Court of Australia, Italian Reservists- Giovanni Ferrando, NAA: MP 367/1 592/4/115.
5 Meeting of Italians at Trades Hall, Goulburn Street, Sydney, 3 July 1918; Report by Sgt Mathew Saunders, Royal Consulate of Italy for Australasia, 'Call to Arms and Repatriation', Italian Reservists Mobilization, NAA: MP367/1, 592/4/295.
6 Statement made by Giovanni Ferrando on HMAT *Baraka* in the English Channel, 13 November 1918, Deportation of Italian Reservist G Ferrando, NAA: MP 367/1 592/4/973.

PADDY HAUENSTEIN *(pp. 189–190)*

1 *Evening News*, 23 February 1923.
2 *Riverine Grazier*, 23 February 1923; *Evening News*, 21 February 1923.
3 *Evening News*, 22 February 1923.
4 *Evening News*, 21 February 1923.
5 *Sydney Morning Herald*, 21 March 1923.
6 *Evening News*, 21 February 1923.
7 ibid.

ELSIE TRANTER *(pp. 191–195)*

1 Diary of Sister Elsie Tranter, 26 December 1916, AWM DRL 4081A.
2 ibid, 18 January, 6 February 1916.
3 ibid, 17 December 1916.
4 ibid, 3 March 1917.
5 ibid, 3 April 1917.
6 ibid.
7 ibid, 2 May 1917.
8 ibid, 28 March 1918.
9 ibid, 9 April 1918.
10 ibid, 1, 14 April 1918.

THOMAS HENLEY MANNS *(pp. 196–199)*

1 Medical History, 23 January 1916, NAA: B2455, MANNS, Thomas Henley.
2 NAA: 536/1285 MANNS, THOMAS HENLEY.

JOHN HUTCHINSON *(pp. 200–201)*

1 Red Cross Wounded and Missing file 1DRL/0424, Private John Hutchinson.
2 *City Rhythm*, no 2, June 1982; undated issue of *Klick* magazine, Australian Lesbian and Gay Archives, South Yarra; *Age*, 26 April 1982 The authors thank Gary Jaynes for his guidance through this collection.

ALFRED ATKINS *(pp. 202–203)*

1 *Salisbury Times and South Wilts Gazette*, 23 November 1917.
2 ibid.
3 NAA: B2455, ATKINS, Alfred.

TASMAN MILLINGTON *(pp. 204–206)*

1 *West Australian*, 12 July 1930.
2 *Morning Bulletin*, 11 November 1935; *Sydney Morning Herald*, 6 November 1935.

FRANK ROBERTS *(pp. 207–211)*

1 Diary entry, 13 September 1918, John Garibaldi Roberts Papers, SLV 265/4, MS 9949.
2 We owe this observation to Jay Winter and Annette Becker.
3 Sympathy letters from Annie Denholm, Edgar Peacock, Ian McDougall, Edith Jones, and Annie Duncan, respectively, Roberts Scrapbook, SLV, MS 8508, book 3.
4 Diary entry, 7 August 1920, SLV 265/4, MS 9949.
5 CEW Bean, Visit to Pozieres- Ypres Battlefields, 1951, Records in respect of Dr Charles Edwin Woodrow Bean, AWM, DRL 6673 series 3, file 419.8.1.
6 Peter Stanley, *Men of Mont St Quentin: Between Victory and Death* (Melbourne: Scribe, 2009), p. 256.

DAISY SCHOEFFEL *(pp. 212–214)*

1 Letter from Daisy Schoeffel to Hon. H. Gregory, NAA: CRS 457, item 406/1.
2 Ernest Scott, *Australia During the War: The Official History of Australia in the War of 1914–1918* (Sydney: Angus and Robertson, 1936), p. 105.
3 Cited in Gerhard Fischer, *Enemy Aliens: Internment and the Homefront Experience in Australia, 1914–1920* (St Lucia: University of Queensland Press, 1989), pp. 128–9.
4 Letter from Daisy Schoeffel to Hon. H. Gregory, NAA: CRS 457, 406/1.

FRANCES EDGEWORTH SOMERS *(pp. 215–218)*

1 *Argus*, 28 April 1926
2 Mrs Edgeworth Somers to John Monash, 4 May [date incomplete], Monash Correspondence, Box 35, Folder 324, Mss 1884, NLA.
3 Red Cross Wounded and Missing file AWM 1DRL/0428 Private Gervase Louis Edgeworth Somers and Private Noel Travers Edgeworth Somers.
4 'My Son' by Frances Edgeworth Somers, Mornington Historical Society website. http://www.morningtoncemetery.com/Denominations/Roman-Catholic/Somers/Somers-Park.shtml#tpm1_2.

CECIL TARRANT *(pp. 219–220)*

1 *Richmond River Herald and Northern Districts Advertiser*, 3 May 1921.
2 ibid.
3 ibid.

MARGARET THORP *(pp. 221–225)*

1 *Brisbane Courier*, 11 July 1917.
2 *Woman Voter*, 19 July 1917.
3 *Brisbane Courier*, 10 July 1917.
4 *Woman Voter*, 19 July 1917.
5 ibid.
6 Margaret Thorp, notes entitled 'Eighth Week of Peace Work' and 'The Moral and Spiritual Aspects of War', Margaret Thorp Papers, Society of Friends collection, ML 1209/78. Box 1 SLNSW *The Australian Friend*, 31 August 2014.
7 Security file on Margaret Thorp NAA: A/402/3, W2455, QF1254, pp. 1–2.
8 Aims and Objects of the WPA, Margaret Thorp Papers, Society of Friends collection, ML 1209/78. Box 2, NLA.
9 Letter from Joseph Thorp, *The Australasian Friend*, 16 August 1916, p. 995; reproduced in the Quaker exhibition, *World War One: Quaker Witness to Peace and Non-violence*, Sydney 2014.
10 Manuscript of 'Faith my Shield', Society of Friends collection, ML 1209/78 Box 2, SLNSW.
11 Statement in support of Vietnamese refugees by Margaret Watts et al, Thorp Papers, Society of Friends collection, ML 1209/78. Box 1, SLNSW.
12 Margaret Thorp, 'National Service', *The Voice of Australian Democracy*, vol 1. no.1, 1916, p. 38.

WILLIAM RILEY *(pp. 226–227)*

1 *Australasian,* 20 July 1907.
2 *Argus,* 1 August 1928.
3 Sworn statement by A. Valentine Soul, Probate Jurisdiction, Supreme Court of Victoria, 2 September 1917, in NAA: B2455, RILEY WILLIAM ERNEST.
4 Betty Horskins to Bruce Scates, 27 August 2014, 100 Stories Archive, National Centre for Australian Studies, Monash University.
5 R. Campbell Edwards to Base Records, Melbourne, 21 June 1922, in NAA: B2455, RILEY WILLIAM ERNEST.

HUGO THROSSELL *(pp. 228–231)*

1 *Sunday Times,* 27 July 1919.
2 Ric Throssell, *My Father's Son* (Melbourne: William Heinemann Australia, 1989), p. 74.
3 Suzanne Welborn, 'Throssell, Hugo Vivian Hope', *Australian Dictionary Biography* (Melbourne: Melbourne University Press 1990), pp. 223–224.
4 C E W Bean, *The Story of Anzac*, vol. 2, (Sydney: Angus and Robertson, 1924) p. 724. Recommendation for mention in dispatches in, NAA: B2455, THROSSELL, Hugo; and *Mirror,* 25 November 1933.
5 Medical Reports, Dr C.W. Courtney, 30 March, 30 April 1931 NAA: PP6441/1, M5273.
6 Medical Report, Dr J.S. Yule, 16 January 1929, ibid.
7 R.H. Weddell, 'Report of Captain and Mrs Hugo Throssell', Australian Security Intelligence Organisation, Central Office, NAA: A6119, 42.
8 Throssell, *My Father's Son*, p. 7.
9 Inquest Proceedings, 19 November 1933 NAA: PP6441/1, M5273.
10 *West Australian,* 14 March 1934.
11 *Argus*, 28 November 1933.
12 Katherine Susannah Throssell To Deputy Commissioner Repatriation Commission, 28 January 1934 NAA: PP6441/1, M5273.
13 Australian Peace Ambassadors http://www.anzacsite.gov.au/2visiting/peace-ambassors.html.

LEO GALLI *(pp. 232–237)*

1 *Colac Herald*, 9 July, 1917.
2 *Barrier Miner*, 17 October, 1917.
3 Lt W.W. Paine to Major Leicester, 26 May 1915, NAA: B2455 GALLI, Leo.
4 Statement by Major J.C. Holdrich Leister, ibid.
5 ibid.
6 *Daily Herald*, 28 September 1917.
7 PR Pike to Director General of Recruiting, 16 May 1918 NAA: 582/1/218; *Border Watch* 9 November 1917.
8 *Mullumbimby Star*, 15 June 1916; *Border Watch* (Mount Gambier) 9 November 1917.
9 *Adelaide Advertiser*, 27 September 1917; *Melton Express*, 16 February 1918: *Murchison Advertiser*, 5 April 1918, *Daily Herald* (Adelaide) 28 September 1917.
10 *Daily Herald*, 28 September 1917; *Tale Talk*, 15 March 1917; *Riverine Herald*, 1 May 1918.
11 Unsigned to CD Ross, 11th of September 1917, Galli, Leo C. recruiting sgt, NAA: 1917/2152.
12 *Weekly Times*, 20 April 1918.
13 S Harrison to J.C. Neagle, 16 August 1949.
14 D.P. Kennedy to Military Base Records, Canberra, 2 April 1940, ibid.

JIM SOORELY *(pp. 238–240)*

1 *Maitland Daily Mercury*, 21 September 1918.
2 *Newcastle Morning Herald and Miners' Advocate*, 21 September 1918.
3 *Newcastle Morning Herald and Miners' Advocate*, 19 September 1918.
4 *Watchman*, 26 September, 1918.
5 *Maitland Daily Mercury*, 23 September 1918.
6 ibid.
7 ibid , 25 September 1918.
8 ibid.
9 ibid, 21 September 1918.
10 ibid, 20 September 1918.
11 ibid, 23 September 1918.
12 ibid, 20 September 1918.

DOROTHY GILBERT *(pp. 241–244)*

1 *Register*, 14 March 1919; Women's War Memorial Committee, Minutes of the General Committee, 12 March 1919; Women's War Memorial Committee, *The Women's Memorial to Fallen in the Great War: Objects*, Adelaide nd, Women's War Memorial Committee of South Australia Papers, State Library of South Australia, SRG 89.
2 Women's War Memorial General Committee Minutes, 5 November 1919, ibid.
3 *Register,* 26 April 1923; Dorothy Gilbert to WR Letharby (IWGC), 23 August 1919; Dorothy Gilbert to JE Talbot (IWGC), 18 December 1919, League of Loyal Women Press Clippings, State Library of South Australia, SRG 684/2 for personal details see Dorothy Gilbert, 'Memories of Pusey Vale and the Gilbert Family, 1839–1923', PRG 266/14 Mortlock Library.
4 Dorothy Gilbert to Lord Mayor, 16 January 1920, ibid.
5 ibid; Dorothy Gilbert to W.R. Letharby, 23 August 1919, ibid.
6 ibid.
7 Women's War Memorial Committee, *The Women's Memorial,* Adelaide nd, ibid.
8 *Register,* 24 March 1922.

SAMUEL ROLFE *(pp. 245–247)*

1 O.S. Watkins, Methodist Report, cited in Joy Robert J.T., 'Historical Aspects of Medical Defense Against Chemical Warfare,' in *Medical Aspects of Chemical and Biological Warfare*, (Washington, DC: The Borden Institute, 1997) p. 90.
2 Oliver Lepick, *La Grende Gueere chimique, 1914-1918,* cited in Stéphane Audoin-Rouzeau, '1915: Stalemate', in Jay Winter, (ed) *The Cambridge History of the First World War,* vol. 1 (Cambridge: Cambridge University Press, 2014), p. 70.
3 B. LeRoy Evidence, 3 December 1919; NSW Acting Assistant Commissioner 22 December 1919; Medical Certificate 22 September 1920; NAA: C138 C138/2, C59810.
4 G. Fitzgerald, 'Chemical warfare and medical response during World War I', *American Journal of Public Health*, vol. 98, no. 4, 2008, p. 611; Watkins O. S., Methodist Report, cited in Amos Fries and C. J. West, *Chemical Warfare* (New York: McGraw Hill, 1921), p. 13.
5 Doctor's Report, 5 December 1924, NAA: C138, NC043642-01 Rolfe.
6 ibid.

WILLIAM IRWIN *(pp. 248–250)*

1 *London Gazette*, 10 January 1920.
2 Report from Moree and District Repatriation Committee, 7 February 1917 NAA: B2455, IRWIN WILLIAM ALLEN.
3 Harry Grose [half-brother to William Irwin] to Base Records, Melbourne, 16 May 1920, NAA: B2455 IRWIN, WILLIAM ALLEN.
4 *Koori Mail*, 8 May 1996.

MARGARET BROADHURST *(pp. 251–253)*

1 *Truth*, 20 April 1918.
2 *Leader*, 20 April 1918.
3 *Truth*, 20 April 1918.
4 Kate Holden, 'Imaginary Widows: Spinsters, Marriage, and the "Lost Generation" in Britain after the Great War', *Journal of Family History*, vol 30 no 4, October 2005, pp. 388–409.
5 Virginia Nicholson, *Singled Out: How Two Million Women Survived Without Men after the First World War* (London: Viking, 2007).

THE REVEREND BERNARD LINDEN WEBB *(pp. 254–256)*

1 B. Linden Webb, *The Religious Significance of the War* (Sydney: S.N., 1915).
2 ibid.
3 Robert D Linder, 'Galilee Shall at Last Vanquish Corsica: The Rev. B. Linden Webb Challenges the War-Makers, 1915–1917', *Church Heritage (Historical Journal of the Uniting Church in Australia)* vol. 11, no. 3 (2000).
4 *Methodist,* 26 June 1915.
5 ibid, 26 June 1915.
6 *Riverine Grazier,* 24 October 1916.

RACHEL PRATT *(pp. 257–259)*

1 Sister Rachael Pratt, *Reveille*, 1 August 1933.
2 Medical case notes, 14 December 1938; 19 January 1939, NAA: B73, H5789.
3 Medical case notes, 31 July 1919, ibid.
4 Medical case notes, 3 October, 30 November 1939, ibid.
5 Medical case notes, 20 October 1940, ibid.

REGINALD BIGGS *(pp. 260–264)*

1 Robin Gerster, *Big Noting: The Heroic Theme in Australian War Writing* (Carlton: Melbourne University Press, 1987); this quote is taken from an interview with Reginald Biggs in Launceston in 1987. We thank our colleagues Russell Fewster (writer), Gus Howard (director) and David Foreman (cameraman) for their generous assistance in providing a tape of this video interview and the series of audio tapes that accompany it.
2 Private Ashmead [Reginald Biggs], *That Other War* (Launceston: privately published, 1983). This limited edition is held in the archives of the State Library of Tasmania. We again thank Russell Fewster for providing the same. A journalist himself, Biggs adopted the penname 'Ashmead', a reference to the war correspondent who first reported the Landings at Gallipoli.
3 ibid, p. 13, 100, 121.
4 ibid, pp. 172–3.

5 ibid, pp. 157, 274.
6 ibid, pp. 165, 198, 204, 217.
7 Undated letter Reginald Biggs to Fred Cahill, AWM 3DRL 6037.
8 ibid.
9 ibid.
10 Letter from Reginald Biggs to Fred Cahill, October 1967, ibid.
11 Letters from Fred Cahill to Air Commodore B. Roberts (Ret), 29 January 1968, and Frank Kennedy (RSL Representative in 'Blighty'), 14 October 1967; letter from Frank Kennedy to Fred Cahill, 9 October 1967, ibid.
12 Biggs also modified the American itinerary, suggesting a run up to Niagara Falls instead of 'the waste of time at the United Nations joint'; letter from Reginald Biggs to Fred Cahill, 5 September 1967, ibid.
13 Reginald Biggs interview with Russell Fewster, Launceston 1987.

ABAS BHAWOODEEN GHANSAR *(p265-268)*

1 NAA: B2455, GHANSAR AB.

MARY BOOTH *(pp. 269–273)*

1 W.H. Swancott to OC Base Records, 16 April 1921, NLA Australian Fellowship of Women Papers, MS2864, Box 14.
2 'Gates of Remembrance', unidentified clipping, Anzac Fellowship of Women (AFW), Minutes, 12 October 1927, NLA MS 2864; Centre for Soldier's Wives and Mothers, *Commemoration Service at the Wharf Gates at Woolloomooloo, . . . In the Presence of their Excellencies the Governor General and Lady Foster* (Sydney, 1923).
3 AFW Minutes, 12 October 1927.
4 Case notes of the Centre for Soldiers' Wives and Mothers, NLA MS 2864.
5 ibid, 12 April 1920.
6 ibid, 16 December 1919.
7 ibid, 16 December 1919.
8 ibid, 18 March 1920.
9 ibid, 14 April 1914.
10 For Booth's attitudes on marriage and her sexual politics generally see Jill Roe, 'Booth, Mary (1869–1956)', *Australian Dictionary of Biography*, National Centre of Biography, Australian National University, http://adb.anu.edu.au/biography/booth-mary-5291/text8927, published first in hardcopy 1979, accessed online 25 October 2014.

THOMAS GOODWIN *(pp. 274–278)*

1 Thomas Goodwin diary, State Library of NSW, ML MSS1598, 25 April 1915.
2 ibid, 6 May 1915.
3 ibid, 2 August 1915.
4 ibid, 20–21 June 1915.
5 ibid, 2 August 1915.
6 ibid, 21 July, 15 September 1915.
7 ibid, 27 July 1915.
8 ibid, 25 June 1915.

BERROL MENDELSOHN *(pp. 279–283)*

1 Abbie Mendelsohn to OC Base Records, 19 September 1916, NAA:B2455, MENDELSOHN BERROL LAYAN.
2 Abbie Mendelsohn to OC Base Records, 9 January 1917, ibid.
3 Abbie Mendelsohn to OC Base Records, 19 September 1916, ibid.
4 Red Cross Wounded and Missing file AWM1DRL/0428 Berrol Mendelshon.
5 Abbie Mendelsohn to OC Base Records, 21 May 1921, NAA: B2455, MENDELSOHN BERROL LAYAN.
6 Abbie Mendelsohn to OC Base Records, 9 January 1917, ibid.
7 Abbie Mendelsohn to OC Base Records, 24 April 1919, ibid.
8 Abbie Mendelsohn to OC Base Records, 14 September 1921, ibid.
9 Statement by Professor Oliver Mendelsohn, Berrol Mendelsohn's nephew, cited in Chantal Abitbol, 'Lost Jewish digger identified', *Australian Jewish News,* 18 March 2010, available: http://www.jewishnews.net.au/lost-jewish-digger-identified/12469.

MADAME CHARLOTTE CRIVELLI *(pp. 284–287)*

1 *Punch*, 11 July 1918.
2 *Brighton Southern Cross*, 23 December 1916; *Punch*, 6 January 1916.
3 Ernest Scott, *Australia During the War* (Sydney: Angus and Robertson, 1941), p. 883.
4 *Argus,* 12 November 1915.
5 *Age,* 8 December 1915.
6 *Advocate*, 8 July 1920.
7 Scott, *Australia During the War,* p. 883.
8 *Ovens and Murray Advertiser*, 18 December 1915.
9 *Punch*, 11 July 1918.
10 *The Argus,* 7 May 1919.
11 *The Australasian*, 13 December 1919.
12 *The Argus*, 2 March 1922.
13 Minutes, Victorian Education Department War Relief Fund Meeting, 26 November 1922, PROV VPRS 14009/P0001/1.

ARCHIBALD BAXTER *(pp. 288–292)*

1 Archibald Baxter, *We will not cease: the autobiography of a Conscientious Objector* (Whatamongo Bay: Cape Catley, 1980), pp. 152–3.
2 ibid.
3 ibid. pp. 56–7.
4 ibid. p. 6.
5 ibid, pp. 105–6.
6 ibid, p. 115.
7 Baxter, Archibald McColl Larmond, WW1 47814 – Army, R22273524, Military Personnel Files, New Zealand Defence Force, Personnel Archives, Archives New Zealand.

DAPHNE MAYO *(pp. 293–296)*

1 Ken Inglis, *Sacred Places: War Memorials in the Australian landscape* (Carlton: Melbourne University Press 2008), p. 292.
2 Lloyd Rees cited in 'Cheerful, strong-willed and resolute', *A Significant Women of Her Time,* the Daphne Mayo collection, Fryer Library online exhibition, University of Queensland.
3 Daphne Mayo, transcript of undated radio talk, Daphne Mayo Papers, UQFL119, Fryer Library, University of Queensland.

WALTER DEXTER *(pp. 297–301)*

1 Diary, 6 April 1915, Papers of Chaplain WE Dexter, AWM 92/0176.
2 Diary 26 April 1915, ibid.
3 Diary 28 April 1915, ibid.
4 Diary, 24 May 1915, ibid.
5 Diary, 12, 14 June 1915, ibid.
6 Diary, 11 August 1915, ibid.
7 Unidentified Anzac cited in Bill Gammage, *The Broken Years: Australian soldiers and the Great War* (Ringwood: Penguin, 1975), p. 110.
8 Diary, 5 November 1915, Papers of Chaplain W.E. Dexter, AWM 92/0176.
9 Diary, 16 December 1915, ibid.
10 Citation for Military Cross, B2455; DEXTER W.

JOSEPH BOLTON *(pp. 302–304)*

1 Letter from Mrs Lydia Bolton, 12 June, 1918 and letter from Mr George Bolton, 14 October, 1918 in NAA: B2455 BOLTON J G.
2 *Sydney Morning Herald*, 4 May 1921.
3 Letter from Mrs Lydia Bolton, NAA: B2455 BOLTON J C; Charles Bean to T. Trumble, Secretary, Department of Defence, 18 February 1920, NAA: MP 367, AB446/10/1331; C.E.W. Bean, *Where the Australians Rest* (Melbourne: Government Printing Office, 1922).
4 *Daily News*, 17 May 1924.
5 *Register*, 22 May 1924, p.10.
6 Thomas Donnan Diary 20 May 1924, Rare Book Collection, Monash University.
7 *Melbourne Herald*, 22 May 1924.

CYRIL AND RUFUS RIGNEY *(pp. 305–308)*

1 Red Cross Wounded and Missing file AWM 1DRL/0428 Private Rufus Rigney.
2 Mike Sexton, 'One service charged with extra emotion', *The 7:30 Report*, ABC, 25 April 2005, transcript available: http://www.abc.net.au/7.30/content/2005/s1353096.htm.

ALEXANDRINA SEAGER *(pp. 309–312)*

1 Jean Ashton, 'Alexandra Seager', *Personalities Remembered.* Scripts of the ABC radio series broadcast from 5CL 10:30–10:50 a.m. Sundays, 7 June 1970 to 26 December 1971.
2 Frederick J. Mills, *Cheer Up: A Story of War Work* (Adelaide: Cheer Up Society Incorporated, 1920), pp. 24–5.
3 ibid. pp. 60–1.
4 ibid. pp. 58–9.
5 ibid. p. 71, 154.
6 A. Seager, *Men: A Collection of Verses Written During the War* (Adelaide: np, 1920), p. 6, 55.
7 A. Seager, *Cheer-Up Souvenir to Our Boys* (Adelaide: W.K. Thomas, 1915).
8 ibid. p. 107.

KARANEMAR POHATU *(pp. 313–315)*

1 Edwin Little to Charles Bean, nd, 'Historical Notes – Gallipoli' AWM 38, 3 DRL 8042, item 18. We thank Peter Stanley for his work in uncovering Edwin Little as the original source of this remark.
2 NAA: B2455 COTTERILL, Eric Roland.
3 Tohana Pohatu to Base Records, Melbourne, 5 April 1922, NAA: B2455, STONE, Robert.

ELLIS SILAS *(pp. 316–321)*

1 Ellis Silas, Diary, August, September and October entries, State Library of New South Wales, MLMSS 1840.
2 ibid, December 1914.
3 ibid, December 1914; January 1915.
4 ibid, April, May 1915.
5 ibid, 25 April 1915.
6 *North Western Advocate and the Emu Bay Times*, 6 April 1916; *Farmer and Settler*, 30 May 1916.
7 Ellis Silas, *Crusading at Anzac, AD 1915* (London: British-Australasian, 1916).

THOMAS MURRAY *(pp. 322–327)*

1 See recollections by Betty Martyn in Bryan Fitzgerald, *A Tale of the Lands which Embrace Famous 'Tullaree'* (Traralgon: LV Printers, 1980), pp. 11–12.
2 Thomas Murray to Base Records, 7 September 1915, NAA: B2455, MURRAY THOMAS RICHARD.
3 Base Records to Thomas Murray, 25 September 1915, NAA: B2455, MURRAY THOMAS RICHARD.
4 C.E.W Bean, *Gallipoli Mission* [1948], (Sydney: ABC Books, 1992), pp. 332–4.
5 *Fethiye Times*, 25 December 2014.
6 Report by C.H. Hughes (Imperial War Graves Commission) for Minister of Defence, NAA: A 458 F 337/7; CEW Bean, Gallipoli Report, AWM 38, item 51; NAA: A2909/2 A453/1/3.
7 Fitzgerald, 1980, p. 12.
8 *British Australasian*, 27 May 1920.

THE UNKNOWN PATIENT *(pp. 328–330)*

1 Callan Park Mental Hospital: 14/9395, Case Papers, no. 1918–81.12449, State Records NSW.
2 George Thomas McQuay, R10927130, Archives New Zealand.
3 *Barrier Miner*, 22 March 1928.
4 *Mercury*, 12 March 1928.
5 *New Zealand Truth*, 5 April 1928; *Truth* (Sydney), 25 March 1928.
6 *Western Mail*, 17 May 1928.
7 We owe this quotation to Jen Hawksley, 'Long Time Coming Home: The Unknown Patient of Callan Park', in Martin Crotty and Marina Larsson (eds), *Anzac Legacies: Australians and the Aftermath of War* (Melbourne: Australian Scholarly Publishing, 2010), pp. 70, 77.

KATHLEEN SKINNER *(pp. 331–333)*

1 Carol Fallows, 'War Brides: for the love of an Aussie', *Memento*, no. 31, Winter 2006, pp. 10–13.
2 Diary of Sister Alice Kitchen, SLV, MS 9627.
3 *Soldier*, 12 January 1917.

ALFRED MORRIS *(pp. 334–337)*

1 Diary dated 5 August, 2 September, 16 October 1915, Alfred Prichard Kington Morris Papers, ML MS 2886, State Library of News South Wales.
2 Diary dated 8 August 1915, Morris Papers. Much of this entry is illegible and the punctuation erratic. We have indicated breaks with ellipsis and included full stops and capital letters in the interests of readability.
3 ibid, 9 August 1915.
4 ibid, 11, 16 August 1915.
5 ibid, 16 October 1916.
6 ibid, 23 August 1916.

JOSEPH O'GRADY *(pp. 338–341)*

1 Application for assistance, 11 December 1919, NAA: BP709/1, M198.
2 Medical Report, 24 August 1915, ibid.
3 Medical Report, 11 March 1921, ibid.
4 Medical Reports, 6 August 1918; 16 April 1920; 31 May, 16 August 1921, ibid.
5 Patient's statement, 12 February 1924, ibid.
6 Application for assistance, 11 December 1919, ibid.
7 Police report, 23 June 1943, ibid.
8 Decision of Repatriation Board, 8 September 1943, ibid.

BILL KEARSEY *(pp. 342–345)*

1 Verdun Kearsey to the Repatriation Department, NAA: C138 M55422.
2 Doctor's notes, ibid.

WILLIAM KNOX *(pp. 346–349)*

1 Bill Knox to Mim, 22 September 1915, Baillieu Family Papers.
2 Citation in NAA: B2455: KNOX WILLIAM JOHNTONE
3 Bill Knox to Mim, 2 May 1916, Baillieu Family Papers.
4 Bill Knox to Mim, 20 January 1917, ibid.
5 Bill Knox to Mim, 28 July 1917, ibid.
6 Bill Knox to Mim, 2 January 1917, ibid.
7 Kate Baillieu email correspondence and interview with authors, 10 March 2015.

SELECT BIBLIOGRAPHY

This bibliography lists the key archival sources on which the stories are based. It is offered as a guide to researchers and, as it is a *select* bibliography, does not claim to be definitive or comprehensive. Relevant secondary sources are noted under the sources and further reading guidelines accompanying each story.

NEWSPAPERS, MAGAZINES AND JOURNALS

Adelaide Register; *Advertiser*; *Age*; *Albany Advertiser*; *Argus*; *Australasian*; *Barrier Miner*; *Bathurst Times*; *Border Watch*; *Box Hill Reporter*; *Brighton Southern Cross*; *British-Australasian*; *British Australian and New Zealander*; *Brisbane Courier*; *Burnie Advocate*; *Cairns Post*; *Cardiff Western Mail*; *Casino Kyogle Advertiser*; *Chronicle*; *City Rhythm*; *Colac Herald*; *Cootamundra Herald*; *Daily Herald*; *Daily News*; *Daily Observer*; *Donald Mail*; *Evening News*; *Farmer and Settler*; *Geelong Advertiser*; *Globe and Sunday Times War Pictorial*; *Herald*; *Kalgoolie Miner*; *Klick*; *Koorie Mail*; *Labor Call*; *Leader*; *London Gazette*; *Mail*; *Melton Express*; *Mercury*; *Mirror*; *Morning Bulletin*; *Mullumbimby Star*; *Murchison Advertiser*; *Murrurundi Times and Liverpool Plains Gazette*; *Newcastle Morning Herald and Miners' Advocate*; *Northern Star*; *Nottingham Journal*; *Observer*; *Ovens and Murray Advertiser*; *Port Pirie Recorder*; *Portland Guardian*; *Punch*; *Queenslander*; *Register*; *Register-News Pictorial*; *Richmond River Express*; *Richmond River Herald and Northern Districts Advertiser*; *Riverine Grazier*; *Riverine Herald*; *Rushworth Chronicle*; *Salisbury Times and South Wilts Gazette*; *Singleton Argus*; *Soldier*; *Southern Morning Herald*; *Sydney City Mission Herald*; *Sunday Times*; *Sydney Morning Herald*; *Sydney Mail*; *Table Talk*; *Truth*; *Weekly Times*; *West Australian*; *Williamstown Chronicle*; *Woman Voter*.

FIRST AIF SERVICE DOSSIERS

NAA:B2455
James Josiah Agnew; Thomas Richard Archer; James Arden; Royce Baesjou; Walter Bagenal; Reginald Biggs; David Bisset; Noble Black; Joseph Bolton; William Charles Angus Brown; Joseph Bryson; Herbert Bulmer; Charles Byrne; Bertram Byrnes; Harold Candy; David Carman; Clement Carman; Roland Carman; John Carson; William Cordiner; Eric Roland Cotterill; Herbert Crowle; Cornelius Danswan; Evelyn Davies; Walter Dexter; Thomas Henry Dowell; Thomas Patrick Elliott; James Ferguson; Leo Galli; Sidney Galloway; Abas Bhawoodeen Ghansar; Norman Gibbins; Albert Gilbert; Charles Gilbert; Robert Gilbert; Thomas Goodwin; Douglas Grant; Reginald James Hackett; Dennis Dunbar Hauenstein; Mervyn Higgins; John Hutchinson; George Roy Irwin; William Allen Irwin; Allen Charles Waters Kingston; William Johnston Knox; Rowland Edward Lording; Brian Lyall; John McGrath; Alexander McKinnon; Thomas Henley Manns; Frank Maynard; James Maynard; William Maynard; Richard Mayo; Richard Mellor; Berrol Mendelsohn; Tasman Millington; Edith Moorhouse; Alfred Morris; Vernon Isaac Mullin; Thomas Richard Murray; John Naughton; Arthur Leslie Parkes; Robert Pennington; Rachael Pratt; Charles Rae; Donald Rae; William Rae; Peter Rados; Cyril Rigney; Rufus Rigney; William Riley; Frank Roberts; Samuel Rolfe; Edward Sadler; John Sadler; Ellis Silas; Gervase Louis Edgeworth Somers; Noel Travers Edgeworth Somers; Harold Alfred Southern; Robert Stone; Cecil William Tarrant; Frank Thomas; Hugo Throssell; Timothy Tovell; Elsie Tranter; Gordon Wallace; Bernhardt Walther; Adam Wardrop; Frederick Weir; John Whealy; Allan Whittaker; Frank Wilkinson.

FIRST AIF REPATRIATION RECORDS

NAA: B73
Thomas Henry Dowell, M41646
Bernard Haines, R14400
John McGrath, H12398
Vernon Isaac Mullin, M27111
Rachael Pratt, H5789
Elsie Tranter, R45567
Gordon Wallace, M61609

NAA: C137, C138, C138/1, C138/2, C/138/3 & C138/4
Nobel Black, C29645
Charles Byrne, M3444
James Dann, C314427
Cornelius Danswan, R54054
Douglas Grant, C70396
Bernard LeRoy, C59810
Samuel Rolfe, NC043642-01
Cecil Tarrant, R90115

NAA: D363
Walter Beauchamp Bagenal, H029717-01
Harold Joseph Candy, R14615

NAA: PP18/1
Royce Baesjou, R3317

NAA: P107
Reginald Biggs, H12148 PART 1 and 2

NAA: NAA PP6441/1
Hugo Vivian Hope Throssell, M5273

NAA: PP645/1
Rowland Lording, M34291

NATIONAL ARCHIVES OF AUSTRALIA

A1: 1920/3508, Ettie Rout - Question of admission to Australia
A11489/1: 2350/2, Arrangements in Connection with Graves of the Fallen Australian Soldiers Buried in Europe
A2909/2: A453/1/3, Imperial War Graves Commission, Minutes of proceedings
A1608, F27/1/7 Part 1, War Graves - Visits To Part 1
A/402/3: W2455, QF1254 Margaret Thorp
A432: 1929/3484 PART 25, Various Papers Re Applications for Permission to use the Word 'Anzac'
A458/1: R337/7, Graves Visit of Mr [Stanley Melbourne] Bruce
A458: F 337/7, Report by C.H. Hughes (Imperial War Graves Commission) for Minister of Defence
A6119: 42, 'Report of Captain and Mrs Hugo Throssell', Australian Security Intelligence Organisation, Central Office
B741: V/3124, Abas Ghansar – Application for repatriation to Bombay, India
MP16/1, Intelligence Report, Melbourne, 25 December 1915, 'Miss Maud Butler, stowaway'
MP427/1: 3/14/8389, Fund for benefit of relatives and crew of submarine *AE1*
MP42/1: 1/14/7490, Expression of sympathy in connection with loss of submarine *AE1*
MP4271/1: 16/14/8314 Loss of submarine *AE1*
MP376/1: 446/10/1840, Court of Inquiry to Inquire into and Report upon certain matters in connection with the Australian Graves Services
MP367/1: 582/1/218, Galli Leo, Recruiting Serg
MP367/1: 592/4/295, Italian Reservists Mobilization
MP367/1: 592/4/1116, Italians- Enlistment in AIF and Calling up of Italian Reservists
MP367/1: 592/4/973, Deportation of Italian Reservist G Ferrando
MT1139/1: 536/1285, MANNS Thomas Henley - Munitions Worker Number 2152
SP1297/2, 'The Story of Douglas Grant, the Black Scotsman' by John Thompson and Brian Hungerford [ABC radio feature script; box c21]

ARCHIVES NEW ZEALAND

R22273524, BAXTER, Archibald McColl Larmond - WW1 47814 – Army
R10927130, McQUAY, George Thomas- WW1 12/2582 – Army

NATIONAL ARCHIVES, UNITED KINGDOM

PRO FO 141/520, Foreign Office Records

AUSTRALIAN RED CROSS SOCIETY WOUNDED AND MISSING ENQUIRY BUREAU FILES AUSTRALIAN WAR MEMORIAL

1DRL/0428:
David Bissett; Joseph Bolton; Charles Bruce Campbell, Claude Clement Carman; Thomas Patrick Elliott; Norman Gibbins; Albert Gilbert; Charles Gilbert; Robert Gilbert; Douglas Grant: Mervyn Higgins; John Hutchinson; George Roy Irwin; Thomas Henley Manns; Berrol Mendelsohn; Vernon Isaac Mullin; William Rae; Rufus Rigney; Gervase Louis Edgeworth Somers; Noel Travers Edgeworth Somers; Bernhardt Hermann Walther.

AUSTRALIAN WAR MEMORIAL

Sister Leila Brown, AWM Nurses Narratives, AWM41: 946
Ethel Campbell Papers, 3DRL/2110
Herbert Walter Crowle Papers 1DRL/0227
Mary Chomley Papers, 1DRL/0615
Evelyn Davies Papers, 3DRL/3398B
Chaplain WE Dexter Papers, AWM 92/0176 and PR00248
Norman Gibbins Papers, PR02053
Alfred Thomas Sharp Papers, PR04809
Hugo Vivian Hope Throssell Papers PR85/361 and 1DRL/0581
Henri Heremene Tovell Papers, PR87/199
Elsie Tranter Papers, 3DRL/4081(A)
Bernhardt Hermann Walther Papers PR00937
Grace Wilson Papers, 3DRL/7819
Rose Venn Brown Papers, 2DRL/0598
CEW Bean, Gallipoli Report, AWM38, item 51
36th Battalion Papers, 3DRL/6037
CEW Bean Papers, AWM, Series 5, 3DRL/8042, item 51
CEW Bean, DRL 6673 series 3, 419.8.1
'Historical Notes – Gallipoli' AWM 38, 3DRL/8042, 18
Prisoner of War Statements, 1914-18 War, AWM30
3rd Australian Pioneer Battalion Diary AWM 14/15/18
10th Australian Light Horse Regiment Diary, AWM4/10/15
10th Field Company, Australian Engineers Diary, AWM 14/29/15
New Guinea Campaign Records 1914-1918 War [German New Guinea] Admiral PATEYS report on the participation by the Australian seagoing fleet in the operations in the Pacific, AWM33
Records of Naval Establishment, AWM50 (18/PARTS 1-4)
Roll of Honour Circulars, AWM 131.

STATE RECORDS OF NEW SOUTH WALES

Returned Soldiers Settlement files:

Noble Black, 12/7421
Charles William Angus Brown, 12/7274
Charles Byrne, 12/7305
James Newman Dann, 12/7293
Cornelius Danswan, 12/7052
Frederick Weir, 12/7286

STATE RECORDS OF SOUTH AUSTRALIA

Police Reports to the Coroner 1879-1982, GRG 1/44, 242

PUBLIC RECORDS OFFICE VICTORIA

Inquest Deposition Files

VPRS24:
Frank, Elizabeth and Isabella Wilkinson, 1927/1017
Henri Tovell, 1928/675
Allan Whittaker, 1929/428

Closer [and Soldier] Settlement Files

VPRS 5714:
Frank Wilkinson, unit 1473, 4147/12

Victorian Board for the Protection of Aborigines Correspondence Files

VPRS1694:
P/0000, unit 000002; 000003; 00004

Civil Case Files

VPRS267:
Broadhurst v Archer, unit 1652, 1917/308

VPRS 14009:
Minutes (Victorian Education Department Patriotic League) P0001/1

NATIONAL LIBRARY OF AUSTRALIA

Anzac Fellowship of Women Papers, MS2864
Henry Higgins Papers, MS1057
Higgins Papers, MS2525
Sir John Monash Papers, MS1884
Society of Friends Papers, ML1209

STATE LIBRARY OF NEW SOUTH WALES

Goodwin Papers, ML MSS1598
Alfred Prichard Kington Morris Papers, ML MS2886
Ellis Silas Papers, ML MSS1840

STATE LIBRARY OF SOUTH AUSTRALIA

Dorothy Gilbert Papers, PRG 266/14
Mrs Alexandrina Seager Papers, SRG6/34/1
League of Loyal Women Press Clippings, SRG684/2
Women's War Memorial Committee of South Australia Papers, SRG89

STATE LIBRARY OF VICTORIA

Chomley Papers, MS11000
Dairy of Sister Alice Kitchen, MS9627
Lyall Papers, MS10132
Joyce McGrath Papers, MS 14583
G.R. Roberts Newspaper Clippings, MS8509
G.R. Roberts Scrapbooks, MS8508
G.R. Roberts Diaries and Correspondence, MS5782-5786; MS8183; MS9105

STATE LIBRARY OF WESTERN AUSTRALIA

Young Australia League Records, 7292A

CHARLES STURT UNIVERSITY REGIONAL ARCHIVES AND UNIVERSITY ART COLLECTION

Walter Campbell Memorial Trust archive

MONASH UNIVERSITY, RARE BOOKS COLLECTION

Young Australia League World Tour 1924 Papers

UNIVERSITY OF QUEENSLAND

Daphne Mayo Papers, UQFL119

UNIVERSITY OF TASMANIA

Olive Pink Collection

ROYAL AUSTRALASIAN COLLEGE OF SURGEONS ARCHIVES

William Kearsey Medical Case Sheet
Gordon Wallace Medical Case Sheet

BRITISH RED CROSS

Minutes of the British Red Cross 1914-1918 and various uncatalogued holdings

PRIVATE FAMILY PAPERS

Baesjou Family Papers
Baillieu Family Papers
McGrath Papers
Walker Family Papers
Wilkinson Family Papers

LIST OF NAMES

VIKING

UK | USA | Canada | Ireland | Australia
India | New Zealand | South Africa | China

Penguin Books is part of the Penguin Random House group of companies whose addresses can be found at global.penguinrandomhouse.com.

Penguin Random House Australia

First published by Penguin Group (Australia), 2015

10 9 8 7 6 5 4 3 2 1

Design by Laura Thomas © Penguin Group (Australia)
Front cover photograph: Australian War Memorial (P00867.001)
Back cover photographs: Ethel Campbell and crowd/National Library of Australia; Remembrance Day badge/Melbourne Museum; Returned Servicemen's badge/Australian War Memorial (REL34983); Portrait of Narelle Hobbes/Australian War Memorial (PR03708); Will Dyson *Stretcher bearers near Butte de Warlencourt* (1917), charcoal, pencil and wash on paper/Australian War Memorial (ART02266); Portrait of Douglas Grant/National Archives of Australia (SP1011/1, 2176); Ettie Rout and soldiers/Australian War Memorial (H03654); Military for Australia badge/Walter Barber.
Poppy images: p. vii jara3000/Shutterstock.com, p. 370 Kuznetsov Alexey/Shutterstock.com
Typeset in Garamond Premier Pro
Colour separation by Splitting Image Colour Studio, Clayton, Victoria
Printed and bound in China by Toppan Leefung Printing Limited

National Library of Australia
Cataloguing-in-Publication data:

World war one: a history in 100 stories / Bruce Scates, Rebecca Wheatley and Laura James.

ISBN: 9780143799986 (hardback)

World War, 1914-1918.
World War, 1914-1918--Personal narratives.
Soldiers--Australia--Correspondence.
World War, 1914-1918--Women--Australia.
World War, 1914-1918--Participation, Aboriginal Australian.
Australia--History, Military.

940.31

penguin.com.au

The engagement is announced of Miss Margaret (Dolly) Broadhurst, only daughter of Mrs. G. Broadhurst, of Chatsworth-road, East Prahran, and the late W. F. Broadhurst, North Carlton, to Mr. Thomas R. Archer, second son of Mr. and Mrs. Charles Archer, "Iona," Windsor.
DOING A LINE !!
("Behind the Line")
AUSTRALIAN IMPERIAL FORCE.
Attestation Paper of Persons Enlisted for Service Abroad.
CANCELLED
CANCELLED
Rope round post only.
1925
LIMBLESS SOLDIERS APPEAL
COMMONWEALTH ARTIFICIAL LIMB FACTORY.
THE MAN
BEHIND THE MAN
BEHIND THE GUN
FOR
AUSTRALIA
AUDAX AT FIDELIS